The Wind from the East

OTHER BOOKS BY RICHARD WOLIN

Walter Benjamin: An Aesthetic of Redemption

The Politics of Being: The Political Thought of Martin Heidegger

The Heidegger Controversy: A Critical Reader

The Terms of Cultural Criticism: The Frankfurt School, Existentialism, Poststructuralism

Labyrinths: Critical Explorations in the History of Ideas

Karl Löwith, Martin Heidegger and European Nihilism (editor)

Heidegger's Children: Karl Löwith, Hannah Arendt, Hans Jonas, and Herbert Marcuse

*The Seduction of Unreason: The Intellectual Romance with Fascism from Nietzsche to
    Postmodernism*

Herbert Marcuse, Heideggerian Marxism (coeditor)

The Frankfurt School Revisited and Other Essays on Politics and Society

The Wind from the East

French Intellectuals, the Cultural Revolution, and the Legacy of the 1960s

Richard Wolin

PRINCETON UNIVERSITY PRESS   *Princeton & Oxford*

Requests for permission to reproduce material from this work should be sent to Permissions, Princeton University Press

Published by Princeton University Press, 41 William Street, Princeton, New Jersey 08540

In the United Kingdom: Princeton University Press, 6 Oxford Street, Woodstock, Oxfordshire OX20 1TW

LIBRARY OF CONGRESS CATALOGING-IN-PUBLICATION DATA

Wolin, Richard.
  The wind from the east : French intellectuals, the cultural
revolution, and the legacy of the 1960s / Richard Wolin.
        p.   cm.
  Includes bibliographical references and index.
  ISBN 978-0-691-12998-3 (hardcover : acid-free paper)
  1. Intellectuals—France—History—20th century. 2. Intellectuals—
France—Political activity—History—20th century. 3. France—
Intellectual life—20th century. 4. Communism—France—History—20th
century. 5. China—History—Cultural Revolution, 1966–1976—
Influence. 6. Mao, Zedong, 1893–1976—Influence. I. Title.
  DC33.7.W75 2010
  305.5'52094409046—dc22   2009041630

British Library Cataloging-in-Publication Data is available

This book has been composed in Bembo and Helvetica Neue

Printed on acid-free paper. ∞

press.princeton.edu

Printed in the United States of America

10 9 8 7 6 5 4 3 2 1

For my students at the University of Paris
and the University of Nantes, 2005–2008

There are now two winds blowing in the world: the Wind from the East and the Wind from the West. According to a Chinese saying: either the Wind from the East will triumph over the Wind from the West, or the Wind from the West will triumph over the Wind from the East. In my opinion, the nature of the present situation is that the Wind from the East has triumphed over the Wind from the West.

—*Mao Tse-tung*

Contents

Prologue / ix

Introduction: The Maoist Temptation / 1

PART I — THE HOUR OF REBELLION

1. Showdown at Bruay-en-Artois / 25

2. France during the 1960s / 39

3. May 1968: The Triumph of Libidinal Politics / 70

4. Who Were the Maoists? / 109

Excursus: On the Sectarian Maoism of Alain Badiou / 155

PART II — THE HOUR OF THE INTELLECTUALS

5. Jean-Paul Sartre's Perfect Maoist Moment / 179

6. *Tel Quel* in Cultural-Political Hell / 233

7. Foucault and the Maoists: Biopolitics and
   Engagement / 288

8. The Impossible Heritage: From Cultural Revolution to
   Associational Democracy / 350

Bibliography / 371
Index / 385

Prologue

According to an oft-cited maxim, all history is the history of the present. Try as they might, historians are incapable of abstracting from contemporary issues and concerns. In fact, were they to do so, their work would surely reek of antiquarian sterility. At best, historians can make their biases clear to ensure they do not exercise an overtly disfiguring influence on their presentations and findings.

The "presence of the past" is especially true of the 1960s. Analysts and commentators have heatedly debated their meaning and import, but nearly all agree that the decade was a watershed. Whatever their ultimate meaning, the 1960s were a caesura that signified the impossibility of returning to the status quo ante. Thus, today the 1960s remain an inescapable rite of passage for those who seek to fathom the nature of the political present. First, their range and extent was genuinely international. In an age of instantaneous, mass communication, virtually no corner of the globe could remain immune from their influence and legacy. Second, the decade's effects, rather than being confined to one specific manifestation or mode, were, to invoke French anthropologist Marcel Mauss, a "total social phenomenon." The 1960s and their after-effects influenced—and left permanently transformed—the realms of politics, society, fashion, art, and music.

By the same token, it would be impossible to deny that the 1960s have also become historical. Thus the decade has provided fertile ground for interpreters who are seeking to distill and comprehend the origins and bases of contemporary politics and society. Yet, as history, the 1960s—whose study threatens to metastasize into another academic growth industry—possess a temporality with a peculiar and profound bearing on the historical present. As such, as a cultural and political phenomenon, the decade remains a pivotal way station on the road toward comprehending who we are and what we would like to become. Hence, to contribute to the historicization of the 1960s is at the same time a method of coming to grips with the "history of the present."

According to one celebrated maxim, the 1960s are an "interpretation" in search of an "event." Indeed, a dizzying vortex of interpretations has emerged seeking to fathom and clarify what transpired and why. Having both studied these events and lived through them as a youth (although, admittedly, many memories remain enshrouded in a Hendrix-esque "purple haze"), at this point, when asked about their ultimate meaning, I am often tempted to fall back on Chinese premier Zhou En-lai's immortal response when asked to comment on the historical import of the French Revolution: "It's too soon to tell."

Yet, if pressed to define the "rational kernel" of the 1960s, I would say that it was quite simply the era that rediscovered the virtues of participatory politics. The 1950s had witnessed the triumph of political technocracy. At the time, it had become an intellectual commonplace that government by elites—in most cases, white, male elites—was preferable to the perils and risks of popular participation. Political mobilization from below was viewed as irrational and untrustworthy, a prelude to totalitarianism in either its "right" or "left" variant. The 1950s were a decade when the so-called welfare-warfare state was ascendant, culminating in the debacle of Vietnam and kindred foreign policy disasters that often resulted in massive and abhorrent human rights violations. (Sadly, in many cases, the promissory note on such violations remains past due.) In the United States and elsewhere, the 1960s signified an attempt to wrest control of "the political" from elites: to counter the ills of "technocratic liberalism" via recourse to logics of grassroots political engagement and thereby to restore confidence in basic democratic norms.

But the 1960s were also, significantly, the moment when the valence of the political itself underwent a significant transformation and expansion. Henceforth, politics no longer remained confined to the trappings

and rituals of electioneering: registering to vote, canvassing, mass rallies, "sound bites," televised debates, and the culminating, frequently
anticlimactic, solitary act of the secret ballot. Instead, politics was redefined to incorporate *cultural politics*. Politics began to include acts of
self-transformation and the search for personal authenticity. Citizens
realized (and here, the American civil rights movement stands out as
Exhibit A) that they were not cut from the same mould. Politics became part and parcel of a new quest for personal identity, a quest that is
also reflected in much of the literature of the period, for in the modern
world identities no longer arise preformed and ready-made. Instead,
they must be created, fashioned, and nurtured. This development helps
to account for the new proximity between culture and politics. Today, culture has become one of the primary vehicles of political self-
affirmation and group self-expression. Thus, one of the 1960s' crucial
legacies is the idea of cultural politics. The lesson we have learned is
that the *cultural* is the *political*.

As such, I consider *The Wind from the East* foremost a political book.
It is not—or I hope it is not—an exercise in what Nietzsche excoriated as "antiquarian history." Instead, it takes its methodological bearings from Walter Benjamin's recommendation that the historian, rather
than seeking to portray the past "as it really was" (an unattainable ideal
in any event), "actualize" the epoch or event, with an eye toward its
actuality or contemporary relevance. In Benjamin's view, this recommendation meant that the historian interprets the past "in order to
blast a specific era out of the homogenous course of history—blasting a
specific life out of the era or a specific work out of the lifework." Benjamin utilized the notion of *Jetztzeit,* or "now-time," as his benchmark or
criterion, which he associated with the theological idea of "a Messianic
cessation of happening." As heirs to the spectacular failures of political
messianism, our political criteria must conversely be immanent, secular, consensus oriented, and democratic.[1]

The Wind from the East represents a modest attempt to capture the
meaning of the 1960s via "indirection": through attention to an exotic,

---

[1] Walter Benjamin, *Illuminations,* trans. Harry Zohn (New York: Schocken Books,
1969), 263.

alternately serious and playful political detour taken by French youth—
or a prominent segment thereof—during the late 1960s and 1970s, the
infatuation with Cultural Revolutionary China and, more generally,
with what came to be known as Mao Tse-tung Thought. The Maoist
fascination began as a marginal phenomenon. But soon, and in ways
unforeseeable to the actors themselves, it transformed into a general
cultural-political intoxication. At a certain point, it seemed that *le tout
Paris* was in the grips of the Maoist contagion. By the time the dust
had cleared, many of France's leading intellectuals—Michel Foucault,
Jean-Paul Sartre, the *Tel Quel* group—had been swept up in this giddy,
left-wing political vortex.

But, importantly, as it ran its course, the Maoist phenomenon underwent significant alterations and modifications. Ultimately, what began
as an exercise in revolutionary dogmatism was transformed into a Dionysian celebration of cultural pluralism and the right to difference. At
issue was a political learning process via which French youth cured itself of its infantile revolutionary longings in order to focus on more circumscribed tasks pertaining to the transformation of everyday life and
the regeneration of civil society. Although French Maoism cannot take
sole credit for this salutary redirection of political energies, it remains
an integral part of the story. It also had a strangely beneficial effect on
French intellectuals, curing this mandarin caste of its residual elitism
and thereby helping to promote a new, more modest, and democratic
cultural sensibility, for in the aftermath of the May revolt, when Maoism had reached its zenith, French intellectuals learned to *follow* as well
as to *lead*. Much of this development was captured by Foucault's felici-
tous coinage: the *specific* intellectual had supplanted the *universal* intellectual. In a further nuance or twist, the *democratic* intellectual would
replace the *vanguard* intellectual of the Jacobin-Bolshevik mould.

One of the most gratifying aspects of writing contemporary history
is that many of the protagonists remain alive and often motivated to
speak—at times, volubly—about their experiences. I have benefited
immensely from conversations with Daniel Cohn-Bendit, Jean-Pierre
Le Goff, former Situationist Mustapha Khayati, Tony Lévy (brother of
the late Gauche prolétarienne leader Benny Lévy), Alain Touraine, as

well as numerous bystanders and foot soldiers of the May movement. Both Cohn-Bendit and Touraine composed on-the-spot analyses of the May events (*Obsolete Communism: The Left-Wing Alternative* and *The May Movement*, respectively) that, to this day, remain indispensable points of reference for anyone seeking to comprehend what happened and why. At one point, Cohn-Bendit vowed he had "nothing more to say" about May. I would like to thank him for generously ignoring this pledge. Touraine is one of the premier sociologists of our time. His theory of the "return of the actor" has drawn many of the right conclusions and insights from the May events. The course of history is not unalterable. "Events" happen and meaningful historical change occurs, something that the structuralist generation had denied. This change is initiated by people acting in concert who seek to reassert meaningful control over their lives and over the pace of historical change.

Chapter 7, "Foucault and the Maoists: Biopolitics and Engagement," was cowritten with Ron Haas, a former student and friend whose intimate knowledge of the French May and the corresponding *gauchiste* (leftist) milieus and *groupuscules* has never ceased to amaze me. Ron and I first began discussing these events ten years ago at Rice University. Since then, he has completed his own study of one of the relatively unsung heroes of the post-May era: the pioneer of homosexual liberation, Guy Hocquenghem. When published, Ron's study of Hocquenghem will undoubtedly add much to our overall grasp of the era and its significance.

During the last few years I have had the privilege of teaching in France, where I had the opportunity to discuss the ideas contained in this book with numerous French students and colleagues. I would like to thank my hosts Professors Emmanuel Faye (University of Paris X Nanterre) and Muriel Rouyer (University of Nantes) for their kind invitations—and for patiently enduring my unbeautiful, American-accented French. Professor Philippe Raynaud of University of Paris-II and the Institut universitaire de France added some extremely valuable insights during the final stages of writing. I would also like to thank my friend Ed Berenson, director of New York University's Institute of French Studies, for inviting me to present a preliminary version of my argument at that wonderful haven of francophone urbanity.

I would like to thank my colleagues at the Graduate Center of the City University of New York for their unfailing solidarity and sociability. In particular I would like to thank History Program Executive Officer Josh Freeman and President Bill Kelly for their unstinting support and encouragement. At the Graduate Center I have been blessed with the punctual aid of research assistants Ran Zwigenberg and Scott Johnson. The New York Area Seminar in Intellectual and Cultural History, which I co-convene with my friend and colleague Jerry Seigel, has proved to be a constant and welcome source of intellectual stimulation. I would also like to acknowledge the assistance of my former student Martin Woessner for helpful comments on an earlier version of the manuscript.

The revised version of the manuscript has benefited immeasurably from two very insightful anonymous readers' reports commissioned by Princeton University Press. Although at this point their identities have become somewhat less anonymous, I would like to publicly acknowledge how perspicacious their remarks have proved. At a crucial stage, Martin Jay (University of California, Berkeley) and Carolyn Dean (Brown University) read the chapter on *Tel Quel* with insight and discernment and helped me to reformulate my interpretation. My nonpareil editor at the Press, Brigitta van Rheinberg, provided a thoughtful and detailed, chapter-by-chapter (virtually line-by-line) commentary on an earlier manuscript draft. Without Brigitta's keen eye for intelligibility and coherence, the final version of this book would undoubtedly be infinitely poorer. At this point, she has selflessly and graciously edited three of my books. With any luck, she will be willing to edit three more.

Last but not least, I would like to thank my wonderful children, Emma, Seth, and Ethan, for being who they are—and for being so alive!

New York City
January 2009

The Wind from the East

The Maoist Temptation

> It is true enough: millions of people have jobs which
> offer no reason for living; neither production nor
> consumption can provide existence with meaning. . . .
> If the present phase of history can be defined in terms
> of ballistic missiles, thermo-nuclear weapons, the
> moon race and the arms race, should we be surprised
> that part of the student population wavers between
> the negation of the hippies, an aspiration towards
> redemptive violence, and escape towards a new utopia?
>
> —Raymond Aron, *La révolution introuvable*

It is a remarkable fact that some forty years later, the year 1968 remains an obligatory point of reference for contemporary politics. During the 2008 presidential election, one of Barack Obama's campaign pledges was that he would elevate American politics to a plateau of unity beyond the divisiveness of the 1960s. The John McCain campaign, for its part, tried repeatedly to tarnish Obama's luster by dramatizing his association during the early days of his political career with former 1960s radical William Ayers. Similarly, during the 2007 French presidential campaign, both main candidates felt compelled to take a stance on the heritage of May 1968. For the eventual winner, Nicolas Sarkozy, the May events served as a negative touchstone. Playing on the nation's insecurities following a series of riots in immigrant suburbs, Sarkozy labeled May 1968 as a turning point in French history when respect for authority declined and moral anarchy gained the upper hand. Conversely, the Socialist candidate Ségolène Royale made a point of holding her final election rally in the Charléty Stadium, which had been the site for one of the May revolt's largest political rallies.

In Germany, too, the 1960s have served as an important point of reference for making sense of contemporary politics. In 2001 photos surfaced showing Foreign Minister and ex-sixty-eighter Joschka Fischer angrily hurling a brick at a policeman during a 1973 demonstration. Among conservatives the image—depicting a confrontation that had occurred nearly thirty years earlier—provoked a flood of accusations alleging that Fischer was unfit for office. More generally, the episode gave rise to a groundswell of national soul-searching about how to historicize the unsettling political tumult of three decades earlier.

In many respects the year 1968 was an annus mirabilis with global political repercussions. The specter of revolution materialized in Peking, Mexico City, New York, Chicago, Berlin, Warsaw, and Prague, where, tragically, hopes for "socialism with a human face" were brutally crushed under the tread of Soviet tanks.

In France, however, events unfolded according to a somewhat different logic. As elsewhere, the revolt was begun by students. But one of the May uprising's unique aspects was that, within a fortnight, French workers decided to join forces with the student demonstrators. This potent student-worker alliance led to a massive general strike that paralyzed the central government and, at one point, compelled President Charles de Gaulle to flee. When the smoke had cleared, eight to nine million French men and women had joined in the strike. France had experienced its greatest social unrest since the 1930s.

The *Wind from the East* represents a modest contribution to making sense of these challenging and tumultuous events. By focusing on one of May 1968's neglected backstories—the wave of Sinophilia that crested in France later that decade—it seeks to illuminate the whole.

The story begins with a small group of *gauchistes*—political activists who had positioned themselves to the left of the French Communist Party—who were students of Marxist philosopher Louis Althusser at the prestigious Ecole normale supérieure. Fascinated and impassioned by political events that were transpiring nearly half a world away, they began to identify profoundly with Mao's China, which they came to perceive as a panacea for metropolitan France's own multifarious political ills.

None spoke Chinese, and reliable information about contemporary China was nearly impossible to come by, since Mao had basically forbidden access to outsiders. Little matter. The less these *normaliens* knew about contemporary China, the better it suited their purposes. Cultural Revolutionary China became a projection screen, a Rorschach test, for their innermost radical political hopes and fantasies, which in de Gaulle's France had been deprived of a real-world outlet. China became the embodiment of a "radiant utopian future." By "becoming Chinese," by assuming new identities as French incarnations of China's Red Guards, these dissident Althusserians sought to reinvent themselves wholesale. Thereby, they would rid themselves of their guilt both as the progeny of colonialists and, more generally, as bourgeois.

Increasingly, the "real" China ceased to matter. Instead, at issue were questions of political eschatology. The "successes" of Chinese communism—or its imagined successes—would magically compensate for the abysmal failures of the Communist experience elsewhere. The young gauchistes viewed themselves as *pur et dur*— true believers who refused to compromise with the sordid realities of contemporary France. In their eyes there could be no going back to the faded glories of French republicanism—a tradition that, in their view, had been fatally compromised by the legacies of colonialism and Gaullist authoritarianism. One senses that if the Cultural Revolution did not exist, the gauchistes would have had to invent it. Mao's China offered the students a way to perpetuate the intoxications of the French revolutionary tradition—the glories of the Bastille, of Valmy, and of the Paris Commune—in an era when the oppressive nature of "really existing socialism" had reached undeniably grotesque proportions.

The French Communist Party took pleasure in belittling the Maoists, owing to their small numbers, as a *groupuscule*—a little group. Were it not for the political maladroitness of the Pompidou government, which in the spring of 1970 abruptly arrested the Maoist leaders and banned their newspaper, their story, when set against the overall tapestry of the May events, would probably rate a minor footnote. But owing to the authorities' heavy-handedness, overnight the unheralded Maoists became a cause célèbre. None other than Jean-Paul Sartre took over the Maoist newspaper, in bold defiance of the government's arbitrary and brutal political sweep. At one point the Rolling Stones' frontman, Mick Jagger, interrupted a concert at the Palais des Sports Stadium to plead for the imprisoned Maoists' release. Suddenly and unexpectedly, Maoism had acquired immense cachet as political chic. It began attracting prominent intellectuals—Michel Foucault as well as *Tel Quel* luminaries Philippe Sollers and Julia Kristeva—who perceived in Maoism a creative solution to France's excruciating political immobilism. After all, the Socialist Party was in total disarray. The Communists had become a "party of order." The Gaullists, with Pompidou now at the helm, pointedly refused to relinquish the reins of power. Yet, here was a left-wing groupuscule active in the Latin Quarter that in many respects had become the heir of May 1968's emancipatory quest.

As a result of the May events and their contact with the Maoists, French intellectuals bade adieu to the Jacobin-Leninist authoritarian political model of which they had formerly been so enamored. They ceased behaving like mandarins and internalized the virtues of democratic humility. In May's aftermath, they attuned themselves to new forms and modes of social struggle. Their post-May awareness concerning the injustices of top-down politics alerted them to the virtues of "society" and political struggle from below. In consequence, French intellectual life was wholly transformed. The Sartrean model of the engaged intellectual was upheld, but its content was totally reconfigured. Insight into the debilities of political vanguardism impelled French writers and thinkers to reevaluate the Dreyfusard legacy of the universal intellectual: the intellectual who shames the holders of power by flaunting timeless moral truths.

The Maoists' story is worth telling insofar as it represents a paradigmatic instance of a *constructive political learning process*. The Maoists started out as political dogmatists and true believers. But they soon found it impossible to reconcile their pro-Chinese ideological blinders with the emancipatory spirit of May. Once they ceased deluding themselves with revolutionary slogans, they began to understand politics in an entirely new light. The idea of cultural revolution was thereby wholly transformed. It ceased to be an exclusively Chinese point of reference. Instead it came to stand for an entirely new approach to thinking about politics: an approach that abandoned the goal of seizing political power and instead sought to initiate a democratic revolution in mores, habitudes, sexuality, gender roles, and human sociability in general.

Ultimately, the gauchistes came to realize that human rights and the values of libertarian socialism, rather than operating at cross-purposes, were complementary. It was the French, after all, who back in 1789 had invented the rights of man and citizen. Under the more contemporary guise of human rights, it was to this legacy they would now return.

AN INTERPRETATION IN SEARCH OF AN EVENT

It has often been said, perhaps only half in jest, that May 1968 in France is an "interpretation" in search of an "event," so concertedly have historians, pundits, and politicians struggled to impose intellectual sense on a sequence of events that at every turn seemed to defy tidy conceptual coherence.

In both France and the United States, the idea that the 1960s were an unmitigated catastrophe has become a staple of conservative ideology. On this side of the Atlantic, one of the commonplaces of neoconservative history-writing is that the social disequilibrium of the postwar period—urban riots, drug use, accelerated divorce rates, and declining respect for authority—can uniformly be traced to the 1960s, purportedly one of the most disastrous decades in American history. Norman Podhoretz, one of neoconservatism's founding fathers, believes that the 1960s witnessed a process of irreversible cultural demise: "Auden's low dishonest decade, of course, was the 1930s; its clever hopes centered on the construction of a workers' paradise in the Soviet Union. Our counterpart was the 1960s, and its less clever hopes centered not on construction . . . but on destruction—the destruction of the institutions that made up the American way of life."[1] In the eyes of Newt Gingrich, American history possessed a 350-year narrative coherence until the

---

[1] Norman Podhoretz, "America at War: 'The One Thing Needful,'" Francis Boyer Lecture, American Enterprise Institute for Public Policy Research, Washington, DC, February 13, 2002.

1960s, when, owing to the excesses of liberal elites and counterculture hedonism, everything unraveled.[2] Straussian political philosopher Allan Bloom takes this argument a step further, suggesting that the New Left was, in essence, Hitler Youth *redivivus*. "History always repeats itself," observes Bloom. "The American university of the 1960s was experiencing the same dismantling of the structure of rational inquiry as had the German university in the 1930s."[3] Bloom's account offers us disturbing images of universities besieged by violence-prone African American student groups. Typically, the liberal university administration spinelessly kowtows to their demands. The mass of students, like sheep or lemmings, spurred by irrational partisanship, simply go along for the ride. Meanwhile, the knowledgeable elite—Bloom and his compadres—possessing "right reason," are marginalized and shunned. Like the protagonist of Plato's cave allegory, they have seen the sunlight—they alone know where truth really lies—but the hoi polloi, blinded by passion, refuse to heed their counsel. However, when it comes to assessing the violence and depredations of the forces of order, Bloom's book is curiously silent.

Bloom's account conveniently abstracts from the excesses of the times: pervasive racism, the unresponsiveness of political elites, urban decay predominantly affecting minorities and the underclass, and, last but not least, an unjust war, fought by palpably immoral means: napalm, indiscriminate aerial bombardments, and ruthless search-and-destroy missions. In the course of the American drive to halt the spread of communism in Southeast Asia, some two million Vietnamese, most of whom were civilians, lost their lives. In neoconservative lore, the Vietnam conflict was ultimately a "good war." Yet the American will

---

[2] Quoted in "The Revenge of the Squares: Newt Gingrich and Pals Rewrite the 1960s," by Fred Barnes, *New Republic*, March 13, 1995, 23: "The Great Society messed everything up: don't work, don't eat. . . . From 1965 to 1994, we did strange and weird things as a country. Now we're done with that and we have to recover."

[3] Allan Bloom, *The Closing of the American Mind: How Higher Education Has Failed Democracy and Impoverished the Souls of Students* (New York: Simon and Schuster, 1987), 313. For a more detailed look at the neoconservative view of the 1960s, see Peter Steinfels, *The Neoconservatives: The Men Who Are Changing America's Politics* (New York: Simon and Schuster, 1979), 44–48.

to fight was treacherously undermined by liberals, protesters, and draft dodgers. Ultimately, the generational war at home tragically and ineluctably sabotaged the war effort abroad, depriving America of victory against a godless and noxious geopolitical enemy.

If one seized the neoconservative "conventional wisdom" about the 1960s generation and stood it on its head, one would probably be much closer to the truth. Instead of being the fount of a proliferating immorality, the 1960s generation was in fact singularly moral. For many activists, the imperatives of social justice became an obsession, and "living in truth" a veritable credo. The neocon brotherhood overlooked the fact that it required profound wellsprings of civil courage to become a freedom rider in the Jim Crow South; to risk arrest for the sake of free speech or freedom of assembly; to demonstrate against an immoral war; to burn one's draft card as an act of conscience; and to voluntarily emigrate rather than kill innocent civilians, as the armed forces often required.

A BREAKDOWN OF CIVILIZATION?

In France rancor vis-à-vis the 1968 generation and its legacy has been equally widespread. As the May events reached their zenith, President Charles de Gaulle set the tone, lamenting: "Reform, yes; sheer disorder, no!" In the general's view, the student activists had set forth no discernible political goals. They had provoked an eruption of pure anarchy. The forces of order had completely lost control of the situation, resulting in a "breakdown of civilization" that only a draconian restoration of political authority could remedy. Among Gaullists, the idea of a global "crisis of civilization" gained popularity. In this view, it was not de Gaulle's trademark autocratic leadership that was to blame. Instead, France was the unfortunate victim of a more general planetary disorder. The rate of technological advance—the pace of "modernization"—had accelerated beyond citizens' capacities to adjust morally and psychologically. These adaptational difficulties resulted in various forms of anomic behavior: riots, protests, rebellion, and generalized social unrest. De Gaulle rued the unwillingness of French youth to embrace the blandishments of modern consumer society. But he also harbored fears that a more general "mechanization" of life had taken hold, in which the individual could not escape being crushed.[4]

The most influential conservative interpretation of the May revolt was set forth by the doyen of the French Right, Raymond Aron. In a series of articles written for *Le Figaro* as the events unfolded, Aron, with characteristic insight, depicted the student uprising as a "psychodrama," a "quasi-revolution." Aron's detractors have assumed that he sought to trivialize the May uprising as a rebellion among disaffected and maladjusted youth. Instead of taking the students' political demands seriously, he purportedly sought to shift the discussion to the "clinical" plane of adolescent social psychology.

Aron's critique captured something essential about the May movement that few other observers had noted. Although the insurgents repeatedly paid lip service to the ideals of the French revolutionary tradition, these allusions were largely rhetorical. They remained on the plane of citation or pastiche. The sixty-eighters were aping their eighteenth- and nineteenth-century progenitors. The May events were a grandiose instance of revolutionary pantomime. Hence, the chasm between the revolt's rhetorical dimension and the actors' real intentions, which were "reformist" rather than "revolutionary." Aron recognized that the May insurrection represented not the culmination of the French revolutionary tradition but its last dying gasp.

Equally hostile to May's legacy were the revolt's republican detractors. Among republicans, the May movement signified the moment when French youth relinquished respect for authority in favor of a self-indulgent hedonism. Heretofore, French society had been structured by venerable social institutions: the university system, the Catholic Church, the army, trade unions, political parties, and so forth. With the triumph of May's antiauthoritarian credo, these institutions suddenly lost their legitimacy. The May revolt accelerated France's transformation into a centrifugally fragmented, atomistic society: a polity of self-absorbed, narcissistic individuals. Worse still, it was the moment of France's permanent and irreversible "Americanization."

[4] Boisseau, *Pour servir le générale*, 89.

In this view, in May's aftermath, it became impossible to form mean-ingful and lasting attachments. Social solidarity had been perma-nently eroded, sacrificed on the altar of American-style possessive individualism.[5]

The republican execration of May enjoyed a resurgence during the 1990s, in part owing to the popularity of novelists such as Michel Houellebecq and Michel Le Dantec. Houellebecq's novels are inhabited by a rogue's gallery of dysfunctional personality types. They wander desultorily from mind-numbing jobs—often in the high-tech sector or sex tourism industry—to dispassionate, unfeeling relationships suf-fused with anonymous, mechanical sex. Unable to emote or to con-nect, Houellebecq's protagonists lead lives of quiet desperation, which the novelist depicts with eloquent candor:

> Your tax papers are up to date. Your bills are paid on time. You never go out without your identity card. Yet you haven't any friends. . . . The fact is that nothing can halt the ever-increasing recurrence of those moments where your total isolation, the sen-sation of an all-consuming emptiness, the foreboding that your existence is nearing a painful and definitive end, all combine to lunge you into a state of real suffering. . . . You have had a life. There have been moments when you were having a life. Of course you don't remember too much about it; but there are pho-tographs to prove it.[6]

Although Houellebecq's characters are too young to have been sixty-eighters, their psychological and emotional failings are meant to reflect the era's disastrous political and cultural legacy.

Undoubtedly, one of the May revolt's immediate repercussions was to significantly raise the bar of utopian political expectations. Leftists

[5] For the predominant representatives of this perspective, see the works by Debray, *Le pouvoir intellectuel en France*; Ferry and Renaut, *68–86*; Le Goff, *Mai '68*; and Li-povetsky, *L'ère du vide*. For a good account of the generalized animus against the 1960s, see Lindenberg, *Le rappel à l'ordre*.

[6] Houellebecq, *Extension du domaine*, 8.

were convinced that a "radiant utopian future" was only months away and that the lifespan of de Gaulle's imperious Fifth Republic was distinctly limited. Soon, the imagination would accede to power, as the well-known May slogan, "L'imagination au pouvoir!" had prophesied.

French society *did* change radically in the May uprising's aftermath, although undoubtedly the transformation was not as far-reaching or thoroughgoing as many former sixty-eighters had hoped. The changes were more subtle and long term, more *evolutionary* than *revolutionary*. For the most part they transpired in the more indeterminate realm of cultural politics, which helps to account for the significance that the Chinese Cultural Revolution assumed in the eyes of various leftist student groups. The transformation in question pertained to modes of sociability and the perception of social roles, to questions of sexuality, claims to authority, and the status of heretofore underrepresented or marginalized social groups—women, immigrants, gays, and the unemployed.

At base, the May revolt effectuated a sweeping and dramatic transformation of everyday life. The politics of everyday life functioned as an exit strategy, allowing French youth to escape from the dogmas of orthodox Marxism as well as the ideological straitjacket the French Communist Party imposed. It enabled the activists to address a variety of prepolitical, "existential" concerns: issues pertaining to psychology, sexuality, family life, urbanism, and basic human intimacy. Via the discourse of everyday life the student militants were able to renew the lexicon of contemporary social criticism, making it relevant for the peculiar challenges of the modern world.[7] One of the activists' central problems was that under conditions of late capitalism, domination was no longer confined to the wage labor–capital dyad that had been central for Marx. Instead, in advanced industrial society the logic of commodification—the process whereby relations among persons become quantifiable, opaque, and thinglike—had surpassed the workplace, penetrating and suffusing social life in its totality.

---

[7] For two classic texts on the politics of everyday life, see Lefebvre, *Everyday Life in the Modern World*, and Vaneigem, *Treatise on Living*. For the intellectual background of the May uprising, see the indispensable contribution by Epistémon, *Ces idées*.

THE OTHER HALF OF THE SKY

During the 1960s Maoism's popularity went hand in hand with the intoxications of third worldism. After all, China—the "other half of the sky"—was the world's most populous nation. In 1949, following two decades of protracted struggle, Mao successfully expulsed Chiang Kai-shek's Nationalists from the mainland. Thereby, he succeeded in providing the world with a new model of revolution based on the central role of the peasantry, a model that seemed well suited to an era of global anticolonial struggle. Soon, the attractions of Chinese "peasant communism" were amplified through Castro's seizure of power in Cuba and Vietnam's heroic efforts to throw off the yoke of American imperialism.

The 1960s were a time of acute disenchantment with Western modernity. Denizens of advanced industrial society discovered that not only did affluence fail to coincide with happiness, but that the two often seemed to operate at cross-purposes. A dizzying array of consumer choices led to a heightened anxiety about status. By defining themselves through their purchasing capacity, Westerners had lost sight of human essentials: family, friendship, and an ability to enjoy oneself apart from the prefabricated amusements of the so-called culture industry.[8] In a 1968 speech, presidential candidate Robert Kennedy eloquently encapsulated the widespread and deep-seated generational discontent:

We will find neither national purpose nor personal satisfaction in a mere continuation of economic progress, in an endless amassing of worldly goods. We cannot measure national spirit by the Dow Jones Average, nor national achievement by the Gross National Product. For the Gross National Product includes air pollution, and ambulances to clear our highways from carnage. . . . The Gross National Product includes the destruction of the redwoods and the death of Lake Superior. It grows with the production of napalm and missiles and nuclear warheads. . . . It includes . . . the

[8] See Horkheimer and Adorno, "The Culture Industry: Enlightenment as Mass Deception," in *Dialectic of Enlightenment*, 120–67.

broadcasting of television programs which glorify violence to sell goods to our children. . . . It does not allow for the health of our families, the quality of their education, or the joy of their play. It is indifferent to the decency of our factories and the safety of our streets alike. . . . It measures everything, in short, except that which makes life worthwhile.[9]

Journalists, scholars, and intellectuals wondered aloud whether the Chinese approach to industrialization might be a viable path to modernization, one that might circumvent the upsets and dislocations of the predominant Western models. Chinese socialism thus doubled as a projection screen for disillusioned Westerners of all political persuasions and inclinations.

Beginning with the Sino-Soviet rift in the early 1960s, Mao tried to wrest the banner of revolutionism from Russia. The Soviets were derided as "social imperialists" and "revisionists"—a regime more interested in furthering its own geopolitical aims than in advancing the ends of world revolution. Mao's doctrine of New Democratic Revolution sought to transpose China's model of revolutionary struggle to other developing nations suffering from the injustices of Western imperialism. His theory proposed a two-stage process that harmonized well with the anticolonialist zeitgeist. The first stage was defined by struggles of national liberation against colonial oppression. The second stage would undertake the political and economic transition to socialist rule.

Among left-wing sympathizers, China's star rose as the Soviet Union's fell. Revelations concerning forced labor camps, the cruel suppression of the 1956 Hungarian uprising, as well as Khrushchev's flirtations with the heresies of "peaceful coexistence" combined to discredit the Soviet experiment in "really existing socialism." It became increasingly clear that Soviet Marxism had forfeited all progressive claims. It had degenerated into a repellent, authoritarian "science of legitimation" (Rudolf Bahro). Conversely, the repute of Communist China benefited from

[9] Robert Kennedy, speech at the University of Kansas, March 18, 1968, in *RFK: Collected Speeches*, ed. Edwin O. Guthmann and Jeffrey Shulman (New York: Viking, 1993) 330.

misleading images of a simple but joyous people working shoulder to shoulder to construct a genuinely humane version of socialism.

Maoism's global prestige was further enhanced when, in 1966, the Great Helmsman launched the Great Proletarian Cultural Revolution. To outsiders, the Cultural Revolution seemed like a laudable effort to reactivate Chinese communism's original revolutionary élan, thereby avoiding the bureaucratic ossification afflicting Soviet communism. The fact that reliable information concerning the Cultural Revolution's manifold sanguinary excesses was hard to come by worked distinctly to China's advantage. Western journalists' celebratory accounts depicting the glories of the Chinese road to socialism helped to reinforce existing pro-Chinese predispositions and convictions.

Unlike the Soviets, China never sought to orchestrate an international Communist movement. With the experience of the Comintern (dissolved in 1943), the Russians had too much of a head start. Moreover, the volatility of China's domestic politics, as illustrated by the abrupt alternation of policy declarations—from the "Let 100 Flowers Bloom" campaign (1956–57) to the "Great Leap Forward" (1959) to the "Cultural Revolution" (1966)—with the accompanying social turmoil, made China seem like a less-than-desirable political model.

Maoism was nevertheless able to gain favor among many advocates of third world revolution, especially in South America and Asia. Convinced that Mao's notion of peasant communism could be fruitfully transposed to Latin America, the Peruvian Sendero Luminoso, or Shining Path, invoked a Maoist pedigree. In Nepal, Maoist guerrillas are still active in antiroyalist struggles.[10] During the 1960s, Maoism also made tangible inroads among Western leftist circles. In Germany a dogmatic, Stalinized version of Maoism took root among the numerous so-called K groups (K = Kommunist) that mushroomed during the 1960s and 1970s.[11] In Italy, too, certain Italian Communist Party dissidents evinced an attraction to Mao's populism.

[10] See Somini Sengupta, "Where Maoists Still Matter," *New York Times Magazine*, October 30, 2005.

[11] For a discussion of these groups and their activities, see Kühn, *Stalins Enkel*. It is worth noting that the founding document of the German Red Army Faction—colloquially known as the Baader-Meinhof Gang—"The Concept of the Urban Guerrilla"

In the United States, Maoism enjoyed cachet among the Black Panthers, who, during the 1960s, financed firearm purchases by selling the Little Red Book at Berkeley's Sproul Plaza. The militants' daily, *The Black Panther*, was suffused with Maoist slogans. The Panthers believed that Mao's strategic elevation of the downtrodden masses to a position of revolutionary centrality had important parallels with the lot of oppressed African Americans. Yet, a good part of Maoism's attraction had less to do with strictly doctrinal matters than with the aesthetics of political militancy. Charismatic Panther leaders like Huey Newton and Eldridge Cleaver were enamored of Maoist slogans such as "Political power grows out of the barrel of a gun" and "A revolution is not a dinner party."

In France, disillusionment with the Soviet Union and with the French Communist Party (PCF) caused Maoism's stock to rise. The PCF had a heroic political past as resistance fighters during the Nazi occupation. In France's first nationwide elections following the Liberation, the Communists were the leading vote-getters. The PCF enjoyed a comfortable niche in the French political system, habitually accruing some 20 percent of the vote. Yet, in the eyes of many on the Left, the Communists had become excessively complacent. Conventional electoral success seemed to trump its commitment to radical political change. Moreover, the PCF enjoyed the dubious distinction of being the most resolutely Stalinist among the European Communist parties. Its servility to Moscow was notorious. The 1950s and 1960s were a time of legendary cultural ferment—the era of the new novel and the New Wave cinema. In Left Bank circles, existentialists and structuralists waged a storied battle for intellectual predominance. The PCF, for its part, seemed mired in anachronistic debates dating from the 1930s. The party's intellectual stagnation was palpable and

---

(1971), bore as its motto the following citation from Mao's Little Red Book: "It is good if we are attacked by the enemy, since it proves that we have drawn a clear line of demarcation between the enemy and ourselves. It is still better if the enemy attacks us wildly and paints us as utterly black and without a single virtue; it demonstrates that we have not only drawn a clear line of demarcation between the enemy and ourselves but achieved a great deal in our work"; Mao Tse-tung, *Quotations from Chairman Mao Tse-tung* (Peking: Foreign Languages Press, 1966), 15.

undeniable. More worrisome still was the fact that its leadership was encountering great difficulties in recruiting new members, especially among French youth.

Hence, when the Sino-Soviet dispute erupted in the early 1960s, in the eyes of many, the Chinese Communists' efforts to equate Soviet Marxism with a lackluster "revisionism" seemed persuasive. In 1964 a number of ex-Communists formed their own breakaway pro-Chinese cell, the Fédération des cercles marxistes-léninistes. In 1966, as Mao inaugurated the Cultural Revolution, the same group, with Beijing's official blessing, rebaptized itself the Mouvement communiste français marxiste-léniniste (MCF-ML) and transformed itself into a veritable party. However, it would not get far in its rearguard effort to revivify Marxist orthodoxy—in the eyes of the MCF-ML stalwarts, the French Communist Party's major sin was that it had remained *insufficiently Stalinist*. The MCF-ML never succeeded in attracting much of a following. It was feted in Beijing and by China's lone European ally, Enver Hoxa's Albania, but it was destined to remain an insignificant blip on the French political landscape.

It is estimated that in 1968, France had approximately fifteen hundred Maoists. About thirty-five of them were concentrated on the rue d'Ulm, the seat of France's most prestigious university, l'Ecole normale supérieure. Among French students, the normaliens were la crème de la crème; yet, by and large, they were alienated from the Fifth Republic's lethargic political institutions and radicalized by the neocolonial horrors of the Vietnam War. In their eyes, the United States had merely picked up in Indochina where France had left off in 1954. The normaliens' pro-Chinese delusions were immortalized in an idiosyncratic agitational film directed by the wunderkind of New Wave cinema Jean-Luc Godard: *La Chinoise*. Today, many ex-Maoists, having undergone the "long march through the institutions," have become luminaries of French cultural and political life: philosophers, architects, scholars, and advisers to the Socialist Party.

Curiously, in the spring of 1968, as the May events unfolded, the Maoists were nowhere to be found. Prisoners of their own ideological dogmatism, they had difficulty fathoming the idea that what had begun as a student revolt might become a catalyst for a general political uprising. Their misjudgment of May's political import would haunt many of them for years to come. Were the narrative of French student Maoism to break off in 1968, the story would constitute little more than a curious political footnote to a more general social upheaval.

The Maoists would not hit their political stride until the post-May period. Their support of a desultory coalition of marginal groups—immigrants, the unemployed, prisoners, gays—gained them considerable publicity and admiration. The French government, with de Gaulle's successor, Georges Pompidou, now at the helm, felt that they could be effectively neutralized were their leaders arrested and their publications impounded. Yet, by proceeding thus, the French authorities succeeded only in turning them into martyrs.

THE HOUR OF THE INTELLECTUALS

During the early 1970s major intellectuals such as Sartre, Foucault, and the *Tel Quel* group gravitated toward Maoism as the most effective way of realizing the values of "engagement." Following the spring 1970 arrest of leading Maoist militants, Sartre would become the titular head of several Maoist newspapers. He would accompany the Maoists during a number of their protests and "actions." Publicly flaunting his Maoist political allegiances, Sartre hawked copies of one banned Maoist newspaper on the boulevards of Paris, all but daring the French authorities to arrest him. Sartre wrote the preface to an anthology of Maoist autobiographical writings and published an extended volume of political conversations, *On a raison de se revolter* (It's Right to Rebel), with Maoist student leader Pierre Victor. He would also open the pages of his prestigious intellectual-political monthly *Les Temps Modernes* to his Maoist *confrères*. Along with Maoist Serge July, he cofounded a left-wing press agency, Libération. Within a few years, this modest journalistic undertaking blossomed into one of France's largest mass circulation dailies.[12] For the aging philosopher, the marriage of convenience with

[12] See Lallemont, *Libé*.

the "pro-Chinese" leftists represented a political rebirth following an epoch in which the structuralists had openly proclaimed him to be a "dead dog."

During May 1968 Foucault was teaching in Tunisia. His partner, Daniel Defert, kept him apprised of the developing situation in Paris by phone. Upon returning to Paris, he became chair of the philosophy faculty of the new "experimental" University of Vincennes, where Foucault eagerly staffed the department with Maoist militants: Alain Badiou, Jacques Rancière, André Glucksmann, and Jacques-Alain Miller. For a time Foucault was shadowed by police agents, who assumed he must be the leader of a Vincennes-based Maoist sect.[13]

Foucault would extract a seminal political lesson from the May events. He understood that the boundaries of "the political" had permanently expanded. Politics could be reduced neither to "class struggle" nor to bourgeois ideals of negative freedom and civil liberty. Instead, the new political stakes pertained to the way in which regimes of knowledge translated into specific institutional practices: techniques of incarceration, population control, and purportedly neutral scientific methods of classification—normal versus abnormal, deviance versus conformity, and so forth.

Foucault's tenure at Vincennes was short-lived. In 1970 he was accorded France's highest academic accolade: a professorship at the Collège de France, where the only requirement was that he lecture every two weeks on his current research. Ironically, at the precise moment of his intellectual canonization, Foucault committed himself wholeheartedly to political activism with the Maoist Groupe d'information sur les prisons (GIP). GIP began as a support group for imprisoned Maoist militants, many of whom were actively engaged in hunger strikes across France. But soon this loose confederation of intellectuals and Maoist activists burgeoned into a nationwide prisoners' advocacy group.

Although GIP was founded by intellectuals, its inspiration largely derived from the libertarian Maoist group Vive la révolution! GIP's

---

[13] See Macey, *Lives of Michel Foucault*, 228. As Macey attests, "Foucault's thought naturally gravitated toward the Maoists."

infrastructure and organizational praxis were thoroughly Maoist. It was Maoists who provided the mimeograph machines, the equipment, and meeting halls. Its method of gathering information on French prison conditions was based on the favored Maoist tactic of the *enquête* (investigation): immersing oneself among the masses—"going to the people"—in order to allow the oppressed to describe their predicament in their own language, a practice that was in keeping with the Maoist maxim, "One must descend from the horse in order to smell the flowers."

Foucault's period of Maoist-inspired political militancy has been little scrutinized. However, if one seeks to gain insight into the gestation of Foucaultian concepts such as "genealogy," "biopower," and the "disciplinary society," an understanding of this period is crucial, for it was as a result of his work with the Maoists that Foucault arrived at the notion of "microphysics of power," which would become the hallmark of his later work. Thereafter, Foucault no longer conceived "power" according to the juridical model, as the capacity to repress, deny, or refuse. Instead, he viewed power as productive, a mechanism of social control that leaves a discernible, positive imprint on bodies, mores, and patterns of thought.

Under the stewardship of Philippe Sollers, *Tel Quel* began as a literary challenge to Sartre's notion of *engagement*. In *Tel Quel*'s view, by seeking to subordinate art to politics, Sartre risked bypassing or distorting art's genuine specificity, which had less to do with "changing the world" than with advancing certain intrinsic formal features and traits. *Tel Quel* began by celebrating the *nouveau roman* as exemplified by the work of Alain Robbe-Grillet and Nathalie Sarraute. Thereafter, it caught the structuralist wave, opening its pages to the likes of Foucault, Derrida, and others. However, as the Left Bank began to erupt with anti–Vietnam War protests, Marxism came back into fashion. From this new political vantage point, Sartre's ideal of "commitment" seemed to merit a fresh look.

At first, *Tel Quel* sought to join forces with the French Communist Party—an alliance that, in light of the PCF's disparagement of the May events, proved to be a tactical blunder. In the post-May period Sollers and others sought to atone for their misdeeds by aligning the journal with Maoism. *Tel Quel*'s pro-Chinese phase was sui generis. The group scorned the Maoist student organizations with which Sartre and Foucault had cast their lot. Instead, it wanted its Maoist commitment to remain as pure and uncompromising as its earlier alliance with Soviet communism had been. *Tel Quel* began publishing special issues on the Cultural Revolution. Sollers and Julia Kristeva learned enough Chinese to translate Chairman Mao's poetry into French. In 1974, accompanied by Roland Barthes, the group made a pilgrimage to Communist China, although by then it had become clear that China's experiment in political utopianism had soured.

THE INTELLECTUALS REPENT

Since the eighteenth century French writers and intellectuals have enjoyed the status of a lay aristocracy. In republican France they functioned as arbiters of the true, the right, and the good. The high-water mark of this trend occurred during the Dreyfus Affair, when, under Emile Zola's tutelage, intellectuals helped to reverse the miscarriage of justice that had victimized the unjustly imprisoned colonel.

The May insurrection provided French intellectuals with a lesson in humility. None had anticipated it. The structuralists had famously proclaimed that historical change was illusory. "Events," they declared, were a thing of the past. The mainstream Left looked to the French working class to play its assigned historical role as capitalism's gravedigger. But in truth French workers were quite content to enjoy the fruits of postwar affluence: *les trentes glorieuses,* or the thirty glorious years. Hence, when the May revolt erupted, intellectuals were relegated to playing a series of bit parts and supporting roles—menial tasks to which this proud guild was largely unaccustomed. The *marxisant* bias of postwar French political culture was still predominantly focused on the workplace. Yet, the revolt had broken out elsewhere: Nanterre, the Sorbonne, and the oblique byways of the Latin Quarter. The only intellectuals who had accurately foreseen the transformed parameters of revolt were those located to the "left of the Left": the gauchistes who were associated with innovative avant-garde organs such as the

Situationist International, Arguments, and Socialism or Barbarism. One of the hallmarks of the May revolt was that ideals of direct democracy and worker control migrated from the periphery to the center.

Looking back, it is easy to mock French intellectuals' overly credulous Maoist political indulgences. Today the excesses and brutalities of the Cultural Revolution have been well documented. China itself has long departed from the revolutionary course charted by the Great Helmsman. Mao may have been a gifted military strategist, but once in power, his policies were capricious, self-serving, and propelled by an ideological fervor that precipitated widespread chaos and ruined millions of lives.

Were the story of French intellectuals and Maoism purely a tale of political folly, it would hardly be worth recounting. In retrospect, the Maoist intoxication that gripped France during the early 1970s stands out as a generational rite of passage. Among students and intellectuals, the identification with Cultural Revolutionary China became an exit strategy to escape from the straitjacket of orthodox Marxism. Early on, revolutionary China ceased being an empirical point of reference. Instead, it became a trope: a projection of the gauchiste political imaginary. As the Maoists themselves later explained, the issue became the "China in our heads." The figure of Cultural Revolution was detached from its Asian geopolitical moorings. In a textbook case of unintended consequences, it fused unexpectedly with the "critique of everyday life" as elaborated by the 1960s French cultural avant-garde.

The May movement signaled the twilight of the "prophetic intellectual": the celebrity writer or thinker who claimed to possess privileged insight into the course of history and who prescribes the line of march for the benighted masses. The student activists helped to reinvent the lexicon of political radicalism. By virulently opposing the idea of a revolutionary vanguard, they took an important step in consigning the Leninist model to the dustbin of history.

The new spirit of humility would find expression in Foucault's conception of the "specific intellectual" who undertakes acts of "contestation" in concrete, local struggles. Foucault and his allies thereby jettisoned the traditional revolutionary expectation of a radiant utopian future in favor of "resistance" that was always situated and site-specific.

Yet, Foucault's endorsement of the specific intellectual would not be the last word. The sixty-eighters realized that they could not entirely dispense with the Dreyfusard ideal of the universal intellectual who morally shames the powers-that-be by confronting them with higher ideals of justice and truth. Solzhenitsyn's devastating exposé of the Soviet Gulag, which was first published in France in 1974, along with macabre revelations about the Killing Fields in Cambodia—another experiment in cultural revolution that drastically miscarried—helped convince French intellectuals that the idea of human rights merited renewed attention. Few believed that human rights represented a political panacea. Yet most conceded that the rule of law acted as a "magic wall"—a juridical-political stopgap—that kept despotism in check and thereby helped to avoid the worst. In this way, the May movement's antiauthoritarian spirit nourished the development of a thoughtful and sustained antitotalitarian political credo.

PART I   The Hour of Rebellion

Showdown at Bruay-en-Artois

> We made war and revolution in our imaginations. We
> pretended to believe. It was like birth pangs without
> giving birth, without passing over to the act. The suffering
> was internal. It was all theatrical. And that permitted us
> to remain outside the gates of hell—that is, murder.
>
> —Roland Castro, Maoist student leader

April 6, 1972. The scene was a mining town in provincial Normandy, Bruay-en-Artois. A young working-class girl, Brigitte Dewevre, had been sadistically murdered, her mutilated, unclothed corpse left in a vacant field. The crime scene bespoke a level of brutality to which France was entirely unaccustomed. Adding to the event's macabre nature was the fact that Brigitte's body was discovered the next day by her younger brother in the course of a pickup soccer match.

Within a fortnight of the murder, the police had arrested a local notable, Pierre Leroy. Leroy was a notary public who specialized in real estate transactions and was a prominent member of the local Rotary Club. There was considerable circumstantial evidence linking the suspect to the crime. Earlier in the day, Leroy's white Peugeot had been observed near the crime scene. Brigitte's body had been found in a field adjacent to the villa of Leroy's fiancée, Monique Mayeur. Shortly before her disappearance, Brigitte had been seen talking to a man in a turtleneck sweater. Leroy had been sporting a turtleneck that day. That night, Leroy's mother had washed his clothes by hand with ammonia instead of taking them to the dry cleaners as usual. There was also a telltale fifteen-minute gap in the suspect's alibi. Moreover, there were rumors that Leroy had been a prodigious consumer

of pornography. Recently, he had been involved in a number of shady
real estate transactions.

Nevertheless, in lieu of more concrete findings explicitly linking Leroy to the victim or the murder scene, the examining magistrate realized
he had a relatively weak case. Thus, shortly after he was arrested, Leroy
was released. Once again he walked the streets of Bruay-en-Artois a
free man.

The Maoists wished to spare Brigitte a second death—this time, at the
hands of a class-based judiciary system—by ensuring that her murderer
was brought to justice. To the brain trust of the pro-Chinese Gauche
prolétarienne, Leroy's guilt was never in doubt. His release was a typical
instance of the fecklessness of bourgeois justice. The plotline was simple,
one that the Maoists had observed time and again: a bourgeois kills a
member of the working class, and no charges are pressed. The culprit is
released with impunity. For the Maoists, although there were some dissenting voices, Leroy's guilt was a foregone conclusion. As a bourgeois,
he was *objectively* guilty. His crime was merely a logical extension of the
everyday injustice members of the working classes endured at the hands
of their bourgeois tormentors. ("First they kill us at the bottom of the
mines; now they kill and mutilate our children," lamented the miners
upon learning of Brigitte's death.)[1] Adding to the Maoists' outrage was
the fact that in recent years several women in the same region—all of
humble origin—had been murdered in similar fashion. In each case,
although the women had not been raped, their torsos had been mutilated. The police felt seemingly little pressure to apprehend the culprit.
In each instance, insinuations surfaced implying that the victims were
"loose women"—a widespread assumption in the region about miners'
daughters—hence, intrinsically blameworthy. Ironically, the Maoists
themselves were nearly all normaliens—students of the elite Parisian
Ecole normale supérieure. As such, their backgrounds were preponderantly upper middle class. Were they, then, seeking to expiate their own
guilt as sons and daughters of the bourgeoisie? Who could doubt it?

---

[1] Philippe Gavi, "Bruay-en-Artois: Seul un bourgeois aurait pu faire ça?" *Les Temps Modernes* 312–13 (July–August 1972): 196.

The Maoist daily *La Cause du Peuple*, with Jean-Paul Sartre as its titular editor, sprang into action to defend Brigitte's honor as well as that of her class. The inflammatory headline of the May 1 issue screamed: "Bruay: And Now They Are Massacring Our Children!" The Maoists sought to transpose the discussion from the plane of criminality to that of class struggle. They lambasted Leroy's and Mayeur's alleged prurient sexual exploits, as well as (somewhat laughably) their purported culinary extravagances: "Who in Bruay-en-Artois buys lobster, under the proviso that both antennae remain attached? Price is no object; one must have quality, even if it costs 300 to 400 francs a week. . . . Who ate 800 grams of meat the night of the crime? Leroy! A daughter of the working class who has just peaceably visited her grandmother is beaten to shreds: it's an act of cannibalism."

A sidebar proclaimed: "Only a bourgeois could have done this!" The youthful gauchistes, or leftists, remained wedded to a Manichaean opposition between "bourgeois" and "proletarian" that bore only a vague resemblance to the realities of contemporary French society. In postwar France, the working class, whose revolutionary potential Marx had glorified, had ceased to be a dominant political and economic force. It had been largely replaced by "salaried employees" (*salariés*), composed of white-collar workers and middle managers (*cadres*). The Maoists' conception of the proletariat was a highly idealized image inspired in part by Louis Althusser's books and seminars.

At one point, the court inexplicably issued a search warrant for the Dewevre family home. A group of irate miners promptly invaded Leroy's garden, demanding justice and fulminating verbal threats. They intemperately suggested that only a death equal in brutality to the one Brigitte had endured would be suitable. Rocks were hurled at the Mayeur estate adjacent to the crime scene. A few days later, a group of miners' wives directly petitioned the examining magistrate, Henri Pascal: "We speak from the bottom of our hearts as mothers. Brigitte was our child. The bourgeoisie treat our children like chattel. If they want to have a good time, they do with our children what they want."[2] Ultimately, the French Supreme Court of Appeal (Cour de cassation) found

---

[2] Ibid., 188.

Judge Pascal biased against Leroy and, to the outrage of local residents, removed him from the case.

A commemorative plaque was placed near the empty lot where Brigitte's body had been found. Beside it lay an appeal to the townspeople to form an independent committee for truth and justice. A brainchild of the Maoists, the committee was intended to keep pressure on the examining magistrate and to ensure that Brigitte's murderer was brought to justice. The GP activists acted as catalysts. In keeping with the Maoist doctrine of the "mass line," according to which truth resides with the people, they shunned an active leadership role. Town elders, siding with Leroy, with whom many had business dealings, actively sought to disrupt the committee's activities. One miner's daughter told of being taken into custody while distributing leaflets and detained for two hours at a local police station. "They threatened to send us to the District Court in Béthune [a neighboring town]," she explained. "The police commissioner told us that we did not have the right to distribute such literature."[3]

The Maoists had already planted several militants in the area, who jockeyed with the pro-Communist trade union, the CGT (Confédération générale du travail), to win over working-class loyalties. In the Maoists' view, manifestations of working-class rage were an unequivocally positive development. It meant that the miners had surmounted their normal state of inert passivity—or, to employ the terminology of Sartre's *Critique of Dialectical Reason*, their "serialization"—and had found the courage to openly denounce class injustice.

The issue of "people's tribunals" had first surfaced in the aftermath of a February 1970 mining disaster near Lens, in which, following a methane gas explosion, sixteen miners had perished. Predictably, the local judiciary dragged its heels when it came to prosecuting mining officials for numerous safety violations, although it did see fit to indict six working-class militants who had thrown a Molotov cocktail at the mining company's offices. In December Sartre arrived to convene a popular tribunal in order to apply public pressure with an eye toward bringing those responsible for the explosion to justice. Medical experts

[3] Ibid., 190.

testified concerning the condition of advanced silicosis, or black lung disease, affecting the deceased.

The Lens tribunal found the state-owned mining company, Houllières, guilty of murder for having placed profits ahead of worker safety. Sartre, employing the idiom of Hegelian-Marxism, argued that the Houllières directorship "intentionally chose output over safety, which is to say, the production of *things* over *people's lives*."[4] The French judiciary remained unmoved, and no one was ever indicted for the catastrophe. At Lens, Sartre's one modest achievement was to secure the acquittal of the six activists who had been charged with arson.

Two months earlier, Michel Foucault and Gauche prolétarienne leader Pierre Victor (nom de guerre of the Egyptian-born Jew Benny Lévy), smitten with the ethos of revolutionary third worldism, debated the merits of popular justice in Sartre's *Les temps modernes*. For the student generation, Che, Mao, and Ho Chi Minh had become the new political idols. Che's slogan "One, two, many Vietnams," was a litany recited by left-wing youth worldwide. Who could doubt that the Vietnamese struggle against American imperialism was intrinsically just? Student radicals hoped that third-world radicalism would inject meaning and substance into an otherwise moribund global revolutionary project. A casual glance at the Kremlin's ossified, septuagenarian leadership helped explain this desperate political wager.

In the debate with Foucault, Victor argued that because of the existing court system's manifest class biases, the Left needed to establish its own revolutionary people's tribunals. He had fully imbibed the "populist" spirit of China's Cultural Revolution: its mistrust of experts and bureaucrats ("better Red, than expert" had been a popular slogan), its Rousseauian veneration of the popular will. Victor excelled at pushing radicalism to its absolute limits. It was this capacity that had won him acclaim among his fellow gauchistes.

Yet, in this particular instance, it was Foucault who outdid Victor in revolutionary zeal. Foucault placed little trust in the existing legal

[4] For Sartre's conclusions, see "Prémier procès populaire à Lens," in *Situations,* vol. 8, *Autour de '68.* See also the account in Simone de Beauvoir's *La cérémonie des adieux* (Paris: Gallimard, 1981), 25.

system, or in any future "proletarian" legal system, for that matter. After all, Stalin's purge trials during the 1930s, in which an estimated one million people lost their lives, had become a permanent blot on the record of Soviet communism. Thus, on the one hand, like Victor, Foucault favored the summary elimination of bourgeois legality. On the other hand, he argued vigorously against the creation of the people's tribunals favored by Victor, Sartre, and other GP activists. Such organs, he believed, represented too much of a formal constraint on the spontaneity of popular will. To employ the jargon of the times, such tribunals risked congealing into an "ideological state apparatus" (one of Althusser's pet terms). Thereby they threatened to create a needless divide between the masses and the official repositories of power.

The model of justice Foucault proposed harked back to the halcyon days of the French Revolution: the September massacres of 1792, when hundreds of helpless prisoners were put to death for fear that, with counterrevolutionary armies amassing on France's eastern frontier, the criminals might threaten the Revolution's integrity. Foucault's logic was antiseptic and chilling:

> Now my hypothesis is not so much that the court is the natural expression of popular justice, but rather that its historical function is to ensnare it, to control it and to strangle it, by re-inscribing it within Institutions which are typical of a state apparatus. For example, in 1792, when war with neighboring countries broke out and the Parisian workers were called on to go and get themselves killed, they replied: "We're not going to go before we've brought our enemies within our own country to court. While we will be out there exposed to danger they'll be protected by the prisons they're locked up in. They're only waiting for us to leave in order to come out and set up the old order of things all over again." . . .

The September executions were at one and the same time an act of war against internal enemies, a political act against the manipulations of those in power, and an act of vengeance against the oppressive classes. Was this not—during a period of violent revolutionary struggle—at least an approximation to an act of popular justice; a response to oppression which was strategically useful and politically necessary?[5]

In Foucault's eyes, spontaneous mass action possessed the added advantage of transcending the "bourgeois" division of labor between judge and executioner. Henceforth, the masses would assume *both* functions. In terms of the logic of revolutionary one-upmanship, Foucault won the debate hands down. Victor was unused to being ideologically outflanked. He could hardly believe his ears and retreated in shock.

Back in Bruay, journalists throughout France descended upon the depressed little mining town, which could have served as the setting for Zola's *Germinal*. A miner's life expectancy was short. Black lung disease was widespread, and the living conditions squalid. In 1906 a mine collapse at a nearby pit had cost 1,101 lives. Miners told gruesome stories of coworkers who had been trapped in cave-ins. One was decapitated. The bosses demanded that the miners keep working rather than pay their respects to the deceased. Many of the accidents in question were avoidable, the result of placing profits above worker safety. As one miner explained: "In the mines, only one thing counts: your ability to work and the state of your health. You're in a situation where the older you become, the less you earn. When your health deteriorates and you lose the ability to work, you're placed at the bottom of the scale. You can make 70 francs a day for ten years and then 30–40 for the next twenty."[6]

In the eyes of the press it was Leroy's arrest rather than Brigitte's murder that was the real scandal. The *Journal de Dimanche* claimed it was inconceivable that someone of Leroy's educational background and social standing could have committed so heinous a crime. Even *Le Monde* glossed over the Bruay residents' outrage over Brigitte Dewevre's tragic demise. For France's newspaper of record, the injustices of class were

---

[5] Foucault and Victor, "On Popular Justice: A Dialogue with the Maoists," in *Power/Knowledge*, 1–2.

[6] Gavi, "Bruay-en-Artois," 118.

inconsequential. Instead, Brigitte's murder was trivialized as a *fait divers*, a "human interest story."

Outraged by Leroy's abrupt release, the Maoists decided to convene an independent truth and justice commission. The GP leadership, along with fellow travelers such as Sartre and Foucault—known as "democrats," since despite their "pro-Chinese" sympathies, they stopped short of becoming full-fledged Maoists—traveled to Bruay in full force. If the French justice system, in collusion with the local bourgeoisie, failed to mete out just retribution for Brigitte's brutal slaying, GP activists would ensure that the people's will was carried out.

The GP inclination toward militancy had been stoked by the February slaying of a young Maoist, Pierre Overney, at a Renault factory on the outskirts of Paris. Weeks earlier, factory officials had uncovered several Maoist militants who had infiltrated the plant for organizing purposes. Once they were discovered, the undercover Maoists were promptly dismissed. A wave of violent confrontations and protests ensued. The Maoists outfitted themselves in riot gear. Victor himself could often be seen leading the charge.

Overney's death, at the tender age of twenty-three, precipitated a major crisis among the Maoists. For years, in keeping with their self-understanding as militants, they had glorified the virtues of revolutionary violence. This ethos of uncompromising revolutionism in part distinguished the Maoists from the reformist orientation of the French Communists (not to mention the openly reformist Socialists) who, since the Liberation, had enjoyed a comfortable niche in the French electoral system. But with Overney's senseless murder, the Maoists were forced to face up to the political implications of their own rhetorical excess. They realized that their own doctrine of violent class confrontation was indirectly responsible for the young worker's senseless death. Many Gauche prolétarienne activists were justly horrified when they were forced to confront directly the sanguinary repercussions of their own political radicalism. According to some reports, the intrepid Victor was observed leaving the Renault factory scene convulsed with tears.

Several days later, Overney's corpse was interred at the Père Lachaise cemetery. Remarkably, a cortege of two hundred thousand mourners followed the casket to its final resting place. At the head of the procession marched a number of high-profile Maoist sympathizers: Sartre, Simone de Beauvoir, future Socialist prime minister Michel Rocard, as well as the actresses Simone Signoret and Jane Fonda. (Fonda was in Paris during the filming of Jean-Luc Godard's ode to the recent spate of French factory occupations, *Tout va bien*.) There could be no mistaking the fact that Maoism, which began as the brainchild of a few wayward normaliens, had in the meantime acquired considerable cultural cachet as radical chic. Yet, as the godfather of French Maoism, Louis Althusser, aptly observed on the occasion of Overney's funeral: "Today they are not burying Pierre Overney; they are burying gauchisme."[7]

In retaliation for Overney's killing, the Gauche prolétarienne's "military wing," the so-called Nouvelle résistance populaire (NRP), kidnapped the Renault plant foreman, Robert Nogrette, only to release him two days later, unharmed.[8] Until then, the Maoists were perceived as victims of government repression and had enjoyed broad popular support. However, the decision to abduct Nogrette backfired egregiously. The Maoist "action" was roundly condemned by the "bourgeois" press but also by other gauchistes.

The political mood in France had perceptibly changed. The public's tolerance for demonstrative acts of violence was negligible. It had observed the consequences of left-wing terrorism in the neighboring lands of Italy and Germany and found them wholly distasteful.[9]

Later on, the Maoists claimed that the weapons they had used during the Nogrette abduction had not been loaded. A similar attraction and revulsion vis-à-vis the lure of revolutionary violence would characterize Maoist militancy throughout all its phases. That the term "résistance" figured in the group's name was hardly an accident. It bespoke the gauchiste conviction that under de Gaulle's rule (and, as of 1971, under Pompidou's), the French were living under a right-wing dictatorship. According to the Far-Left political optic, France was an "occupied" country that needed to be "liberated."

[7] Althusser, *L'avenir dure longtemps*, 197.

[8] See the fictionalized account of the Maoist Popular Resistance movement by Rolin, *Paper Tiger*.

[9] For more on the relationship between leftism and terrorism, see Sommier, *Violence politique*.

Coming on the heels of Pierre Overney's death, for French gauchisme the showdown at Bruay-en-Artois represented a point of no
return. Memories of the unprecedented revolutionary upsurge that
was May 1968 were rapidly receding. A period of political normalcy
had set in. Many Gauche prolétarienne activists had begun to doubt
whether they were still living in a revolutionary age. Moreover,
several prominent Maoists—among them, the philosopher André
Glucksmann—had serious doubts concerning Leroy's guilt. They felt
that, by prejudging him, their comrades had proceeded rashly and
irresponsibly.

How would the Maoists act in the event they adjudged Leroy guilty?
Would they cross the line to political murder, or terror, as their opposite numbers in Germany and Italy had already done?

Victor, channeling Saint-Just, observed that under the circumstances
revolutionary violence was entirely justified. As he commented in the
pages of La Cause du Peuple:

> It is necessary to pose the question: if Leroy is set free, would the
> population be justified in seizing him? We respond: Yes! In order
> to reverse the authority of the bourgeoisie, the humiliated popu-
> lation would be right to institute *a brief period of terror and to strike*
> *at a handful of contemptible, hateful individuals.* . . . A principle of
> "popular" justice that would suppress that natural course of justice
> on the part of the population would be a principle of oppression
> that would reproduce the principle of all the judiciary apparatuses
> based on exploitation. . . . For us, class hatred is creative. It is the
> necessary point of departure.[10]

Surprisingly, one of the "democrats" who argued vigorously for restraint was Sartre. On the one hand, Sartre wholeheartedly endorsed
the Bruay miners' involvement in the struggle to determine Leroy's
guilt or innocence. Their activism proved that they refused to be
duped by the system, that class consciousness was alive and well. On
the other hand, Sartre strenuously objected to the inculpatory tone of

[10] Victor, *La Cause du Peuple*, May 17, 1972; emphasis added.

the *Cause du Peuple* articles. In "Lynching or Popular Justice?" he expressed his concern that the miners' visceral class hatred would trump the presumption of innocence.[11] After all, the evidence for Leroy's guilt remained sketchy. Moreover, as Sartre pointed out, lynching was a reactionary form of justice, a species of mob violence that had been popularized in the American South. As such, it was hardly a model for committed leftists to emulate. Sartre also claimed that it would be a tragic error to allow the dictates of class belonging to determine an individual's fate. Thereby, he remained true to his later philosophical mission: reconciling existentialism's focus on individual freedom with Marxism's emphasis on the dynamics of history and class struggle. In lieu of convincing proof of Leroy's guilt, the Maoist position remained little more than an incitement to vigilantism.

Nevertheless, led by Victor, the Maoists remained immovable. Replying to Sartre in the same issue of *La Cause du Peuple*, they accused him of driving a wedge between the bourgeoisie as a class and Leroy the individual. Thereby, the editors insinuated that by defending Leroy and the norms of due process, Sartre's analysis, like his philosophy in general, remained beholden to an ethos of "petty bourgeois individualism." They contended that Sartre had lost sight of the "class character" of the Leroy affair. The editors claimed that in the mind of the average Bruay resident, the "Leroy gang" and the "bourgeoisie" had become synonymous.

But was class justice in the name of the downtrodden genuinely preferable to bourgeois class justice? The lessons of history associated with the names of Stalin, Mao, and Pol Pot—who, during the 1950s, learned the Marxist catechism at the finest Parisian universities —suggested otherwise. One observer correctly noted: "What type of political power will this revolution produce if it succeeds in imposing a 'Communist catechism' that . . . proves conducive to an oppressive authoritarianism in its will to extirpate laziness, 'perversity,' and marginality? The perfect society would be that of honest families, good workers, devoted comrades, heroic *résistants*, courageous women,

---

[11] Sartre, "Lynchage ou justice populaire," *La Cause du Peuple*, May 17, 1972, 12.

[and] noble laborers."[12] The intemperate leftists risked substituting the Communist definition of "normalcy" for bourgeois "normalcy." The resultant "right-thinking" individuals would seem little more than pale imitations of their bourgeois counterparts. In the post-May period, French leftists realized that it was impossible to reconcile the austere tenets of dialectical materialism with the "joyful wisdom" (Nietzsche) sought by the counterculture.

Such dilemmas would impel a number of prominent GP stalwarts to become staunch human rights advocates. They had experienced the excesses of leftism firsthand and recoiled in horror at what they had seen. One could say that the ethos of *droit-de-l'hommisme* that flourished during the 1970s and 1980s was one of the primary, if unintended, consequences of the gauchiste experience.

After Judge Pascal was removed from the case, the new judge failed to convene a grand jury to review the evidence, and Leroy never stood trial for Brigitte's slaying. Sadly, to this day, her death remains an unsolved crime, and her murderer has never been found.

Bruay-en-Artois had turned into a mini-laboratory of left-wing political correctness. Soon, the fault lines of leftism stood fully exposed, and the delusions of gauchisme began to unravel. Remaining faithful to the Maoist doctrine of the "mass line," the GP leadership held that truth lay with the masses. In opposition to Sartre, they insisted that were popular justice exposed to the formal hindrances of rules and procedures, the "natural movement of justice on the part of the population" would be fatally impeded. As a result, a formal judicial apparatus "external to the masses" would gain the upper hand.[13]

Since Foucault, like Sartre, was a prominent Maoist sympathizer, he was numbered among the so-called democrats, or well-disposed fellow travelers. Foucault's attitude toward the Bruay-en-Artois affair was rife with ambivalence. On the one hand, he was convinced that Leroy was guilty. On the other hand, the situation's political explosiveness made

---

[12] Gavi, "Bruay-en-Artois," 200.
[13] Victor, *La Cause du Peuple,* May 17, 1972.

him distinctly uncomfortable. He therefore resigned himself to the role of an onlooker or observer.[14]

Although in the debate with Victor, Foucault had posed as an advocate of popular justice, in Bruay, having observed the phenomenon from up close, he was revolted by what he saw. In his view, the Bruay protests risked degenerating at any moment into the crudest form of unthinking mob violence. Thus, despite his theoretical attraction to the September massacres, ultimately Foucault realized that this was not a political model to be emulated or encouraged. Instead, he came to view the potential for unmediated popular violence he had witnessed as distinctly fascistic. He began to wonder: was not the gauchiste intoxication with revolutionary violence merely a left-wing analogue of fascism's fascination with political sadism? After all, had not critics of totalitarianism long suggested that left- and right-wing dictatorships were merely mirror images of one another? In his preface to Deleuze and Guattari's *Anti-Oedipus,* written later that year, Foucault formulated his thoughts on these challenging political themes. As he inquired: "How does one keep from being fascist, even (*especially*) when one believes oneself to be a revolutionary militant? How do we rid our speech and our acts, our hearts and our pleasures, of fascism? How do we ferret out the fascism that is ingrained in our behavior?"[15] Here was an authoritarian temptation from which left-wing militants were by no means immune.

At Bruay a growing contingent of Maoists suddenly refused to follow Victor's lead. In essence, Victor was confronted with a palace revolution. Among the prominent defectors were André Glucksmann, Christian Jambet, and *Cause du Peuple* editor Jean-Pierre Le Dantec. They rejected the claim that the Leroy affair was the turning point in working-class history that Victor and his allies had made it out to be. Victor felt that, at Bruay, his puritanical ideological line had been undermined by Maoism's "libertarian" current. Shortly after the May 1968 uprising, French Maoism had split into two groups: a more

---

[14] For Foucault's views, see Claude Mauriac, *Une certaine rage* (Paris: Laffont, 1977), 254. See also Hamon and Rotman, *Génération* 2:428–39.

[15] Foucault's preface to Deleuze and Guattari's *Anti-Oedipus*, ix.

dogmatic, neo-Leninist, orthodox wing, represented by Victor and the
Gauche prolétarienne, and a "Dionysian" current that focused on the
"politics of everyday life": women's liberation, homosexual identity,
and experimentation with alternative lifestyles. In retrospect, Victor
viewed the crisis at Bruay as the revenge of French Maoism's so-called
libidinal wing.

For years the Maoists strove to construct an alternative political
reality to compensate for the paucity of creditable domestic political
choices. In this way, the GP leadership had fabricated a delusory, eschatological image of the proletariat as the "solution to the riddle of
history" (Marx). Amid the hysteria and confusion of Bruay-en-Artois,
such delusions proved unsustainable.

CHAPTER 2

France during the 1960s

> Who would honestly believe that, at age 67,
> I would start a new career as a dictator?
>
> —Charles de Gaulle (1958)

> One cannot reign innocently.
>
> —Louis-Antoine Saint-Just (1792)

THE MAN OF JUNE 18

From 1958 to 1969 General Charles de Gaulle wholly dominated the landscape of French politics. One cannot understand France during the 1960s, as well as the nature of the political system against which the sixty-eighters rebelled, without examining the general's central role. By the same token, the political closure the general had mandated engendered a trenchant body of oppositional cultural criticism that ultimately succeeded in undermining Gaullism's credibility as a political model. As the decade evolved, pathbreaking works of fiction, film, and theory emerged, forming a cultural template through which the sixty-eighters viewed the shortcomings of postwar French society.

As of the spring of 1958, the Algerian War had raged for four years. On both sides atrocities had become commonplace. The National Liberation Front (FLN) regularly perpetrated terrorist acts against European settlers, who numbered approximately one million, as part of their effort to gain independence. In view of the French government's intransigent refusal to negotiate, the FLN felt it had no choice.

That year, the rebels crossed a threshold by targeting military sites on French soil. The French army, for its part, routinely engaged in acts of torture in defiance of international law. According to a September 1957 report, as many as three thousand Algerians taken for questioning "were never seen again, some dying under torture, some finished off to prevent their lodging unofficial complaints, and others summarily executed or shot 'attempting to escape.'"[1] It was anything but a "clean" war. Instead, savage acts of reprisal had become everyday occurrences.

In May 1958 events suddenly took a sinister turn. Just as French politicians had seriously begun entertaining the idea of negotiations, throngs of settlers stormed the Algerian capital, overthrowing the colonial administration. This was the signal that the French military—still licking its wounds from its humiliating defeat at Dien Bien Phu four years earlier—had seemed to be waiting for. At this point the generals entered the picture. Perhaps in Algeria they could regain the honor that had been tarnished in Indochina. Following the civilian insurrection, on May 13 they stepped in to declare the previous regime null and void. Led by Generals Jacques Massu and Raoul Salan—and following the script of a questionable republican tradition—they proclaimed the rule of a Committee of Public Safety, to be headed by General Salan.

The generals' political aims were twofold. First, they hoped they could block the impending ministry of Pierre Pflimlin, a political moderate who in a recent interview had raised the prospect of resolving the crisis via a negotiated settlement. Their other goal was to pave the way for de Gaulle's seizure of power. Two of de Gaulle's supporters, Léon Delbecque and Jacques Soustelle, had already entered into secret negotiations with Massu and Salan. The generals sought to force the hand of a severely weakened government, precipitating a crisis that only a military strongman like de Gaulle could resolve.

Since the colonial generals had ceased to obey their civilian leaders and had opted for rebellion, authorities in Paris were now confronted with sedition. But just when it seemed that the situation had reached a nadir, metropolitan France appeared to be at risk. Rebellious paratroopers invaded Corsica, where they formed a Committee of Public

---

[1] Maurice Larkin, *France since the Popular Front, 1936–1986* (New York: Cambridge University Press, 1988), 260.

Safety—in essence, a junta. Could the French mainland be next? In fact, the generals were already planning Operation Resurrection, a military coup targeting Paris that was scheduled for May 27. Political analysts saw eerie parallels with Franco's seizure of power some twenty years earlier. In that case, too, a general had used an African base to foment civil war in the metropole. The end result had been thirty-seven years of dictatorial rule.

Throughout its life, the Fourth Republic had been plagued by interminable parliamentary jockeying. The Communists, who, by virtue of their prestige as résistants, were one of the Fourth Republic's leading parties, delighted in playing the role of "spoiler," seizing every available opportunity to undermine prospects for political consensus. But it was the Algerian War and the May 1958 military putsch that proved to be the straw that broke the camel's back. No one believed that the republic's familiar cast of well-meaning political mediocrities could resolve the crisis. Their credibility had been permanently tainted by the Fourth Republic's rickety performance at home and abroad. The situation seemed to demand a political savior, and only one figure could plausibly play that role: Charles de Gaulle, the "man of June 18, 1940." As a *Le Monde* journalist put it, "The Republic had only one defense between it and Fascism, and that lay in the physical person of Charles de Gaulle."[2]

Eighteen years earlier, as France lay prostrate before the goose-stepping conquerors from across the Rhine, de Gaulle, in a landmark radio broadcast from London, summoned the nation to permanent resistance. De Gaulle was, to be sure, an autocrat. But unlike Pétain, he was a *republican* autocrat. In 1946 he abruptly abandoned the Fourth Republic, whose parliamentary constitution and "party system" he scorned. Twelve years later, as France tottered on the brink of civil war, de Gaulle seemed to be a figure whom both sides felt they could trust.

---

[2] Quoted in Berstein's *Republic of de Gaulle*, 8. The Fourth Republic had also been tarnished by the fiasco of the Suez affair. Following Nasser's nationalization of the Suez Canal in the fall of 1956, a joint British-French expeditionary force tried to expel the Egyptians under the cover of ensuring "freedom of navigation." The force was withdrawn following a barrage of harsh international criticism.

After he was summoned to lead in May 1958, the general engineered a brilliant political coup de théâtre. During a visit to Algeria he announced to the insurrectionary colonials: "I have understood you!" (Je vous ai compris!). The French Algerians interpreted this declaration as an endorsement of their cause—an affirmation of Algeria's undying Frenchness. Yet the statement was sufficiently ambiguous to permit de Gaulle to placate both sides. De Gaulle's return had temporarily solved the Fourth Republic's political crisis, but the dispute over Algerian independence would require another four years to resolve.

Although de Gaulle had managed to bring the so-called ultras, or putschists, back into line, by trying to play both sides of the Algerian question he was merely postponing the inevitable. The Algerian independence movement had occurred at the peak of the decolonization fervor. In recent years France had ceded independence to Indochina, Morocco, and Tunisia. A fully sovereign Algeria, where natives outnumbered Europeans by ten to one, seemed to be merely a question of time. In 1961 a group of disaffected generals once again attempted to seize power in Algiers. That same year, the Organisation de l'armée secrète (OAS) rocked metropolitan France with a series of vicious terrorist attacks. In September de Gaulle himself narrowly escaped assassination. A year later, a pro-Algerian demonstration by French Muslims was brutally suppressed by the Paris police. The death toll was well over one hundred.

To resolve the May 1958 crisis, de Gaulle was granted emergency powers. He was also licensed to formulate a new constitution whose precepts drew upon his 1946 Bayeux program. Its hallmark was a strong executive branch. Whereas France's two previous republics had been resolutely parliamentary, the Fifth Republic would be a *presidential* republic. De Gaulle's prestige was enhanced by the fact that he had reemerged from self-imposed exile to find the traditional party system in tatters. Both the Socialists and the Radicals had disappointed their followers over their irresolute handling of the Algerian crisis. Their leaderships further split over whether to accept the mixed blessing of de Gaulle as the republic's savior.

In September the new constitution was presented to the nation for approval in a referendum. Few voters wished to return to the earlier,

unstable parliamentary model, and the new constitution gained 80 percent of the vote. Of course, the recourse to plebiscites was one of the
hallmarks of twentieth-century authoritarian rule. It was one of de
Gaulle's favorite tactics, since it allowed him to circumvent parliament
and appeal directly to the nation or people.

In December de Gaulle was elected by a wide margin as the Fifth
Republic's first president. In due course, the "presidential republic"
would metamorphose into an "imperial presidency." During his tenure the presidential residence (the Elysée Palace) was justly known as
"le chateau." Although the zeitgeist was profoundly youth-oriented,
for the ensuing ten years France would be ruled by a haughty septuagenarian. Yet, no other contemporary political figure could rival the
general's charisma. De Gaulle's dramatic return from the "wilderness
years" at Colombey-les-Deux-Eglises confirmed a time-honored cycle
of French political culture: the oscillation between revolutionary upsurge and autocracy.

The bloody and divisive Algerian conflict had a profound impact on
the current generation of *lycéens,* or high school students. Rather than
viewing de Gaulle as a savior, they perceived him as someone who had
irresponsibly allowed the tragedy to persist for an additional four years.
During "les années noirs" of 1940–44, France had been the victim of a
brutal occupation. In the eyes of French youth, the Algerian War, with
its attendant cruelty and sadism, had transformed France from a nation
of victims to a nation of perpetrators. In Algeria the French themselves
had become the "occupiers." The conflict reinforced French youth's
sense of political alienation, its antiauthoritarianism, and bred a pervasive cynicism concerning the Fifth Republic's political institutions. Its
disaffection from mainstream politics set the stage for the emergence of
gauchisme: the proliferation of micropolitical groups that would stake
out terrain to the left of the Communists and their allies.

By no means did the Algerian conflict bring out the best among
France's vaunted caste of intellectual mandarins. Sartre wrote an inflammatory preface to Franz Fanon's *Wretched of the Earth,* in which he celebrated the redemptive qualities of political violence. He contended that
for the colonized to kill Europeans was an essential act of political self-
affirmation. Yet, by virtue of his refusal to distinguish between civilians

and combatants, Sartre's preface tacitly underwrote FLN terrorism. He failed to appreciate the fact that FLN violence had become the raison d'être for the systematic excesses perpetrated by the French army.

Camus, who had been born and educated in Algeria, seemed trapped in an ethical and political no-man's-land. Initially, he cautioned restraint on both sides, a message that few were prepared to accept. His compassion for the lot of the oppressed native Algerians was genuine. By the same token, Camus never came out with the unambiguous declaration of support for Algerian independence that so many on the Left had hoped for. His admirers were disappointed by the fact that his 1957 Nobel Prize acceptance speech made no mention of the Algerian conflagration. In retrospect, Camus failed to live up to the two precepts of intellectual integrity he had specified in his Nobel address: (1) the refusal to lie about what we know and (2) resistance against oppression.

Upon accepting the prize, Camus made a telltale verbal slip. When asked for his opinion about the conflict, he declared that although he believed in justice in the case at hand, he felt it was more important to defend his Algerian-born mother, thereby implying uncritical solidarity with the colonists. "When confronted with the war in Algeria and the agonizing decision it meant for him as a *pied noir*, Camus could not simply live up to his own definition of intellectual responsibility."[3] Three years later, Camus died the consummate existential death: the victim of a senseless traffic fatality.

Among French students, the Algerian War was an important run-up to the May events. At the time, the Union nationale des étudiants français (UNEF), or national student union, acted heroically in protesting against the war, supporting Algerian self-determination, and denouncing the French army's widespread use of torture. The UNEF also sponsored numerous teach-ins to heighten student awareness about the conflict, a practice it would revive at the height of the Vietnam War protests. In retrospect, the UNEF's political acumen far surpassed that of the established Left—Communists, Socialists, and Radicals—whose representatives pursued a more measured and cautious approach. The

---

[3] David Schalk, *War and the Ivory Tower: Algeria and Vietnam* (New York: Oxford University Press, 1991), 61.

UNEF was also a prominent participant in the February 1962 anti-OAS protest, when a police charge at the Charonne metro station resulted in nine deaths and more than 150 injuries.[4]

During the 1960s French society continued to modernize at an unprecedented pace. Conversely, the French political class, with de Gaulle at the helm, remained drastically out of sync. In many respects, the political system was an atavism: it had been conceived at the time of the Third Republic, whereas by the 1960s France was well into its Fifth. This marked disjunction between society and politics was one of the May uprising's root causes. One might say that, in May, French civil society avenged itself against the political system's reprehensible aloofness.[5]

"LES TRENTES GLORIEUSES"

In France the years 1945–75 have frequently been described as "les trentes glorieuses" (the thirty glorious years)—a reference to the unprecedented explosion of economic growth and consumer affluence. Commentators have characterized this period as nothing less than a second French Revolution, so vast and sweeping was the metamorphosis French society experienced. Observers have claimed (hyperbolically) that only following World War II did France finally emerge from the "Middle Ages," for it was only after 1945 that France ceased to be a predominantly rural-agrarian society and fitfully became "modern."

In his book *Les trentes glorieuses,* sociologist Jean Fourastié begins with a parable.[6] He contrasts the social condition of two rural French villages, Madère and Cessac. Madère is a paragon of underdevelopment, to the point where it could conceivably be located in the Balkans or

[4] For a good account, see A. Belden Fields *Student Politics in France: A History of the Union Nationale des Etudiants de France* (New York: Basic Books, 1970).

[5] See Serge Berstein, "Les forces politiques: Récomposition et réappropriation," in *Les années 68: Le temps de contestation,* ed. Geneviève Dreyfus-Armand (Brussels: Editions complexe, 2000), 487: "Viewed from the side of the parties, the 1968 events appear as a brute vindication of society . . . unfiltered by the mediation of political language that would resolve [problems] by [the traditional means of] republican debate."

[6] Jean Fourastié, *Les trentes glorieuses* (Paris: Arthème Fayard, 1979).

southern Europe. The inhabitants of Madère are practicing Catholics and attend church regularly. Most of them were born within a five-mile radius of the village and will spend their entire lives there. Of Madère's 574 inhabitants, 274 are actively employed. Among the latter, 208, or approximately 75 percent, work in agriculture. Their methods of cultivation have remained traditional. The entire village possesses only two tractors. Agricultural production is Madère's sole source of income. Its inhabitants are, by any stretch of the imagination, poor. They can afford to eat meat only once a week. They rarely consume butter. The only cheese they eat must be produced locally, since the villagers cannot afford to purchase it from the outside. As Fourastié makes clear, Madère has changed very little over the course of the previous one hundred years. The dominant patterns of private and vocational life resemble models that were established in the mid-nineteenth century.

Cessac, conversely, is a paragon of bustle and middle-class upward social mobility. The standard of living is four to five times that of Madère. Of 215 actively employed citizens, only 50 work in agriculture. The majority—102—work in the service or tertiary sector. They are office workers or administrators in finance or commerce. The adoption of modern agricultural production techniques has greatly enhanced the villagers' productivity. It takes Cessac farmers only one hour to produce what their counterparts in Madère produce in twelve. Fifty years ago, on Sunday mornings the local church would fill up twice. Nowadays, this occurs only on religious holidays. But not all the changes in Cessac have been for the better. As with other big cities, the town's streets are often choked with traffic and afflicted with noise pollution. Parking is scarce.

At the end of this edifying study in contrasts, Fourastié confesses that he has been having some fun at his readers' expense. The two towns he has been comparing are fictional. The differences he describes are, in fact, longitudinal rather than latitudinal. The sociologist portrays the modernization of *one particular village*, Douelle en Quercy, from 1945 to 1975. If one were to assess Douelle's dramatic socioeconomic ascent during this period—the reduction in mortality rates and needless physical suffering; the increased availability of education, information, and culture; easy access to state-of-the-art material and creature comforts—one may be tempted to conclude that one of Charles Fourier's social utopias has been realized.

Douelle's case was paradigmatic. Over a span of thirty years, France had become a hypermodern, postindustrial polity. The population swelled from forty-two million to fifty-six million. Whereas in 1945 one-third of French workers toiled in the agricultural sector, by 1975 a mere 10 percent did so. The demise of the peasantry, which traditionally had been one of the mainstays of French social and political life, as well as the backbone of *la France profonde*, signaled a permanent and dramatic sociological shift.

The urban working class was another casualty of France's rapid modernization. As in other Western societies, during les trentes glorieuses France's core industrial sectors, such as mining and metallurgy, experienced a rash decline. Automation favored unskilled over skilled labor, rendering apprenticeships superfluous and undermining class cohesion. The deskilling of industry also meant that many posts could now be filled by the rising influx of North African immigrants, which further altered traditional working-class composition. By the 1980s many workers who had traditionally voted for the Communists transferred their allegiance to Jean-Marie Le Pen's anti-immigrant National Front. During the 1960s, women entered the workforce in unprecedented numbers.

The structural transformation of work and the attractions of the affluent society combined to render the traditional Marxist notion of class struggle antiquated. *Farewell to the Working Class*, the title of a 1982 study by André Gorz, aptly summarized the French Left's resignation. If the proletariat was no longer a viable agent of revolutionary transformation, Marxism had become bereft of meaning.

By the 1970s, 85 percent of the French workforce earned its daily bread as salaried employees (*salariés*), a broad rubric that included professionals, service-industry workers, civil servants, teachers, and middle managers. This group would become the leading constituency of François Mitterrand's Socialist Party. Their support would account for the Socialists' stunning electoral victory of May 1981, which has often been viewed as a post hoc confirmation of May 1968.

As the number of salaried employees rose, smallholders—shopkeepers, the self-employed, and independent farmers—a traditional French occupational "strength," became increasingly scarce. At the same time, a major new professional grouping emerged: *cadres,* or the managerial class. When all is said and done, during les trentes glorieuses France underwent a more radical social and cultural transformation than it had experienced during the entire previous century.

During this period a vast metamorphosis of everyday life occurred. As a nation, the French were both enthralled by the seemingly boundless expansion of possibilities and unsettled by the breathtaking pace of social and cultural change, which disrupted so many well-ingrained, traditional assumptions about custom, family, place, and belief.

"BANALIZATION"

The "thirty glorious years" witnessed the proliferation of mass-market paperbacks, youth culture, and the rise of consumer society (*la société de consommation*). The advertising industry's influence seemed omnipresent: billboards, magazines, and cinema houses sung the praises of consumer affluence. The semiotics of publicity implored citizens to partake of the new ethos of socially administered hedonism. One prescient critic writing in the early 1950s observed:

> A mental disease has swept the planet: banalization. Everyone is hypnotized by production and conveniences—sewage system, elevator, bathroom, washing machine. This state of affairs, arising out of a struggle against poverty, has overshot its ultimate goal—the liberation of man from cares—and become an obsessive image hanging over the present. Presented with the alternative of love or a garbage disposal unit, young people of all countries prefer the garbage disposal unit. It has become essential to bring about a complete spiritual transformation by bringing to light forgotten desires and by creating entirely new ones. And by creating *an intensive propaganda* in favor of these desires.[7]

[7] Ivan Tchechgov, "Formulary for a New Urbanism," in *The Situationist Reader*, ed. Ken Knabb (Berkeley, CA: Bureau of Public Secrets, 1980).

The hardships of the laboring society had ceded to the blandishments of the affluent society. Faced with the enticements of modern
consumerism, orthodox Marxism seemed flatly outdated. The epicenter of alienation no longer resided in the workplace, as Marx had contended. It lay with the sphere of circulation. Little wonder that during
this period semiotics—the study of signs—became intellectually fashionable. As a paradigm, semiotics alone seemed capable of doing justice
to the omnipresence of "consumer choice" as an expression of "false
consciousness."

In *Mythologies* Roland Barthes brilliantly analyzed the appearance
world of late-modern commodity fetishism: the wrestling matches, de-
tergent boxes, cinematic delusions, travel guides, and best sellers that
had become icons of totemistic veneration. And in *The System of Objects*, Jean Baudrillard insightfully described the erotic core of modern
consumerism:

> Advertising serves as a permanent display of the buying power,
> be it real or virtual, of society overall. Whether we partake of it
> personally or not, we all live and breathe this buying power. . . .
> The mechanics of buying, which is already libidinally charged,
> gives way to a complete eroticization of choosing and spending.
> Our modern environment assails us relentlessly, especially in the
> cities, with its lights and its images, its incessant inducements to
> status-consciousness and narcissism, emotional involvement and
> obligatory relationships. We live in a cold-blooded carnival atmo-
> sphere, a formal yet electrifying ambience of empty sensual grati-
> fication wherein the actual process of buying and consuming is
> demonstrated, illuminated, mimicked . . . much as the sexual act
> is anticipated by dance.[8]

Increasingly, it seemed that the world of things flourished while
their owners languished. The austere, impersonal world conjured up by
Alain Robbe-Grillet's antipsychological novels appeared to be a perfect

[8] Jean Baudrillard, *The System of Objects*, trans. James Benedict (London: Verso,
1996), 172.

illustration of this trend. In works such as *The Erasers* and *The Voyeurs,* the object world seemed to gain the upper hand. Persons had become supernumeraries—superfluous appendages. The nouveau roman portrayed a society "in which the individuals . . . have lost all their truly primordial importance and have fallen to the level of mere anecdote." Corresponding to this diminution of the importance of character was the "strengthening of the autonomy of objects."[9]

The structuralist vogue reflected similar tendencies. As an intellectual paradigm, structuralism's ascent corresponded to humanism's demise. Structuralism sought to offset the delusions of human autonomy, the narcissistic pretense that thought and action had a meaningful impact on the world. Instead, structuralism suggested that subjectivity was conditioned by a sequence of immutable cultural constants: language, myth, and the unconscious. But what structured structuralism? As many commentators have observed, structuralism's rise correlated with the Fifth Republic's acute sociopolitical impasse, the feeling that de Gaulle's presidency had hardened into an immovable autocracy. By declaring subjectivity null and void, were the structuralists not generalizing their generation's deep-seated political frustrations?

Little wonder, then, that the sixty-eighters—colloquially known as the "children of Marx and Coca-Cola"—placed cultural concerns at the center of their revolt. It was also unsurprising that they found the heritage of surrealism—a movement that had embraced Rimbaud's slogan "Change life!" (Changez la vie!)—so congenial. One of the keys to understanding May 1968 politically is that it was less concerned with seizing political power than with rescuing everyday life from the sinister clutches of the "hidden persuaders" who had colonized it. Marx prophesied that working-class immiseration would be the revolution's driving force. But the May revolt erupted paradoxically amid a climate of unprecedented affluence.

The striking disjunction between cultural modernization and France's endemic political traditionalism, as embodied by de Gaulle's imperial presidency, was undoubtedly one of the major precipitating

---

[9] Lucien Goldmann, "The Nouveau Roman and Reality," in *Toward a Sociology of the Novel*, 134.

factors subtending the May revolt. With the ravages of the Algerian War still fresh in mind, the postwar generation had simply lost confidence in the Fifth Republic's capacity to reform itself.

France remained a highly traditional society in other respects as well. A smug coterie of elites monopolized the corridors of power as well as the venues of cultural prestige. Prospects for upward social mobility remained correspondingly circumscribed.[10]

The system of higher education was a dinosaur. The curriculum was woefully traditional, and its stifling Napoleonic centralization meant that it remained badly out of touch with the cultural concerns of contemporary youth. Educational methods reflected an arid Cartesian formalism that discouraged creativity and individual initiative. Whereas broader cultural trends encouraged immoderation and the joys of immediate gratification, French pedagogy remained didactic and austere. Professors assumed that students had nothing to contribute to the educational process. Hence, dialogue between the two groups was rare. Students mocked universities as "knowledge-vending machines" and "diploma factories."

Between 1955 and 1967 the student population had increased by 300 percent—from 150,000 to 510,000. Heretofore, higher education had been reserved for the social elite. However, given recent demographic changes, these expectations were no longer realistic. An open admissions policy—a democratic legacy of French republicanism—formally guaranteed a place for every student who had successfully completed the *baccalauréat*. Plans for expansion were belated and halfhearted. Enrollment in the humanities had soared, yet very few practical provisions had been made to accommodate the increase. It was anyone's guess whether graduates would find employment matching their sophisticated educational training. Thus, especially in the humanities, student anxieties ran high. In 1967 the government responded maladroitly by proposing the Fouchet reforms (named after Minister of Education Christian Fouchet), recommending "selective admissions" as a way of paring down France's

[10] See the classic study by Pierre Bourdieu and J-C Passeron, *The Inheritors: French Students and Their Relation to Culture*, trans. Richard Nice (Chicago: University of Chicago Press, 1979).

burgeoning student population, a gambit that catapulted student anxiety into overdrive. In many respects the university system was a time bomb waiting to explode. In a prescient 1964 article, the philosopher Paul Ricoeur glimpsed the writing on the wall: "If the country does not monitor the growth of the university in reasonable fashion, it will experience a student explosion as a national cataclysm."[11]

THE PERSISTENCE OF THE OLD REGIME

Atavistic traces of "court society" suffused French social and political life. France's paternalistic administrative culture was a perfect case in point. In *The Old Regime and the Revolution,* Alexis de Tocqueville bemoaned the French administrative system, which attempted to "foresee everything, to take care of everything, always better aware of the citizen's interests than the citizen himself, ever active and sterile."[12] The situation had changed very little since Tocqueville's day. The dominant mentality of French organizational life remained hierarchical, combined with a marked aversion to participatory decision making. The result was a seemingly unbridgeable gulf between administrative elites and their minions. Input that challenged the elites' decision-making monopoly was rejected a priori. Lower-level employees, to accommodate their superiors, would voluntarily adopt a policy of self-censorship. Why bother to provide higher-ups with unwelcome information? they reasoned. Those in positions of power thereby ended up foolishly depriving themselves of the information they needed to make informed and intelligent decisions. As one analyst lamented, "Centralization and stratification are such insuperable barriers to communication that the [adverse] consequences of 'bureaucratic' decisions take a long time to become apparent. The system cannot learn from its mistakes, and it

---

[11] Paul Ricoeur, "Faire l'université," *L'Esprit* (May–June 1964) 1163.
[12] Alexis de Tocqueville, *The Old Regime and the French Revolution,* trans. Stuart Gilbert (Garden City, NY: Doubleday, 1955), 291.

has a constant tendency to close in upon itself."[13] It was this ossified organizational mould that the sixty-eighters sought to overturn.

The postwar stress on managerial expertise meant that French society was increasingly subjected to the machinations and designs of aloof state-planning bureaus. From a democratic perspective, it seemed that technocracy had supplanted politics, and experts had replaced citizens. Higher education was fully implicated in these developments. The Ecole nationale d'administration (ENA), for example, was a mandarin institution charged with training political and administrative elites. Graduates were colloquially known as "énarques." In the eyes of critics, its ideal of a perfectly ordered society seemed like an Enlightenment experiment gone haywire. As one skeptical commentator remarked, "The history of the *énarques* is the history of Paris's decline."[14] According to the ENA's detractors, its graduates were soulless technocrats, direct descendants of T. S. Eliot's "hollow men." These new "organization men" were now running France.

In an age of specialization, one of the university's main functions was to provide government and industry with managers and experts. Knowledge had forfeited its prior innocence. As Foucault suggested in several pathbreaking works, knowledge was hardly neutral or value-free. It was involved in the maintenance of social power, a sine qua non for the reproduction of the "disciplinary society." Among French students, the field of sociology was a chief offender. Its reliance on quantitative methods and empirical research meant that it had become

[13] Michel Crozier, *The Stalled Society*, trans. Rupert Swyer (New York: Viking/Compass, 1970), 79. Crozier continues:

> If, in this light, we look at the practical results of the French administrative system in terms of cost, we will quickly see that it is more and more obsolete. First, it fails to offer good possibilities of communication and participation and, consequently, cannot make effective use of its human and material resources; second, it adapts to change slowly and with great difficulty; lastly, it is a system tending to intellectual impoverishment and a loss of capacity for self-renewal and innovation. (87)

[14] Louis Chevalier, *The Assassination of Paris*, trans. David Jordan (Chicago: University of Chicago Press, 1994), 122.

little more than a "data provider"—a handmaiden to the forces of "governmentality."

It was hardly a coincidence that a number of prominent sixty-eighters had been sociology majors. A few months prior to the May rebellion, Daniel Cohn-Bendit published an essay entitled "Why Sociologists?" ("Pourquoi des sociologues?"), which addressed the relationship between the social sciences and the evils of political technocracy. Rule by professional politicians and experts, who viewed the populace as fodder for managerial control, negated the ideal of self-determination that is democracy's normative crux.

Another one of Cohn-Bendit's targets was the burgeoning field of industrial sociology. Increasingly, social scientists were being hired as corporate consultants to boost industrial efficiency. The information society craved technical expertise, and in university-trained social scientists, it found a bountiful supply of willing accomplices. Cohn-Bendit was especially critical of the 1927–32 Mayo experiments at Chicago's Western Electric Hawthorne Works, which demonstrated how industrial output could be enhanced by isolating workers in small groups. In Cohn-Bendit's view, Mayo's narrow-minded focus on data collection remained oblivious to the values of social philosophy—that is, sociology's ability to articulate substantive questions and concerns—and inaugurated the age of empirical sociology. By banishing normative considerations while seeking objectively to register "facts," empiricism nurtured a mentality of political passivity. As Cohn-Bendit observed:

> The transformation of academic sociology into a [branch] of independent study with scientific pretensions, corresponds to the transformation of competitive capitalism into a state-controlled economy. From that point, the new social psychology has been used by the bourgeoisie to help rationalize society without jeopardizing either profits or stability. The evidence is all around us. Industrial sociology is chiefly concerned with fitting the man with the job; the converse need to fit the job to the man is neglected. Sociologists are paid by the employers and must therefore

work for the aims of our economic system: maximum production for maximum profit.[15]

Since the university played a central role in adapting knowledge to meet the new requirements of managerial efficiency, among students with a developed social conscience, it became a natural target of criticism.

Paradoxically, although during the postwar years the French had achieved an unprecedented level of material well-being, as a people they seemed remarkably discontent. In fact, the denizens of Madère—that fictive archetype of sociocultural backwardness—were undoubtedly more content with their lot than their sophisticated metropolitan counterparts. Despite its limitations, traditional French society possessed the virtues of stability and familiarity. Conversely, the affluent society of the 1960s presented citizens with a dizzying array of pseudochoices: cultural choice, vocational choice, lifestyle choice, and consumer choice. By the same token, as de Gaulle's tenure in office persisted, French citizens felt they had been all but deprived of meaningful political choice.

In a few short decades, France was transformed from a regimented class society into a stratified agglomeration of atomized individuals. Expectations of material well-being had increased dramatically. Yet, as a people, the French seemed increasingly dissatisfied, for in and of itself affluence has no natural stopping point. No matter how economically well-off the middle class became, there always seemed room for further improvement. French society appeared glued to a treadmill of acquisitiveness. Enhanced material satisfaction translated into a diffuse yet undeniable existential queasiness. The French soon realized that happiness could not be quantified.

In March 1968 an article appeared in *Le Monde* declaring "the French are bored" (les français s'ennuient).[16] It seemed that France was at risk of becoming a society of nondescript, impersonal functionaries focused on an endless series of meaningless bureaucratic tasks.

[15] See Cohn-Bendit, *Obsolete Communism*, 36–37.
[16] Pierre Viansson-Ponté, "Quand la France s'ennuie," *Le Monde*, March 15, 1968.

Social life had congealed into a congeries of stultifying and familiar routines—a condition aptly summarized by the phrase *metro-boulot-dodo* (metro-job-sleep). On the eve of the May revolt, a Situationist International tract proclaimed: "We don't want to live in a world that guarantees not dying of hunger at the cost of dying of boredom."[17] In the same spirit a celebrated May 1968 graffito declared: "Boredom is counterrevolutionary!"

Ironically, the same month that the article in *Le Monde* appeared, the Nanterre campus erupted with a student strike—the celebrated March 22 Movement—which, in a few weeks, spread to the heart of the Latin Quarter. As faculty member Didier Anzieu, writing under the pseudonym Epistémon, put it, "I'm not bored anymore!"[18]

THE REVOLUTION OF EVERYDAY LIFE

One of the central motifs of 1960s cultural criticism was the "critique of everyday life" (la critique de la vie quotidienne). Under conditions of classical capitalism, domination was largely confined to the workplace. One's private life—or what remained thereof following a sixteen-hour workday—was one's own. But the demands of consumer capitalism had altered the picture entirely. There was no longer anything "private" about private life. Under the guise of "leisure time," it had been colonized by the forces of industry—pervaded by enticements to consumer affluence, as it were. Everyday life had been stripped of its naturalness, its informality, and thus its integrity. Whether one rode the metro, went to the cinema, strolled the grand boulevards, or watched television, the iconography of consumption had become total and inescapable. In the postwar years, French material culture had been transformed to the point of unrecognizability. As Henri Lefebvre observed in his influential study *Everyday Life in the Modern World*: "We are undergoing a painful and premature revision of our old 'values'; leisure is no longer a

---

[17] Raoul Vaneigem, *Traité de savoir-vivre à l'usage des jeunes générations* (Paris: Gallimard, 1968), 8.

[18] Epistémon, *Ces idées*, 12.

festival, the reward of labor, and it is not yet a freely chosen activity pursued for itself. It is a generalized display: television, cinema, tourism."[19]

Leftism (gauchisme) developed an interpretive framework that allowed the student radicals to articulate their aspirations for political change in light of (1) communism's epic historical failures and (2) the new ways that power had begun to infiltrate the interstices of everyday life. Through its insights into the debilities of Soviet Marxism, leftism developed a theory of radical democracy. Inspired by the tradition of worker self-management, it advocated a "horizontal," egalitarian model of democratization: the self-organization of society. Leftism's political bête noir was Leninism and its doubles: Stalinism, Trotskyism, and Maoism. They were viewed as forms of left-wing authoritarianism that had repeatedly quashed rival leftist movements that strove for worker autonomy. At the same time, in one of the ironies of the cross-cultural transposition of ideas, the critique of everyday life would ultimately merge with the Maoist notion of Cultural Revolution. Importantly, this conceptual fusion helped to promote the idea that, in opposition to the pieties of orthodox Marxism, cultural themes were a legitimate object of emancipatory struggle.

The Socialism or Barbarism (S or B) group began as a Trotskyist organ, adhering to the Fourth Internationalist view that the Soviet Union was a "degenerate workers' state," which implied it could be transformed from within. Soon, however, the group understood that the limitations of Soviet communism, far from being Stalin's work alone, were traceable to Lenin's conception of the party as an authoritarian vanguard responsible for inculcating proletarians with "class consciousness." The group concluded that the Soviet Union, far from being "objectively socialist," was instead a perversion of Marxism's original emancipatory promise. In the eyes of Socialism or Barbarism founders Claude Lefort and Cornelius Castoriadis, it represented a new form of political domination: "bureaucratic state socialism."

[19] Lefebvre, *Everyday Life in the Modern World*, 54. On the influence of the French New Left, see Ingrid Gilcher-Holtey, "La contribution des intellectuels de la Nouvelle Gauche à la définition du sens de Mai 68," in *Les années 68,* ed. Dreyfus-Armand, Frank, Lévy, and Zancarini-Fournel, 89–98.

Eventually, in S or B's critical framework, the standard Marxist opposition between bourgeois and proletarians gave way to the more general antithesis between leaders and led, rulers and ruled. Influenced by
Max Weber's analysis of "bureaucratic authority," the S or B group
perceived bureaucracy as an independent form of domination that was
neither dependent on nor reducible to the market.

These insights translated into a systematic mistrust of the French
Communist Party and its allies (for example, the Communist-dominated trade union Confédération générale du travail). At a later point,
Castoriadis would arrive at the more radical conclusion that the failures
of Marxist regimes needed to be traced back to the shortcomings of
Marxist doctrine itself. As a philosophy of history, Marxism betrayed
an emphasis on totality and unity that was incompatible with the diversity of the human condition as well as the plurality of forms of historical
struggle. Castoriadis and his associates realized that contemporary reality could neither be understood nor progressively transformed via concepts of orthodox Marxism.[20] Insight into the shortcomings of Marxist
thought led the group to conclude that the critique of bureaucracy and
domination should be transposed to "the family and sexuality, education and culture—in sum, the critique of everyday life."[21] However,
Castoriadis and his colleagues refrained from drawing the logical conclusion from this train of argumentation: if Stalinism, Leninism, and
Marxism were ideologically contaminated forms, was not the idea of
revolution itself contaminated—hence, invalid?

Having broken with Marxism, Castoriadis's later thought centered on the notion of the self-instituting society. Here, his thinking
was profoundly influenced by the idea of *autogestion,* or worker self-
management, which had gained favor amid the proliferating factory
occupations at the time of the May revolt. The bureaucratically reg-
ulated society must become self-regulating, the administered society
self-administered, argued Castoriadis. He observed in 1961:

[20] Cornelius Castoriadis, "Marxism and Revolutionary Theory," in *The Castoriadis
Reader,* ed. David A. Curtis (Cambridge, MA: Blackwell, 1997), 139–95.

[21] Cornelius Castoriadis, introduction to *Socialisme ou barbarie* (1961; repr., Paris:
Union Générale des Editions, 1979), 8.

The majority of individuals, whatever their level of skill or remuneration, have been transformed into salaried executors of piecemeal labor, who openly sense the alienation of their work and
the absurdity of the system and incline toward revolt against it.
Salaried employees and office workers—members of the so-called
tertiary sector—are increasingly less distinct from manual laborers and are beginning to struggle against the system in analogous ways. Similarly, the crisis of culture and the decomposition
of values push important segments of capitalist society—above
all, students and intellectuals . . . toward a radical critique of the
system.[22]

Little wonder that in his book *Obsolete Communism*, Cohn-Bendit, enu-
merating the virtues of leftism, openly declared himself a disciple of
Castoriadis and Lefort's innovative political doctrines.[23]

In the case of the like-minded Arguments group (1956–62), the break
with orthodox Marxism was much more abrupt. In 1951 founding editor Edgar Morin was purged from the French Communist Party for
disseminating heretical views. His sin? Publishing an article mildly
critical of the party in the news and opinion weekly *France-Observateur*.
The suppression of the Hungarian uprising—an experiment in worker
self-management that was brutally quashed by Warsaw Pact tanks—
five years later left few doubts in the eyes of the Arguments group
concerning the merits of "really existing socialism."

The Arguments editors affirmed that they were interested in "arguments" rather than "dogma." Thereafter, the floodgates opened
to all manner of heterodox intellectual experimentation. The group,
whose number included Henri Lefebvre, Kostas Axelos, and Pierre
Fougeyrollas, openly proclaimed themselves to be "revisionists" vis-à-
vis the political correctness of Soviet orthodoxy.[24] Their antipathy to
organized communism made them averse to political sectarianism and

[22] Cornelius Castoriadis, *Socialisme ou barbarie* 6 (33) (December–February 1961): 84.
[23] Cohn-Bendit, *Obsolete Communism*, 16.
[24] See, for example, *Arguments* 14 (1959): 1–19.

groupthink. They found philosophical inspiration in the renaissance of Marxist humanism (Arguments published pioneering translations of leading "Western Marxists" such as Georg Lukács and Karl Korsch), which they viewed as a constructive alternative to orthodox Marxism's self-understanding as a form of scientific determinism.

The Arguments group were averse to the political implications of Sartre's declaration in *What Is Literature?* that intellectuals must be "committed" (engagé). Instead, its members were content to act as un-committed, "free-floating" intellectuals. By the same token, by accept-ing the individual as a valid starting point for social philosophy, their enterprise bore distinct affinities with Sartre's existential Marxism.

The Arguments group realized that given the decline of the manu-facturing sector, in postindustrial society the proletariat was ill suited to playing the eschatological role it had been assigned by orthodox Marx-ism. They realized that instead of waiting for a "radiant utopian future" that was destined never to arrive, progressive social change must be spurred by the actions of small avant-garde groups. In this respect, they came to view Lefebvre's association with the surrealists during the 1920s as a model. The surrealists firmly believed that the spirit of poetry should infuse the practice of everyday life. Inspired by the sur-realists, Lefebvre developed a "theory of moments": situations in which the sublime could temporarily break through the reified continuum of daily life, where "lived time" could provisionally penetrate the "dead time" of alienated labor, or the commodity-producing society.

Another one of the Arguments group's innovations was to incor-porate the methods of the social sciences for the ends of a critique of the historical present. They realized that since under late capitalism the forms of domination had expanded, a new pluralistic interpretive framework was required. In this respect their approach bore distinct similarities to that of the Frankfurt School, a fraternal society of "un-orthodox Marxists."

The innovative political doctrines of the Socialism or Barbarism and Arguments groups were the point of departure for Guy Debord's *So-ciety of the Spectacle,* one of the most influential exemplars of pre–May social criticism. In *Capital,* Marx defined "commodity fetishism" as "a definite relation between persons that assumes, in their eyes, the fantastic form of a relation between things."[25] The result was an inverted social world in which "things," qua commodities, took precedence over persons. Whereas during the nineteenth century commodity fetishism remained confined to the workplace, under late capitalism its influence had spread to the superstructure, or cultural sphere.

In *Society of the Spectacle* Debord analyzed the extension of reification from the factory to the so-called image sphere. Commodification had assumed an all-encompassing, totalizing quality. It produced a world in which the quest for authenticity was subverted at every turn by superficies or appearances. Modern life entailed a series of nefarious inversions or substitutions: the sign for the thing, image for reality, appearance for essence. The sixty-eighters felt that only an ethos of total contestation could recapture a fully alienated lifeworld. As the most recent manifestation of the "reification of consciousness" (Lukács), under late capitalism the "spectacle" had become the defining modality of "false consciousness." Under its influence the denizens of modern society seemed reduced to a state of somnambulant compliance, or, as Debord observed, the spectacle was the "sun that never sets on the empire of modern passivity."

> The spectator's alienation from and submission to the contemplated object works like this: the more he contemplates, the less he lives; the more readily he recognizes his own needs in the images of need proposed by the dominant system, the less he understands his own existence and his own desires. The spectacle's externality with respect to the acting subject is demonstrated by the fact that the individual's own gestures are no longer his own, but rather those of someone else who represents them to him. The spectator feels at home nowhere, for the spectacle is everywhere. [26]

[25] Karl Marx, *The Marx-Engels Reader*, ed. Robert Tucker (New York: Norton, 1978), 294.

[26] Guy Debord, *Society of the Spectacle*, trans. Donald Nicholson-Smith (Cambridge, MA: MIT Press, 1995), 23.

For intellectuals devoted to the values of social contestation, such developments raised a troubling specter: the working class, instead of actively opposing capitalism's injustices, had been bought off by tantalizing material incentives. Class consciousness had been defused by the baubles and trinkets of consumer society. As Lefebvre remarked: "Alienation is spreading or becoming so powerful that it *obliterates all consciousness of alienation.*"[27] Despite its penurious material circumstances, the traditional working class had at least been allowed to think its own thoughts. It seemed that the denizens of late capitalism no longer possessed this luxury. Authenticity had been redefined by the lures of consumer hedonism. In the guise of *l'art pour l'art,* culture had served as the repository of humanity's utopian aspirations and longings. Conversely, in the postwar period, culture had become a handmaiden of advanced industrial society.

THE ASSASSINATION OF PARIS

In the postwar years Paris was dramatically transformed. France's remarkable population increase—a net rise of 33 percent—provoked a corresponding building frenzy. On Paris's western outskirts the monolithic glass and steel towers of La Défense arose. Their only virtue was to have temporarily spared central Paris similar ravages.

Soon the blight of modern urban planning reached Paris as well. Although some of the more egregious architectural calamities did not occur until the 1970s, the conceptualization and planning took place during the 1960s.

Les Halles, a lively and colorful market located in the heart of the Right Bank, was bulldozed to make room for an ultramodern shopping complex. As one Francophile rued, "With les Halles gone, Paris is gone."[28] Insofar as les Halles' destruction was symbolic of a grow-

---

[27] Lefebvre, *Everyday Life in the Modern World,* 94.
[28] Cited in Chevalier's *Assassination of Paris,* 246.

ing trend, the lamentation was entirely apposite. A similar fate befell Le Marais, one of Paris's oldest districts, when the Centre Pompidou desecrated the neighborhood. Ostentatiously sporting its plumbing on the outside, Beaubourg (as it was colloquially known) was, by critical consensus, a garish, hypermodern monstrosity.

Eventually, the plague of architectural disfiguration spread to the Left Bank as well. In the heart of the Montparnasse District—a traditional haven for writers and artists—rose the fifty-eight-story Tour Montparnasse, dwarfing surrounding street life like an insatiable Moloch. Thus, by the early 1970s the Paris landscape was besmirched by a series of unsightly towers that threatened to consume their surroundings like monsters from a Japanese horror film. Le Corbusier's conception of the modern city as an industrialzed "machine for living in" had taken a distinctly dystopian turn.

Unfortunately, such neobrutalist eyesores were merely the tip of the iceberg. The postwar years also witnessed the proliferation of retail chain stores, branch banking, self-service restaurants, and the first soulless, ultrasleek supermarkets. None of Paris's traditional quartiers remained unaffected. The title of cultural historian Louis Chevalier's 1977 book, *The Assassination of Paris*, felicitously captured these trends. For artists and literati, from Baudelaire to the impressionists, Paris had been an inspirational landscape, a literary personage in its own right. For the surrealists, its streets and byways had been repositories of the "marvelous": a locus of unexpected encounters and "objective chance." Suddenly, all of this changed. Paris had become a site of lost innocence. As Chevalier observes:

> Nothing brings the consumer society home more forcibly to Parisians . . . than the newness of things, the absence of the familiar. And nothing can be clearer than its responsibility for the disfigurement and—eventually—the destruction of their city. . . . These new buildings are the great beasts, man-eating ogres, and they have already taken their first big bite. All things considered, even if they continue, here and there, to ravage and sometimes devour neighborhoods, the evil they are capable of has largely

been accomplished. All that can be done now is to curse them, to refuse them forgiveness, and also to try to contain them.[29]

In the literature and film of the period, this sense of acute social and cultural dislocation became a central leitmotif. In 1966 Simone de Beauvoir published *Les belles images*, which she described as a novel about "the technocratic society"—an amorphous social reality that was seemingly everywhere and nowhere. As de Beauvoir explains: "It is a society that I keep as much as possible at arm's length but nevertheless it is one in which I live—through newspapers, magazines, advertisements and radio; it hems me in on every hand."[30]

De Beauvoir's protagonist, Laurence, works for an advertising agency—the Orwellian "Pub-Info." Her job is to contrive enticing slogans and images in order to induce consumers to purchase wares they might otherwise scorn. One day she arrives at the office and opens the file for one of her current projects. She experiences an existential revelation, a *prise de conscience*, about the unbearable professional tedium she must endure on a daily basis. As Laurence recounts, it was all "wearisome [and] depressing. Smoothness, brilliance, shine; the dream of gliding, of icy perfection; erotic values and infantile values (innocence); speed, domination, warmth, security. Was it possible that all tastes could be explained by such primitive phantasms?"[31]

Laurence realizes that she has been living life on the surface of things. It was a hollow existence, befitting the depthlessness and impersonality of a Robbe-Grillet novel. (Nevertheless, de Beauvoir proceeds to mock Robbe-Grillet as a writer who avoids plot. Such authors, she continues, "write to write, as you might pile up stones one on top of the other, for the pleasure of it.") Did it even deserve to be called "living"? The "phantasms" had taken over. The "beautiful images" are in fact anything but beautiful. Laurence suffers from an acute case of dissociation. As the narrator remarks: "She has known some bitter rifts,

[29] Ibid., 71.

[30] Simone de Beauvoir, *All Said and Done*, trans. Patrick O'Brian (New York: G. P. Putnam's Sons, 1974), 122.

[31] Ibid., 51.

a certain irritation, grief, bewilderment, emptiness, boredom. Above all, boredom. There are no songs about boredom."[32] *Laurence s'ennuie.*

Laurence's ten-year-old daughter poses a simple question about the meaning of life—"Why do people live?"—which takes Laurence aback. She has no satisfactory answer. Her husband attempts to fill the conversational void with some meaningless clichés about "progress." In twenty years' time, he suggests optimistically, science will have eliminated the material causes of human unhappiness. But he neglects to say how should we occupy ourselves in the meantime.

The "phantasms" have also taken over the sphere of leisure time, as the following conversation between Laurence, her husband (Jean-Charles), and two friends (Gilbert and Dufrène), suggests:

"You must come on Friday. I want you to hear my new hi-fi. . . . It really is astonishing," said Gilbert. "Once you've heard it, you can't listen to music on an ordinary system anymore."

Laurence: "Then I don't want to hear it. I love listening to music."

Jean-Charles seemed deeply interested. "How much must you reckon, at the lowest figure, for a good hi-fi installation?"

"At the minimum, the strict minimum, you can get a mono setup for three hundred thousand old francs. But it's not the real thing, not the real thing at all."

"To have something really good, I suppose you have to pay about a million?" said Dufrène.

"Listen: a good system in mono costs between six hundred thousand and a million. In stereo, say two million. I advise mono rather than not very good stereo. A worthwhile combination–amplifier costs something in the neighborhood of five hundred thousand."

"That's what I said, a minimum of a million," said Dufrène, sighing.

"There are sillier ways of spending a million," said Gilbert.[33]

[32] Simone de Beauvoir, *Les belles images*, trans. Patrick O'Brian (New York: G. P. Putnam's Sons, 1968), 26.

[33] Ibid., 16. For additional studies of May 1968's literary precursors, see Margaret Atak, *May 68 in French Film and Fiction: Rethinking Society, Rethinking Representation*

In certain respects Laurence is a female version of Roquentin, Sartre's protagonist in *Nausea*. Yet, whereas Roquentin is overwhelmed by "facticity"—the refractoriness of Being or things—Laurence's alienation is social: the imagery generated by the "society of the spectacle" obviates wholeness, the attainment of authentic selfhood. Only youth—as personified by Laurence's daughter, Catherine—remains immune from the baneful effects of total socialization. In this respect, too, de Beauvoir's novel prefigures the logic of the May revolt, when, for a brief shining moment, French youth seized the political stage.

In 1965 Georges Perec's novel *Les choses: Une histoire des années soixante* (Things: A History of the 1960s) appeared. Like de Beauvoir's Laurence, Perec's characters inhabit a universe where everyday life is dominated by an ethos of consumer hedonism; a universe in which being has ceded to the materialist imperatives of having.

The protagonists of *Les choses*, Sylvie and Jerôme, are twenty-something Parisians. Both are recent college graduates and hail from the middle class. By profession, Sylvie and Jerôme are "psycho-sociologists": aspiring mind managers. In Perec's words, they are budding "technocrats halfway along the road to success."[34] They spend their days formulating and analyzing "motivational" questionnaires that explain why people develop particular consumption habits.

Sylvie and Jerôme are eager to climb on the bandwagon of the acquisitive society, where a dazzling world of consumer choice awaits them. "They passionately loved those objects that only the taste of the moment considered handsome: fake Epinal prints, English-style engravings, agates, spun-glass tumblers, neo-barbarian knickknacks, pre-scientific bric-a-brac. . . . It seemed to them that they were more and more masters of their desires: they knew what they wanted; they had clear ideas. They knew what their happiness, their freedom, would be like."[35] Their leisure time is devoted to contemplating the limitless prospect of acquiring "things": for convenience, for prestige, or for the

---

(Oxford: Oxford University Press, 1999); and Patrick Combes, *La littérature et le mouvement de Mai 68* (Paris: Seghers, 1984).

[34] Georges Perec, *Les choses*, trans. Helen Lane (New York: Grove Press, 1967), 41.
[35] Ibid., 24.

sheer joy of acquisition. One might describe them as aspiring connois-
seurs of the thing-world. The accumulation of objects is their raison
d'être. Perec characterizes the world of profligate material excess they
inhabit as follows:

> In the world that was theirs, it was practically a rule always to
> desire more than one could acquire. It was not they who had so
> decreed; it was a law of civilization, a given fact of which adver-
> tisements in general, magazines, the art of display, the spectacle of
> the streets, and even, in a certain way, the whole of those produc-
> tions commonly called cultural, were the truest expression.[36]

The choices available to them were all false choices. The only option at their disposal was to freely submit to the glamour and allure of
"things."

Socially critical elements also suffused the language of cinema. During the course of the 1960s, nouvelle vague humanism, as represented
by François Truffaut's *The 400 Blows* and *Jules and Jim*, ceded to topical
films with a sharp political edge, with Jean-Luc Godard leading the way.

As Godard's career progressed, the filmmaker concluded that traditional narrative cinema had been thoroughly co-opted by Hollywood,
to the point where it had become wholly unserviceable as a medium
of critique. If the image sphere of late capitalism was predominantly
a vehicle of social conformity, then cinema, too, was entirely compromised. In Godard's view, it had become a "cinema of illusion."
It furthered social passivity by reinforcing the reigning mentality of
unbending compliance.

Godard concluded, paradoxically, that the only way to "save" cinema was to destroy it—at least in its present incarnation. Hence, one
of his main concerns as a cineast was to dismantle film as a purveyor
of harmonious and pleasing images.[37] He had become a convinced foe

[36] Ibid., 40.

[37] See Colin McCabe, *Godard: A Portrait of the Artist at Seventy* (New York: Farrar
Strauss, 2004): "In intellectual terms, what is striking about Godard in 1968 is that
within a decade he had traveled from a position of pure classicism (using established

of the bourgeois ideal of the self-contained, well-wrought work of art. There seemed something intrinsically suspect about the fact that bourgeois civilization promoted the idea of aesthetic perfection while society itself was allowed to languish in squalor. To combat this ideal, Godard increasingly relied on a variety of techniques drawn from the repertoire of the twentieth-century avant-garde. One of his favorites methods was Bertolt Brecht's alienation effect (*Verfremdungseffekt*), which ensured a measure of critical distance from the art object. Godard viewed Soviet filmmakers such as Sergei Eisenstein and Dziga Vertov as his cinematic role models, as opposed to the Hollywood directors he had lionized during his years at *Cahiers du Cinéma*.

Godard's *Weekend* (1967) was a transitional film—the director's last fling with the conventions of narrative cinema, which, by the same token, he was at pains to disrupt throughout the film. *Weekend*'s satirical thrust takes aim at the clichés and conventions of Hollywood film. By demolishing cinema as a self-contained realm of pleasing illusion (*les belles images*)—as an extension of art for art's sake, as it were—Godard hoped to facilitate its rebirth as a vehicle of political education. As the film's final title aptly proclaims, "End of Story, End of Cinema."

Weekend concludes with a spectacular eight-minute tracking shot of a titanic traffic jam stretching on a country road as far as the eye can see. Of course, nothing was more symbolic of postwar French society's cult of technological perfection than the automobile. Yet, increasingly the automobile culture's attendant ills came to light: choked thoroughfares, toxic emissions, noise pollution, as well as horrific collisions resulting in the indiscriminate commingling of metal and human flesh. As a symbolic object, the automobile stood for "the materialism and aggression of a society being crushed by its own fetishized commodities."[38] Godard's legendary tracking shot culminates in a violent accident scene. Mangled corpses litter the road, but the camera refuses to linger,

---

genres and an accepted language to address an established audience) to one of pure modernism (deconstructing established genres and grammars to address an ideal audience)"; 207.

[38] David Sterritt, *The Films of Jean-Luc Godard: Seeing the Invisible* (New York: Cambridge University Press, 1999), 93.

thereby suggesting that modern society has perversely embraced such carnage as a natural and acceptable part of everyday life.

Cinema, an ingrained French passion, had an even more direct role in the events leading up to the May explosion. In February 1968 the French authorities abruptly dismissed Henri Langlois, the beloved director of Cinémathèque française, Paris's storied repertory screening room located at Palais de Chaillot. Langlois was an incomparable film connoisseur and archivist. During the 1950s it was at the Cinémathèque that the leading nouvelle vague directors such as Truffaut, Godard, Claude Chabrol, and Alain Resnais received their education in the history of cinema. In response to the closing, a major protest movement arose—a mobilization that, in retrospect, stands out as an important precursor of the May events.

In hindsight, the years of quiet desperation between 1962, when the Algerian conflict was resolved, and the May uprising were merely the calm before the storm. French society had attained an unprecedented level of material well-being. Yet beneath the veneer of beautiful appearances, a pervasive existential discontent seethed. The affluent society's triumph occurred at the expense of other, substantive political and cultural values the French held dear. The Fifth Republic's presidential system suited crisis situations. But under conditions of political normalcy, it seemed patently undemocratic. During the 1960s French youth longed to express its political aspirations and will, but under Gaullism they were effectively deprived of a meaningful voice. To compensate, they would need to invent utopian political forms corresponding to their hopes and dreams.

CHAPTER 3

May 1968: The Triumph of Libidinal Politics

> The replacement of the pleasure principle by the reality principle is the great traumatic event in the development of man. . . . But the unconscious retains the objectives of the defeated pleasure principle. Turned back by external reality . . . the pleasure principle not only survives in the unconscious but also affects in manifold ways the very reality which has superseded the pleasure principle. The return of the repressed makes up the tabooed and subterranean history of civilization. . . . This *recherche du temps perdu* becomes the vehicle of future liberation.
>
> —Herbert Marcuse, *Eros and Civilization*

> We have experienced an impossible revolution: a revolutionary moment without revolution. We must not confuse revolutionary self-expression in an extra-territorialized Sorbonne with political preparation for a real social revolution. Revolutionary consciousness cannot take the place of revolution.
>
> —Alain Touraine, *The May Movement*

"THE YEAR OF THE HEROIC GUERRILLA"

Prescient political prognostications were never Fidel Castro's forte. But in his 1968 New Year's Day speech, the Cuban revolutionary leader seems to have more or less "gotten it right." Reeling from Che

Guevara's summary execution the previous year at the hands of Boliv-
ian military authorities, Castro foresaw that 1968 would be "the year of
the heroic guerrilla." His prophecy would not be far off.

By any stretch of the imagination, 1968 was an annus mirabilis—
a year of *événements,* or events. Historians have repeatedly sought to
fathom how it was possible that within a span of twelve months spectacular youth revolts managed to break out across four continents. And
although the students' aims and demands varied greatly from country
to country, these worldwide political uprisings indubitably possessed
something in common. But what, exactly?

For students the world over, a major focal point was the war in
Vietnam, a sine qua non for almost all that followed. The war featured
the world's major industrial power employing the most lethal technological methods to force a hapless developing nation into submission.
As a result of the United States's effort to "save" Vietnam from the
menace of communism, some one to two million Vietnamese civilians
perished. Time and again, the plucky Vietnamese, playing David to
America's Goliath, resisted heroically, despite their inferior weaponry
and materiel. From the standpoint of world public opinion, America's
anti-Communist crusade in Southeast Asia had backfired egregiously.
It managed to breathe new life into the Marxist theory of imperialism
as the "highest stage of capitalism." Images of American atrocities—
carpet bombing by dreaded B-52s, napalm attacks, gruesome civilian
massacres—appeared on the nightly news worldwide.

In January 1968 the Vietcong launched the Tet Offensive, timed to
coincide with the Vietnamese Lunar New Year. The attacks included a
brazen nighttime assault on the United States Embassy in Saigon. From
a military standpoint, the results were counterproductive. By the time
the smoke had cleared, the North Vietnamese were forced to relinquish
nearly every position they held. Yet, as a symbolic act and propaganda
coup, Tet represented an unequivocal turning point. American military
commanders had repeatedly described the war as being well in hand.
The offensive proved that such claims were fallacious. The generals
looked like fools, and the plucky Vietnamese appeared indomitable.

The greatest military machine in history was on the run. Condem-
nation of the Vietnam War became a central rallying point for the

International Left. In France, Vietnam Committees (CVB, or Comités Vietnam de bases) attracted thousands of activists who would play a pivotal role during May 1968 and its aftermath.

The pace of the year's political events seemed dizzying. In the United States 1968 was a year of history-altering political assassinations: Martin Luther King in April; Robert Kennedy in June. Both incidents represented irremediable setbacks for the cause of American liberalism, whose luster had already been severely tarnished by the war in Vietnam.

In August the Czech experiment in "socialism with a human face"—the so-called Prague Spring, led by Alexander Dubček—was brutally suppressed by Warsaw Pact troops. Across Eastern Europe the disheartening realization set in that henceforth it would be impossible to ameliorate communism's ills from within.

In Mexico City throngs of students assembled to protest encroachments upon university autonomy and to call attention to the mistreatment of political prisoners. Soon, world attention would be focused on the Mexican capital, where the summer Olympic Games were scheduled to take place. On October 2 tens of thousands of students assembled in Tlatelolco Plaza to press their concerns. The police panicked and a massacre ensued. Hundreds of unarmed student demonstrators were slain. The official accounting would begin only three decades later.[1]

What might these disparate political events have in common? Part of the explanation lies with demographics. The post–World War II period witnessed a dramatic population surge, the baby boom. This generation reached maturity during the mid- to late 1960s, at a moment when, throughout Europe and North America, a commitment to political radicalism took hold. Youth, as a distinct transitional phase between childhood and adulthood, became an autonomous cultural and political variable. The postwar economic boom had obviated the need for youth to enter the workforce immediately. Instead, middle-class youth had at its disposal the leisure time necessary for self-reflection and self-cultivation.

---

[1] James McKinley, "Mexico Charges Ex-President in '68 Massacre of Students," *New York Times,* June 30, 2006, A3.

Via music, dress, and morals, postwar youth carved out a distinct cultural niche. The rapid expansion of higher education meant that contemporary youth was, intellectually and culturally, growing more sophisticated. The 1960s generation refused to acquiesce passively vis-à-vis questionable decisions that were imposed from on high by political elites. Instead, as informed citizens, it began actively to seek out avenues and possibilities for political participation. Advanced industrial societies claimed to be democracies. Should they not be forced to live up to their own egalitarian political claims?

The revolution in mores initiated during the 1960s has been described as a turn toward postmaterialist values. One observer explains: "Advanced industrial societies are undergoing a shift from economic and physical security . . . toward greater emphasis on belonging, self-expression, and quality of life."[2] This was a generation—once again, perhaps the first in history—for which the imperatives of material necessity ceased to dominate everyday life. Thus, unlike previous generations, postwar youth was increasingly able to turn its attention toward qualitative and spiritual pursuits. The unprecedented affluence of les trentes glorieuses afforded it the leisure and material comfort to do so.

THE END OF ART AND THE BEGINNING OF CONTESTATION

For two years student activists protested against American military involvement in Vietnam. The war in Indochina radicalized French students in much the same way the Algerian conflict had ten years earlier. During the 1960s French students also sought to address their own specific, existential, generational concerns—concerns bearing on the "politics of everyday life."

In 1966 a dress rehearsal for the May revolt occurred at the University of Strasbourg. The Strasbourg events centered on the publication and distribution of a pamphlet, *On the Poverty of Student Life*, by an obscure avant-garde group known as the Situationist International (SI).

[2] Inglehart, *Culture Shift*, 11.

Although at the time the Strasbourg episode seemed to be a relatively minor affair, in retrospect it stands out as an uncanny anticipation of May's unique blend of libidinal-political fervor.

The Situationist International was founded in 1958 by Guy Debord. It emerged from two earlier cultural groupings, Potlatch and the International Movement for an Imagist Bauhaus. The problem that preoccupied both 1950s SI prototypes was, what is the role of culture after the end of art? To proclaim the end of art seemed portentous. How might it be claimed that "art" has "died"? Debord and the Situationists had something very specific in mind. They were reflecting on the fact that modern art, especially surrealism, had patently lost its capacity to shock. Instead it had become something familiar and nonthreatening. The once-provocative avant-garde had found a respectable niche within the canon of twentieth-century culture. Art had become "presentable." The Situationists held that art and social respectability operated at cross-purposes. Since the nineteenth century, art had functioned as modern society's "bad conscience." It unmasked hypocrisy, bad faith, and the evils of social conformity. Now that the avant-garde had become canonical, where might one find a substitute that could fill its socially critical role?

Having lost his faith in culture, Debord experimented with various forms of "anti-art" reminiscent of Dada, thereby hoping to resuscitate culture's critical social function. In 1952 his film *Howlings in Favor of Sade* premiered. As the screen oscillated between imageless white and black backgrounds, selected quotations and theoretical tidbits punctuated interminable stretches of silence. "Cinema is dead. Films are no longer possible," declared a voice during the opening sequence. "If you want, let's have a discussion."[3] After twenty minutes, the audience left. In another notorious incident, the Situationists provoked a scandal at Notre Dame Cathedral when one of their number dressed up as a priest and, mounting the pulpit as the faithful looked on in horror, proclaimed, à la Nietzsche, the death of God.

Yet, somehow these neo-Dadaist provocations fell short of the mark—jejune illustrations of the "end of art" thesis. A different strategy was needed. What if art's demise was not amenable to an *aesthetic*

[3] See the account of the incident in Jappe's *Guy Debord*, 49.

solution? What if instead the problem could be resolved only via re-course to *radical political change*?

During the 1960s the Situationists' focus altered accordingly. Instead of bemoaning the deficiencies of contemporary culture, they began exploring the historical and philosophical bases of radical politics. Along with Cohn-Bendit's anarchism, the Situationist critique of everyday life would become one of the most important theoretical influences on the May activists.

In the fall of 1966, the Strasbourg branch of the national students' union, incited by a handful of leftists, decided to fund the publication of *On the Poverty of Student Life*, a radical pamphlet by the Situationist Mustapha Khayati.

Khayati presented a no-holds-barred exposé of student illusions. Students liked to think of themselves as autonomous. But in reality they were dependent on the university as their ersatz family. They saw themselves as critics of the university's role as a professional school for middle managers and technocrats. Yet most of their proposals for reform would simply reinforce that role rather than genuinely challenge it. One would merely end up with a more efficient university structure rather than a qualitatively different one. After all, one of the chief objectives of the current round of reforms was to streamline university admissions procedures to facilitate a better interface between higher education and private industry. Students thought of themselves as adepts of avant-garde cultural goods—nouvelle vague cinema, Camus, and Althusser—without realizing the conformist nature of their allegiances and choices. (The Situationists took special aim at Godard, whom they viewed as toying with revolutionary ideas and themes rather than demonstrating genuine commitment.)[4] As consumed within a university setting, moreover,

[4] See Guy Debord, "On the Role of Godard," in *Situationist International Anthology*, 177–78:

> Godard's critiques never go beyond innocuous, assimilated nightclub or Mad Magazine humor. His flaunted culture is largely the same as that of his audience which has read exactly the same pages in the same drugstore paperbacks. . . . His successful ascension from the provinces is exemplary at a time when the system is striving to usher so many "culturally deprived" people into the respectable consumption of culture– even "avant-garde" culture.

these avant-garde cultural constructs remained depotentiated and sterile. Khayati observes:

> The student is a stoical slave: the more chains authority heaps upon him, the freer he is in fantasy. He shares with his new family, the University, a belief in a curious kind of autonomy. Real independence lies in a direct subservience to the two most powerful systems of social control: the family and the State. He is their well-behaved and grateful child, and like a submissive child he is over-eager to please. He celebrates all the values and mystifications of the system, devouring them with all the anxiety of the infant at the breast.[5]

Sixteen thousand students were enrolled at the University of Strasbourg. Leftist students used student body funds to publish ten thousand copies of Khayati's intemperate Situationist diatribe and then proceeded to distribute them during a convocation. All the town notables, from the mayor to the bishop, were present. The Strasbourg gauchistes also disrupted classes on occasion—particularly those of a psychology professor known for his contributions to the science of "urban population control."[6] The students also reproduced a Situationist political comic strip, *The Return of the Durutti Column* (a reference to an anarchist brigade during the Spanish Civil War) and proceeded to distribute it campuswide. The strip mocked rival leftists and advocated "theft" as a means of countering the logics of commodification. *The Return of the Durutti Column* exemplified one of the Situationists' favored techniques, *détournement*: seizing on an otherwise conventional cultural object and reconfiguring it for radical political ends.

Strasbourg is a fairly conservative and traditional milieu. When the local press got wind of these protests and disruptions, it pounced. The leading Parisian dailies—*L'Aurore, France-Soir,* and *Le Monde*—followed

---

[5] Situationist International, *On the Poverty of Student Life* (Berkeley, CA: Contradiction, 1972), 2.

[6] For the Situationist account of this episode, see "Our Goals and Methods in the Strasbourg Scandal," in *Situationist International Anthology,* 204–12.

suit. Their headlines denounced the new reprehensible breed of "ultra-revolutionaries," "beatniks," and "Situationists" who had managed to commandeer and corrupt an otherwise respectable organ of student governance. *Le Monde*'s reaction was typical: "This pamphlet, with its high tone, must be considered a systematic rejection of all social and political organizations as we know them in the West and of all the groups that are currently trying to transform them."[7] (The irony of *Le Monde*'s complaint about another publication's "high tone" is too good to let pass unremarked.) The press suggested that, from their perch in Paris, the Situationists were "conspirators" who had engineered a student government coup behind the scenes. In fact, *On the Poverty of Student Life* had been published wholly within the bounds of existing student government regulations. During a faculty assembly, one professor declaimed: "I'm all in favor of freedom of speech. . . . But if there are Situationists present, they must leave!"[8] In other words, freedom of speech should be granted to everyone but the Situationists!

One of the remarkable aspects of the May uprising was that a series of student protests swiftly metamorphosed into a general assault on the perceived failings and inadequacies of French society. Situationist literature was critical in demonstrating that the crisis of the university was an integral part of a larger social crisis. In the post-May period, the Situationist focus on everyday life fused with the Maoist notion of cultural revolution. In this way, the project of a revolution of everyday life was born. "Revolution" no longer meant seizing power or socializing the means of production. It connoted instead a grassroots transformation of interpersonal relations and living conditions.

THE UNIVERSITY IN CRISIS

With respect to the French university system, the Strasbourg incident was merely the tip of the iceberg. At Antony, a suburban university on

[7] *Le Monde*, December 9, 1966.
[8] See the account in *Situationnistes et mai '68*, by Dumontier, 90. See also Daniel Lindenberg, "1968 ou la brèche du situationnisme," *L'Esprit* (May 1998): 127–40.

the outskirts of Paris, protests repeatedly broke out over regulations governing dormitory visitation privileges. Male students were forbidden access to female residence halls after 11:00 p.m. Women could visit the men's residences as long as they were twenty-one years old. Guardhouses, which served as surveillance posts, were ominously stationed throughout the campus to ensure that the visitation regulations were stringently enforced.

In most other respects, the students were viewed as adults. The consumer society employed sexual imagery to sell everything from lingerie to automobiles to bars of soap. The sexual revolution was in full swing. Yet, the French university system was anachronistically trying to uphold an outmoded, Pétainiste moral code that was woefully out of step with broader social tendencies and trends. De Gaulle himself seemed wholly indifferent to the students' concerns, remarking on one occasion: "They really only need to see each other in the lecture halls."[9] The Ministry of Education had set itself up for a fall.

In 1962 frustrated Antony students destroyed one of the detested surveillance lodges. Three years later, fifteen hundred students signed a petition demanding liberalized visitation rights and affordable housing. The university administration, however, remained unmoved, fearing that any compromise might set a precedent for universities nationwide. Demonstrations ensued. In an anticipation of the May events, French authorities imprudently summoned riot police, thereby turning what had been a civil-protest movement into a scenario rife with potential for violent confrontation. The police arrested eight demonstrators. Five were expelled from the university, two others were suspended for a year, and one was released. Predictably, in a new round of demonstrations, students began to protest the expulsions. These were followed by renewed police intervention, resulting in a new wave of arrests.

Antony was merely a microcosm of the problems confronting the French university system in general. The protests there were an uncanny harbinger of the May 1968 events.[10]

---

[9] Joffrin, *Mai '68*, 44.
[10] See Seidman, *Imaginary Revolution*, 37–43.

The government was painfully aware that it had a crisis on its hands. To remedy the situation, in 1967 it announced the Fouchet reforms, named for Minister of Education Christian Fouchet. One of the students' major issues was horrendous overcrowding. Since the 1960s, university enrollment had essentially doubled. From the authorities' standpoint, one reason for the overcrowding was the open admissions system. Anyone who passed the nationwide qualifying exam—the *baccalauréat*—could attend university.

One of the main remedies the Fouchet reforms envisaged was a competitive admissions system. But this would solve one problem by creating another. In an era when higher education had increasingly become a sine qua non for cadres and professionals, to restrict university access risked undermining France's economic competitiveness. The so-called Grandes écoles—l'Ecole normale and l'Ecole nationale d'administration—already practiced competitive admissions. But sociological studies showed that such admissions procedures played a major role in perpetuating the class biases of French society; according to one estimate, a mere 6 percent of university students hailed from working-class backgrounds.[11] The proposal for competitive admissions sent the wrong signal to the current generation of students. In essence, the minister of education responded to the crisis by taking away something they already had.

During the fall of 1967 the mood at the Nanterre campus west of Paris was extremely tense. Earlier that year, a protest concerning residence-hall visitation privileges had been rudely disrupted by the police. The campus itself was an impersonal glass-and-steel wasteland. Transportation to Paris was sporadic and unreliable. The last bus from the city to Nanterre departed at 9:00 p.m. In the evenings the students had nothing to do. When the campus opened in 1964, the university did not have a single functioning library. In November 1967 sizable demonstrations erupted to protest the shabby working and living conditions. Hervé Hamon and Patrick Rotman describe the situation at Nanterre in the following terms:

[11] See the classic study by Bourdieu and Passeron, *Héritiers*.

If, at the beginning of the 1960s, a perversely minded sociologist had imagined a geometrical locus where all of the contradictions of Gaullist France would intersect, the site of the new
university—Nanterre—would have easily fit the bill. It was built
on a small patch of several hundred acres where the urban and the
suburban, opulence and misery, the manual and the intellectual,
were conjoined. Adjacent to the sinister gates of the public housing projects, which stood out amid the smog generated by the
factory chimneys, the excavation for the new regional railway
line . . . where the bulldozers created a din with their incessant
tunneling, the shantytown huts, which had been bastions of the
FLN [Algerian Liberation Front], and, lost in the chaos of industrial warehouses, of railway lines, lay the sanctuary where allegedly spirits would soar and science would triumph.[12]

In January 1968 Minister for Youth and Sport François Missoffe
visited the campus to help defuse the situation. Missoffe presided over
the opening of a new swimming pool on campus, testifying to the
government's good faith in trying to redress the students' manifold
grievances.

An altercation followed between him and student leader Daniel
Cohn-Bendit, which has become part of May 1968 lore. As Missoffe
began to leave following his triumphant unveiling of the pool, he was
accosted by Cohn-Bendit, who, alluding to the previous fall's demonstrations, demanded: "And what about our sexual problems?" Missoffe
responded with Gaullist high-handedness: "If you have sexual problems, go jump in the pool!" Cohn-Bendit rejoined, in keeping with
the antifascist spirit of the times: "That's what the Hitler Youth used
to say!"[13]

In retrospect, the exchange stands as a classic example of generational
mistrust. At the time few could have imagined that it would serve as
the flash point for a nationwide youth rebellion. But it was owing to

[12] Hamon and Rotman, *Génération* 1:385.
[13] This incident has been recounted many times. See Daniels, *Year of the Heroic Guerrilla*, 155.

this exchange, and to his willingness to confront unwarranted authority, that Cohn-Bendit would emerge as a cult figure among contemporary French youth. The hour of the *enragés* had struck!

It is hardly an accident that the altercation that set the May events in motion centered on questions of sex. The students wished to be treated as adults. They viewed the in loco parentis laws regulating intimacy on French university campuses as profoundly infantilizing. In a classical case of Eros versus civilization, the students wanted the legitimacy of their desires to be recognized. Moreover, they strongly felt that French universities were being turned into impersonal and highly bureaucratized "knowledge factories." To offset the hyperrationalizing tendencies of the age, the students sought to affirm their status as libidinal beings—or, as Deleuze and Guattari would phrase it following the May events, as "desiring machines." This theme would become one of the May movement's guiding threads.

THE MARCH 22 MOVEMENT

Cohn-Bendit was the May movement's leading political figure and its most charismatic. His parents were German Jewish refugees who had settled in France during the 1930s. In 1959 he opted for German citizenship to avoid French military service. Consequently, his legal status in France was precarious, since as a noncitizen he possessed only a student visa.

In late May 1968 Cohn-Bendit would leave France for Berlin to participate in a demonstration. French authorities seized the occasion to bar his reentry. This served as a rallying point for the student protesters. The French Communists, who were threatened by Cohn-Bendit's charisma as well as by his resolute antiauthoritarianism, disparaged him as "a German anarchist." The government stooped to Jew baiting, characterizing him as little more than a "Juif allemand," a German Jew. The students, to their credit, refused to be hoodwinked by such anti-Semitic canards, proclaiming, "We are all German Jews!" (Nous sommes tous les juifs allemands!), thereby turning Cohn-Bendit's "otherness" into a positive rallying cry.

Cohn-Bendit possessed a sophisticated understanding of twentieth-century left-wing politics. One of the Russian Revolution's fateful turning points had been Trotsky's suppression of the 1921 Kronstadt Uprising, which had been directed against the dictatorial nature of Bolshevik governance. A year earlier Lenin published a harsh polemic criticizing left-wing Communists such as Anton Pannekoek and Hermann Görter, who had embraced the direct democratic ideal of "workers' councils." Cohn-Bendit fully understood that Bolshevik rule—from Lenin to Stalin to Brezhnev—had been an unbroken history of repression. Moreover, this repression was not just confined to enemies on the Right—which might have been bad enough—but was also mercilessly directed against perceived enemies on the Left.

Cohn-Bendit's insights into Bolshevism's historical shortcomings meshed with the May movement's libidinal-libertarian component. The critique of authoritarian communism well suited a politics of emancipated desire. As a well-known May 1968 graffito proclaimed: "We take our desires for reality because we believe in the reality of our desires." However, practically speaking, the problem was that at times the movement's studied aversion to authority and hierarchy translated into a rejection of organization *tout court*. As one of the revolt's protagonists explained, "[Our movement] has a number of 'leaders' in the sociological sense of the term, but no 'chiefs,' no executive, even less bureaucracy. Anyone in it can speak 'to the four winds'; the meeting does not vote, it sorts out a number of lines of force and any of the movement's militants can express them."[14]

Cohn-Bendit developed a critique of the university that complemented the Situationist perspective. Enrollment statistics confirmed the boom in humanities majors. Yet, there was a profound tension between this humanism and the technocratic vocational ends that the government sought to promote. As Cohn-Bendit expressed this dilemma:

The liberal university allows its students a measure of liberty, but only so long as they do not challenge the basis of university education: the preparation of a privileged minority for a return to the

[14] Cited in *French Student Revolt*, ed. Bourges, 54.

ranks of the ruling class from which they have taken temporary leave of absence. The university has, in fact, become a sausage-machine which churns out people without any real culture, and who are incapable of thinking for themselves, and instead trained to fit into the economic system of a highly industrialized society. The student may glory in the renown of his university status, but in fact he is being fed "culture" as a goose is fed grain—to be sacrificed on the altar of bourgeois appetites.[15]

In Cohn-Bendit's view, the challenge was not to repair a university that had lost its direction and fallen into disarray, but to mend the society that had engendered the university and its intractable array of problems.

Following the swimming-pool incident, reports circulated that the government had initiated deportation proceedings against Cohn-Bendit. The students also feared that plainclothes detectives were secretly monitoring their rallies and activities. A new round of protests arose, and once again the police were summoned.

In March the National Vietnam Committee staged a major antiwar rally. The American Express office in central Paris was also attacked. Six students were arrested, four of them dragged by police from the confines of their own homes. The enragés, led by Cohn-Bendit, sprang into action to protest the arrest of their comrades. They baptized themselves the March 22 Movement to commemorate the date of the arrests.

The student arrests that preceded the March 22 Movement signified a point of no return. It was the episode that galvanized a large swath of disaffected, yet heretofore apolitical, students. At Nanterre enrollment was approximately 12,000. At the assembly that launched the March 22 Movement, a mere 140 students attended. Yet, just ten days later, on April 2, when German SDS (Sozialistischer Deutscher Studentenbund) leader Karl-Dietrich Wolff came to speak at the university, some 1,200 students jockeyed for space in the crowded lecture hall.

Heretofore, the students had focused on campus-related "quality of life" issues: overcrowding, antidemocratic governance structures, an

---

[15] Cohn-Bendit, *Obsolete Communism*, 27.

obsolete curriculum, and oppressive in loco parentis regulations. However, following the March arrests, the students began to connect their
personal concerns with broader social questions.[16] Teach-ins proliferated. An alternative, or "parallel," university structure evolved so that
students could address pressing political issues: the Vietnam War, government repression, and the international student movement. In this
spirit, on March 29, a Critical University Day was convened.

At this point faculty members Henri Lefebvre, Edgar Morin, Paul
Ricoeur, and Alain Touraine, repulsed by police brutality, broke ranks
with the administration. In the eyes of the left-liberal professorate, the
students had many legitimate concerns and demands. To respond to
these concerns with repression was unacceptable. Touraine, who would
write one of the best books on May 1968, summarized the mood
among dissident faculty members when he observed: "*The French are of
no interest to their leaders.*"[17]

Thus, within a matter of weeks, the Nanterre campus had become
a hotbed of student militancy. Still, the movement had yet to spread to
other Paris-area campuses. The Nanterre-based enragés planned another round of teach-ins for late April and early May. In April German
SDS leader Rudi Dutschke was gravely wounded by a right-wing fa-
natic. Protests erupted across Germany. Throughout Europe, the level
of political tension escalated correspondingly.

On April 27 Cohn-Bendit was arrested by the police while leaving his apartment. Prime Minister Pompidou, fearing that his im-
prisonment would turn him into a martyr, ordered him released the
following day. Glorying in his newly won celebrity, upon his release
Cohn-Bendit held a press conference mocking his timorous captors.
Who, then, was running the show?

Meanwhile, in Paris, the Maoists clashed with a Far Right, anti-
Communist group, Occident. The rightists were severely beaten and
vowed prompt revenge. The Maoists countered with a banner that read:
"Paras [short for paratroopers], you may have escaped Dien Bien Phu,
but you won't escape Nanterre" (the anticipated site of an impending

[16] Dumontier, *Situationnistes et mai '68*, 97–110.
[17] Touraine, *May Movement*, 50; emphasis added.

confrontation). Individual Maoists had already lent their support to the March 22 Movement.

Dean Pierre Grappin had hoped that the two-week Easter break would sap the students' ardor. His expectations were rudely dashed, however. Cohn-Bendit and seven other students had been summoned to face a mandatory disciplinary hearing scheduled for May 6. The students had announced a massive teach-in for May 2–3. In view of the heightened political tensions, Grappin, an ex-*résistant* and a man of the Left, abruptly closed the university. The enragés and their supporters had no choice but to move their activities to the Sorbonne, in the heart of the Latin Quarter.

PARIS IS BURNING

"Whoever controls Paris controls France" is an adage that has frequently been invoked as a geopolitical explanation for the nation's robust revolutionary tradition. France's inordinate administrative centralization, dating from the days of Mazarin and Louis XIV, meant that the mastery of Paris is tantamount to the mastery of France. In French history this scenario would play itself out time and again: in 1789, 1830, 1848, and 1871. The May events would attest to this maxim's staying power.

On May 3 Cohn-Bendit and some three hundred students assembled in the main courtyard at the Sorbonne to discuss recent events: police repression, the closing of Nanterre, and the spate of student arrests. What the government feared most would soon come to pass: the Nanterre disruptions were spreading from the suburbs to central Paris. Prime Minister Pompidou, who had consistently favored a policy of conciliation, had recently embarked on a ten-day trip to Iran and Afghanistan, leaving Minister of the Interior Christian Fouchet in charge. De Gaulle, who had just turned seventy-seven, informed Fouchet that he wanted a prompt and immediate halt to the student agitation, but it was unclear what steps the minister might take without aggravating an explosive situation.

Once again the authorities acted maladroitly. This time, the consequences were irreversible. Sorbonne rector Jean Roche, fearing a repeat of Nanterre, sent a written order to Police Commissioner Maurice Grimaud requesting that the Sorbonne courtyard be "cleared." The police, accompanied by units of the dreaded CRS (Compagnies républicaines de securité) riot police, who were outfitted with truncheons and shields, descended en masse. The students, vastly outnumbered, negotiated a brief truce. The police methodically cordoned off the area and proceeded to arrest some six hundred students, whom they trundled into the backs of waiting paddy wagons. In their view, it was better to arrest too many than too few.

The massive arrests proved to be the final straw. Hundreds of student bystanders, infuriated by the arbitrariness of the arrests, began pelting the police vans with stones in the hope of liberating their imperiled comrades. The police responded by firing off rounds of tear gas. Next, they began clubbing and apprehending civilian bystanders at random. Commuters emerged from local metro stations only to find themselves immersed in melees that were erupting throughout the Latin Quarter. In several cases they, too were arrested. To protect themselves from retaliation, the students began loosening paving stones from the street and erecting makeshift barricades.

This scenario would occur repeatedly over the course of the ensuing fortnight. Soon, the number of student demonstrators swelled to tens of thousands. Two British journalists who witnessed the May 3 Sorbonne altercation described the events as follows:

These first few minutes of the insurrection set a pattern which was to be tragically repeated throughout the month The authorities had blundered badly by penetrating the Sorbonne, and taking into custody scores of young people, whose only offense had been to make a little noise. They had then compounded the error by parading their prisoners in front of their comrades. As was so often to happen, repression bred violence, rather than stifled it. The immediate effect of the authorities' crude display of strength was to unite the mass of uncommitted students—and their teachers— behind the *enragés*. . . . Combat in the street, the simple act of reaching for a stone and throwing it at a police officer, the lightning solidarity bred in a fighting crowd—this was the instant political education which turned the student population into an army of rebels.[18]

Although most of the students who had been arrested were released the following day, over the weekend four were sentenced to two months in prison. In response, the main student leaders, Alain Geismar (SNESUP), Jacques Sauvageot (UNEF), and Cohn-Bendit (March 22 Movement), announced a major protest for Monday, May 6. The students articulated three demands: (1) the reopening of the Sorbonne; (2) the withdrawal of all police units from the Latin Quarter; and (3) the immediate liberation of their imprisoned comrades.

This was the worst rioting France had experienced since the Algerian War. Parisians were repulsed by the flagrant display of police brutality, much of which occurred beneath their very windows. Significantly, by midweek the tide of public opinion had shifted dramatically against the forces of order and toward the various student groups. A May 8 public opinion poll showed that four out of five Parisians favored the students. At virtually every turn, the student cause was energized by the government's miscalculations and overreactions. De Gaulle decreed that the state display firmness and resolve in the face of disorder, and his ministers sought to follow suit. Yet, it was no longer Algerian immigrants whom the Paris police were brutalizing. It was the sons and daughters of the French middle classes.

With the prime minister incommunicado in rural Afghanistan, the government found it difficult to pursue a coordinated response. Did ultimate jurisdiction fall to the minister of education or the minister of the interior? No one knew for certain. The ministers acquiesced to the students' first two demands—the reopening of the Sorbonne and the withdrawal of the police—but little progress was made toward freeing the imprisoned students. (According to later reports, de Gaulle himself personally intervened to reject this point.)

In the meantime, the momentum of the student protest movement increased exponentially. Protests in support of the Parisian students burgeoned throughout rural France. Student leaders called for a major

[18] Seale and McConnville, *Red Flag, Black Flag*, 69.

demonstration on Friday, May 10, to protest government intransigence and press the case for their jailed *confrères*.

The May 10 protest—the so-called Night of the Barricades—has become a legendary event in French political history, a bona fide *journée* in the French revolutionary tradition. By now, student forces in the French capital had swelled to nearly forty thousand. *Lycéens* were well represented and set forth their own political demands. Neither they nor university students enjoyed freedom of political speech.

The demonstration began like any other, with the students amassing at the vast Denfert-Rochereau intersection. Their intention was to march across Paris to the site of French radio and television headquarters, the ORTF. Soon, word arrived that the forces of order had blockaded all the major bridges leading to the Right Bank. Barred from their primary destination, the student leaders were forced to improvise. They made an impromptu pass at the Santé Prison, where they believed their jailed fellow activists were being held. Next, they marched down the Boulevard Saint-Germain under the watchful eye of the police and the CRS, who appeared to be shunting them back toward the narrow byways of the Latin Quarter.

A turning point had been reached. The police clearly had the upper hand. They had succeeded in blocking the demonstrators' path, and now the marchers were in danger of becoming dispirited. The student leaders realized that they must somehow retake the initiative or return home downtrodden and defeated. They received the disheartening news that eleventh-hour negotiations between acting prime minister Louis Joxe and Cohn-Bendit had broken down.

Facing the prospect of another police assault, the students spontaneously began constructing barricades, using paving stones as well as urban detritus. As one observer put it, "The barricades were a response to a social order reduced to the mute, massive power of the police."[19] The students employed this tactic in part to protect their own turf. The police were occupying the Sorbonne. Now, the rest of the Latin Quarter would belong to them! But the *pavés*, or paving stones, also served as a symbolic link with the French revolutionary tradition. For a

[19] Touraine, *May Movement*, 176.

brief moment, the students had become sansculottes and communards. Within a few hours, as many as sixty of these improvised minifortresses sprouted in the neighborhood adjacent to the Sorbonne. Cohn-Bendit instructed his troops to break up into small groups in order to better defend themselves against the anticipated police charge. He believed it was imperative to cultivate a mentality conducive to responsible collective action. He sought to disrupt the passivity and "serialization" (Sartre) that can befall mass movements lacking coherence and purpose.

The barricade construction was a consummate act of revolutionary romanticism, an act of sheer joy. In his memoir, Cohn-Bendit describes this event with suitable lyrical enthusiasm:

> In a society which seeks to crush the individual, forcing him to swallow the same lies, a deep feeling of collective strength had surged up and people refused to be browbeaten. We were no longer thousands of little atoms squashed together but a solid mass of determined individuals. . . . The "rashness of youth" did not spring from despair, the cynicism of impotence, but on the contrary from the discovery of our collective strength. It was this feeling of strength and unity which reigned on the barricades. In such moments of collective enthusiasm, when everything seems possible, nothing could be more natural and simple than a warm relationship between all demonstrators and quite particularly between the boys and the girls. Everything was easy and uncomplicated. The barricades were no longer simply a means of self-defense: they became a symbol of individual liberty.[20]

The students' joy would be short-lived. The riot police were poised for an assault. Around midnight, they received the green light from Ministers Joxe and Fouchet and the new minister of education, Alain Peyrefitte.

The police opened their attack by firing volleys of tear gas. A vicious pitched battle ensued. Blood flowed. One eyewitness described the chaotic scene as follows:

[20] Cohn-Bendit, *Obsolete Communism*, 63.

[It is] 2 a.m. It is now obvious that police are preparing a powerful
attack. Radio announces we are surrounded and that government
has ordered police to attack. . . . In front of us we turn over cars
to prevent police from charging with their buses and tanks (Radio said tanks were coming, but we never saw any). . . . I must
insist again that the general mood was defensive, *not* offensive;
we just wanted to hold the place like an entrenched sit-down
strike. . . . Their tactics are simple: at 100 yards' distance they
launch gas grenades by rifle which blind, suffocate, and knock us
out. This gas is MACE (Vietnam and Detroit Mace). Also explosive
grenades. One student near us picked up one to throw it back;
it tore his whole hand off. . . . But then police attack at three
points simultaneously: at two extremities of [rue] Gay-Lussac, at
our barricade, and at the rue d'Ulm. . . . Finally, we are forced
back. Our barricade burns. At this point all I can remember is that
I faint from lack of air.[21]

Innocent bystanders caught in the melee were senselessly beaten.
Local residents tried to assist the students by providing them with
water, bandages, and shelter. In many cases the police pursued their
prey directly into private residences. In one instance they attacked a
young woman who had not even participated in the demonstrations
and expelled her into the street naked.[22] The fighting continued until
the early morning, when the students finally disbanded and went home
to dress their wounds. Three hundred and seventy students had been
injured and 460 arrested.

The authorities still assumed that they were facing a student revolt
they could safely contain by a show of firmness and resolve. They refused to release the four imprisoned protesters for fear of alienating the
police—the only force standing between the government and sheer
"anarchy."

Yet after the Night of the Barricades, these assumptions ceased
to hold. From then on, the authorities would face a massive social

[21] Jean-Jacques Lebel, "The Night of 10 May," *Black Dwarf*, June 1, 1968.
[22] Seele and McConnville, *Red Flag, Black Flag*, 88.

movement emanating from virtually every quarter of French society. As Raymond Aron observed, it must have come as quite a shock to the Gaullist regime, which had staked everything on the precepts of authority and order, to realize that it was so widely loathed.[23] When a regime has lost its legitimacy in the eyes of its citizens, repression becomes its only recourse.

Heretofore, the Communists had belittled the student insurrection as a revolt led by spoiled "daddy's boys" (*fils à papa*)—hence, from a working-class standpoint, irrelevant. But on May 10 another bloody massacre had occurred in the heart of Paris. Now the PCF feared competition from the Left. Owing to their refusal to enter the fray, the Communists had begun hemorrhaging political capital. Their leaders were behaving like the timorous "revisionists" the Marxists-Leninists had accused them of being. It was time to act and thereby perhaps to steal some of the students' insurrectionary thunder for their own political benefit.

The Communist-dominated Confédération générale du travail (CGT) boasted a membership of some two million workers. The PCF leadership announced a general strike in support of the students for Monday, May 13. The Left-Catholic Confédération française démocratique du travail (CFDT) followed suit.

That weekend the student leaders announced a large demonstration on Monday. The Communists agreed to accommodate them by participating. They conceded that the triumvirate of Cohn-Bendit, Geismar, and Sauvageot would lead the march. And what a march it was. According to the most reliable estimates, three hundred thousand people participated! The hour of the groupuscules had struck. Fittingly, one of the banners accompanying the demonstration sarcastically announced: "We Are a Groupuscule" (Nous Sommes un Groupuscule!)—yet this time, a groupuscule comprising hundreds of thousands.

May 13 signified a remarkable vindication of the enragés, who from inauspicious beginnings were suddenly thrust onto the political center stage. Following the uprising of May 3–6, the PCF daily, *L'Humanité*, derisively mocked Cohn-Bendit and the March 22 Movement in the

---

[23] Aron, *Elusive Revolution*, 9.

following terms: "Irresponsible Leftists use the pretext of government inefficiency and student unrest in order to subvert the work of the faculties and to impede the mass of students from sitting for their examinations. These false revolutionaries behave objectively as allies of the Gaullist authorities and represent a policy that is objectionable to the majority of students."[24] With these words there could be little doubt that the PCF had abandoned political struggle and become a "party of order."

Seven days later, the enragés headed the largest demonstration Paris had seen since the Popular Front era, with the Communists and their allies, the CGT, trailing contritely behind. Cohn-Bendit later recounted: "What made me happy was to be at the head of a march where the Stalinist SOBs were serving as the baggage handlers at the end of the queue."[25]

A SELF-LIMITING REVOLUTION

In the end de Gaulle's endemic revulsion for "disorder" nearly brought down the regime. Thus the stage was set for an unforeseeable chapter in the unfolding narrative of the May revolt. What had began as a student uprising in the Paris suburbs had metamorphosed into a mammoth anti-Gaullist student-worker alliance. The worker-student coalition was an unprecedented development. At no other point during 1968—not in the United States, not in Latin America, nor elsewhere in Europe—did an analogous front materialize.

Political scientists had discounted the possibility of revolution in an advanced industrial society, in which considerations of technological efficiency purportedly trumped "ideology." The May events falsified such prognoses. The student leaders wisely declined to overplay their hand. They refrained from proposing grandiose political demands—for example, threatening a "seizure of power." Their express political objective was the removal of Gaullism. Hence, the slogan of the May 13 demonstrations: "Ten years is enough!" (May 13, 1968, was the tenth

[24] Cited in Cohn-Bendit's *Obsolete Communism*, 58.
[25] Joffrin, *May '68*, 139.

anniversary of de Gaulle's reemergence during the Algeria crisis.) All in all, the students proposed a series of modest and reasonable political claims. Thereby, they set a trap for the authorities, who obliged at nearly every turn by overreacting.[26]

The May revolt signified a new political phenomenon. Along with the American civil rights movement, it represented perhaps the first instance of a "self-limiting revolution." This phrase was immortalized by Polish dissident Adam Michnik to describe efforts to carve out an autonomous civil society—"spheres of liberty"—in the face of state socialism's near-total political domination. In May student activists similarly sought to develop autonomous spheres of action vis-à-vis Gaullism's well-nigh monolithic political predominance. One important dimension these two revolutionary movements shared was an inherent distrust of the Jacobin model of centralized state power. According to this schema—which was, as it were, "perfected" by Lenin—the state functioned as the sole legitimate political actor. Both the May movement and the Eastern European dissidents strove vigorously to combat political centralization by nurturing alternative forms of political contestation, that is, forms that derived from the sphere of an independent civil society.[27]

---

[26] One testimony to the student leaders' sober ability to gauge the objective political situation–their "realism"–is the interview Sartre conducted with Cohn-Bendit in *Le Nouvel Observateur*. There, Cohn-Bendit points out time and again that the May crisis is not a classical, old-style revolutionary situation:

> I am not interested in metaphysics, in ways to "make the revolution." As I have said, I think we are moving toward a perpetual change of society, produced by revolutionary actions at each stage. A radical change in the structure of our society would be possible if, for example, a serious economic crisis, the action of a powerful workers' movement and vigorous student activity suddenly converged. These conditions have not been realized today. At best we can hope to bring down the government. We must not dream of destroying bourgeois society. That does not mean there is nothing to be done; on the contrary, we must struggle step-by-step, on the basis of the global challenge.
>
> (Cohn-Bendit et al., *French Student Revolt*, 76–77)

[27] See Michnik, "The New Evolutionism," in *Letters from Prison*. For a comparison of the sixty-eighters with the Eastern European dissident movement, see Berman, *Tale of Two Utopias*.

By embracing antiauthoritarianism and by forcefully renouncing
étatisme, or "statism"—a political form venerated by Gaullists, Communists, and Republicans alike—the student revolutionaries harked
back to the subterranean political tradition of anarchism. In the nineteenth century, its most eloquent spokesman had been Pierre-Joseph
Proudhon. Proudhon had begun as a Saint-Simonian but was soon
repulsed by the Saint-Simonians' glorification of state authority. He
justly reproached them for seeking to replace one form of political despotism—monarchical absolutism—with a more modern, technocratic
variant. Proudhon revered the French Revolution's libertarian beginnings, but he viewed the Jacobin dictatorship of Year II (1793–94) as a
betrayal of the Revolution's incipient emancipatory promise. Proudhon
perceived France's subsequent political history—Napoleon, the Restoration, the Second Empire—as further proof of centralized political
authority's intrinsic evils.

In surveying the flaws of French political culture, Proudhon laid
much of the blame on Rousseau's absolutist conception of sovereignty.
In opposition to such enduring statist longings—in both their right-
and left-wing variants—Proudhon celebrated the notion of local,
decentralized democracy, thereby anticipating the ideal of "workers'
control." As Proudhon observes, when "work is self-organized, no longer requiring either legislator or sovereign, the workshop will replace
government."[28]

During his own lifetime, Proudhon's doctrines were scorned. He
was the butt of Marx's denunciations in *The Poverty of Philosophy* and
was outmaneuvered by Marx's followers at the inception of the First International (1864). His vindication would arrive belatedly in the form
of twentieth-century anarcho-syndicalism, a movement that rejected
trade unions and political parties in favor of the political self-organization of labor.

In retrospect, Proudhon stands out as an important forerunner of
the antiauthoritarian, workers' self-management currents that proliferated in the aftermath of May 1968. Not only did his doctrines anticipate

[28] Pierre-Joseph Proudhon, *Idée générale de la révolution au dix-neuvième siècle* (Paris:
Garnier Frères, 1851), 395.

anarcho-syndicalism, but they also presaged the *autogestion* vogue that inspired the "Second Left" and the CFDT trade union during the 1970s.[29]

Where, then, were the Maoists during the political conflagrations of May 3–10, which turned the normally peaceable Latin Quarter into a veritable battleground? After all, the normaliens' rue d'Ulm was located a mere stone's throw away from the Sorbonne environs, where the street fighting had been most intense.

In a characteristic gesture of normalien arrogance, the Maoists dismissed the student revolt due to its deficient class character. Since, in their view, the uprising lacked the requisite "proletarian content," it failed to measure up to the theoretical strictures of orthodox Marxism. The Marxist-Leninist catechism repeatedly stressed that the revolution would be made by the working class, not by a group of middle-class youth whose central grievance concerned dormitory visitation rights. The Maoists, conversely, as a self-styled revolutionary vanguard, prided themselves on their asceticism.

The Maoists issued a directive instructing their supporters to abandon the Latin Quarter and to "agitate" instead in outlying working-class districts.[30] The normaliens may have been brilliant, but they often lacked the Socratic virtue of self-knowledge. In most cases they were far more privileged than were the Nanterre and the Sorbonne students, whose political motivations they so haughtily dismissed.

During the pivotal clashes of May 3–6, the Maoist leadership was smugly tucked away in its rue d'Ulm sanctuary. By this point, what had begun as a localized student uprising had rapidly gained momentum. The entire nation's attention—and, soon, that of much of the world—was intently focused on the Latin Quarter. Was it, then, time for the Maoists to change their political course?

On Tuesday, May 7, Maoist leader Robert Linhart summoned an assembly at the Ecole normale to discuss these questions. The Maoist leaders were all in attendance: Pierre Victor, who would succeed

[29] Hayward, *After the French Revolution*, 177.

[30] See the documentation in Kessel's *Mouvement maoïste*; see especially "Et maintenant, aux usines! Appel du UJC (ML) et des cercle servir le peuple," May 7, 1968, 41–44.

Linhart in the post-May period; Tiennot Grumbach, nephew of former Radical Party prime minister Pierre Mendes-France and future coeditor of the influential post-May organ *Vive la Révolution!*; and Christian de Portzamparc, a graphic arts major at l'Ecole des beaux-arts. In 1994 Portzamparc would win architecture's most coveted award, the Pritzker Prize.

The meeting's goal was to discuss how the Maoists should respond to the recent political events. In accordance with the Maoists' ideological line, Linhart recommended that the next round of demonstrations shift to the suburbs, where most of the working class lived, in order to bring students and workers together. In the ensuing days, the Maoists proceeded to distribute a plodding political pamphlet, *And Now to the Factories!*, throughout the Latin Quarter. But as far as joining forces with the student protest movement was concerned, Linhart remained immovable.

Amid the frenetic political agitation of recent days, Linhart, like other student leaders, slept little. Undoubtedly, this fact adversely affected his judgment and allowed certain political delusions to take root. Under Linhart's leadership, the Maoists were convinced that both the Gaullists and the Socialists were conspiring to lure the French working class into the streets, where, in a scenario reminiscent of the June Days or the Paris Commune, they would be brutally massacred by the forces of order.

The Maoists thought of themselves as revolutionary true believers— as "pur et dur," hardened Marxists-Leninists. Psychologically speaking, it was nearly inconceivable for them to admit that other political factions might be right and that they could be wrong. Yet, there may have also been a more practical and self-interested reason for Linhart's political stubbornness, for should the UJC-ML belatedly join forces with the other major student groups—the Nanterre enragés, Sauvageot's French Students' Union, or the Trotskyists associated with Alain Krivine's Jeunes communistes révolutionnaires—the admission of error would threaten to undermine their entire revolutionary credo. Thereby, the self-proclaimed revolutionary avant-garde would be exposed as political latecomers—a revolutionary *derrière-garde*.

Thus, as Linhart delivered his May 7 peroration, none of his key lieutenants—neither Lévy/Victor, nor Tiennot Grumbach, nor Roland

Castro—openly contradicted him, despite the fact that many of them had begun to have serious doubts about the UJC-ML's political course. Clearly, at this particular juncture, one of the major issues at stake was Linhart's increasingly tenuous credibility as leader. To avow that he had misjudged the student movement's import and potential at this point was nearly inadmissible.

Toward the end of the discussion, a woman's voice rang out from the back of the room. It was Nicole Linhart, Robert's wife. She passionately intoned: "Robert, the students are fighting outside. It's foolish to stay here, behind closed doors. It's time to join in. . . . The proletariat *wants* to join the demonstrations and, following the students' example, to go on strike!"[31]

Linhart's heartless response was: "Leave! You don't have the right to speak here. Get out!" Nicole left the room in tears. Robert followed her out, trying to apologize by invoking untoward circumstances (sleeplessness, unbearable political pressure, and so forth), to no avail.

Thus the Maoists would remain entirely on the sidelines until the week of May 13, when the Communist party called for a general strike.

FROM THE LATIN QUARTER TO THE FACTORIES

Although students and workers marched arm in arm on May 13 and would strive to maintain their alliance during the weeks that followed, they were hardly natural allies. Nevertheless, the wave of wildcat strikes that over the ensuing weeks brought French occupational life to a standstill was a striking and unprecedented development. The Communists had wagered that following the general strike their constituency would dutifully return to the shop floor. But their expectations were dashed. Traditionally, the French labor movement had displayed a marked anarchist streak. Inspired by the Night of the Barricades and the enragés' incendiary rhetoric, during May this strain of political radicalism vigorously reemerged. Following the May 13 demonstration, worker-student action committees formed to spread the gospel of

[31] See the account in Hamon and Rotman, *Génération* 2:368–70.

revolt.[32] Within a few days, some two million workers were on strike. By May 22 the number had risen to approximately nine million.

Among French workers an awareness dawned that the trade unions had failed to represent their interests. In general, French workers were pathetically ill remunerated.[33] While the middle classes enjoyed the advantages of consumer affluence, the working class had been distinctly slow to benefit. The May events suggested that rather than continuing to rely on ineffectual union representation, they would be better off taking affairs into their own hands.

Wildcat strikes began in western France. Workers at the Sud Aviation plant near Nantes seized control and began running the factory according to the strictures of worker self-management, or *autogestion*. Next, workers at several Renault plants went out: Cléon, Flins, Le Mans, and Boulogne-Billancourt on the outskirts of Paris. At Cléon and Boulogne-Billancourt, the workers sequestered the foremen and proceeded to manage the factories themselves.

The class composition of French workers had changed markedly. Increasingly, what mattered was technological competence and managerial proficiency. This better-educated stratum of workers was more receptive to the claims of the student activists. During May, among both groups, it was qualitative demands that mattered. Skilled workers and students sought to challenge the quasi-feudal, hierarchical structure of French organizational culture. Having demonstrated their abilities, both groups felt they merited more say in the way French institutional life was managed. Analysts showed that skilled workers were less concerned with material benefits than with the injustices of management's administrative prerogatives.[34]

Yet, once the qualitative demands of France's new class of experts were met, the new "worker aristocracy" rapidly returned to the fold.

---

[32] See Vienet, *Enragés et situationnistes.*

[33] Seale and McConnville, *Red Flag, Black Flag,* 155: "Before the May–June wage settlements, a quarter of French workers earned less than 500 francs per month ($110) and a third earned less than 720 francs ($144); about 1,500,000 wage earners on the bottom of the scale—unskilled industrial laborers and agricultural workers—made little more than 400 francs a month ($80)."

[34] See Mallet, *Essays on the New Working Class.*

Their professional interests lay with the preservation and improvement of the existing system. As an aspiring managerial elite, France's "new class" was genuinely Saint-Simonian. The student radicals, on the other hand, proved more difficult to placate.

One of the French working class's distinctive features had been its aversion to revolution. For decades, the French proletariat's interests had been well served by the Communist Party and its trade union allies. Thus, in France for the most part class conflict had been successfully institutionalized. The decline of traditional industrial sectors like coal and steel helps explain the predominantly "defensive" nature of working-class demands. The mainstream working class had little interest in so-called qualitative issues or concerns—although, under the influence of the May events, amid the outbreak of wildcat strikes and factory occupations, this attitude began to change. Thus, typically, labor's focus had been economic or quantitative. Workers sought better remuneration, increased benefits, and improved working conditions. These issues were addressed during the Grenelle negotiations of late May, which succeeded in getting workers off the streets and back into the factories.

May was a watershed insofar as it signaled a transition to social struggles of a new type. The old type of struggle concerned demands for higher wages and improved working conditions. The new struggles revolved around two main themes:

1. the dismantling of authoritarian patterns of social control and the resultant democratization of society, and
2. the struggle for inclusion on the part a variety of groups—women, gays, immigrants, and prisoners—who had heretofore subsisted on the social margins.

Following May, their struggles and demands would occupy center stage.

THE GENERAL'S RETURN

May 29, 1968, was undoubtedly one of the strangest days in French political history. On that day de Gaulle informed his staff that he would leave Paris for his country retreat at Colombey-les-Deux-Eglises—a strange decision for a leader faced with a full-blown insurrection. For two weeks the French capital had been paralyzed by a massive general strike. In the eyes of many, to leave Paris under the circumstances was tantamount to surrender.

But the general did not go to Colombey that day. Instead, he traveled to Baden-Baden, Germany, to meet with General Jacques Massu, the head of French forces stationed there. (Ten years earlier General Massu had led the "revolt of the generals" in Algiers, an event that precipitated the political crisis that facilitated de Gaulle's return to power.) The general's trip to Baden-Baden has been the subject of endless speculation. What could the French president possibly hope to gain from such a trip?

For France's seventy-seven-year-old head of state, the political situation appeared unmasterable. He felt he had exhausted all political options and contemplated stepping down. As the general lamented to Massu: "Everything is ruined! The Communists have precipitated a paralysis throughout the country. I am no longer in charge of anything. I have decided to step down; and since I feel threatened . . . I have sought refuge with you in order to decide what to do."[35]

For his part, Massu sought to shore up de Gaulle's resolve. This was no time for surrender, observed Massu, but a moment that demanded renewed decisiveness. In his memoirs Massu immodestly credits himself with having single-handedly deterred the general from resigning.

Yet, there may have been another reason behind the general's mysterious excursion to Baden-Baden. De Gaulle was, after all, a military man. Since he could see no way out of the deteriorating political situation, he entertained the option of summoning French troops to Paris to restore order. As one historian of the May movement affirms: "Behind the trip to Baden-Baden lay the . . . highly real threat of civil war and an appeal to the military."[36] De Gaulle never publicly avowed having contemplated this option. To admit to having considered using the

[35] Massu, *Baden 68*, 79–80.
[36] Joffrin, *Mai '68*, 283.

French army against citizens of the republic would have tarnished his reputation for decades. But the trip to Baden-Baden was no random act of flight. It was part and parcel of a carefully considered strategy.

Whatever the real truth behind this strange sojourn, upon his return to Paris de Gaulle was able to right the ship of state. On May 30 he took to the airwaves of French radio (the same medium he had utilized three decades earlier to rally the nation following France's "strange defeat" at the hands of the Nazis), declaring with firmness that under no circumstances would he resign. He described himself as the embodiment of "republican legitimacy" and insisted that he would fulfill his mandate. He announced that he was dissolving the National Assembly and that new elections would be held in June. Then he deftly played the anti-Communist card, claiming that the May uprising had been provoked by a certain party with totalitarian political designs. As in 1940, France was once again threatened by "dictatorship"—however, this time from the political Left. Only de Gaulle possessed the wherewithal and fortitude to save the nation from this ignominious fate.

That evening, the Gaullists organized a massive demonstration in support of the embattled general on the Champs-Elysée, from the Tuileries to the Place de l'Etoile. The rally was a prominent symbolic indicator that the political tide had begun to turn in the government's favor. Amid the dozens of pro–de Gaulle and anti-Communist banners, one in particular stood out: "Cohn-Bendit à Auschwitz."

De Gaulle's performance was a political masterstroke. The general realized that since his popularity had eroded considerably, a referendum on his presidency would be ill advised. Yet, he was also keenly aware that the French middle classes had grown weary of strikes and demonstrations and of the deterioration of social conditions that accompanied them. The average "right-thinking" Frenchman and -woman craved a return to political normalcy—and that is exactly what de Gaulle pledged to provide.

The Grenelle Accords, negotiated between the government and the major trade unions, resulted in a 35 percent rise in the minimum wage, a 10 percent wage increase, a reduction in social security payments, and one hour's decrease in the workweek. In May the Communist

Party lived in constant fear of being outflanked on the Left by the various groupuscules: anarchists, Maoists, and Trotskyists. The Grenelle agreement had the desired effect of defusing working-class militancy, an outcome that worked to the political advantage of both the Communists and the Gaullists. As one commentator has aptly noted, "The Communist Party was profoundly Gaullist, devoted to 'order,' to authority, to transmitting commands from above, to the cult of personality, to channeling popular aspirations into tidy 'agreements.'"[37]

The June parliamentary elections resulted in a stunning victory for the Gaullists. The associated Left (Federation of the Left, PCF, and the Socialists) lost more than one hundred seats. Conversely, the Center Right parties gained nearly one hundred. As one historian has observed, "The June 1968 election was all about fear."[38] The French electorate had had enough of political experimentation and longed for a return to stability. Perhaps "boredom" was not so bad after all. Its confidence buoyed, the government employed troops to forcibly evict strikers from occupied factories in the greater Paris region. In July de Gaulle rewarded Pompidou, who had been a voice of moderation and sobriety throughout the conflict, by handing him his walking papers. Pompidou was replaced by the nondescript Maurice Couve de Murville. With Couve de Murville heading the government, at least the general ran little risk of being outshone.

De Gaulle interpreted the June 1968 electoral results as a mandate analogous to the one he had received ten years earlier, in December 1958. But on this count he seriously erred. Gaullism's electoral triumph was little more than a political stopgap that returned France to a holding pattern. None of the deep-seated structural problems that underlay the May revolt had been resolved. Flush with confidence, in March 1969 de Gaulle announced a new referendum. This time his proposals were roundly and summarily rejected. In April the general left Paris for Colombey-les-Deux-Eglises—this time for good.

[37] Caute, *Year of the Barricades*, 250.
[38] Berstein, *Republic of de Gaulle*, 224.

THE CONFLICT OF INTERPRETATIONS

The May revolt caught commentators and intellectuals wholly off guard. Within weeks a coterie of professional and amateur scribes sought to retrace the key events and decipher their meaning. A robust cottage industry arose over how best to interpret the revolt. Many of the contemporary accounts, written either by the historical actors or by reflective eyewitnesses, have retained their vigor and lucidity.[39]

Jean-Pierre Le Goff has aptly described May's legacy as "an impossible heritage."[40] Along with the Fourth Republic's rash implosion that precipitated de Gaulle's political return, the May revolt remains the key political event of the postwar era. Correspondingly, the political and ideological stakes involved in interpreting the May events are keen. At issue is the legitimacy of the Fifth Republic's various political incarnations—Gaullist, Center Right, Socialist, and so forth.

The conservative interpretation of May has been best represented by Raymond Aron. At the time, Aron wrote a series of on-the-spot opinion pieces for the Center Right daily *Le Figaro*. On the one hand, Aron soberly acknowledged that aspects of French society, such as the universities, were badly in need of reform. On the other hand, like de Gaulle, he abhorred the May uprising's tendential anarchism. In a critique redolent of Edmund Burke's *Reflections on the Revolution in France*, Aron blamed the revolt on the circulation of abstract, utopian ideas emanating from the pens of the Left Bank's *maîtres penseurs*: Althusser, Lacan, Lévi-Strauss, and Sartre. Thus, in Aron's view the May revolt was a classic example of the "treason of the intellectuals" (an allusion to Julien Benda's 1927 classic *La trahison des clercs*).[41] Jettisoning all professionalism, the left-wing professorate engaged in thoughtless and brazen

---

[39] In addition to the books by Cohn-Bendit, Seale and McConnville, and Touraine that have already been cited, studies by Aron (*May '68: The Elusive Revolution*), Cornelius Castoriadis, Claude Lefort, and Edgar Morin et al. (*La brèche*) also fall within this category. For a good overview, see Weber, *Vingt ans après*.

[40] Le Goff, *Mai 68*.

[41] Benda, *Trahison des clercs*.

acts of political partisanship. In an oft-cited observation, Aron characterized the revolt as a "psychodrama," implying that the movement's
protagonists were psychologically maladjusted. They were in the throes
of a "left-wing emotionalism" and as such in need of a cure.

The most sophisticated left-wing analysis of the May revolt, also written in the heat of battle, was *La brèche* (The Break), coauthored by Edgar
Morin, Claude Lefort, and Jean-Marc Coudray (Cornelius Castoriadis'
pseudonym).[42] In their view the May uprising was a tangible refutation
of theories of social technocracy, which claimed that revolution was no
longer possible in the modern world. The May movement demonstrated
that advanced industrial societies were vulnerable to new democratic
logics of social contestation. From the authors' perspective May constituted a breakthrough insofar as students and workers, mistrusting traditional forms of political representation such as parties and trade unions,
had spontaneously organized themselves into autonomous, egalitarian
collectives: "soviets," or "councils." In their eyes the spirit of worker
self-management, or *autogestion,* represented a left-wing alternative to
authoritarian approaches to socialism that, heretofore, had been historically dominant. Perhaps, the authors hoped, May was the dawn of a new
variety of libertarian socialism, whose historical precedents had been
the Paris Commune, the Kronstadt revolt, the anarchist collectives of
the Spanish Civil War (1936–39), and the Hungarian uprising (1956).

During the 1970s, as the May events receded and France returned
to political normalcy, a cynical interpretation of the revolt found favor
among disillusioned former leftists. In this account May 1968 signified
little more than a way station on France's relentless march toward societal modernization. As we have seen, during the 1960s French organizational life remained in the grip of a quasi-feudal traditionalism. By
challenging the hierarchy, the May movement putatively helped speed
the transition to a more streamlined and efficient organizational culture. The May revolt's paradoxical end result was to advance capitalist
modernization by helping to eliminate atavistic cultural blockages. The
revisionist view of May 1968 implicitly followed Tocqueville by arguing that these events were not discontinuous with long-term social and

---

[42] Morin, Lefort, and Coudray, *Brèche.*

political trends but merely a further step on the march toward democratization qua social leveling.

The cynical critique of the May movement also bemoaned the rise of a "new individualism," which the events' detractors viewed as an expression of the consumer society *simpliciter*.[43] They claimed that the May insurrection had been a false dawn. By stressing logics of cultural revolt and identity politics, the May movement had done little more than pave the way for an expanded spectrum of vacuous and ephemeral "lifestyle choices." No longer locked into an identity predetermined by social class, individuals were free to choose among a new range of cultural pseudo-options. From this perspective, the ideals of libertarian socialism were little more than a utopian afterthought. Instead, the "culture of narcissism" had arrived in full force. In *Democracy in America,* Tocqueville famously described the softening of morals (*moeurs*) coincident with the triumph of democratic political culture. In *Era of the Void* and other writings, Gilles Lipovetsky, one of Tocqueville's latter-day heirs, described the post-May analogue as follows:

> May '68 was a "soft" revolution, without deaths, traitors, orthodoxies, or purges. Indeed, it manifested the same gradual softening of social mores that Tocqueville first noticed in personal relations characteristic of an individualistic and democratic age. . . . The spirit of May recaptured what historically has been the central tenet of the consumer society: *hedonism*. By emphasizing permissiveness, humor, and fun, the spirit of May was largely molded by the very thing it denounced in politics . . . : the euphoria of the consumer age.[44]

[43] Ferry and Renaut, *68–86*.

[44] Gilles Lipovetsky, "May '68, or The Rise of Transpolitical Individualism," quoted in *New French Thought*, ed. Mark Lilla (Princeton: Princeton University Press, 1994), 214–15, 216. Of course, politicians, too, have frequently proffered their opinions. In 2002 Finance Minister Nicolas Sarkozy offered the following dismissive interpretation of May: "It's time to turn back the clock on this period when all values lost their meaning, when there were only rights, but no duties, when no one respected anyone else, and when it was 'forbidden to forbid.'" Quoted in "Faut-il rompre avec l'esprit de 1968?" *Le Monde*, May 19, 2002.

Ironically, here, *les extrêmes se touchent,* as the left-wing and conservative excoriations of the May events' political legacy join forces. For former leftists such as Régis Debray, the fact that following May the goal
of revolution was abandoned in favor of piecemeal, social evolutionary
change meant that the revolt's outcome was, by definition, retrograde.
But Debray's perspective offers a false choice between pure revolutionism and wholesale conformism. Here, strong traces of the former
Althusser student's Marxist superego are showing.[45] Similarly, conservative republican thinkers such as Lipovetsky, Luc Ferry, and Marcel
Gauchet, operating under Tocqueville's spell, assumed that the rise of
individualism meant that French political culture had succumbed to
the centrifugal debilities of its Anglo-American counterparts: liberalism, possessive individualism, and multiculturalism. The republican
credo, conversely, excoriated all manner of communitarian particularism. It also scorned mediating bodies or institutions, demanding instead that the individual sacrifice herself for the greater good of *la patrie.*
Hence, viewed from a neorepublican standpoint, the rise of individualism and the breakdown of the earlier republican consensus meant that
French "exceptionalism"—its steadfast rejection of Anglo-American
liberalism—had been one of the main casualties of the post-May era.

Both left-wing and republican critiques misconstrued May's political specificity. The May movement's uniqueness lay in the challenges
it posed to traditional forms of political struggle, be they Marxist, liberal, or republican. The May revolt corresponded to a new, multivalent
political dynamic that transcended the Manichaean oppositions of a
class-based society. Students and workers invoked norms of *openness,
publicness,* and *direct democracy* in order to contest new technocratic models of social control. As such, those who were involved in the May protests possessed an acute awareness concerning the altered modalities of
domination and the restrictive nature of contemporary social roles. As

---

[45] See Régis Debray, *Teachers, Writers, Celebrities: The Intellectuals of Modern France*
(London: New Left Books, 1981), where Debray's many perceptive insights are offset
by sweeping and untenable exaggerations: "We are seeing the university corps and,
at a more general level the intellectual corps, voluntarily relinquish its own logic of
organization, selection and reproduction and adopt the market logic inherent in the
workings of the media" (46–47).

one commentator put it, "We are what we do and what others do to us, the roles that we play in the social apparatus. Work is no longer merely activity, production, and profession. It is relationships, communication, and status. Leisure is no longer withdrawal into oneself, one's family, or one's neighborhood group. The culture is controlled and transmitted centrally."[46]

The May activists recognized that "commodity fetishism"—a "definite relation between persons, that assumes, in their eyes, the fantastic form of a relation between things"—had been transposed from the workplace to social relationships in general.[47] With the consumer society's triumph, not even the once-sacrosanct realm of human intimacy had been spared. The student militants sought to remedy and offset these developments, realizing all the while that in advanced industrial societies to abandon bureaucracy in its entirety was a sociological impossibility. Hence, the May movement targeted impersonal, bureaucratic, and highly formalized modes of socialization that operated "without regard for persons" (Max Weber). As a result, everyday life in France was permanently transformed. The May activists succeeded in overturning an institutional culture that unthinkingly glorified social rank and technocratic expertise. Following the May revolt, that culture would never possess the same unquestioned self-evidence. Contra Tocqueville, democracy does not merely signify "social leveling. Instead, it indicates a political approach requiring that authority be discursively legitimated from the bottom up, rather than quiescently accepted.

In this respect, the authors of La brèche, who understood the May events in terms of the emergence of new logics of individual and collective autonomy, were not far off the mark,[48] for the May revolt sought to recalibrate the basic dynamics of socialization in advanced industrial societies. It represented an attempt to shift the locus of social power away from "alienated institutions" and toward the control of associated individuals. In the post-May period, these individuals regrouped

[46] Touraine, *May Movement*, 59.
[47] Ibid., 132.
[48] See Castoriadis, *Philosophy, Politics, Autonomy.*

themselves in various social movements: feminism, ecology, worker autonomy, citizens' initiatives, prisoners' rights, and gay rights. It is in this regard that Alain Touraine has justly described the post-May period in terms of a "return of the actor."[49] To conceptualize these developments in Marxist or neorepublican terms is to misconstrue their scope and import.

[49] Touraine, *Return of the Actor.*

CHAPTER 4

Who Were the Maoists?

> We confused everything: the political commissar-
> philosopher's machine gun, the big-hearted anarchist
> prostitutes, the cunning of the Hegelian concept,
> the Spanish Civil War, Kyo in [André Malraux's] *La
> Condition humaine* . . . Jean Jaurès and Lenin, [Paul]
> Nizan and [Louis] Aragon, the Resistance and the war
> in Algeria. . . . In sum, I became a Communist because
> I believed it was the only way to live life like a novel.
>
> —Jean-Paul Dollé, ex-Maoist

"A CIVIL WAR WITHOUT GUNS"

In May 1966 Mao Tse-tung launched the Great Proletarian Cultural
Revolution, pitting youthful Red Guards against Chinese Communist
Party stalwarts and city dwellers suspected of bourgeois habitudes.[1] To
much of the outside world, the Cultural Revolution appeared as a noble
attempt to reignite Chinese communism's fading revolutionary ardor.
Thereby, perhaps China could escape the bureaucratic sclerosis that had
afflicted the Soviet Union and its Eastern European allies.

However, we now know that Mao was rapidly losing his grip on
power. His credibility as a leader had suffered greatly from the debacle
of the Great Leap Forward: the disastrous agricultural modernization
scheme that from 1958 to 1961 caused some twenty million senseless, famine-related deaths. Moreover, Mao was aging, having recently
turned seventy-three. His rivals in the party hierarchy, Deng Xiaoping,

---

[1] The epigraph is from "Les illusions fécondes de Jean-Paul Dollé," *Le Monde Dimanche*, October 2, 1983.

Peng Zhen, and Liu Shao-qi, were gradually shunting him aside. To underscore his youthful vigor, in July 1966 Mao took a widely publicized swim in the Yangtze River. Thereby, he sought to convince skeptics that the revolution's fate was inextricably tied to his personal status as hero and leader.

Thus, in part, the Cultural Revolution was a naked power grab, rife with persecution and abuse for anyone who was suspected of being insufficiently revolutionary: "revisionists," "Khruschevites," and "bourgeois roaders." Mao instructed the Red Guards: "Do not be afraid to make trouble. The more trouble you make and the longer you make it, the better. Confusion and trouble are always noteworthy. . . . Trouble-making is revolutionary."[2] Such "instructions," or "notifications," would prove a recipe for mass anarchy. It was a strategy Mao set in motion to avenge his political enemies—above all his chief rival, Liu Shao-qi, who in 1959 had succeeded Mao as the People's Republic of China's head of state. At the same time, the Cultural Revolution represented a declaration of war against putative "rightist" tendencies within the Communist Party. The Great Helmsman feared that the party was in danger of producing a new elite of self-satisfied technocrats. As he warned the party leadership in 1965: "The life of sitting on sofas and using electric fans will not do."[3]

In recent years, Mao had followed developments in Soviet politics with great apprehension: Khrushchev's 1956 Twentieth Party Congress speech denouncing the "crimes of the Stalin era," as well as the Soviet leader's abrupt October 1964 dismissal by the politburo. Communist China's political legitimacy was openly predicated on the Stalinist-authoritarian model. From Mao's vantage point, Khrushchev's 1956 assault on Stalin's "cult of personality" struck close to home. He perceived de-Stalinization as an ignominious ideological retreat that threatened the success of communism worldwide. Although Mao had been openly at odds with the Soviet leader, reviling him as a "revisionist," Khrushchev's ouster raised the specter that before long an analogous fate could befall Mao himself. For all of these reasons Mao felt that the time was

[2] See Mao, *Mao Papers*, 26–29.
[3] Cited in Wakeman, *History and Will*, 306.

ripe to unleash a bold new political initiative that would double as a preemptive strike against potential enemies and rivals.

Significantly, the Cultural Revolution's shock troops, the Red Guards, were composed of high school and university students. They had been issued red armbands, allowing them to wreak havoc with impunity. Their motto, as proclaimed by numerous wall posters, was: "Beat to a pulp any and all persons who go against Mao Tse-tung Thought—no matter who they are, what banner they fly, or how exalted their positions may be."[4] And so they did.

At one point, Mao abruptly suspended the school system, thereby freeing up millions of students to do his bidding throughout the country. All atavisms of tradition that stood in the way of the socialist system and the dictatorship of the proletariat were fair game. At the instigation of Mao, the students proceeded to "demolish old buildings, temples, and art objects in their towns and villages, and to attack their teachers, school administrators, party leaders and parents."[5] During the Cultural Revolution victims were forced to march through the streets in dunce caps and with demeaning placards around their necks, proclaiming their guilt before large hostile crowds. Others were made to stand for hours on end "with backs agonizingly bent and arms outstretched in what was called the 'airplane position.'"[6] Intellectuals especially were frequently beaten and disgraced. Many others committed suicide after enduring unbearable public humiliation. Millions of urban dwellers were forcibly relocated to the countryside, where they were subjected to the "purifying" influence of backbreaking labor.

Mao conceived the Cultural Revolution as the Chinese equivalent of the Paris Commune. It would be, he once claimed, a "nationwide civil war without guns."[7] One of its goals was to eliminate the risks of class conciliation—for example, revisionist shibboleths concerning "peaceful coexistence"—and to underscore the insuperable "contradiction" (a keyword in the Maoist lexicon) between bourgeois and

[4] MacFarquhar and Schoenhals, *Mao's Last Revolution*, 104.

[5] Spence, *Search for Modern China*, 575.

[6] Ibid.

[7] Mao Tse-tung, "Vice Chairman Lin's Instruction," *JPRS* (90): 19.

proletarian classes. As modern Communards, the Red Guards would smash the bourgeois state apparatus and reestablish Chinese communism on a secure ideological footing. (Here, one of the ironies was that despite the official appellation "the Great Proletarian Cultural Revolution," the Chinese working class played a negligible role.) In December 1968, at a point when the social anarchy that had been unleashed seemed unmasterable, Mao reversed course by banishing the Red Guards to the countryside in order to learn "proletarian consciousness" from the peasantry. Mao Tse-tung Thought was nothing if not a mass of contradictions.

The ensuing chaos retarded Chinese economic development by some fifteen years. In the official history of the Chinese Communist Party published in 1981, the Cultural Revolution is described as being responsible for the "severest setbacks and the heaviest losses suffered by the Party, the state and the people since the founding of the People's Republic."[8] One of the jokes that circulated following Mao's death was that the Cultural Revolution's goal was to do away with culture.

One of Mao's chief theoretical texts was "On Contradiction" (1937). There Mao sought to address the asymmetrical relationship between base and superstructure. Given the primacy that dialectical materialism traditionally bestows on the economic base, is it a violation of Marxism, Mao inquires, to ask how one should respond when political and cultural factors assume primacy? "No!" Mao responds emphatically, for while acknowledging the primacy of social being over consciousness, we must also recognize "the reaction of mental on material things, of social consciousness on social being and of the superstructure on the economic base."[9]

One of the political intentions of Mao's treatise on materialist epistemology was to elevate China's standing in the avant-garde of revolutionary struggle, despite its manifest social and economic backwardness. After all, China was a nation that had only recently begun to

---

[8] *Resolution on CPC History, 1949–1981* (Beijing: Foreign Languages Press, 1981), 32.
[9] Mao, *On Contradiction*, 36–37.

emerge from its feudal past. Although factories could be found in the large cities, the vast majority of China's population remained peasants—a far cry from the scenario of proletarian revolution envisioned by Marx or even Lenin, who, despite Russia's sizable peasantry, had always attributed a leading role to the working class.

Thus, in an intellectual maneuver that would have significant repercussions for third worldism, Mao's theoretical writings endowed the peasantry with the same potential for class consciousness that Marx had attributed to the working class. Marx had famously maintained that class consciousness was a function of one's relationship to the means of production—hence, the proletariat's putatively privileged revolutionary vantage point. The Great Helmsman updated Marx to suit Chinese circumstances by declaring that class consciousness need not be so narrowly sociologically construed. He contended that class consciousness was a function of a group's *ideological* standing. Since under feudalism and imperialism the peasantry had been brutally oppressed, it, too, had ample incentive to rebel. Mao's stress on the superstructure's relative autonomy also provided license for the revolutionary leadership to indoctrinate workers and peasants to the point where their class consciousness became historically adequate. In essence, it underwrote a theory of educational or cultural dictatorship.

Yet, how exactly might one determine which contradiction plays the leading role at a given historical moment? At this point Mao's "voluntarism" comes into play—a voluntarism that, from Robespierre to Lenin, represented one of the hallmarks of the Jacobin revolutionary tradition. At every key juncture, one needed a knowledgeable revolutionary elite to sort out the various contradictions and to identify the path to genuine class consciousness. Thus, Maoist political thought oscillated between celebrating the virtues of the "mass line"—that is, taking one's lead from the disposition and orientation of "the people"—and revolutionary vanguardism à la Lenin and Robespierre. In a time of crisis, Mao was quick to stress the virtues of political leadership. Ultimately, when it came to revolution, the people were well-meaning amateurs. The party cadres, conversely, were knowledgeable and trustworthy professionals.

"THE YEAR 1967 WILL BE CHINESE"

The year 1967 was Chinese.[10] In Paris signs of Maoism's popularity
abounded. Mao-collared suits—"les cols Maos"—had become immensely fashionable. Try as they might, the clothing boutiques in
Paris's tony sixteenth arrondissement could not keep them in stock.
For their part, Left Bank booksellers were perpetually selling out of
Quotations from Chairman Mao. Lui, the French equivalent of *Playboy,* decided to jump on the pro-Chinese bandwagon by featuring
an eight-page spread of scantily clad models in straw hats, red stars,
and Red Guard attire. The accompanying captions were culled from
the Little Red Book. One striking image portrayed a young woman,
unclad and equipped with an automatic rifle, emerging from an enormous white cake. "The revolution is not a dinner party," read the
legend.[11]

In the world of cinema Jean-Luc Godard's *La Chinoise,* an alternately
whimsical and propagandistic attempt to fathom the wave of Sinophilia
cresting in Paris that year, became a succès de scandale. Godard was at
the zenith of his cinematic talents. *Weekend,* his breakthrough portrayal
of bourgeois decadence, had been released to immense critical acclaim
that spring.

Godard described his intentions in an August 1967 interview in *Le
Monde*:

> Why *La Chinoise*? Because everywhere people are speaking about
> China. Whether it's a question of oil, the housing crisis, or ed-
> ucation, there is always the Chinese example. China proposes
> solutions that are unique. . . . What distinguishes the Chinese
> Revolution and is also emblematic of the Cultural Revolution is
> *Youth*: the moral and scientific quest, free from prejudices. One

[10] Hamon and Rotman, *Génération* 1:329.

[11] Han Suyin, "La Chine aux mille vertus," *Lui,* June 1967, 36. I am very grateful
to Ron Haas for pointing out this side of the Maoist intoxication in his dissertation
"The Death of the Angel" (PhD diss., Rice University, 2006).

can't approve of all its forms . . . but this unprecedented cultural fact demands a minimum of attention, respect, and friendship.[12]

La Chinoise was filmed almost entirely in a private apartment at 15, rue Miromesnil, in Paris. The spatial isolation made the film seem something like a gauchiste Robinsonade. The young Maoists had completely turned their backs on the corruptions and lures of bourgeois society. As such, the film became a laboratory experiment or testing ground for the viability of left-wing ideology.

Godard had originally intended to examine the respective merits of Chinese and Soviet Marxism. However, by the time he started filming, the senescence of the Soviet model seemed self-evident.

To the annoyance of viewers with more conventional cinematic expectations, much of *La Chinoise* consisted of didactic political harangues culled from the texts of Saint-Just, Lenin, and, of course, the Great Helmsman himself. It was a tactic Godard had imbibed from Brecht's so-called didactic plays (*Lehrstücke*) and was intended to up-end the pretensions of cinematic and theatrical realism. Godard employed the technique to discomfit or "alienate" the viewer: to strip the filmgoer of his or her most reassuring illusions. Plot, narrative, character development—these were some of the vestiges of bourgeois "affirmative" cinema that Godard summarily jettisoned as ideologically compromised. By highlighting the constructed or fabricated nature of cinematic experience, the director hoped to disrupt the complacency with which cinemagoers customarily viewed films. Thereby, Godard sought to remove cinema once and for all from the world of entertainment or modern consumerism.

Fortunately, *La Chinoise* also contained moments of levity reminiscent of the director's pathbreaking nouvelle vague films, as in the scene where the young philosophy student Véronique (played by Godard's wife, Anna Wiazemsky) declares: "The Revolution is an uprising, an act of violence whereby one class overthrows another. As for me, I'm

---

[12] Jean-Luc Godard, interview with Jean Baby, *Le Monde,* August 24, 1967, 10.

in philosophy class." At that point the screen cuts to an image of the philosopher Maurice Merleau-Ponty.

La Chinoise ends with a lengthy political debate between Véronique and her real-life Nanterre philosophy professor Francis Jeanson—a "Sartrean" who had won notoriety during the Algerian War as a "porteur de valise," or money handler, for the FLN[13]—over the merits of revolutionary violence. At one point Véronique impetuously declares that she wants to "shut down the university with bombs." Jeanson points out that when he was a militant he had an entire people backing his actions. Conversely, Véronique and her fellow Maoists are politically isolated. "I think you are heading down a path that is a perfect dead end," Jeanson concludes resignedly, although, for his part, Godard would later claim that at the time he was more sympathetic to Véronique's point of view.[14]

La Chinoise went a long way toward boosting Maoism's political-chic quotient. Within a few years, numerous celebrities would clamber on board the Maoist bandwagon. As one observer cynically observed, among Left Bank intellectuals "radical chic became a form of moral tax deduction."[15] What filmmaker apart from Godard could get away with including the following Althusserian rhetorical gem in a feature film: "The idea of permanent revolution is only valid if the diversity and determination of the teams of political economists allow them to overcome the uncertainties of the conjuncture."[16]

Godard went on to make several other pro-Chinese films—including *The Wind from the East* (1969) and *See You at Mao* (1971)—during his stint as a "guerrilla filmmaker" with the Dziga Vertov group, which Godard cofounded with fellow director Jean-Pierre Gorin. In 1970, when the Maoist daily *La Cause du Peuple* was impounded by the Pompidou government and its editors imprisoned, Godard was among the prominent French intellectuals who defied the ban by hawking the proscribed broadsheet on the boulevards of Paris.

[13] See Hamon and Rotman, *Porteurs de valise.*
[14] Godard, *Jean-Luc Godard*, 303.
[15] Caute, *Year of the Barricades*, 259.
[16] Godard, *Made in USA*, 1967.

If by filming *La Chinoise* Godard's aim had been to ingratiate himself with the Maoist student militants, who had pointedly refused to appear in the film, his efforts fell short. A celebrated May 1968 graffito mocked the Swiss director as "le plus con des suisses pro-Chinois" (the biggest ass among the Swiss pro-Chinese).

THE "NORMAL SCHOOL"

The Maoist temptation began among a group of Louis Althusser's students at the Ecole normale supérieure. The ENS is a training ground for France's intellectual elite. Those who are accepted receive a four-year stipend. Jean-Paul Sartre, Simone de Beauvoir, Maurice Merleau-Ponty, Raymond Aron, Louis Althusser, and Michel Foucault were all ENS graduates.[17]

The students' attraction to Maoism had been piqued by the Sino-Soviet rift of the early 1960s. In 1963 the Central Committee of the Chinese Communist Party had openly challenged the Soviet Union's leadership of the international Communist movement. The Soviets abruptly recalled some fourteen hundred technicians and experts from China, seriously disrupting Chinese industrial development.

The PCF, headed by a group of unregenerate Stalinists, had become the embodiment of ideological rigidity. In 1956, to the dismay of fellow travelers like Sartre, it unhesitatingly backed the brutal Soviet invasion of Hungary. By the mid-1960s, however, its servility to Moscow had become something of an embarrassment. Increasingly, it had difficulty finding recruits among France's vaunted caste of intellectual mandarins. The PCF recycled the same old "workerist" political line. But increasingly, its slogans were out of touch with the realities of French occupational life, where the ranks of white-collar and service-industry workers were swelling. Moreover, the party was consistently tone-deaf

---

[17] For the relevant background, see Henri Bourgin, *L'Ecole normale et la politique: De Jean Jaurès à Léon Blum* (Paris: Fayard, 1938). See also Diane Rubenstein, *What's Left? The Ecole normale supérieure and the Right* (Madison: University of Wisconsin Press, 1990).

to the political novelties of the 1960s: decolonization, third worldism, not to mention the attractions of "cultural revolution," which fascinated the student generation. Where, then, might young leftists turn to find a viable oppositional political model?

For a time many of the ENS Maoists tried to make a go of it within the French Communist Party student organization, the Union des étudiants communistes (UEC). They hatched a Machiavellian scheme, known as "entrisme," to transform the UEC along less dogmatic lines from within. For this reason, they came to be known as the Italians, since among West European Communists, the Italian Communist Party displayed the greatest independence from Moscow. But once their plot was uncovered, they were, in good Bolshevik fashion, summarily purged. In 1966 the student Maoists started their own organization, the Union des jeunesses communistes marxistes-léninistes (UJC–ML). The "marxiste-léniniste" suffix was a sign of the times. It indicated that UJC adherents were genuine revolutionaries, unlike the PCF "revisionists," who seemed more concerned with electoral success and trade union gains than the virtues of armed struggle.

Hence, curiously, while America's "best and brightest"—the Harvard graduates who served in the Kennedy and Johnson administrations—were prosecuting the Vietnam War, their opposite numbers in France, the so-called Ulmards (the Ecole normale was located on the rue d'Ulm, in the heart of the Latin Quarter) were planning trips to China, copiously citing the Little Red Book, and praising the virtues of a "war of position" against the bourgeois enemy.[18]

REDISCOVERING MARXISM WITH ALTHUSSER

Recent political developments had placed the Maoists' spiritual mentor, Louis Althusser, in an awkward position. Althusser was a devout Communist who revered Stalinism as the movement's glorious pinnacle. He viewed Khrushchev's Twentieth Party Congress speech, exposing

[18] See André Glucksmann, "Strategy and Revolution in France 1968," *New Left Review* 52 (1968).

the "crimes of the Stalin era," as a departure from orthodoxy that had opened the door to the flaccid heresies of revisionism. Already during the 1950s, Althusser sensed the threat that the new antiscientific Marxist lexicon represented to the standpoint of Soviet orthodoxy. In Eastern Europe, Marxist humanism, in the guise of "socialism with a human face," would culminate in the ill-fated Prague Spring of 1968. Althusser's theoretical efforts (under the aegis of structuralism) to restore Marxism's respectability as "science" were directed against the threats posed by the growing popularity of "Marxist humanism," whose chief French representatives were PCF philosopher Roger Garaudy and Sartre. In Althusser's view the softening of the party line, the retreat from "science" in favor of the effete philosophical standpoint of "Western Marxism," risked effacing the all-important difference between genuine communism and social democracy.[19]

In the PCF, dissent was tantamount to sacrilege, grounds for expulsion. Althusser's dilemma was clear. Following the Sino-Soviet rift, one could not be both a card-carrying member of the PCF and pro-Chinese. It was a case of either-or. When, in 1967, the ENS students published a special issue of their journal praising the achievements of the Cultural Revolution, Althusser contributed, but without affixing his byline, lest he run afoul of party authorities. For their part, the students decided to overlook the tension between their own political "voluntarism"—their exaltation of "revolutionary will"—and Althusser's inflexible structuralism, which belittled human agency in favor of indubitable scientific axioms. As one commentator aptly noted, the peculiar alliance between Althusser and the gauchistes "made possible a paradoxical bringing together of an often mad political voluntarism—a desperate activism—and the notion of a subjectless process that resembled a mystical commitment."[20]

The normaliens wagered that by sacrificing themselves as autonomous "subjects" and integrating themselves with the "logic of history," they would be redeemed. As an additional benefit, they would thereby

---

[19] See the discussion of "Western Marxism" in Maurice Merleau-Ponty's *Signs*, trans. Richard McCleary (Evanston, IL: Northwestern University Press, 1964).

[20] Dosse, *History of Structuralism* 1:299.

negate the taint of their own bourgeois class background. In their approach to Marx, the UJC militants craved an element of certainty that structuralist thinkers—Fernand Braudel, Ferdinand de Saussure, and Claude Lévi-Strauss—had been able to confer on other disciplines and fields. The austerity of Althusser's philosophical doctrines projected an air of uncompromising theoretical rigor that the young normaliens found seductive. They yearned for an absolute, and Althusser's iron-clad distinction between "science" (Marxism) and "ideology" (the delusions of bourgeois humanism) provided it. But was not structuralism, with its inordinate focus on "discourse" and "theory," in the end patently "idealistic"—hence, incompatible with the requirements of Marxism qua materialism? The normaliens rationalized this dilemma with loose speculation about the "materiality of the signifier."

At the time, Hegelianism and phenomenology—as dominated by the three *H*s, Hegel, Husserl, and Heidegger—were the leading strands of French philosophy. From an intellectual standpoint, Althusser's structuralism offered a novel, nonacademic approach that students found refreshing vis-à-vis the shopworn pieties of republican humanism. Structural linguistics attacked the delusions of authorship (we do not speak language; instead, "language speaks us"); structural anthropologists and psychoanalysts attacked the paradigm of "consciousness"; Althusserians, for their part, sought to "joyfully bury humanism like the pitiful remnants of a bygone era of triumphant bourgeois thinking."[21]

Althusser's structuralism stressed Marxism's status as a self-enclosed, autochthonous conceptual system. Marx's theoretical corpus contained absolute truth—as long as one knew how to read it and what to look for. By emphasizing Marxism's internal coherence, Althusser sought to safeguard its doctrinal purity, no matter how badly the theory might play out in reality. Stalin may have committed egregious crimes; the Soviet Union might be a degenerate workers' state; yet Marxism's pristine theoretical truths would persevere unscathed. But what sense did

---

[21] Ibid., 291. Apropos of Lévi-Strauss: an oft-told anecdote places him at a Berkeley restaurant following a campus lecture. When the Lévi-Strauss party arrives to claim its reservation, the owner quips: "The blue jeans manufacturer or the anthropologist?"

it make to embalm Marxism as a body of pristine a priori truths when it was intended as an explanation of real history?

In retrospect, it seems clear that subtending Althusser's "scientism" lay a nostalgia for Stalinism: a deep-seated intolerance for aleatory perspectives and views. In many respects, Althusser's structuralism did for Marxist philosophy what Zhdanov's doctrine of socialist realism had done for the arts in the 1930s. During the 1930s Althusser belonged to a militant Catholic organization, Action catholique. Commentators have speculated that following World War II, the philosopher transposed his fervent quest for absolute truth from the church to the Communist Party. Was it mere coincidence that toward the end of his life Althusser lobbied the Vatican for a private audience with Pope John Paul II?[22]

The French Communist Party viewed structuralism disparagingly, since it scorned history in favor of timeless constructs. Marxism prided itself on its theory of history, which prophesied capitalism's decline and the proletariat's inevitable triumph. Nevertheless, since at the time structuralism was enjoying such an unparalleled vogue—France's leading thinkers, Barthes, Braudel, Foucault, Lacan, and Lévi-Strauss, were all structuralists—the party tolerated Althusser's theoretical views as a much-needed source of intellectual prestige. His regeneration of Marxist theory might offset the taint that communism had in the eyes of French intellectuals following the 1956 Hungarian debacle.

Althusser was sympathetic to aspects of Chinese communism. In his view, under Mao's leadership China's leaders displayed a revolutionary vitality that had long ceased to exist among their geriatric counterparts in Eastern Europe. Paradoxically, one of the main reasons Althusser admired Chinese communism was that its leaders had remained unwavering Stalinists. Khrushchevism, with its conciliatory rhetoric of "peaceful coexistence," had opened Pandora's box to all manner of political slackness. Hence, some of Althusser's early texts featured guarded allusions to Chinese developments.

---

[22] According to sources familiar with the story, Althusser's request was granted. But a few weeks later, he strangled his wife, Hélène, and the plans were promptly abandoned.

Althusser's 1962 essay "Contradiction and Overdetermination" is a good case in point.[23] Although Mao's name appears nowhere in the article, the essay is an extended commentary on the Great Helmsman's disquisition "On Contradiction." Since to cite Mao directly would have constituted grounds for immediate expulsion, as a substitute Althusser invoked an 1890 letter by Engels claming that the economic "base," though indispensable, is far from being all-determinant, thus allowing for the quasi-autonomy of cultural and political developments. Althusser rightly sensed that Soviet Marxism had congealed into an inflexible economic determinism. The virtue of Mao's essay was that it acknowledged that "base" and "superstructure" did not always stand in a direct, causal relationship. Instead, often they stood *in contradiction to one another.* In pursuing this tack, Althusser sought to expand the purview of Marxist theory so that it would be capable of engaging new cultural and intellectual challenges.

Althusser's students, conversely, operated under no such prohibitions. Their enthusiasm for revolutionary China was zealous and unqualified, although almost none of them could read Chinese, and reliable information about contemporary China was extremely scarce. As of 1965—Althusser's annus mirabilis, when both *For Marx* and *Reading Capital* appeared—the students began airing their radical political views in the self-published *Cahiers marxistes-léninistes.* The editors were Robert Linhart, Jacques-Alain Miller, and Jacques Rancière. In 1967 epistemologist Dominique Lecourt took over as editor-in-chief. The student activists came to view their four-year ENS stipend as a subvention that allowed them to militate full-time.

French Maoism operated at a dangerous remove from the reality principle. Mao's China became a projection—a Rohrschach test—for the students' overheated revolutionary fantasies. With Soviet communism substantially discredited, revolutionary China, along with other third-world experiments in state socialism (North Vietnam, Cuba, and so on), seemed to embody the last best hope for a left-wing alternative to the dislocations of Western modernity: overcrowded cities, urban

---

[23] Althusser, "Contradiction and Overdetermination," in *For Marx.*

blight, ghetto uprisings (in the United States, at least), industrially scarred landscapes, and massive pollution.

Looking back, a leading Maoist militant, Roland Castro, explained the basis underlying the students' attraction to Maoism as follows:

> The first message we received from China: *revolution within the revolution*. The second message we received (though fewer of us this time): *revolution of civilization*. The third message we received: Seven hundred million Chinese people is not a kibbutz; it's not a phalanstery; it's not a splinter group. It's a quarter of the world, an empire in the center of the world, in the center of the world that it was about to implode. We could hear the implosion.[24]

"Revolution within the revolution" meant that by stressing the primacy of cultural and ideological themes, Maoism had beneficially broadened the scope of revolutionary struggle. Revolutionary discourse was no longer governed by the administrative-managerial mentality of Eastern European socialism. *"Revolution of civilization"* meant that radical politics no longer pertained to questions of social engineering, as in Lenin's infamous definition of "socialism" as "the Soviets plus electrification." Instead it bespoke a qualitative transformation of everyday life. Hence, the popular May 1968 slogan, borrowed from Rimbaud, "Changer la vie!" (Change life!) "Seven hundred million Chinese people is not a kibbutz" meant that the Cultural Revolution could not be dismissed as an epiphenomenon or a blip. At stake were events of epochal significance that portended nothing less than a wholesale transformation of humanity's capacity for political self-organization.

REVOLUTIONARY TOURISM

In August 1967 the UJC-ML leadership—Robert Linhart, Jacques Broyelle, Christian Riss, and Jean-Pierre Le Dantec—made a life-transforming pilgrimage to China. Upon their return, in *Garde Rouge*

[24] Castro, *1989*.

they praised China's first hydrogen bomb detonation as "An immortal victory for Mao Tse-tung thought."[25] Since the People's Republic of China was itself in the throes of an immense political purge (the Cultural Revolution), Linhart decided his group should follow suit and extirpate the last vestiges of the "petty bourgeois intellectualism." It was at this point that the Maoists, in vintage Oedipal fashion, turned against Althusser, who had repeatedly refused to renounce his Communist Party membership and join forces with the UJC-ML.

The pro-Chinese activists who made pilgrimages to the People's Republic of China engaged in blind acts of "revolutionary tourism." They visited prefabricated Potemkin villages and were perpetually accompanied by party-appointed "handlers." They returned to France to publish florid reminiscences praising the superiority of the Chinese path to socialism.[26] As the Italian Communist writer Maria-Antonietta Macciocchi enthused in her travel memoir *De la Chine*,

[Here is] a people marching with a light step and with fervor toward the future. This people may be the incarnation of the new civilization of the world. China has made an unprecedented leap into history. . . . Mao is essentially antidogmatic and antiauthoritarian. He prizes the initiative of the masses over the primacy of the [production] apparatus, he insists on the principle of equality, he repeats that the party cannot be a substitute for the masses and that the masses must liberate themselves.[27]

The complexities and sordid realities of contemporary Chinese politics mattered little. What counted was that the illusion of a radiant utopian future was preserved. Thus, for all their rebelliousness, the Maoist *normaliens* merely repeated the mistakes of a previous generation of leftists, who, led by prestigious literati such as Henri Barbusse

[25] Bourseiller, *Maoïstes*, 81. For an excellent overview, see Julian Bourg, "The Red Guards of Paris: French Student Maoism of the 1960s," *History of European Ideas* 4 (31) (2005): 472–90.

[26] See, for example, the influential account of Claudie Broyelle, *La moitié du ciel* (Paris: Denoël-Gonthier, 1973).

[27] Macciocchi, *De la Chine*, 466; see also Moravia, *Révolution culturelle*.

and Romain Rolland, had uncritically sung the praises of Stalinist Russia during the 1930s.[28]

Long after his initial visit to the People's Republic, Jacques Broyelle, one of the UJC-ML leaders, returned to confront his party-appointed chaperone. "You only showed us the positive side of Chinese communism," complained Broyelle. "We showed you what you wanted to see," his Chinese counterpart retorted.

The students' Maoist intoxication testified to an enduring trope of French cultural life, Orientalism—the idea that an infusion of "primitive" energies from non-Western lands would offset European decadence and revitalize France qua metropole-in-decline. Eugène Delacroix's sprawling depictions of Oriental decadence, André Malraux's revolutionary romanticism in *La condition humaine* (set during the early phases of the Chinese civil war during the late 1920s), and Paul Nizan's youthful memoir, *Aden, Arabie*, all fit the mold. At odds with their elders, frustrated with metropolitan France's cultural insularity, politically homeless under de Gaulle's eleven-year autocratic reign, the student militants sought out an alternative political reality light-years removed from the prosaic historical present in which they felt trapped.

It seemed that the less information the students possessed concerning the People's Republic and the greater China's geographic and cultural remove from Europe, the more leeway they had to project their own utopian hopes and dreams. Still, important aspects of their pro-Chinese worldview were reality based. They venerated Mao as one of the titans of the twentieth-century revolutionary tradition. He was perceived as a creative interpreter of Marxist doctrine, someone who was both an activist and a theorist. His interpretation of class struggle incorporated the peasantry, an innovation that was central for Asian and South American third worldism. Moreover, the Great Helmsman's personal saga as a figure who, following countless military and political setbacks, persevered until he finally succeeded in driving Chiang Kai-shek's Kuomintang from the mainland, was a narrative that fascinated revolutionary romantics worldwide.

---

[28] See Hourmant, *Au pays de l'avenir radieux*. To his credit, Gide, in *Retour de l'URSS*, sounded a skeptical note.

In addition to being a gifted military strategist, Mao was an intellectual—among the habitués of Left Bank society, an inestimable source of prestige. Along with his capacious theoretical writings, he also wrote poetry! Among the Parisian literati, the fact that Mao had unleashed a *cultural* revolution carried great weight. It accounted for the innovative character of Chinese communism vis-à-vis its drab, *dirigiste* Soviet counterpart. Among the normaliens and their sympathizers, the fact that Chinese students had been called upon to play the role of a revolutionary avant-garde appeared to cinch matters. Thus, from a French perspective the Cultural Revolution seemed to strike all the right chords.

From its inception the Cultural Revolution generated global support and admiration for the Chinese cause, and not just among leftists. Sinologists, foreign service officers, and amateur China watchers worldwide believed that revolutionary China represented an alternative path to modernity, one that avoided the West's dismal excesses and missteps. As Harvard Sinologist John K. Fairbank wrote in 1972: "The people seem healthy, well fed and articulate about their role as citizens of Chairman Mao's new China. . . . The change in the countryside is miraculous. . . . The Maoist revolution is on the whole *the best thing that happened to the Chinese people in centuries.*"[29]

During the 1960s a deep-seated disenchantment with Western modernity prevailed. The consensus was that something had drastically gone wrong. The ghettos of major American cities—Chicago, Detroit, and Los Angeles—were periodically consumed in flames. Anarchists and student revolutionaries rocked Europe's capitals with violent protests. In Germany and Italy terrorist cells engendered a siege mentality. For many observers China became the beneficiary of the West's loss of self-confidence.

Under Mao's benevolent tutelage, China had learned how to harness the power of the masses. It pursued an approach to industrialization that was self-evidently more humane. The new China seemed to provide something for everyone: "for the puritan, a hardworking, simple,

---

[29] John K. Fairbank, "The New China and the American Connection," *Foreign Affairs* (October 1972): 31, 36; emphasis added.

efficiently modernizing country; for the cultural connoisseur, thousands of years of Chinese culture; for the frustrated leftist, a Marxist-Leninist regime restoring the good name of Marxism; above all, and for most visitors, there was a land of mystery, beauty, purpose, and order, a former victim acquiring power and dignity."[30] While the West coped with endless social and political strife, under Mao's leadership, revolutionary China seemed to embody a refreshing unity of purpose. It was hard to argue with the robust political enthusiasm of seven hundred million Chinese.

Like many gauchistes, the Maoist student radicals were self-avowed sectarians. Alienated from mainstream French society, their political zealotry provided their lives with purpose and meaning. From a social-psychological standpoint, Maoism allowed a gifted contingent of French youth to resolve problems of identity formation amid a turbulent and confusing era. Involvement with the UJC—and later on, with its successor, the Gauche prolétarienne (GP)—provided student activists with an integral credo or worldview. In their devotion to their chosen political cause, the Maoists exhibited the fervor of true believers. Moreover, the role that bourgeois self-hatred played in their pro-Chinese worldview was inestimable.

The ethic of total commitment protected adherents from the risks of social atomization. Among diehard militants, Maoism became a vehicle of what Max Weber called "inner-worldly salvation." As believers, the activists were "saved" or "redeemed." As Jacques Broyelle acknowledged in retrospect: "The UJC-ML was a totalitarian society in miniature, with one significant difference: we didn't have the power to manipulate the material parameters that, in a socialist country, determine people's lives. Moreover, it was a servitude to which we consented voluntarily."[31]

The student Maoists seized on aspects of Chinese Communist doctrine they found congenial to their ends. Mao's voluntarism—his belief that revolution depended not on objective conditions but on heroic acts of will—well suited their own youthful insurrectionary

---

[30] Hollander, *Political Pilgrims*, 287.
[31] Quoted ibid., 337.

exuberance.[32] Owing to their belief in spontaneity, among PCF supporters the Maoists were derisively known as "les Maos-Spontex."
Spontex also happened to be the name of a widely advertised, fast-
cleaning sponge. Mao was widely viewed as a genuine populist
who kept the people's interest foremost in mind. His political texts
brimmed with praise for the "masses," who possessed an innate revolutionary potential waiting to be tapped by politically enlightened
cadres. Last, Mao's notion of "permanent revolution" also resonated
among denizens of Paris's Left Bank. It would ensure that, unlike its
Soviet counterpart, Chinese communism would not succumb to the
heresies of "revisionism."

For its part, the French Communist Party was endemically conservative. It had become so successful in the Fifth Republic's party system
that it hesitated to rock the boat. The PCF greeted the May student
revolt with incomprehension and condescension, dismissing the student militants as irredeemably bourgeois. Their "class character" meant
that they were intrinsically unserviceable for revolutionary ends. If the
student insurrection lacked an identifiable proletarian component, why
bother to support it, reasoned the Communists.

THE SAGA OF THE *ETABLIS*

The Maoists' political itinerary is inseparable from the saga of the
établissements—literally, the "shop floor." As we have noted, Mao
identified the masses as the touchstone of political authenticity. On
many occasions he instructed party members to commingle with the
rural masses as a method of raising political consciousness. He declared in a 1957 speech: "We recommend that intellectuals go among
the masses, in the factories, in the countryside. . . . Our politicians,
our writers, our artists, our teachers, and our scientific workers must

---

[32] As Spence aptly notes in *Search for Modern China*, 546: "The roots of Mao's radical
thinking had always lain in the voluntaristic, heroic workings of the human will and
the power of the masses that he had celebrated in his earliest writings."

seize every occasion available to enter into contact with workers and peasants."[33]

The student Maoists took this suggestion to heart. In keeping with Mao's slogan "One must get down from the horse in order to pluck the flowers," they consigned themselves to arduous factory work in the provinces. There, they would blend in with the proletarian milieus, all the while trying to redirect the workers' focus away from trade union demands (salary increases and improved working conditions) and toward the ends of political struggle. The situation placed the student activists under considerable psychological stress, for in order to gain acceptance among their fellow workers, they were forced to conceal their backgrounds as sons and daughters of privilege and as normaliens.

Among the Maoists, to "establish" oneself in a provincial factory became a rite of passage, an act of political self-sacrifice that doubled as a test of one's revolutionary mettle. At its height, some two to three thousand students participated in the *établi* movement, though not all were Maoist. The établi phenomenon was a vehicle via which leftists could divest themselves of their bourgeois origins and demonstrate their proletarian bona fides. The Maoists prided themselves on their dedication to "practice," as opposed to "theory," which was ironic, since as normaliens they represented France's intellectual elite. Moreover, the stress placed on proximity to the masses entailed a marked anti-intellectual dimension. UJC-ML leader Robert Linhart commented that during his stint as an établi he once went two years without cracking open a book.

During the 1980s many ex-Maoists, including Linhart, wrote revealing memoirs recounting their experiences as établis. Often, the working conditions were excruciating. Hailing from privileged backgrounds, many of them had never done a day's manual labor in their entire lives. Thus, they frequently had great difficulty completing their assigned tasks. One young Maoist recounted how she obtained work in a factory that manufactured copper plating. By midafternoon, her hands were bloody. The foreman politely recommended that she find

---

[33] Cited in Dressen's *De l'amphi à l'établi*, 7.

alternative employment. She left the factory in tears.[34] Another memoir insightfully depicts the mind-numbing, Sisyphean drudgery at a provincial automobile plant:

> As soon as the car has been fitted into the assembly line it begins its half-circle, passing each successive position for soldering or another complementary operation, such as filing, grinding, hammering. . . . A few knocks, a few sparks, then the soldering's done and the car's already on its way out of the three or four yards of this position. And the next car's already coming into the work area. And the worker starts again. Sometimes, if he's been working fast, he has a few seconds' respite before a new car arrives; either he takes advantage of it to breathe for a moment, or else he intensifies his effort and "goes up the line" so that he can gain a little time, in other words he works further ahead, outside his normal area, together with the worker at the preceding position. And after an hour or two he's amassed the incredible capital of two or three minutes in hand, that he'll use up smoking a cigarette. . . . Short-lived happiness: the next car's already there: he'll have to work on it at his usual position this time, and the race begins again, in the hope of gaining one or two yards, "moving up" in the hope of another peaceful cigarette. . . .
>
> Through the gaps in this gray, gliding line I can glimpse a war of attrition: death versus life and life versus death. Death: being caught up in the line, the imperturbable gliding of cars, the repetition of identical gestures, the work that's never finished. If one car's done, the next one isn't, and it's already there, unsoldered at the precise spot that's just been done, rough at the precise spot that's just been polished. . . . The aggressive wear and tear of the assembly line is experienced violently by everyone: city workers and peasants, intellectual and manual workers, immigrants and Frenchman [sic]. It's not unusual to see a new recruit give up after his first day, driven mad by the noise, the sparks, the inhuman pressure of speed, the harshness of endlessly repetitive work, the

---

[34] Bourseiller, *Maoïstes*, 84.

authoritarianism of the bosses and the severity of the orders, the dreary prison-like atmosphere which makes the shop so frigid.[35]

The UJC-ML militants were known as a groupuscule. This was an insult coined by PCF officials to mock the Maoists' paucity of adherents. Who, after all, read the jargonized articles that appeared in *Cahiers Marxistes-Léninistes*? At one point the UJC-ML leadership lobbied Beijing for official recognition but were politely rebuffed. The student revolutionaries' numbers (approximately thirty-five militants in 1967) were too small. In response, the Maoists organized a nationwide anti–Vietnam War protest movement among *lycées* and universities throughout France, Comités Vietnams de bases (CVBs). The number of pro-Chinese activists swelled to two thousand.

In keeping with another precept of Mao Tse-tung Thought, "Unless one has made an investigation, one doesn't have the right to speak," the Maoists also conducted "investigations" (*enquêtes*) of working-class conditions to familiarize themselves with the habitudes and mind-set of the class that, according to orthodox Marxist catechism, represented humanity's future.[36] There follows the testimony of one UJC-ML activist about the enquête he and his fellow militants undertook in the Vosges region of eastern France. The description of his blind ideological devotion and the difficult choices he faced as an établi are fairly typical.

I joined the UJC-ML in 1967. At the time one felt that if one wanted to understand something about working-class reality, one

[35] Robert Linhart, *The Assembly Line*, trans. Margaret Crosland (Amherst: University of Massachusetts Press, 1981), 15, 17, 26.

[36] For Mao's explanation of this idea and its importance, see *Quotations from Chairman Mao*, 230:

Everyone engaged in practical work must investigate conditions at the lower levels. Such investigation is especially necessary for those who know theory but do not know the actual conditions, for otherwise they will not be able to link theory with practice. Although my assertion, 'No investigation, no right to speak,' has been ridiculed as 'narrow empiricism,' to this day I do not regret having made it; far from regretting it, I still insist that without investigation there cannot be any right to speak.

had to go directly there, to plunge in. . . . As Chairman Mao once said: "One can't understand the working class if one keeps it at arm's length." I didn't undertake the decision to live in a factory on theoretical grounds. It was a collective decision I made with my comrades in the UJC–ML. At this point in time [1967], our primary focus was studying the works of Chairman Mao, who repeatedly said that one must think in line with the majority. The "majority" is the people. One can't think about revolution without understanding the people's opinion. Thus, that summer, we launched our enquêtes about country life. We went there to live among the farmers. We called it: *Investigations in the Countryside.*

By the end of the summer, we decided that one of us should remain to continue the enquête. I volunteered. I thought it would suffice to remain close to the workers, so I took a job as an apprentice at a school that trains construction workers and masons. By the end of the month I realized that I would understand nothing about the reality of workers' lives in this region . . . unless I worked in a factory. So long as I was content to sit in a café, or to stand by the factory gate, I would understand nothing. I had to go inside the factory, with the workers.

I stayed for six months. It was hard! I didn't know how to manage the work. I had read Mao's books, but that was all. . . . It was the dead of winter. I had to get out of there![37]

LOST ILLUSIONS

Ultimately, the UJC–ML's ideological inflexibility proved to be its undoing. When 1968 rolled around, the militants' servile reverence for Maoist doctrine led them to misapprehend the nature and scope of the May revolt. They had become prisoners of their own political dogmatism.

Since the May uprising was initially a *student* revolt, and since the students were predominantly *bourgeois*, the Maoists dismissed the

[37] Manceaux, *Maos en France*, 54–56.

rebellion as politically irrelevant. The insurrection failed to conform to their narrow-minded ideal of political class. They misunderstood the futility of transposing a model of political struggle conceived in a rural, semifeudal developing nation such as China to a hypermodern society like France.

Unlike China, France was hardly a peasant society. As countless studies attested, by the 1960s French occupational life was highly strati-fied. Hence, it bore little resemblance to the sociological presupposi-tions of classical Marxism: a mass of destitute proletarians on one side and a handful of affluent capitalists on the other. The French working class, although oppressed, was far from impoverished. Moreover, its numbers were rapidly shrinking, and a new class of salaried employees, largely in the tertiary or service sector, was on the rise.

The May uprising's goal was not to seize political power à la Lenin and the Bolsheviks, but to democratize decision-making processes in government, education, and the workplace. In the main, it targeted the authoritarian disposition of French administrative elites. Rather than focusing on the traditional concerns of class politics, the student pro-testers targeted qualitative issues pertaining to the "politics of everyday life": the rise of consumer society, the accelerated pace of moderniza-tion, and the dilapidated condition of French universities.

Over the course of the previous decade, the terms of political strug-gle had been redefined. Left-wing groupuscules like the Situationist International addressed these problems directly. But since none of these issues and concerns had been treated in the Little Red Book, for the UJC-ML brain trust they remained immaterial. In the words of Pierre Victor: "We were profoundly mistrustful vis-à-vis the student move-ment. We had a very, very narrow proletarian perspective. We thought: if the students don't go to the factory gates, they have no future; their future will be that of the bourgeoisie."[38] Caught entirely off guard by the May uprising, the Maoist leadership elected to condemn it.

For the Maoists, things would only get worse before they got better. Uncertain as to how they should react to the May insurrection, like true sectarians, the leadership began to succumb to political paranoia. Their

[38] Ibid., 188.

official political line held that the student uprising was a plot hatched by
de Gaulle and the French state to ensnare and crush the French proletariat. They feared that if the working classes allied themselves with the
student protesters, the government would use it as a pretext to carry out
a major wave of repression: a massacre reminiscent of the "June days"
of 1848 or the Paris Commune, when some twenty thousand workers
were slain by the National Guard.

Just when it appeared that things could not get any worse, as the
May events crested UJC-ML leader Robert Linhart suffered a nervous
breakdown. On the Night of the Barricades (May 10–11), as the student
radicals tried to seal off the Latin Quarter from an impending attack by
the riot police, Linhart made an emergency visit to the Chinese embassy, detailing the implausible entrapment theory just outlined. The
Chinese diplomats looked on in bewilderment. Under the pressure of
the moment, and seeing no way out, Linhart panicked and boarded a
train to the provinces. His collapse required months of hospitalization
and subsequent medical treatment.

By May 13, when the working class joined the student protesters in
full force, individual Maoists had begun participating in the immense
demonstrations that were convulsing metropolitan France. But during the uprising's first week, from May 3 to May 10, the Maoists were
AWOL. The greatest revolutionary upsurge in postwar Europe had
taken place, and the Maoists had missed it. They had learned the Maoist
revolutionary catechism by heart, but when their generation's defining
political moment occurred, they failed to recognize it, even though it
had transpired directly beneath their dormitory windows in the heart
of the Latin Quarter.

In June Minister of the Interior Raymond Marcellin warned in a
nationally televised speech, "In all countries of the world . . . there are
Maoist parties and Marxist-Leninists. . . . It is reasonable to say—and
the information at my disposal allows me to say it—that the ringleaders
know one another. It is easy to imagine who the ringleader of Maoism
and Marxism-Leninism might be."[39] Of course, it was none other than
Mao himself! Marcellin insinuated that the Maoists represented a fifth

[39] Cited in Bourseiller's *Maoïstes*, 99.

column that was secretly in the pay of Beijing.[40] He proceeded to ban the UJC-ML as a subversive organization.

For the Maoist normaliens, the summer of 1968 was a time for soul-searching—and, in good pro-Chinese fashion, a period of collective self-criticism. The UJC-ML leadership was filled with self-reproach. Under Linhart's guidance, they had followed a narrowly "ouvriériste" political line, thus misapprehending the student uprising's political nature and import. The realization had gradually taken hold that although working-class concerns remained significant, other political struggles were equally deserving of attention. The crisis of French society that exploded during May suggested that political radicalism far transcended the strictures of the Marxist-Leninist orthodoxy. Above all, the Maoists had misjudged the nature of the "cultural revolution" that had been building up in the years prior to 1968. As one repentant Maoist would acknowledge, "For a long time a sectarian ideology dominated our ranks, holding the students in contempt and underestimating their capacity to revolt against bourgeois society."[41] For the Maoists this realization became one of May 1968's foremost political lessons. The post-May era witnessed the emergence of a plethora of new political struggles and social movements: the women's movement, gay liberation, prisoners' rights, and environmentalism. Henceforth, it would prove increasingly difficult to claim that any one of these struggles merited exclusive priority.

The May events had convinced militant Tiennot Grumbach (nephew of former prime minister Pierre Mendès-France) that it was the *libertarian* side of the student revolt that represented the movement's enduring contribution. He and a handful of Nanterre enragés founded a new group, Vive la révolution! Inspired by Situationist doctrines, it focused on "cultural politics" and "everyday life." In the 1969 inaugural issue of their publication, Grumbach and his fellow "anarcho-Maoists" realized that their servile adherence to Mao Tse-tung Thought had led them badly astray. They sought to definitively jettison the sectarian mind-set that they had once held dear:

[40] See Marcellin's mémoir, *L'importune verité.*
[41] See the detailed UJC-ML self-critique "Projet d'autocritique," in Kessel's *Mouvement maoïste,* 96–107.

We disagree profoundly with those who seek to turn the page as quickly as possible as if nothing had happened. This time we do not want to squander an opportunity for understanding by hastily reconstituting a groupuscule [the UJC-ML] that would once again isolate us from the main movement, that would render us incapable of responding to questions, that would render us impervious to reality. . . . Many comrades have cursed the organization [the UJC-ML] that forbade them to participate in the mass movement of May '68 or to help it to develop. . . . The general will of our comrades has been not to reconstitute groupuscules but to avoid the "groupusculization" of the movement in order to preserve the May movement's unity. . . . Prior to May, to be a Marxist-Leninist was on the whole very simple: every time a problem presented itself, one could resolve it by citing Chairman Mao and then going peacefully off to bed. After May things became a lot more complicated: to cite Mao no longer made an impression on anyone.[42]

The UJC-ML split into two factions. One group, the "liquidationists," concluded that the May revolt had foundered for lack of a vanguard party to lead the way. As the authors of *Vers la guerre civile* observed, "In May—and still today—the mass movement's absence of a center deprived this movement of an instrument of struggle and knowledge. This absence . . . is also indicative of the movement's current weakness."[43] But before rushing out to found yet another political party, the group needed to steep itself in Marxist theory. Thereby, it could be certain that the party would have the proper theoretical foundation. The so-called liquidationists repaired to the ENS library to study and read. During the post-May period, the popularity of Lenin's 1902 Bolshevik manifesto *What Is to Be Done?* reputedly soared. In this way, this faction, led by ex-teachers' union president Alain Geismar, returned to its Marxist-Leninist roots.

[42] *Vive La Révolution!* 1 (July–August 1969): 74. The FER, or Fédération des étudiants révolutionnaires, was an offshoot of the Lambertist Trotskyist CLER group (Comité de liaison des étudiants révolutionnaires), which was established on April 28, 1968.

[43] Geismar, July, and Morane, *Vers la guerre civile*, 15.

In addition to the UJC-ML, Marcellin barred several other left-wing groups, including the rival Maoist PCFML (an offshoot of the PCF that was officially allied with Beijing) and the Trotskyist Ligue communiste révolutionnaire (LCR). In June 1968 his ministry sent in riot police to summarily quash the residual factory occupations. Following the elections that month, the Gaullists triumphantly returned to power. The elections, and the wave of repression that had preceded them, convinced the Maoists that "French fascism" was setting in. They believed that France was on the verge of becoming another Portugal, with General de Gaulle playing the role of Salazar, who ruled Portugal with an iron fist from 1932 to 1968. Between 1969 and 1970 a total of forty-three films were banned by the French minister of culture on the grounds of "mental toxicity." By 1970 French authorities had placed more than one hundred activists behind bars.

The second UJC-ML faction, numbering forty or fifty militants, formed the Gauche prolétarienne. With Pierre Victor at the helm, it reaffirmed the group's earlier political line. Now more than ever, militants needed to merge with the urban and rural masses, who embodied humanity's glorious revolutionary future. In Victor's eyes the May events proved what he and like-minded militants had wanted to believe all along: advanced industrial society was eminently susceptible to massive revolutionary upheaval. The June Days that followed the May uprising were punctuated by wildcat strikes at factory plants throughout the Paris region. The working class had not been wholly seduced by the blandishments of the "affluent society." Undoubtedly, before long, another revolutionary upsurge would be in the offing. It was a revolutionary militant's solemn task to prepare for this eventuality. Victor compared the Maoists' temporary retreat following the setbacks of June 1968 to the Chinese Communists' 1934 Long March, when Mao's army trekked some four thousand miles to escape annihilation by Kuomintang forces at Jiangxi. Out of an original one hundred thousand troops, a mere seven thousand survived.

And thus, out of the UJC-ML's ashes rose the Gauche prolétarienne (GP), which was established by Victor and several others in September 1968. One lesson the GP militants had learned from the May-June factory occupations pertained to the issue of working-class stratification—not only the division between unskilled and skilled workers (known as "OS," or *ouvriers specialisés*) but also the important differences between indigenous workers and the estimated 3.5 million immigrant laborers currently residing in France. In the post-May period, the GP would increasingly turn its attention to the plight of the latter group, whose material circumstances were for the most part lamentable.

In the spirit of the *enquête,* GP activists investigated the ethnic composition of the immigrant workers at the mammoth Renault manufacturing plant at Billancourt, on the outskirts of Paris. Among a total of 8,500 immigrant laborers, 4,500 were Moroccans, 2,000 Portuguese, and 800 sub-Saharan Africans (with significant ethnic and tribal differences), in addition to Yugoslavs, Spaniards, and Tunisians. Wide-ranging ethnic and cultural disparities made it extremely difficult to mobilize assembly-line workers as a group, both in the automobile industry and elsewhere.

Two examples will suffice to illustrate the type of "actions" the Maoists favored in the post-May period to catalyze working-class solidarity among these otherwise disparate groupings. In the spring of 1970 GP activists seized on a fare increase in the public transport system to mobilize the largely immigrant workforce at the Renault plant at Billancourt. At the workday's end hundreds of workers, spurred by the Maoists, occupied the Billancourt metro station, demonstrating against the fare hike and protecting their fellow workers as they jumped the turnstiles in protest. When the police finally materialized, Maoist activists mobilized additional workers. These incidents received widespread press coverage and helped to preserve the spark of proletarian militancy kindled during the May-June uprising.

A similar enquête in the provincial town of Meulan uncovered a sizable black market in work permits for foreign workers. The Maoists occupied city hall to protest the scandal and, more generally, to call attention to the sorrowful plight of France's immigrant workforce. The events in Meulan were soon reported by the mainstream press and proved to be a major source of embarrassment for the Pompidou government. Prime Minister Jean Chaban-Delmas took to the national airwaves, vowing that in two years the nation would be cleared of slums—a pledge that was never honored. Nevertheless, the Meulan action succeeded in bringing to a halt the illegal trafficking in work permits and helped focus national attention on the woeful lot of the immigrant community.

Another favored Maoist tactic during this period was the sequestration of factory bosses. During these actions, plant managers were locked in their offices for several hours. Sequestrations were viewed as antidotes to worker passivity. In the language of Sartre's social theory, such acts were meant to counter proletarian entropy, or "serialization." One GP activist, evidently well versed in the lexicon of "existential Marxism," offered the following rich phenomenological description of shop-floor alienation:

> Everything is arranged so that the workers are stripped of their intelligence. Both the machine and the boss are there to say to the worker: shut up, don't think, it's superfluous and pointless. In thrall to the assembly line and the machine, the worker is intentionally isolated. As an isolated consciousness, he becomes a machine like the others. In this way, he loses all self-awareness. The factory rebellions develop as a way of counteracting this state of alienation. To become self-aware is a way of breaking with this isolation; it's a way of inventing a mode of collective self-expression against the assembly line, against the machine, against the boss.[44]

Factory sequestrations were intended to encourage proletarian self-reliance by demonstrating that the managers were superfluous and that workers could run the factories themselves. These tactics sought to rekindle the spirit of worker self-management, or *autogestion*, one of the May revolt's pivotal political legacies. As wildcat actions, they were intended to be a direct challenge to the authoritarian structure of the French trade unions—above all, the Communist-dominated Confédération générale du travail (CGT).

---

[44] See the special issue of *Les Temps Modernes*, "Nouveau fascisme, nouvelle démocratie," 42.

In the spring of 1970, French authorities arrested *La Cause du Peuple* editors Jean-Pierre Le Dantec and Michel Le Bris and impounded the newspaper. The last time a newspaper editor had been arrested in France was 1881. A few weeks later, GP spokesperson Alain Geismar was also incarcerated without cause. The government believed that by decapitating the GP leadership, the organization would collapse. But they had severely miscalculated. Thanks to the rash arrests licensed by Marcellin and company, the GP's status would change from that of a handful of unknown militants to a cause célèbre whose plight was passionately embraced by *le tout Paris*.

Simone de Beauvoir and the writer Michel Leiris immediately organized an advocacy group to support the interned Maoists, Les amis de *La Cause du Peuple*. In her memoir of the period, *All Said and Done*, de Beauvoir echoed the attitude of many French intellectuals vis-à-vis the Maoists when she observed:

> Despite several reservations—especially, my lack of blind faith in Mao's China—I sympathize with the Maoists. They present themselves as revolutionary socialists, in opposition to the Soviet Union's revisionism and the new bureaucracy created by the Trotskyists; I share their rejection of these approaches. I am not so naive as to believe that they will bring about the revolution in the near future, and I find the "triumphalism" displayed by some of them puerile. But whereas the entirety of the traditional Left accepts the system, defining themselves as a force for renewal or the respectful opposition, the Maoists embody a genuinely radical form of contestation. In a country that has become sclerotic, lethargic, and resigned, they stir things up and arouse public opinion. They try to focus "fresh forces" in the proletariat—youth, women, foreigners, workers in the small provincial factories who are much less under the influence and control of the unions than those in the great industrial centers. They encourage action of a new kind—wildcat strikes and sequestrations—and sometimes they foment it from within. . . . I shall never regret whatever I may have done to help them. I should rather try to help the young

in their struggle than to be the passive witness of a despair that has led some of them to the most hideous suicide.[45]

FROM HISTORICAL TO HYSTERICAL MATERIALISM

In the post-May period the Maoists reveled in the seducements of libidinal politics that had suffused the student-worker uprising. In the fall of 1970 Maoists affiliated with the Vive la révolution! (VLR) group parted ways with the GP to found *Tout!* ("Ce que nous voulons: Tout!" What We Want: Everything!), a biweekly that celebrated the May movement's libertarian spirit. The brain trust behind *Tout!* realized that the May events had gone far in redefining the meaning of "revolution" along "cultural political" lines. The *Tout!* Maoists had imbibed the critique of the vanguard revolutionary model proffered by the Nanterre enragés and Paris Situationists. May's predominant political orientation had been avowedly antiauthoritarian. Why, the breakaway Maoists reasoned, should the critique of authoritarian politics stop at the doorstep of the political Left?

Under the direction of ex–Gauche prolétarienne leader Tiennot Grumbach, the activities of *Tout!* embraced the full range of "alternative" political themes that had crystallized during the post-May period. The "occupation movement" that coincided with the May revolt—factories, offices, schools, and universities—had culminated in the idea of revolution-as-festival. It was this resolutely libertarian political heritage that *Tout!* sought to develop and preserve.

In a spirit of post-May cultural-revolutionary pluralism, the *Tout!* editorial staff opened its pages to new forms and varieties of political contestation. Why, the editors of *Tout!* reasoned, should the "liberation of desire" remain limited and defined by the terms of heterosexual desire? What about the broad range of proscribed and marginalized sexualities? Was *homosexual* desire somehow less valid than *heterosexual* desire? Why challenge the economic and political aspects of bourgeois

[45] De Beauvoir, *Tout compte fait*, 419.

society while leaving its culture, mores, and predominant social psychological modalities unchallenged? The *Tout!* editorial board expressed
these concerns in the following programmatic statement of principle:

> Capitalist society has not only colonized and employed to its ad-
> vantage the productive powers of our bodies and our brains. It has
> also made off with our desires and our ability to love. It has de-
> ported them to a forced labor camp called the family. . . . When
> I have officially accepted to only love a person of the opposite
> sex, and one person alone, with the avowed goal of reproducing
> the species . . . when by virtue of my parental authority I repro-
> duce all the laws of the species in my own children, stressing fear,
> possessiveness, obedience, competitiveness, and hierarchy, when I
> timidly surrender my sons and daughters to the school system, to
> television, and thus to the ideology of the dominant classes, what
> then remains of my project as a revolutionary? And who benefits?
> The mechanism that perpetuates the bourgeoisie or the classless
> society? . . . We are told that by fighting the repression of the
> body, sexuality, and the mind, capitalist relations of production
> are allowed to persist; that such battles benefit only a privileged
> minority and lead only to individual triumphs. . . . But no revo-
> lution is accomplished unless it is at the same time a revolution
> of desire, of sexuality, of our bodies, and if the struggle against
> economic exploitation consumes all of our energies.[46]

In a series of pathbreaking issues devoted to the question of alternative modes of self-individuation, the *Tout* staff eagerly sought to explore
the nature of these alternative practices and themes. The review proved
especially receptive to both feminism—as represented by the MLF, or
Mouvement libération des femmes—and gay rights, as promoted by
FHAR, or Front homosexuel d'action révolutionnaire.

For French feminists, 1970 was the year zero. On August 26, the fiftieth
anniversary of American women's suffrage, a group of twelve feminists,

---

[46] *Tout!* 12 (1970): xx.

having first alerted the press, gathered at the Arc de Triomphe for a demonstration at the Tomb of the Unknown Soldier. Emerging from the local metro station as the television cameras rolled, they unfurled their banners: "One out of every two persons [*hommes*] is a woman." "There's someone more unknown than the soldier: his wife." The twelve were promptly arrested and carted off in police vans. The activists were affiliated with and drew their inspiration from the Maoist Vive la révolution! group, a fusion of ex-UJC-ML activists and Nanterre militants. In this way the Mouvement libération des femmes was born. This seemingly minor incident had a sensational nationwide impact. Although France was certainly used to demonstrations and protests, it was unaccustomed to protests by feminists who explicitly called attention to women's issues.

That fall the glossy weekly *Elle* tried to organize a "women's estates general" in order to promote a "civilized," that is, nonfeminist, discussion of women's issues. To remain on the safe side, the list of panelists was heavily weighted toward male speakers. The organizers of the meeting had distributed an anodyne questionnaire to gain information about women's tastes and consumption habits. Soon, a group of radical feminists called Les petites marguerites arrived to disrupt the event. The marguerites distributed their own "alternative" inquiry, featuring questions such as "Do you wear makeup (a) out of self-loathing? (b) to look less like yourself and more like what you are expected to look like?"[47] Another question was: "Who is best suited to decide the number of children you have?—(a) The pope, who doesn't have any; (b) the president, who's having a hard enough time with his own; (c) the doctor, who values the life of your fetus more than your own life; (d) your husband, who plays with them for a few minutes each day when he returns from work; (e) you, who carry, bear, and raise them."[48]

But the event that went farthest toward raising awareness about feminist issues was the manifesto of the 343 women who had undergone illegal abortions. Entitled "Our Wombs Belong to Us!" the manifesto appeared in the April 5, 1971, issue of *Le Nouvel Observateur*. Among

[47] Cited in Duchen's *Feminism in France*, 10.
[48] Cited in Picq's *Libération des femmes*, 22.

the signatories were Simone de Beauvoir, Catherine Deneuve, Marguerite Duras, Violette Leduc, and Jeanne Moreau.

De Beauvoir's *The Second Sex* was a milestone in the development of modern feminist consciousness. She made short shrift of biological determinism, famously declaring, in a ringing affirmation of existential subjectivity: "One is not born a woman, one becomes one." Yet, by the time the MLF burst onto the scene circa 1970, her brand of egalitarian feminism seemed tame and outdated. Although she never personally had an abortion, rumor suggested that on occasion she allowed them to be performed in her apartment.

The manifesto of the 343 began: "One million women undergo abortions each year in France. They do this under dangerous conditions, owing to the clandestine circumstances to which they are condemned, although this operation, when practiced under medical supervision, is one of the simplest. One passes over the fate of these one million women in silence."[49] At the time, abortion remained illegal in France, which, since World War I, had been obsessed by a stagnating birthrate. According to the French penal code, abortion was an offense punishable by six months to three years in prison. Contraception had been legalized in 1967, the year the so-called loi Neuwirth was passed. Until then, medical personnel who provided information about contraception were subject to prosecution.

French feminism's emergence was a heady and confusing time. In France it was the high point of gauchisme. Male leftists feared that by independently pursuing women's issues, feminists would detract from the larger stakes of the class struggle. French feminists themselves displayed multiple political loyalties. Many had begun as left-wing activists and were uncertain as to how they might reconcile their Marxist commitments with their newly acquired feminist convictions. Some solved the problem by simply declaring that men were bourgeois and women were proletarian. Since so many male militants remained uncomprehending, not to mention manifestly unsympathetic, vis-à-vis their motivations and aims, MLF activists decided early on to exclude men from

[49] *Le Nouvel Observateur*, April 5, 1971, 42.

their meetings. "Since when must the oppressed demand from their oppressors permission to revolt?" they inquired rhetorically.[50]

Whereas mainstream feminists pursued rights-oriented issues—better child care, equal pay, abortion rights—MLF activists viewed feminism as a vehicle for reexamining fundamental questions concerning women's identity—that is, as a key to qualitatively transforming womanhood and femininity in their entirety. In an unsubtle rejection of bourgeois-egalitarian feminism, their slogan became "Down with Mommy's feminism!" Traditional feminism had sought to integrate women within society. The MLF, in keeping with the spirit of the times, sought to "disaggregate" society along with its predominant practices, values, and mores.

One commentator has described the mood of the times in the following terms:

At these meetings, chaos and good humor rather than clarity and order prevailed. . . . At MLF meetings nobody knew quite what was going on. This unstructured format, a reaction against the rigid procedures of male-dominated political meetings, met with mixed response. Some women found it invigorating, others found it irritating. One woman wrote bluntly that "every time I went to a general assembly, I wondered what I was doing there." But another wrote: "it was magnificent, invigorating. You didn't know what was going on, you couldn't really see anything . . . but still there was a liveliness, a joy, that I had never seen anywhere else."[51]

The MLF creatively disrupted an otherwise staid French society. As a result, deeply ingrained patriarchal habitudes and assumptions quickly lost their self-evidence. Traditional mores were challenged by a new set of feminist terms and concepts. The Gazolines were an omnipresent clique of boisterous transvestites. Another group that attained media prominence was the Gouines rouges, or Red Dykes, who flaunted their flamboyance during the 1971 May Day parade. One of the leading

[50] Cited in Picq's *Libération des femmes*, 15.
[51] Duchen, *Feminism in France*, 9.

feminist publications was called *Le Torchon Brûle!* (The Rag Burns!). Its subtitle, *Un Journal Menstruel,* was a play on "mensuel," the French word for "monthly." Inspired by the credo of Maoist populism, *Le Torchon Brûle!* was an offshoot of the Vive la révolution! group. As one member explained: "There was no desire to produce polished journalism, but instead to avoid the division between those who can and those who cannot read and to encourage women to write whether they thought they could or not."[52] Heated ideological debates raged over whether motherhood was a negation of women's autonomy, as Simone de Beauvoir had intimated in *The Second Sex,* or a woman's ultimate fulfillment, as certain strains of "difference" feminism would soon claim.

By the same token, by pursuing an independent agenda the MLF created an irreparable breach in the heart of leftism and thereby contributed to gauchisme's demise. Taking the claim that "the personal is the political" to new extremes, the MLF often flirted with an unhealthy, sectarian narcissism. As Christine Delphy, one of the movement's leading theorists, claimed in the pages of *Le Temps des Femmes*: "We have no desire to fight for our neighbor, be it a man or a woman. Militants used to spend their time fighting on behalf of others such as workers or immigrants. We speak about *ourselves*."[53] Soon, not only would the MLF refuse to collaborate with male comrades, it would also refuse to ally itself with rival feminist groups. Such developments were merely one more indication of how difficult it would be to maintain the fragile post-May coalition of left-wing causes and political groupings.

MLF politics had become avowedly anti-intellectual. A "politics of feeling"—"thinking with one's gut"—triumphed over a "politics of the intellect," now denigrated as "masculinist" and "phallocentric." The net result was that, paradoxically, the MLF's focus took on a distinctly nonpolitical cast. The outside world ceased to count. In their discussions, militants seemed unable to transcend the parameters of their own group dynamics and personal feelings. As one observer has noted, "Politics was reduced in value, dissolving in the unlimited expression

[52] Ibid., 10.

[53] Delphy, "Je ne vois pas pourquoi un mouvement s'arrêtait de grandir," *Le Temps des Femmes* 12 (Summer 1981).

of women's individual and relational problems—or, more precisely, those of specific MLF members."[54] In this way, the MLF consummated the transition from "historical" to "hysterical" materialism.

STONEWALL IN PARIS

The gay rights or homosexual liberation movement encompassed both men and women. Gay men openly attended the first MLF meetings to share their problems and concerns. Only later would their respective paths diverge.

At the forefront of the struggle for homosexual rights was the Maoist organ *Tout!* A groundbreaking issue published in April 1971 featured a woman's backside on its cover. In keeping with the irreverent spirit of the times, it proclaimed: "There's plenty of ass for everyone." Following in the footsteps of the surrealists, as well as the American yippies, both the MLF and the Front homosexuel d'action révolutionnaire (FHAR) employed to maximum effect the strategy of deliberate provocation to call attention to their cause. The writings and actions of Guy Hocquenghem, author of the pioneering manifesto *Homosexual Desire*, are a perfect case in point. In the April 1971 issue of *Tout!* Hocquenghem's contribution, "Manifesto of 343 Fags Who Admit to Having Been Buggered by Arabs" (an unsubtle allusion to the celebrated "abortion" issue of *Le Nouvel Observateur*), reverberated throughout the hexagon.

Using the pages of *Tout!* as a sounding board, FHAR militants actively called into question inherited conceptions of bourgeois sexual normalcy: "What you identify as 'normal' is, for us, a source of oppression. All normality harasses us [*nous hérisse*]—even ideals of revolutionary normalcy."[55] FHAR activists proceeded to carry this argument a step farther, celebrating the superiority of "homosexual desire."[56]

[54] Le Goff, *Mai 68*, 310.

[55] "Les pédés de la révolution," *Tout!* 12 (April 23, 1971).

[56] See Hocquenghem's classic manifesto *Homosexual Desire*. My account of FHAR is indebted to Haas's formulations in "Death of the Angel."

Heterosexuals, they claimed, had denatured their own polymor-
phous libidinal potential by arbitrarily limiting the range of their sexual
options and practices. If as a political radical one strove to systematically challenge received notions of behavioral normalcy, then why not
call heterosexuality into question as well? After all, did not homosexual
desire creatively undermine a panoply of bourgeois "family values," the
nuclear family, patriarchy, monogamy, virility, and so forth? Sodomy
was revolutionary, FHAR activists contended, insofar as it violated a
series of bourgeois moral conventions and taboos.[57] Or, as Hocquenghem expressed this thought with characteristic bravado, "Our assholes
are revolutionary!"[58]

The homosexual liberation issue of *Tout!* was a resounding success.
Observers noted that at last French homosexuals had experienced their
own May 1968. Several spin-off publications resulted, including the journal *Le Fléau Sociale* (The Social Plague), an appropriation of an affront
commonly directed against homosexual practices. The *Tout!* articles,
along with several additions, were collected and republished in a popular anthology, *Rapport Contre la Normalité* (Report against Normalcy).[59]
The Pompidou government impounded ten thousand copies of the
twelfth issue of *Tout!*—about one-fifth of the total print run—on the
grounds of obscenity, generating further publicity. *Tout!*'s titular director, Jean-Paul Sartre, was indicted for "outrage against public morals,"
although the charges were later rescinded. Many leftist bookstores refused to stock the issue, widening the rift at the heart of the gauchiste
community over the centrality and import of "cultural politics." Both
the Trotskyists and the Communists dismissed all matters pertaining to
sexual emancipation as a retrograde, petty bourgeois distraction.

Thereafter, gays throughout France began to feel comfortable discussing questions concerning their sexuality. It was as though, following the special issue of *Tout!*, an immense weight had been lifted
from their shoulders. A new homosexual assertiveness was immediately
discernible.

[57] See "Les pédés de la révolution."
[58] Cited in Martel's *The Pink and the Black*, 17.
[59] *Rapport contre la normalité* (Paris: Editions Champs Libre, 1971).

At the next meeting of FHAR, several hundred homosexual militants were in attendance as opposed to the usual several dozen. One prominent activist described a typical FHAR meeting at the Ecole des Beaux-Arts as follows:

> In 1971, the general meetings of the FHAR at the Beaux-Arts became a place for immediate sexual gratification. Militants put revolution into practice: they invented cruising relieved of its furtiveness, and, moving through hallways, surrounded by sculptures, or on the upper floors and in the attic, they experimented with [Charles] Fourier's 36,000 forms of love. . . . The general meetings, an early incarnation of the back rooms designed for quick, anonymous sex that were to spread throughout France in the late 1970s, replaced the Tuileries. . . . In Hocquenghem's words, the FHAR became a "nebula of feelings."[60]

In January 1972 another milestone in the history of gay liberation occurred on the occasion of Hocquenghem's celebrated "coming out" essay, "La révolution des homosexuels," in the mass circulation weekly *Le Nouvel Observateur*. During the 1960s Hocquenghem had traversed the entire spectrum of radical political engagement, starting off as a Communist, then joining the Trotskyists, before ultimately casting his lot, like so many leftists, with the Maoists and Vive la révolution! One commentator has aptly described Hocquenghem's *Nouvel Observateur* article as "a homosexual version of General de Gaulle's appeal of June 18, 1940."[61] Hocquenghem painstakingly recounted his travails as a closeted youth—the unbearable confusion and manifold humiliations—until his "liberation" thanks to the sympathy and patience of a philosophy professor he encountered at Lycée Henri IV. As Hocquenghem movingly reflects, "Each one of us is mutilated in an aspect of our life that we know is essential, that which we call sexual desire or love."[62]

[60] Martel, *The Pink and the Black*, 26.
[61] Ibid., 13.
[62] Hocquenghem, *Homosexual Desire*.

In 1972 the ubiquitous Hocquenghem, who died of AIDS in 1988, published *Homosexual Desire*, the manifesto that single-handedly launched the queer studies movement.

Both the women's movement and FHAR were part of a widespread, post-May cultural current known as the liberation of desire. Taking their cues from the theories of Herbert Marcuse, Wilhelm Reich, and the antipsychiatry movement, activists initiated a sweeping critique of bourgeois normalcy. They sought to show that issues of sexuality had an important *political* dimension that transcended individual consider-ations of sexual preference. As one FHAR pamphlet contended, "We homosexuals are oppressed by the domination of imperialism. Our lib-eration, like that of all oppressed people, is part of a larger political struggle against every from of domination: ideological domination; the domination of women; sexual and racial domination."[63]

Was homosexual desire less acceptable than heterosexual desire? Was the nuclear family, which Freud had exposed as a breeding ground of neurosis and which feminists excoriated as a hotbed of patriarchy, a more desirable model than various alternative living arrangements? Was there a direct relationship between the self-renunciation that bourgeois civilization demanded and the repression of desire, with all of its nega-tive consequences for character formation and personality structure? By posing such questions, FHAR militants initiated a wide-ranging critique of "phallocracy": the tyranny of heterosexual normalcy.

In the end both the MLF and FHAR were remarkably successful in gaining widespread public recognition of their basic cultural claims. As sociologist Henri Mendras has observed, what began as "a revolt of homosexuals led to a rapid and complete reversal of the majority of French people's attitudes toward homosexuality, and, consequently, toward the differences of the Other."[64] Ironically, both the MLF and FHAR imploded once they had succeeded in obtaining broad cultural acceptance of the right to be different.

Yet, the change of focus from "revolutionary politics" to "cultural politics" carried certain risks. Although the ultimate political value of

---

[63] FHAR, Tract 1, Bibliothèque nationale de France, 4 WZ 10828 (1972).
[64] Mendras, *Français*, 122.

feminism, gay liberation, and the various alternative movements remained unquestionable, the *Tout!* editors soon realized that their organ threatened to become a journal of "lifestyle" studies. As the May movement receded from view, "movement politics" increasingly risked sliding imperceptibly into "lifestyle politics." The preoccupation with consciousness-raising and group identity was necessary and legitimate, as were the various groups' demands for social recognition. By the same token, as they began pursuing their separate and often irreconcilable conceptions of emancipation, one began to wonder: what exactly were the values they held in common? If every oppressed group must speak for itself and only for itself, because only it can analyze its own suffering and decide the proper course of action, is there anyone left to speak for the oppressed as a whole?

Among feminists a bitter rift soon developed between rights-oriented feminism, "difference" feminism (stressing women's specificity or particularity), and lesbian separatists, who believed that all contact with men should be studiously avoided. French feminism's inner divisions seemed paradigmatic of a general fragmentation besetting post-May social movements and of the attendant risks of ghettoization. Would the temptations of political inwardness—the seductions of navel-gazing and groupthink—ultimately outweigh the demands of active social contestation? At stake was a delicate balance that in many respects was never satisfactorily resolved. Conversely, more optimistic interpreters of the May movement's legacy viewed this oscillation between public and private as a fruitful tension.

"SEVEN YEARS OF HAPPINESS!"

In part, the new social movements that flourished in the post-May years were victims of their own success. In many instances the grassroots pressures they exerted on the political system were cannily effective in forcing the French government's hand. This strategic shift from an inward-looking cultural politics to an outwardly directed focus on legislation and civil liberties was part of a general trend. The change in focus was true not just for gays, but for many other groups—Jews, immigrants, and feminists—as well. Thus, "after a period of identity politics—centripetal, introverted, and introspective—the discourse evolved and militants turned to defending the rights of the minority group in a quasi-unionist, centrifugal movement."[65]

In 1975, the year after the liberal-centrist Valéry Giscard d'Estaing was elected to office, the so-called loi Veil was passed (after Minister of Health Simone Veil), legalizing abortion in most circumstances, despite vigorous opposition from the Catholic Church and the parliamentary Right. Once abortion became licit, the pressures to fully legalize contraception followed suit. It stood to reason that the more liberally contraception was employed, the fewer abortions would take place. Thus, as part of the loi Veil—and reflecting a widespread transformation of societal attitudes and mores—contraception was at last made generally available. Moreover, the costs were fully reimbursed by the national health care system. The loi Veil's passage was widely perceived as a triumph of Enlightenment values against the forces of reaction: the Enlightenment over tradition, republicanism over monarchy, freethinking over Catholicism.[66] In sum, it was a triumph for the values of *laïcité*, or secularism.

In the lead-up to the 1981 presidential election, Socialist candidate François Mitterrand distinguished himself as a forceful advocate of homosexual rights. In an April 1981 round-table discussion with feminist activists, the Socialist Party (PS) standard-bearer brusquely declared: "Homosexuality must cease to be a criminal offense. The choice of each person must be respected, that's all, but within a normal framework of relations between men and women, or between men, or between women. . . . But no discrimination because of the nature of one's morals; for me, that goes without saying."[67] Thereby, Mitterrand and his fellow Socialists demonstrated a level of tolerance far superior to that of their left-wing rivals, the Communists and the Trotskyists.

Little wonder, then, that homosexuals flocked to support the Mitterrand campaign in droves. On April 4, 1981, ten thousand gays took

---

[65] Martel, *The Pink and the Black*, 127–28.

[66] Picq, *Années-mouvement*, 171.

[67] Choisir, *Quel président pour les femmes?* (Paris: Gallimard, 1981), 98.

to the streets of the Latin Quarter to demonstrate in support of his can-
didacy. After all, the Socialist Party had openly embraced the cultural
revolutionary slogan "Change Life!" (Changez la vie!) as an integral
part of its 1971 Epinay Program, the reconstituted PS's statement of
principles. Some observers believe that, in what proved to be an extremely close election, the homosexual vote may have tipped the balance in the Socialists' favor. The gay community hailed Mitterrand's
election as an event akin to the Second Coming. The headline of the
popular gay weekly *Gai Pied* effused: "Seven Years of Happiness!"

Once in office, the Socialists, who had obtained a solid majority in the
June 1981 legislative elections, demonstrated the courage of their convictions. At the instigation of the Mitterrand cabinet, PS deputies proceeded to reverse a wide range of discriminatory laws and regulations.
Interior Minister Gaston Defferre circulated a memo ordering the police
to dispense with humiliating identity checks in the areas surrounding
gay bars and clubs. The vice-squad unit overseeing homosexual activity
was promptly disbanded. Those who had been arrested for "homosexual
crimes" were amnestied. An antigay clause renters utilized, specifying
that tenants must be "good family men," was struck down.

But the major challenge lay in reversing a Vichy ordinance criminal-
izing homosexual activity prior to the age of twenty-one (during the
1960s the age had been reduced to eighteen), even though the age of
consent for heterosexuals was fifteen. After a series of prolonged and
heated debates, the law was finally overturned in July 1982, thanks to
the perseverance of Minister of Justice Robert Badinter and the legal
acumen of the feminist attorney Gisèle Halimi, who served as the administration's chief counsel.

The irony was that both the feminist and the homosexual liberation movements proved so successful politically that they ultimately
rendered themselves superfluous as movements. Thus, as both groups
increasingly gained broad social acceptance, and as their basic legal and
constitutional agendas were met, they were deprived of their original
raison d'être. So great was the flush of enthusiasm in the aftermath
of the Left's stunning 1981 electoral victory that many activists abandoned society for politics, assuming advisory posts in the new Socialist
government. Therefore the 1980s paradoxically represented the ebb

tide of social movements in France.[68] With the Socialists in power, a
range of conventional and familiar political options—standing for office, promulgating legislation, constitutional reform—that had been
foreclosed under the Gaullists seemed to open up again. Consequently,
with the Socialist victory, the ethos of left-wing militancy that had
flourished in the post-May period under libertarian-Maoist auspices
paradoxically receded.

[68] See the excellent account in Waters's *Social Movements in France*.

On the Sectarian Maoism
of Alain Badiou

As we have seen, when viewed in terms of the longue durée, French Maoism, which spanned the years 1966–74, was a relatively short-lived episode. In most cases revelations of the Cultural Revolution's manifold persecutions and atrocities definitively cured the Maoists, as well as their "democratic" sympathizers, of their pro-Chinese leanings. One of the initial reasons they had turned to China was that the Soviet experiment in "really existing socialism" had been totally discredited. Maoism seemed the last best hope for a utopian alternative to the dislocations and disappointments of "really existing democracy." But already during the early 1970s, the allure of Cultural Revolutionary China had begun to fade. Indeed, the warning signs of political failure seemed omnipresent. Why had Lin Piao, the leader of the People's Liberation Army—one of the Cultural Revolution's mainstays—died in a mysterious plane crash over Mongolia in 1971? Were rumors concerning an aborted coup attempt accurate? What about the damning revelations contained in Simon Leys' (the alias under which the Belgian Sinologist Pierre Ryckmans wrote) exposé of the Cultural Revolution's gruesome excesses, *Chairman Mao's New Clothes,* as well as the equally scandalous material contained in Jean Esmein's memoir *The Chinese Cultural Revolution?*[1] Given the relative strength of the staunchly pro-Soviet French Communist Party and its allied trade union, the CGT (Confédération générale du travail), how realistic was it to think that the French working class would transfer its political allegiances to an

---

[1] Leys, *Habits neufs de président Mao*; Esmein, *Révolution culturelle chinoise*; Esmein in English: *The Chinese Cultural Revolution,* trans. W.J.F. Jenner (New York: Anchor Books, 1973).

Eastern land known for promoting "peasant communism"? The phan-
tasmagorical nature of the French pro-Chinese mentality had become
increasingly obvious. In the aftermath of the Cultural Revolution's
unraveling, many ex-Maoists, spurred by Alexander Solzhenitsyn's
epic exposé of the Soviet prison camp system in *The Gulag Archipelago*,
would become vociferous human rights advocates as a mode of penance
and contrition for their former revolutionary credulity.[2]

One of the few former Maoists to remain not only unrepentant but
to celebrate the Cultural Revolution as one of the twentieth century's outstanding political breakthroughs is Alain Badiou. Like many
of the UJC-ML Maoists and Gauche prolétarienne activists, Badiou
was a normalien and an Althusser student. Yet, for various reasons,
during his student days he kept his distance from both groups. Instead, following May 1968, Badiou joined the Unified Socialist Party
(PSU), which, since its inception in 1960, had sought to outflank the
mainstream Socialists—the SFIO (Section française de l'internationale
ouvrière)—to the left. Diehard anticolonialists, the PSU leadership had
never forgiven the SFIO, under Guy Mollet's leadership, for (1) its vigorous opposition to Algerian independence and (2) its acquiescence
vis-à-vis de Gaulle's 1958 "coup d'état." In 1965 François Mitterrand
had been the joint PSU-PCF presidential candidate, losing to de Gaulle
by 10 percent. From 1967 to 1973 the party was led by future Socialist
Party stalwart Lionel Jospin.

In 1969 Badiou, along with two former GP members, founded a rival
Maoist organization, the Union des communistes français marxistes-
léninistes (UCF-ML). According to Badiou's later avowals, one reason
he decided to establish a competing Maoist group was that he was put
off by the GP's turn to a "politics of everyday life." In Badiou's eyes,
"libidinal politics" was an inferior, middle-class substitute for "real"
politics, whose authentic modalities could be traced to the unshakable
political will of the Jacobins and the Bolsheviks. He also took exception
to the GP's histrionic, revolutionary posturing, which, in his opinion,
led to an unrealistic view of the contemporary political situation. As

---

[2] For an excellent account of the "Solzhenitsyn effect" on French intellectuals, see
Grémion, *Paris-Prague*.

Badiou observes sardonically in a later interview, "Almost everything put out by GP propaganda was half untrue—where there was a kitten, they described a Bengal tiger."[3]

Whereas Badiou considered the Gauche prolétarienne "left deviationists" due to their surfeit of revolutionary voluntarism, he viewed the more orthodox PCFML (Parti communiste français marxiste-léniniste)—a group composed of ex-PCF members who had broken with the party during the early 1960s and had received Beijing's official blessing—as "right deviationists." The PCFML Maoists had objected strenuously to the Soviet Union's "revisionism" under Khrushchev. They lamented the fact that unlike Mao's China, the Soviet Union had remained *insufficiently Stalinist*. (Suffice it to say that in the aftermath of the libidinal upsurge of May 1968, this position's currency diminished significantly.) Thus, Badiou and his fellow UCF militants sought to create a via media between these two rival "Left" and "Right" Maoist factions or groupings.

For Badiou, one of the primary reasons the May movement remained unconsummated was the want of authentic revolutionary leadership. The UCF's rigid, neo-Leninist ideological standpoint can be gleaned from the following programmatic statement taken from its main theoretical organ, *Le Marxiste-Léniniste*: "What must be done, what presents itself as a task for revolutionaries, is to form a party: to form a party for the sake of making the revolution, in order that it is not only the weather that is stormy, but us. The party means that it is we who become genuinely revolutionary and not the weather."[4]

To justify their standpoint, Badiou and his UCF allies were fond of citing the Great Helmsman's maxim "One divides into two," which had been one of the slogans Mao employed to launch the Cultural Revolution. Beginning in 1965, "One divides into two" had served as a rallying cry for true Communist believers to take cognizance of conservative and bourgeois tendencies—"right" deviationists—within the party and to root them out, often by whatever means necessary. Putative reactionaries such as Liu Shaoqi and Deng Hsiao-ping, conversely,

[3] Badiou, "Roads to Renegacy," 125–33.
[4] Cited in Bourseiller's *Maoïstes*, 173.

adhered to the slogan "Two fuse into one" to preserve a semblance of
unity that masked these fundamental ideological differences. Hence,
an epistemological debate that, superficially viewed, pertained to the
true nature of Marxist dialectics—whether antagonism or synthesis
was primary—would have portentous consequences for China's political future.[5] Soon, "One divides into two" became the catch-all rubric
through which Mao would define and crush his political enemies. For
Badiou, who today still proudly views himself as a Maoist, Mao's singular ability to fuse epistemological and political thematics would assume foundational significance.

The UCF-ML was one of several Maoist splinter groups that emerged
after the UJC-ML was banned by government edict following May
1968. By all accounts, its membership never rose above eighty. Rival
Maoist groups viewed it disparagingly as elitist and sectarian insofar as
it allegedly maintained a fairly strict, neo-Leninist separation between
leaders—who, like Badiou, were predominantly intellectuals and college graduates—and the rank and file, who hailed from the working
classes. At the time of the UCF's founding, Badiou, along with a plethora of fellow Maoists, had recently been selected by Michel Foucault
(who chaired the search committee) to staff the philosophy department
at the new "experimental" University of Vincennes, located on the outskirts of Paris. A former UCF central committee member, philosophy
professor Bernard Sichère, recollects: "At the UCF one was well cared
for as an intellectual. . . . [To be part of] the UCF was rather chic."[6]

The UCF leadership was partial to the Latin Quarter. One meeting
on behalf of immigrant workers was staged in a private room at the
luxurious Hotel Lutétia, situated at the fashionable Parisian intersection
of Sèvres-Babylone—a choice of venue that stood in marked contrast
to the group's otherwise militant proletarian theoretical line. Ideologically, the UCF sought to split the difference between an openly "spon-
taneist" approach, which favored gratuitous provocations and "direct
action," and dogmatic *obéisances* to the virtues of *ouvrièrisme* (workerism).

[5] See Badiou's commentary on this debate in *Century*, 58–67.
[6] Cited in Bourseiller's *Maoïstes*, 162. Among the other Maoists who joined Badiou
at Vincennes were Judith Miller, Etienne Balibar, and Jacques Rancière.

Translated into practice, this meant that the UCF frequently worked with immigrants in the shantytowns that dotted the outskirts of Paris, "established" themselves on the factory shop floors (as the UJC rank and file had done earlier under Robert Linhart's leadership), and organized grassroots revolutionary councils (*comités de base*) to prepare for the next revolutionary wave. In 1927 the Great Helmsman had published his *Report on an Investigation of the Peasant Movement in Hunan*, which in many respects set the tone for Chinese "peasant communism." In solidarity with this Maoist ideal, the UCF engaged in detailed investigations of the living conditions of French farmers. As one investigation proclaimed: "It is of prime importance to lead militant investigations on the great revolts of poor peasants, especially in West and Central France."[7] One of their other pet endeavors was the so-called department store project. The idea was to disrupt the normal rhythms of the consumer society by allowing shoppers to exit Paris's "grands magasins," or department stores, without paying. It seems, however, that in most cases these practices devolved into simple looting.[8]

In his student years, Badiou, who was born in 1937, was a self-professed Sartrean; he was convinced that Sartre's notion of phenomenological subjectivity represented a salutary corrective to the objectivism-cum-dogmatism of the reigning varieties of orthodox Marxism—Stalinism, in particular. By the same token, as a normalien, Badiou willy-nilly succumbed to Althusser's influence. He was impressed by the rigor of Althusser's "theoreticism": the idea that Marxism, qua doctrine, embodied a series of stringent and irrefragable epistemological-political truths. Thus, "theory" possessed an indubitable logical cogency to which reality might aspire but which it would never in fact attain—a truism that reflected the basic ontological distinction between "being" and "beings"; that is, the categorical priority of ontology over mere entities. For Badiou fidelity to Marxian doctrinal purity was one way of avoiding

---

[7] Groupe pour la fondation de l'union des communistes français (marxiste-léniniste), *La révolution prolétarienne en France et comment construire le parti de l'époque de la pensée de Mao Tse-toung* (Paris: Maspero, 1970), 46; cited in Bosteels's "Post-Maoism," 580.

[8] Bourseiller, *Maoïstes*, 149.

the temptations and risks of bourgeois "deviationism"—temptations and risks to which so many ex-sixty-eighters would succumb once the revolutionary tide had ebbed.

These two different philosophical standpoints—the perspectives of Sartre and Althusser—proved to be a difficult and at times contradictory set of intellectual allegiances to juggle. However, both of these influences are fundamental to appreciating Badiou's political self-understanding as an unrepentant Maoist. As a result of Sartre's tutelage, Badiou came to venerate the concept of political subjectivity or will. Earlier versions of Marxism had remained too beholden to "historicism," holding that one must patiently allow the dialectic of history to follow its preordained course. In Badiou's view, Lenin's reassertion of the "primacy of politics" had effectively broken with the delusions of political *attentisme* (a "wait-and-see" attitude). Still, there existed the ever-present risk that the revolutionary party would congeal into something objectlike and rigid—in Sartre's idiom, the "practico-inert"—as occurred under Stalinism.

That is why the Cultural Revolution, in tandem with May 1968, represented an authentic political breakthrough, or *novum*. Taken together, these events precipitated Badiou's break with Althusser, who had openly extolled the virtues of "history without a subject" and "science without a subject." Structuralist Marxism had openly impugned the role of political subjectivity as well as historical "events." The political radicalism of the 1960s made structuralism seem politically anachronistic. By fetishizing structure as an unyielding, ontological constant and by dismissing subjectivity as, in essence, one of structure's ideological effects, Althusser and his supporters had rashly discounted the masses' capacity for resistance.

During the Cultural Revolution, under Mao's leadership the party actively sought to replenish its original revolutionary élan by purging itself of entropic, counterrevolutionary elements. (In Mao's political lexicon, retrograde elements within the party represented a "nonantagonistic contradiction," whereas the opposition between the proletariat and the bourgeoisie signified an "antagonistic contradiction.") As a politics and as a doctrine, Maoism's greatness lay in its unshakable belief in the force of political will. In Badiou's eyes, Marxism has both truth and the "Real" on its side. A Lacanian coinage, the "Real" represents a bedrock of ontological certainty that we strive to reach but can never attain due to the mediating forces of "socialization": the symbolic realm, or language. To its credit, Marxism, unlike competing political paradigms with their timorous half measures, displays an unquenchable passion for authenticity: a "passion for the Real."[9] For the sake of truth, this passion must be honored.

Whatever their empirical failings, in Badiou's estimation both the Cultural Revolution and May 1968 stand as living testimonies that revolutionary subjectivity possesses a singular capacity to destroy the obstacles standing in its way. Badiou expresses this idea in his trademark, unbeautiful philosophical prose: "Subjectivation submits to the discourse of belief in order *to shatter the obstacle*. . . . Having confidence in oneself in the mode of the destructive scission of local constraints *generalizes the process of the subject*."[10]

Badiou hones his thesis concerning the nature of revolutionary subjectivity in his 1982 treatise *The Theory of the Subject*. In his later philosophy, one of the central leitmotifs pertains to the dialectic, or

---

[9] See the chapter of *The Century* entitled "The Passion for the Real and the Montage of Semblance," 48–57. Badiou claims at a later point that in its fidelity to history as an objective constant, Marxism was ultimately led astray; thereby, it undervalued subjectivization. Badiou's "post-Marxism" acknowledges that the Marxist claim concerning "class society" is obsolete, as is the notion of the "Party-State" as an emancipatory force. Or, as he asserts in *Metapolitics*, "Marxism doesn't exist. . . . Marxism [is] the (void) name of an absolutely inconsistent set, once it is referred back, as it must be, to the history of political singularities" (58).

The literature on Badiou and politics is metastasizing. See the special issue of *Positions* 13 (3) (2005), which contains translations of many chapters relevant to Maoism from Badiou's *Théorie du sujet*, an important political stocktaking. An English translation of the entire book, *Theory of the Subject*, trans. Bruno Bosteels (New York: Continuum, 2009), has recently appeared. See also "Politics and Philosophy: An Interview with Alain Badiou," in *Ethics*, 95–144. See, in addition, "Politics and Ontology," in *Infinite Thought*. Among the most helpful commentaries are Philippe Raynaud's "Métapolitique de la révolution," in *L'extrême gauche plurielle*, 149–70; and Bosteels, "Post-Maoism."

[10] Badiou, *Théorie du sujet*; English translation: "Further Selections from *Théorie du sujet* on the Cultural Revolution," in *Positions* 13 (3) (2005): 651; emphasis added.

opposition, between "force" and "place." "Force" is vital, dynamic, and allied with "subjectivization."[11] "Place" is sedentary, static, and, at times, well-nigh immovable. It must be *pulverized* by "force."

Badiou's thought is partial to violent philosophical imagery, a tendency that goes hand in hand with his defense of bloodletting, or terror, in the name of "progressive" political causes; the Jacobin dictatorship, the Russian Revolution, Stalin's purges, and the Cultural Revolution are the examples he frequently invokes. At one point, he characterizes his political approach as "terroristic nihilism"—that is, a type of combative, Nietzschean-inspired anarchism.[12] Thus, it is hardly surprising that Badiou is fond of citing Mao's remark "The Revolution is not a dinner party."[13] Badiou's philosophy, as well as his reflections on politics, is suffused with metaphors of destruction. He believes that destruction is philosophically justified and ontologically necessary if one desires to surmount the obstacles of "place"—what Badiou derides as "capitalo-parliamentarian" place in particular. Badiou cheerfully endorses Nietzsche's notion of active nihilism as an effective means of eliminating "semblance" (artifice and inauthenticity) and approximating the Real. Nietzsche quite justly "philosophized with a hammer," believing that if something dilapidated is falling, one should give it a final push. If the powers of nihilism can be diverted to the ends of destroying bourgeois society and its attendant ills, all the better. "*The passion* [for the Real] *can only be fulfilled through destruction*," observes Badiou.[14]

Even well-disposed critics have found a number of Badiou's political judgments—his embrace of Khmer Rouge policies, for example

[11] "Subjectivization" is Badiou's way of avoiding the idea of the "subject." Following Althusser, Badiou believes that the "subject" is an ideological product or effect of the bourgeois "state apparatus." See the discussion in Badiou, *Metapolitics*, where Badiou observes that Althusser's greatness as a thinker lay in his attempt to conceptualize "subjectivity without a subject" (66).

[12] See Badiou, *Century*, 64.

[13] Ibid., 62.

[14] See the discussion ibid., 56: "There exists a passion for the Real that is obsessed with identity: to grasp real identity, to unmask its copies, to discredit fakes. It is a passion for the authentic, and authenticity is in fact a category that belongs to Heidegger as well as to Sartre. *This passion can only be fulfilled as destruction*" (emphasis added).

—"bone-chilling."[15] Badiou, however, remains unrepentant and unbowed. He clearly revels in differentiating his unwavering fidelity to
the great political causes of his youth—the Cultural Revolution and
May 1968—from the "renegade" mentality of his fellow Maoists,
who, as "New Philosophers," hastened to embrace a slack, feel-good
droit-de-l'hommisme.[16]

Badiou holds that whereas the nineteenth century was an epoch of
defeats (the Restoration, the revolutions of 1848, and the Paris Commune), the twentieth century, as measured by the Bolshevik, Chinese,
and Cuban revolutions, emerges as an epoch of victories—at least until
the advent of neoliberalism's disconcerting triumph, following communism's inglorious demise. In his view the twentieth-century cultural and political avant-gardes—both Duchamp *and* Lenin—effected
a remarkable historical achievement: they engendered a civic efflores-
cence that bears comparison with Periclean Athens and Renaissance
Florence. From a political standpoint, there is no need to renounce or
to shy away from the sanguinary excesses of revolution, for violence is
the way of the world and the necessary price of freeing humanity from
the evils of democracy and capitalism. In Badiou's view, these two
social forms are inseparable. They mutually reinforce one another and
are therefore equally objectionable. In a 2002 interview he describes
democracy as the "authorized representative of capital."[17] As Badiou
observes with reference to the Cultural Revolution:

[15] See Jean Birnbaum, "L'épurateur du vingtième siècle," in *Le Monde,* February
18, 2005. In "Métapolitique de la révolution," Philippe Raynaud observes that Badiou
"places his considerable talent in the service of a politics that one would rightfully
judge to be atrocious" (152). Raynaud discusses Badiou's "audacious defense of the
Khmer Rouge" on page 150.

[16] See Badiou, "Roads to Renegacy."

[17] See "Politics and Philosophy: An Interview with Alain Badiou," in Badiou's
Ethics, 99. See also Badiou, "Prefazione all'edizione italiana," *Metapolitica*, trans. Ma-
rina Bruzzese (Naples: Cronopio, 2002), 9–15: "The enemy today is not called Empire
or Capital. It is called Democracy. With this term we mean not only the empty form
of the 'representative system,' but even more the modern figure of equality; reduced
to equality before the offer of the market, rendering every individual equal to any
other on the sole basis of virtually being, like anyone else, a consumer."

What about the violence, often so extreme? The hundreds of thousands of dead? The persecutions, especially against intellectuals? One will say the same thing about them as about all those acts of violence that, to this very day, have marked the History of every somewhat expansive attempt to practice a free politics, to radically subvert the eternal order that subjects society to wealth and the wealthy, to power and the powerful, to science and scientists, to Capital and its servants, and considers worthless . . . the intelligence of workers . . . and any thought that is not homogeneous to the order in which the ignoble rule of profit is perpetuated. The theme of total emancipation, practiced in the present, in the enthusiasm of absolute present, is always situated *beyond Good and Evil. . . . The passion for the Real is devoid of morality. . . . Morality is a residue of the Old World.*[18]

Unlike the numerous sixty-eighters who either joined the revamped Socialist Party or became human rights activists, by virtue of his fidelity to the tenets of Maoism, Badiou seems to have ended up politically in a relatively lonely place. When the Union des communistes français imploded in 1984, Badiou cofounded another marginal left-wing groupuscule, L'organisation politique. His scorn for all variants of contemporary political philosophy—democratic theory, liberalism, republicanism—which, in his view, merely reinforce the logic of capital, seems to have left him with few political allies, apart from the small circle of Maoists left over from his youth.[19] Following Althusser, Badiou holds that what passes for philosophy is, in truth, an ideological "effect," a product or construct of "bourgeois state apparatuses." To try to subordinate politics to philosophy is therefore illicit. In place of political philosophy, Badiou seeks to promote "metapolitics": critical reflections on the political present formulated from the standpoint of a *révolution manqué*, or "missing revolution." However, by rejecting a priori "bourgeois logics of emancipation," Badiou risks trivializing

[18] Badiou, *Century*, 62–63; emphasis added.
[19] See the polemical remarks contained in chapter 1 of Badiou's *Metapolitics*, "Against 'Political Philosophy,'" 10–25.

very real gains in the realms of civic freedom, group autonomy, cultural recognition, and immigrant rights—the significant panoply of social and cultural achievements that represent the political legacy of the post-May era.

One might describe Badiou's political course as an evolution from Maoism to post-Maoism—a trajectory that corresponds to the political realities of postcommunism and post-Marxism.[20] It is perhaps in this sense that Badiou, at long last disillusioned with the criminal excesses of revolutionary vanguardism, describes his later approach as "politics without party." But what sense it might make to adhere to a Jacobin or Leninist conception of politics divested of its trademark "political centralism" is not very clear. Belatedly, Badiou has acknowledged that the conceptual armature of Marxist orthodoxy—the ideas of class and class struggle, for example—is no longer viable. Leninism wagered on the capacity of the party-state to revitalize the masses and spur them to action. But this wager miscarried, as we realize from the frozen political legacy of Stalinism. Although Badiou continues to defend the Cultural Revolution's halcyon days—the purportedly "heroic," Red Guard phase of 1966–68—we now know that, ultimately, the situation became so chaotic the People's Liberation Army had to be brought in to restore order. Thereafter, the Communist Party felt compelled to reassert its leading status, bringing the Cultural Revolution's initial "creative period" to a disappointing close and, as Badiou sees it, paving the way for the "reactionary" triumph of Hua Ko-feng and Deng Xiaoping.

Politics will continue, Badiou asserts, citing the examples of the Soviets during the Russian Revolution and the "liberated zones" that were painstakingly wrested from the enemy during Mao's twenty-year struggle against the Kuomintang.[21] In the wake of the UCF's demise, Badiou's new political organ, L'organisation politique, has embraced a variety of worthy causes: that of the so-called *sans papiers* (or undocumented aliens), the 1995 French public sector strikes, and greater justice for the Palestinians. By the same token, Badiou has been a staunch

[20] See Bosteels, "Post-Maoism."
[21] Badiou cites these instances at the conclusion of *Metapolitics*, 152.

opponent of struggles for cultural or group rights—feminism, homosexual liberation, and all varieties of communitarianism—insofar as
their particularism putatively detracts from the universal truth content
of emancipation. (Badiou is fond of referring to politics as a "universal
truth-event.") Ultimately, these movements fail to qualify as political
insofar as they pose no objective threat to capital.[22]

In "Metapolitics," Badiou's radical alternative to (in his view) the
overwhelmingly conformist bent of contemporary political philosophy, the philosopher stresses the irreducible singularity of politics qua
"event." "Events" are situations that pose a meaningful collective challenge to the political status quo. As such, they manage to breach the
continuum of political normalcy. Yet there seems to be a strange dis-
connect between Badiou's uncompromising theoretical radicalism—as
represented, for example, by his book *Metapolitics*—and his relatively
uncontroversial defense of "progressive" political causes: immigrant
rights (*sans papiers*), the homeless (*sans abris*), the gains of the welfare
state, and so forth. Once the logic of history no longer subtends processes of collective struggle, as with Marxism, by Badiou's own admission one is left with the ebb and flow of "events" qua evanescent,
"multiple singularities." Thus, despite his aversion to postmodernism
and the epistemological relativism it entails, Badiou's recent political
commitments betray a certain random, opportunistic, and eclectic
quality. Since the dialectic of revolution has egregiously miscarried,
culminating in the excesses of Stalinism and Cultural Revolutionary China—hence, Badiou's ultimate embrace of "politics without
party"—with Badiou truth has become avowedly "post-evental"; it has
become entirely "subjective," decontextualized, and, as such, devoid
of consequences. Thus, in the words of a sympathetic commentator,
Badiou's "politics of historically indetermined singular situations becomes akin to the very postmodern fragmentation it sought to resist."[23]

[22] See Badiou's remarks in "Politics and Philosophy," 107–9.

[23] See, for example, the critique of Daniel Bensaid, "Alain Badiou and the Miracle
of the Event," in *Badiou*, 102. As Bensaid observes: With Badiou

> truth has become more fragmentary and discontinuous under the brunt of
> historical disasters, as though history no longer constituted its basic frame-
> work but merely its occasional condition. Truth . . . becomes a post-evental

THE SECTARIAN MAOISM OF BADIOU

By belittling logics of bourgeois emancipation as a swindle, his political framework systematically neglects the advances that democratization and rule of law can provide for the social struggles of both groups (the post-May social movements) and entire polities (the former socialist states of Eastern Europe). In the end his brand of post-Maoism remains politically sectarian and needlessly self-marginalizing.

---

consequence. As "wholly subjective" and a matter of "pure conviction," truth henceforth pertains to the realm of declarations that have neither precedents nor consequences. . . . For Badiou, there can be no transcendental truth, only truths in situation and in relation, situations and relations of truth, oriented toward an atemporal eternity. (95)

Fig. 1. Jean-Paul Sartre and Simone de Beauvoir defying a government ban by illegally distributing *La Cause du Peuple* in the spring of 1970. Photo: Gilles Peress. Source: Magnum Photo.

Fig. 2. Issue of the Maoist daily *La Cause du Peuple* protesting the arrest of spokesman Alain Geismar. Photo: Gilles Peress. Source: Magnum Photo.

André Glucksmann,
la cigarette aux lèvres,
sous la banderole
du journal maoïste
La Cause du peuple
le 1er mai 1968.

Fig. 3. A Maoist rally during May 1968 featuring André Glucksmann in the lower right-hand corner. Photo: Archives Rouges. Source: Magnum Photo.

Fig. 4. Jean-Luc Godard collating copies of the banned Maoist daily *La Cause du Peuple* in the spring of 1970. Photo: Bruno Barbrey. Source: Magnum Photo.

a.

Fig. 5a and b. Sartre and Foucault protesting the treatment of Arab immigrants at the Goutte d'Or quarter in Paris, November 1971. Photo: Gérard Aimé. Source: Magnum Photo.

b.

Fig. 6. François Wahl, Julia Kristeva, Philippe Sollers, and Marcelin Pleynet, along with their Chinese translators, visiting Beijing in 1974. Photo: Archives Philippe Sollers. Source: Editions de Minuit. Magnum Photo.

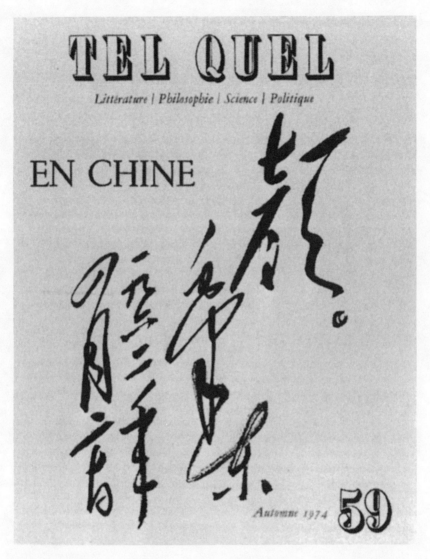

Fig. 7. Special issue of *Tel Quel*, "In China" (1974). Source: Editions de Minuit. Magnum Photo.

PART 2

The Hour of the Intellectuals

The May events took France's vaunted caste of intellectual mandarins entirely by surprise. As we have seen, the theoretical inspiration for the revolt did not come from the intellectual elite—France's so-called Master Thinkers—but from the margins: left-wing groupuscules like the Arguments group, the Situationist International, and Socialism or Barbarism. For French intellectuals, the May revolt was a lesson in humility. To their surprise, and perhaps for the first time, they found themselves in the peculiar position of followers rather than leaders. As such, May sounded the death knell for the prophetic intellectual: the thinker who possesses privileged access to history and thus takes it upon himself to explicate its course to the benighted masses.

Some intellectuals, like Sartre, learned the lesson faster—and better—than others. He was the only intellectual of the traditional stamp whom the sixty-eighters openly embraced. Ironically, their affection for Sartre owed less to his Marxist contributions than to his existentialist writings, which postwar students knew by heart. They sought to escape the ill-fitting corset of orthodox Marxism, whose ideological rigidity failed to meet their intellectual and cultural needs. Conversely, existentialism, with its probing meditations on the problem of individual freedom, possessed an openness that the student activists could calibrate and refashion to suit their pressing contemporary concerns. Gradually, under the impact of the French May, Sartre's long-standing attachments to Marxism receded. When in 1979 he intervened publicly, with great fanfare, on behalf of the Vietnamese boat people, he resembled Voltaire more than he did Robespierre.

The Tel Quel story serves as an important foil to the Sartre episode, for Tel Quel began as a *machine de guerre* directed against the

Sartrean concept of commitment. As such, the Telquelians sought to reintroduce aestheticism—*l'art pour l'art*—to a nation that, following the Algerian War, had become weary of politics. But as the 1960s progressed, it became clear that politics were impossible to ignore. Tel Quel's relationship to Maoism was sui generis. Unlike Sartre and Foucault, the Telquelians had no contact with the vibrant student Maoism of the Gauche prolétarienne. Instead, they took their political cues directly from Beijing—albeit, an imaginary Beijing, the Beijing "in their heads." The saga of Tel Quel's Maoist infatuation is less uplifting than Sartre's or Foucault's insofar as the group merely transposed the dogmatism of its earlier Stalinism (1968—71) directly to its intoxication with Cultural Revolutionary China. By the same token, by the late 1970s the Telquelians, too, had become staunch *droit de l'hommistes*, climbing on the bandwagon of Soviet dissidence and worshiping at the church of Andrei Sakharov and Alexander Solzhenitsyn.

Foucault missed May 1968, since at that time he was teaching in Tunisia. But undoubtedly he was the French intellectual who drew the most probing and far-reaching conclusions from his post-May Maoist engagement. Prior to May, Foucault had been relatively apolitical. Ironically, this situation worked to his distinct advantage, since he had considerably less ideological baggage to cast off than did Sartre or Tel Quel. It was via his contact with the Maoists around the Prison Information Group (GIP) that Foucault discovered "micropolitics": the way that power coursed through the body politic at the microphysical, corpuscular level. In the company of the Maoists, Foucault discovered both the reality of "the social" and the ecstasies of Cultural Revolution. These experiences, as the 1970s drew to a close, sensitized him to the imperatives of human rights.

In this respect Foucault's thought—and French intellectual life in general—came full circle, so to speak. As the brutality of "really existing socialism" hit home, French intellectuals began to rediscover their original métier, that of the universal intellectual of the Dreyfusard stamp: the intellectual who shames power by confronting it with timeless moral truths. The paradigm shift from "antihumanism," as embraced by the structuralists, to the "new humanism," or "French philosophy of the 1980s," was under way.

CHAPTER 5

Jean-Paul Sartre's Perfect
Maoist Moment

During the 1960s the structuralists had declared Sartre, as well as the paradigm of existential phenomenology he represented, obsolete, or "passé." However, May 1968 signified a resounding vindication of Sartre's doctrine of human freedom, for May demonstrated that "events" happened, that history was more than the opaque, frozen landscape the structuralists had made it out to be. Thereafter, Sartre's concerted involvement with the Maoists—at one point, he served as the titular editor of no fewer than three Maoist publications (*La Cause du Peuple, J'Accuse,* and *Tout!*)—catapulted him to the center stage of French political life. Since the May revolt, gauchisme had captured the political imagination of contemporary France. Youth was the wave of the future. Sartre's alliance with the Gauche prolétarienne made it clear that French youth had embraced Sartre.

By the same token, Sartre's collaboration with the Maoists was more than an alliance of political convenience. As with other French intellectuals, Sartre's Maoist episode was a way station and rite of passage that allowed him to escape the political strictures of orthodox Marxism. But even more important, his association with the Maoists allowed him to think through problems concerning the role of the intellectual that had preoccupied him for years. Although Sartre was the consummate twentieth-century French intellectual, he always felt extremely ill at ease in this role. On the one hand, the intellectual claimed to be the exponent of universal values. On the other hand, he or she remained powerless to realize these values in real life. This chasm or breach afflicted the core of the intellectual's being. It accounted for her endemic "bad faith" (*mauvaise foi*). Sartre's Maoist commitment impelled him to view the intellectual's role in an entirely new light. From now on, the intellectual would cease to embody an absolute that was external to the masses. Instead, he or she would be a "friend of the people."

"A MAN LIKE ANY OTHER"

Sartre was that rare breed of intellectual who effortlessly succeeded at virtually every form of literary endeavor: short stories, novels, philosophical treatises, essays, political tracts, interviews, and plays. In 1963 he published, to considerable acclaim, an autobiography, *Les mots* (The Words), an affecting tale of how, from a very early age, deprived of a father and surrounded by devoted women, he was bred for literary success. Working through his own past, the philosopher of freedom came to realize how his character and persona had been indelibly shaped by his familial origins—and how difficult it proved to transcend them. Sartre's narrative was remarkably frank and self-critical. At times it bordered on bourgeois self-hatred. He was, as Simone de Beauvoir once observed, the perfect embodiment of "unhappy consciousness," as defined by Hegel.[1] Looking back with a jaundiced eye at his early literary breakthrough, *Nausea*, Sartre insightfully mocked his own achievement: "I was Roquentin . . . the elect, the chronicler of Hell, a glass and steel photomicroscope peering at my own protoplasmic juices. Later I gaily demonstrated that man was impossible. . . . Fake to the marrow of my bones and hoodwinked, I joyfully wrote about our unhappy state. . . . I doubted everything except that I was the elect of doubt. . . . I regarded anxiety as the guarantee of my security; I was happy."[2]

As a young man Sartre viewed writing as a noble—and ennobling—vocation. Later he became disillusioned. It was next to impossible for an intellectual to surmount the taint and limitations of his class origins. The entire project of "littérature engagée," announced with such fanfare in 1947, had seemingly collapsed. The imaginary, the writer's province, unconscionably left reality untouched and untransformed. When it came to redressing the suffering of an innocent

---

[1] De Beauvoir, *Adieux*, 4.
[2] Sartre, *Words*, 87.

child, literature was impotent, lamented Sartre.[3] If Sartre continued to write—his monumental study of Flaubert, for example—it was more out of force of habit than anything else, he claimed. Still, *Les mots* concluded on a note of modest self-affirmation. Sartre described himself as "a whole man, composed of all men and as good as all of them, and no better than any."[4]

The following year Sartre was awarded the Nobel Prize for Literature, which he proceeded to reject. His refusal created an international clamor and demonstrated that the only way to supersede the world's most esteemed literary accolade is to repudiate it. After all, Nobel Prize winners are legion. In only one other case has someone who had been offered the prize refused it.[5]

Nevertheless, there was a widespread consensus that, at the moment of his canonization by the Swedish jury, the Sartrean juggernaut had essentially run aground. Since the war's end, Sartre had been at the forefront of the major political battles of the day: the cold war, Stalinism, the Soviet invasion of Hungary, and the Algerian War. The prophet of existentialism had redefined the ideal of the committed intellectual— a concept with an estimable French pedigree traceable to the likes of Voltaire, Victor Hugo, Emile Zola, and André Gide.

The high-water mark of Sartre's career as an *intellectuel engagé* was undoubtedly his principled stance against the Algerian War, where the French army had committed atrocities with regularity. In 1961 Sartre demonstratively signed the Manifesto of the 121, which openly urged French troops to desert and which the government therefore viewed as an open incitement to treason. For his efforts, Sartre's apartment on rue Bonaparte in the heart of the Left Bank was bombed—twice. The government, confronting a virtual civil war at home (in 1961 disaffected officers had formed the Organisation de l'armée secrete, which openly challenged de Gaulle's policies and committed terrorist acts on French soil), threatened many signatories with arrest. In a celebrated

[3] Sartre, interview with Jacqueline Piatier, *Le Monde*, April 18, 1964.
[4] Sartre, *Words*, 255.
[5] Le Duc Tho, the Vietnamese negotiator at the Paris Peace Talks, who received the prize in 1973 along with Henry Kissinger.

bon mot, de Gaulle, when confronted with Sartre's open defiance, was alleged to have remarked: "On n'arrete pas Voltaire!" (One doesn't arrest Voltaire!). The French president could hardly have paid Sartre a higher compliment.

Yet, with the Algerian War's end in 1962, the Sino-Soviet rift had permanently split the "anti-imperialist" camp. Fashionable geopolitical talk of "convergence," suggesting that despite their pronounced ideological differences, the American and Soviet political systems were becoming increasingly similar, effectively precluded meaningful outlets for intellectual engagement. France, moreover, was in the throes of a quasi-benign eleven-year presidential dictatorship. De Gaulle's Imperial Presidency (1958–69) would be followed in turn by the five-year rule of Georges Pompidou, his handpicked successor. Prospects for internal political change appeared frozen.

Toward the end of the Algerian War, Sartre published his second major philosophical opus, *Critique of Dialectical Reason*, which he composed over a period of several months in an amphetamine-induced stupor. (Sartre was addicted to the drug corydrane, which at the time was sold over the counter. In a short time this addiction would adversely affect his health.)[6] *Critique* was Sartre's response to the excesses and misdeeds of Stalinism. In it, he speculated about the historical and ontological limits of socialism. Reprising the conceptual framework of *Being and Nothingness*, Sartre speculated about the inevitability of group inertia, a phenomenon he dubbed "serialization." In Sartre's view, among human groups there existed a quasi-anthropological tendency to squander the vitality of an initial revolutionary upsurge. Sartre tried to support his conclusions with historical examples: the French Revolution's Thermidor, when the followers of Robespierre were themselves marched to the guillotine; Stalin's brutal purge of the old Bolsheviks during the

---

[6] In *Force of Circumstance*, Simone de Beauvoir describes Sartre's frenetic modus operandi as follows: "It was not a case of writing as he ordinarily did, pausing to think and make corrections, tearing up a page, starting again; for hours at a stretch he raced across sheet after sheet without re-reading them, as though absorbed by ideas that his pen, even at that speed, couldn't keep up with; to maintain this pace I could hear him crunching corydrane capsules, of which he managed to get through a tube a day"; 385.

1936–37 Moscow show trials; and so on. If Sartre's political specula-
tions were accurate, the future of revolutionary struggle would be ex-
ceedingly dim, if not entirely pointless.[7]

Thus, by the 1960s, existentialism's revolutionary élan seemed de-
pleted. One commentator noted: "Never, during his entire literary
career, had [Sartre] had as few contacts with other intellectuals, his
contemporaries. In Paris, in the Latin Quarter, he seemed rather a
has-been."[8]

One sign of existentialism's demise was a legendary 1960 confrontation between Sartre and Louis Althusser at the Ecole normale—the
PCF philosopher's home turf. Althusser's disciples bombarded Sartre
with questions about whether one could understand history on the
basis of the egocentric framework of existential phenomenology. Was
a historically oriented paradigm like Marxism not necessary to make
sense of the action of social groups? Sartre appeared uncharacteristically
tongue-tied. According to most observers, Althusser won the debate
hands down.[9]

HISTORY WITHOUT A SUBJECT

Sartre had spent the previous decade trying to fuse existentialism with
Marxism, implying that taken by itself, a philosophy of existence was
unserviceable for historical and political ends. At the time, a competing intellectual paradigm had emerged to fill the void that was left in
existentialism's wake: the rigid and impersonal grid of structuralism.
As an approach to the human sciences, structuralism openly mocked
the self-confidence of the Cartesian *cogito*, which had been French

---

[7] See Aronson, *Jean-Paul Sartre*, 257: "Sartre lays down a formal condition which,
in the manner of *L'Etre et le Néant*, is virtually beyond our grasp and foredooms all
efforts to outstrip it. Because of it, the Other will threaten us no matter what. Having paid due respect to Marxism and to the contingency of this 'ultimate' fact, Sartre
has fallen back on his old bogeys. In the analyst of scarcity we once again meet the
philosopher of 'hell is other people.'"

[8] Cohen-Solal, *Sartre*, 449.

[9] See the account of this debate ibid., 450–51.

philosophy's starting point and sine qua non. Invoking the higher authority of "science," structuralism tried to show that the cogito was an epiphenomenal manifestation of deeply rooted, long-term historical constants—so-called deep structures. Just as Freud had shown, via recourse to the unconscious, that the ego was not master of its own house, just as Marx had demonstrated that culture, politics, and law were ultimately the expression of underlying economic determinants, the structuralists mobilized "scientific" arguments to counteract the delusions of autonomy on the part of consciousness, mind, and spirit. Thereby, representatives of the social sciences manned a concerted assault against philosophy's vaunted primacy in French intellectual life—a primacy that since the war's end was inextricably associated with the name of Sartre.

The 1950s were structuralism's gestation period. However, with the onset of the 1960s, Sartre's structuralist opponents began attacking him directly. In *The Savage Mind*, Claude Lévi-Strauss, structuralism's most formidable advocate (his 1955 autobiographical study, *Tristes tropiques*, had been a runaway success), published a blistering, no-holds-barred critique of Sartre's *Critique of Dialectical Reason*. Lévi-Strauss argued from the standpoint of a fashionable, postcolonial anthropological relativism. He believed that in view of colonialism's depredations and massive criminality, not to mention the more recent sins of Auschwitz and Hiroshima, to argue for the West's cultural superiority was myopic. In his celebrated characterization of Marxism as the "unsurpassable horizon of our time," Sartre had succumbed to precisely this trap, Lévi-Strauss argued. The monomania of the Sartrean *Pour-Soi*, or for-itself, Lévi-Strauss contended, bore affinities with the untrammeled narcissism of the savage mind.

In Lévi-Strauss's view—and with the Warsaw Pact's predatory invasion of Budapest fresh in mind—the Marxism Sartre endorsed was merely another specious rationalization of Western cultural dominance. The Belgian-born anthropologist openly preferred the relative tranquillity of premodern, non-Western societies. These primitive communities lived in relative harmony with their environment and wreaked considerably less global havoc. Perhaps the highlight of Lévi-Strauss's critique was the passages in which he compared Sartre unfavorably with a Melanesian savage—someone who, to his credit, remained free of the unbridled and megalomaniac will to power afflicting Western intellectuals such as Sartre.

Shortly thereafter, Michel Foucault, one of the structuralists' up-and-coming luminaries, mounted his own barely veiled assault against the aging "maître" in *The Order of Things*. Foucault wisely refrained from naming names, but it did not require much imagination to discern the real target of his polemical ire. Foucault's book, in the spirit of structuralism, constituted a frontal attack against the illusions of "man," "subjectivity," and "humanism"—that is, against all of the concepts that Sartrean existentialism held dear. In one of the book's most celebrated and lyrical passages, Foucault conjectured that the paradigm of man would be swept away like a sand castle at the edge of the sea. Thereafter, there would exist once again a space in which it was possible to think.[10]

For a younger cohort of French thinkers who had come of age during the postwar period and had endured its political disappointments, Sartre had acquired the status of a generational superego. He was the primal father who had to be slain so that the "sons" might prosper and flourish. When, in *Reading Capital* and *For Marx*, Althusser denigrated Marxist humanism as "ideological" and "prescientific," his real target was the popularity of Sartrean existential Marxism. The growing consensus, strongly reinforced by detractors of humanism such as Foucault, Althusser, and Jacques Lacan, was that the Sartrean paradigm of phenomenological Marxism had foundered. It was time for a major paradigm change, an "epistemological break" (Gaston Bachelard), which the structuralists sought to precipitate.

Sartre's biographer, Annie Cohen-Solal, has aptly summarized these developments as follows:

> For a few years, Sartre had been quite marginal. Structuralism, Lacanism, Althusserianism: not one of these new trends had

---

[10] Foucault, *Order of Things*, 342: "It is no longer possible to think in our day other than in the void left by man's disappearance. For this void is . . . nothing more, and nothing less, than the unfolding of a space in which it is once more possible to think."

elicited any response, recognition, criticism from him. And this was not because he disapproved of his new colleagues—Louis Althusser, Jacques Lacan, Michel Foucault, Roland Barthes, Claude Lévi-Strauss—the new stars of the Latin Quarter. . . . He was simply not there. He accepted them, coexisted with them, let them be. But he remained silent. He was silent when Althusser buried the young Marx's Paris Manuscripts. Silent when Lacan initiated the grand debate on language. He uttered only a few words when Foucault published his two masterpieces on madness and prisons. He was absent as if his contemporaries' intellectual concerns were quite extraneous to him.[11]

In 1964 a memorable confrontation between advocates of the two antagonistic paradigms took place. Sartre was pitted against two of the leading representatives of the structuralist camp, the Telquelians Jean Ricardou and Jean-Pierre Faye. The occasion was a much-anticipated conference at the Mutualité, a large public meeting hall, addressing the theme "what can literature do?" Since its inception in 1960, *Tel Quel*, in manifest opposition to Sartre, had assiduously embraced literary formalism as epitomized by Alain Robbe-Grillet's hermetic nouveau roman. Sartre, for his part, remained a champion of "committed literature." Thus, the stage was set. Sartre immediately went on the attack, criticizing the nouveau roman for its aestheticist complacency. In a world rife with social injustice, literary self-indulgence was a luxury that humanity could ill afford. But the Telquelians more than held their own. Ricardou justly retorted that by virtue of its meaning-generating capacities, literature redeemed human existence from a type of mute anonymity. To its credit, literature registered instances of human suffering that would otherwise pass unremarked. As such, it was, willy-nilly, an exercise in consciousness-raising.[12] Sartre, it seemed, had met his match.

The structuralist ambush seemed to catch Sartre off guard. In 1965 he had turned sixty. It seemed that, apart from Lévi-Strauss and perhaps

---

[11] Cohen-Solal, *Sartre*, 469–70.
[12] See the discussion of this event in Forest's *Histoire de* Tel Quel, 210–11.

Foucault, Sartre never read his structuralist critics very closely.[13] Never-theless, on at least one occasion Sartre attempted to formulate a coher-ent response. In 1966 the French journal *L'Arc* published an interview with the aging doyen of Rive Gauche existentialism. In his rebuttal Sartre insisted that the structuralists' real target was Marxism. Their rejection of history, he continued, ended up suppressing the notion of progressive historical change in toto. In the wake of the structur-alist critique, history became a frozen and ossified landscape, resem-bling an Yves Tanguy painting: a terrain devoid of direction, intention, or meaning. As Sartre commented: "Behind history, of course, it is Marxism which is attacked. The task is to come up with a new ideol-ogy: the latest barrier that the bourgeoisie once again can erect against Marx. . . . In the system of language, there are some things that the inert [that is, structures] cannot give us alone: the mark of *praxis*. Struc-tures impose themselves upon us only to the extent that they are made by others. Thus, to understand how a structure is made, it is necessary to introduce praxis as that totalizing process."[14]

Although Sartre avoided a detailed engagement with the arguments of his structuralist adversaries, it is hard to deny that his critique of structuralism's determinism—which, in Sartre's view, was tantamount to affirming, rather than striving to surmount, the "practico-inert"—displayed foresight and prescience. For structuralism's days, too, were numbered.

A year later François Furet provided a partial confirmation of Sar-tre's diagnosis. Attempting to furnish a historical account of structural-ism's rise, Furet showed that its popularity coincided with Marxism's

---

[13] See the account in Cohen-Solal's *Sartre*, 449:

It was disappointing to hear Sartre or those close to him utter formulas that minimized the importance of Michel Foucault—"a positivist in despair"—or that, in the name of History, passed up ethnography, linguistics, and psychoanalysis. Even though at the time France was excited over Lévi-Strauss, Barthes, Lacan, Althusser, and Foucault, Sartre refused to confront their fertile methods of investigation in any way whatsoever, let alone with the open mind that would have been so useful in such a confrontation.

[14] "Replies to Structuralism: An Interview with Jean-Paul Sartre," *Telos* 9 (Fall 1971): 110–11.

decline. As the French Left's confidence in progressive historical change was sapped by Soviet Marxism's ongoing bureaucratic stultification, it tended to lapse into a historical political fatalism. Structuralism, which was marked by a self-canceling cynicism about prospects for meaningful human betterment, had become the paradigm du jour in an era of extreme political disillusionment.[15]

"SARTRE'S REVENGE"

Within a year May 1968 would demonstrate that "events" were still possible. For an entire month structuralism's platitudes and truisms were refuted daily in the streets and amphitheaters of the Latin Quarter. The intellectual "lessons" of May were aptly summarized by the philosopher Lucien Goldmann, who famously observed, "Structures don't go out in the street to make a revolution." In other words, history was not "frozen." Subjectivity and "events" had reasserted their prerogatives. Sartre, too, was making a political comeback, only a few years after structuralism's leading apostles had demonstrably written him off as a "dead dog."

In many respects, the May events stood as a ringing confirmation of Sartre's ideas, above all his belief in the capacities of men and women to actively influence the course of historical events via sovereign acts of will, despite the disfavor of objective conditions. As University of Nanterre psychologist Didier Anzieu, alluding to Sartre's doctrine of the revolutionary "group-in-fusion," observed: "The May student revolt tried out its own version of Sartre's formula '*The group is the beginning of humanity.*'"[16] It is, then, hardly by chance that, in his magisterial history of the structuralist movement, François Dosse entitles his chapter on May 1968 "Jean-Paul Sartre's Revenge";[17] in his capacity

---

[15] Furet, "French Intellectuals: From Marxism to Structuralism," in *In the Workshop of History.*

[16] Epistémon, *Ces idées qui ont ébranlé*, 83; emphasis added.

[17] Dosse, *History of Structuralism* 2:112.

as an intellectual and political activist, Sartre was involved in the May uprising from the very outset.

On May 10—the legendary Night of the Barricades—Sartre co-signed a manifesto in *Le Monde* vigorously supporting the student demands. The document was noteworthy for the insight it displayed concerning the sociological and existential basis of the student rebellion: French youth's unwillingness to be bought off and seduced by the blandishments and baubles of consumer society. The student malaise could no longer be redressed by piecemeal reforms. Sartre recognized early on, as did a few others, that the student revolt had embraced an ethic of "total refusal." As he and his cosigners declared:

> The solidarity we are here pledging to all the student movements in the world—movements that have suddenly upset the so-called leisure society so perfectly represented in France—is, above all, our answer to all the lies with which all the institutions and political organizations . . . and all the organs of the press and the rest of the media . . . have been trying, now for months, to alter said movements and to pervert them by ridiculing them.[18]

Soon after, Sartre took to the airwaves of Radio Luxembourg to help sway public opinion in the students' favor. The peroration he delivered was vintage Sartre: bold, impassioned, rich, and unequivocal.

> These young people do not want to share the future of their fathers, that is, our own, within a set of themes we know all too well . . . that is, a future that has clearly revealed our cowardice, our weariness, our sluggishness and servility, and our total submission to a closed system. . . . Whatever the regime, *violence* is the only thing remaining to the students who have not yet entered into their fathers' system and who do not want to enter into it. . . . For the moment, the only anti-establishment force in

[18] M. Legris, "M. Jean-Paul Sartre à la Sorbonne: Pour l'association du socialisme et de la liberté," *Le Monde*, May 22, 1968.

our flabby Western countries is represented by the students, but I
hope that it will soon spread to all our young people.[19]

Sartre's insights were immediately reproduced by the students and distributed in flyers throughout the Latin Quarter.

Next, Sartre took to the pages of *Le Nouvel Observateur*. Since his
1964 Tokyo lectures, he had tried to rethink the role of the intellectual.
Sartre believed that in advanced industrial societies the intellectual's
vocation was rent by insoluble contradictions and tensions. On the one
hand, intellectuals claimed to speak from the standpoint of "the universal," or generally valid knowledge. Yet, in fact their activities always stood in the service of particular social interests. Here, Sartre gave
voice to a tension he increasingly felt in his own work, one that formed
one of the self-critical leitmotifs of *Les mots*. Sartre constantly strove
to orient his activities toward emancipatory ends and goals, but he felt
that the systemic constraints of class society continually frustrated his
efforts. Try as he might, it proved well-nigh impossible to transcend
the taint of privilege. Following Soviet communism's failures, it had
become clear to Sartre that the Leninist "vanguard" model was obsolete. Yet how was one to act on this realization without relapsing into
another antiquated intellectual ideal, that of the *littérateur,* or bourgeois
aesthete?

Amid the tumult of May, Sartre interviewed Daniel Cohn-Bendit,
justly ceding the limelight to the charismatic leader of the March 22
Movement. Sartre's act of self-effacement was simultaneously a political
act. It bespoke a new sense of philosophical and personal humility. It
expressed a modest understanding of the intellectual as someone who
knows when to follow and when to lead.

Sartre realized that, with the May uprising, the annals of revolutionism had entered into uncharted territory. He maintained an open mind
and was eager to learn from his student interlocutors. Sartre was acutely
aware of how repressive de Gaulle's presidential dictatorship had been.
For these reasons, he was predisposed to appreciate a revolt that could

[19] *Les écrits de Sartre*, ed. Michel Contat and Michel Rybalka (Paris: Gallimard,
1970), 463–64.

prove a harbinger and catalyst for more sweeping sociopolitical change. In this respect, Sartre demonstrated his superiority to PCF ideologues, who dismissed May as a grandiose case of revolutionary playacting: a rebellion by a spoiled group of "fils à papa," or Daddy's boys.

The interview with Cohn-Bendit had a faintly comical air. At times it resembled a dialogue of the deaf. Sartre repeatedly tried to assimilate the student revolt to a formal organizational mentality that was alien to its uninhibited, spontaneous spirit. Thus, he continually pressed Cohn-Bendit about the students' long-term "programs" and "objectives." Conversely, Cohn-Bendit, a self-professed anarchist with ties to the Left-Communist tradition that was anathema to orthodox Marxists, flatly denied that there were any, to Sartre's dismay and frustration. Sartre was convinced that, barring a successful revolutionary seizure of power, the forces of reaction would merely be strengthened. For his part, Cohn-Bendit harbored no such fears. His aversion to the Bolshevik model led him to doubt whether the idea of destroying bourgeois society was a desirable goal. He realized that in advanced industrial societies, social change needed to be evolutionary and gradualist. He already sensed the necessity of—to quote German SDS leader Rudi Dutschke—the "long march through the institutions." Once one had abandoned Leninism—and this remained the crucial ideological dividing line between the March 22 Movement, on the one hand, and the Trotskyists and Maoists, on the other (although all three "groupuscules" shared a marked antipathy to the French Communist Party)—there were really no other alternatives. Cohn-Bendit was convinced that, whether it succeeded or failed, the student revolt had initiated a turning point in postwar French political and institutional life. From this point on, there would be no turning back. In these respects, Cohn-Bendit showed himself to be both more realistic and more politically astute than Sartre.

From the interview it was clear that Cohn-Bendit had a marked aversion to organized communism's long list of political sins and misdeeds: the Bolsheviks' suppression of the 1921 Kronstadt Uprising, Stalin's show trials of 1936–37, the Warsaw Pact invasion of Budapest in 1956. The very idea of positing strategic objectives was anathema to him. Thus, one of the student rebellion's major strengths—its strong

distaste for ossified, traditional organizational structures—was also one
of its major weaknesses.

As the May events reached their crescendo, Sartre found himself
caught between two competing and contradictory conceptions of political radicalism. His Marxist training suggested—as both the French
Communist Party and the Maoists had repeatedly stressed—that the
proletariat remained the only genuine revolutionary agent. Hence, Sartre was convinced, as were most orthodox leftists, that for a revolution
to take place, the French working class must finish what the students
had begun. Thus, as a political thinker Sartre, despite his commend-
able openness to student concerns, was unable to overcome his residual
ouvriérisme.

By the same token, in a June 1968 article that appeared in *Le Nouvel
Observateur,* "L'idée neuve de Mai 1968" (May 1968's New Idea), Sartre
displayed a percipient awareness of what May's real stakes were. He recognized that the student movement was more than a political "catalyst."
It was simultaneously the harbinger of a new, untrammeled conception of freedom that transcended the hidebound ideological strictures
of traditional Marxism. As Sartre observed, "What I reproach all of
those who insulted the students with is not having seen that they gave
voice to an original claim: that of *sovereignty.*"[20] With this insight, Sartre
acknowledged that May 1968's meaning had nothing to do with the
Blanquist-Leninist fantasy of seizing political power, nor with the orthodox Marxist goal of socializing the means of production. Instead, it pertained to the libertarian ideals of "autonomy" and "self-determination."
The dismantling of rigid hierarchies, vested interests, and unwarranted
social authority were the issues foremost on the student revolutionaries'
minds. Instead of destroying bourgeois society, they sought to make it
live up to its original radical democratic and emancipatory potential.
This was the meaning of the multifarious struggles to democratize the
workplace and the university that proliferated in May 1968's aftermath.
The new "politics of everyday life" actively sought to make quotidian
existence a repository of human fulfillment rather than, qua "leisure
time," a reified extension of consumer society.

[20] Sartre, "Idée neuve de mai 1968," 21.

Shortly after the May revolt ended, Cohn-Bendit paid Sartre the ultimate tribute by identifying his writings and doctrines as a formative influence upon the student revolutionaries: "None of us had read Marcuse. Some had read Marx, of course, and maybe Bakunin, and among contemporary thinkers, Althusser, Mao, Guevara, [Henri] Lefebvre. But the political militants of the March 22 Movement had all read Sartre."[21]

One remarkable testimony to the esteem in which the student revolutionaries held Sartre is the fact that at a momentous May 20 gathering at the Sorbonne, he was the only member of the intellectual "old guard" permitted to address the overflowing assembly hall.[22] Thus, despite their overheated Oedipal impulses, the students eagerly sought out Sartre's approbation. An estimated seven thousand students crammed the lecture hall and the adjacent courtyard solely for the purpose of hearing what Sartre had to say.

Neither Althusser, nor Foucault, nor Lévi-Strauss, nor Lacan really interested them. As a PCF stalwart, Althusser, as a rule, maintained a safe and comfortable distance from the politics of student radicalism, since one factor uniting the coalition of student protesters was their unlimited antipathy to the PCF and everything it stood for. In his autobiography, *L'avenir dure longtemps (The Future Lasts Forever)*, Althusser accords May 1968 a mere *fifteen words*.[23] In return, as the May events unfolded, the student revolutionaries would avenge themselves vis-à-vis structuralist Marxism's dogmatism and vacuity via a clever pun, mocking Althusser's followers as "Althusser-à-riens" (Althusser is worthless). During May Foucault was absent, teaching in Tunis. He received periodic updates on the turmoil from his partner, Daniel Defert. Lévi-Strauss's major concern was that student anarchy would set back the structuralist project by twenty years. He fled the Collège de France in a panic and was neither seen nor heard from for eight days. Most discouraging, perhaps, was Lacan's patronizing attitude toward the students. "You will find a new master!" he famously declared at

[21] Cohn-Bendit et al., *French Student Revolt*, 58.

[22] See Dosse, *History of Structuralism* 2:112–13: "Make no mistake. Jean-Paul Sartre was the only major intellectual allowed to speak in the main lecture hall of the Sorbonne at the heart of the uprising."

[23] Althusser, *L'avenir dure longtemps*, 389–90.

the height of the uprising, thereby implying, in vintage structuralist fashion, that all political change was chimerical. At best, one could succeed only in effectuating a change in leadership.

The students' antipathy to structuralism was thoroughgoing and deep-seated. For them it signified the hermetic discourse of a super-cilious intellectual elite—the new "Master Thinkers." They perceived structuralism's claims to "scientificity" as an ideological expression of the managerial mind-set they were desperately seeking to overthrow. After all, the structuralists had openly declared that history and events had, in essence, ceased to exist. By word and deed, the students strove, via all the means at their disposal, to prove them wrong.

Conversely, the student revolutionaries greeted the author of *Nausea, Being and Nothingness,* and *Les mots* like a messiah. "The philosopher who scorned university laurels, the representative of 'humanism' who, now out of fashion, fifteen months earlier had been entombed, ground to a pulp by the structuralist mill, flattened by the Althusserian steamroller—Sartre now made his comeback."[24] As Hervé Hamon and Patrick Rotman have aptly observed, on May 20 the Sorbonne militants found their Socrates.[25] In the aftermath of the May events, Lévi-Strauss was forced to concede: "In France . . . structuralism is no longer in fashion. Since May 1968, all objectivity has been repudiated. The position of the youth corresponds more to that of Sartre."[26]

In *All Said and Done,* Simone de Beauvoir described the tumultuous scene at the student-occupied Sorbonne as follows:

Neither in my studious youth nor even at the beginning of 1968 could I ever possibly have imagined such a party. The red flag flew over the chapel and the statues of the great men, and the walls blossomed with the wonderful slogans invented some weeks earlier at Nanterre. Every day new inscriptions appeared in the corridors, new tracts, posters, drawings. Clusters of people argued

[24] Hamon and Rotman, *Génération* 1:523.
[25] Ibid., 525.
[26] John Hess, "French Anthropologist at Onset of 70's Deplores the Twentieth Century," *New York Times,* December 31, 1969, 4.

passionately on the stairs or standing in the courtyard. . . . The young and the less young crowded the benches of the amphitheater; and anyone who chose to speak could state his case, explain his ideas or suggest tasks or watchwords, while the audience replied, approved or criticized. Press offices were set up in lecture-rooms, and in the attics, a crèche. Many of the students spent the night there in their sleeping-bags. Sympathizers brought fruit-juice, sandwiches, and hot meals.[27]

Amid the turmoil of the May events, the Sorbonne students peppered Sartre with the following earnest questions about philosophy, politics, and life:

Question: What did you mean when you said "Hell is other people?"
Sartre: We'll lose too much time if we discuss that now.

Question: Is the dictatorship of the proletariat necessary?
Sartre: Until now, the dictatorship of the proletariat has usually meant a dictatorship over the proletariat.

Question: You might be a good artist, but you're a lousy politician.
Sartre: I'm not here as a politician; I'm here as an intellectual.[28]

Addressing the student audience, Sartre offered the following politically astute diagnosis of the May events:

Cohn-Bendit has ensured that the movement remains on the path of contestation that is appropriate for it. It is evident that the current strike movement [in the factories] has its origins in

---

[27] De Beauvoir, *All Said and Done,* 425.
[28] See the account in Legris' "M. Jean-Paul Sartre à la Sorbonne"; "Sartre à la Sorbonne en mai 68," *Le Nouvel Observateur,* May 27–June 2, 1988, 125. See also Drake, "Sartre and May '68," 43–65.

the student insurrection. The CGT's position is one of belatedly joining in [*suivisme*]. It found it necessary to join with the movement in order to stifle it. It wanted to avoid at all costs the grassroots democracy that you have created and that upsets all institutions. For the CGT is itself an institution. Conversely, what is taking form here is a new conception of a fully democratic society, an alliance between socialism and liberty, for socialism and liberty are inseparable.[29]

Sartre recognized that worker-student solidarity was one of the keys to the May movement's success. He realized that, for all its virtues, youth was a transitory stage of life. It might serve as a catalyst for sweeping political change. Yet, if left to its own devices, its scope and aspirations were limited. University reform could be meaningful only as part of a more broadly based social transformation.

Sartre cautioned the students about the ulterior motives of the Communist-dominated trade union, the CGT. In general, the Communists feared anarchy and would try to co-opt the revolt for their own bureaucratic ends. In retrospect Sartre's suspicions were fully borne out. In June the PCF and de Gaulle agreed on a modus vivendi, which brought the May events to a sudden halt.

Until May Sartre had more or less accepted the Leninist political model, which stressed the paramount role of a professionalized revolutionary vanguard. As he once remarked in *Situations*: "The 40 volumes of Lenin represent an oppression for the masses: we can accept that, for the masses have neither the time nor the means today to tackle this type of knowledge, which is an intellectual's knowledge."[30] The theory's classic articulation was Lenin's 1902 *What Is to Be Done?* Yet, Bolshevism had been conceived under political circumstances appropriate to a czarist police state, hence the Bolsheviks' stress on the clandestine operations of a highly trained elite. The applicability of this model to the rest of Europe, where since the late nineteenth century democratic socialism had enjoyed a remarkable string of successes and gains, was dubious. Yet,

[29] Legris, "M. Jean-Paul Sartre à la Sorbonne."
[30] Sartre, *Situations,* vol. 8, *Autour de '68*, 71.

it is hard to argue with success. When the Bolsheviks seized power in October 1917, albeit in a country whose political development had been severely retarded by czardom (serfdom had belatedly been abolished in Russia in 1861), the Leninist model acquired vast prestige among an international Left in disarray after the debacle of 1914.

SARTRE JOINS "LES MAOS"

The saga of Sartre's post-May involvement with gauchisme revolves around his participation in the Gauche prolétarienne (GP)—the most radical among the various post-May groupings.

As we have seen, the GP's forerunner, the UJC-ML (Union des jeunesses communistes marxistes-léninistes), was radically disaffected with the French Communist Party. In their view, the PCF's chief problem was not that it was excessively Stalinist but that it was rife with "revisionist" tendencies and, hence, *insufficiently Stalinist*. In the UJC-ML's eyes, the 1966 PCF congress at Argenteuil was the last straw. On this occasion the PCF openly embraced the precepts of "Marxist humanism"—the young Marx, Georg Lukács, and Roger Garaudy—that had become so influential throughout Europe. The Maoists, for their part, denigrated "Marxist humanism" as a slippery slope toward social democratic reformism. The Maoist normaliens set a high store by ideological purity. In part their dogmatism was intended as a safeguard against the risk of a "relapse" to bourgeois political mores and habitudes. The advantage of Althusser's doctrines, as well as what had come to be known in France as Mao Tse-tung Thought, was that both currents steadfastly resisted the lures of revisionism for the sake of fidelity to Leninist orthodoxy. Althusser tacitly disapproved of the UJC-ML's formation, thereby opening up a significant rift between the *maître* and his students. In his view the PCF was the only authentic revolutionary organ in France. No genuine political change could be achieved outside of it.

When the May 1968 student protests erupted, the UJC-ML militants remained aloof. Insofar as the student revolt lacked a genuinely proletarian character, it was not worth taking seriously—a "nonevent." Their rigid ideological blinders obscured their capacity to appreciate the new modalities of radical protest that had been unleashed. Instead, they remained wedded to a credo of revolutionary vanguardism. In sum, when the most significant revolutionary upheaval of the postwar era erupted, the UJC-ML activists were AWOL, "no-shows."

That summer, the UJC-ML, in prototypical Maoist fashion, undertook prolonged self-criticism sessions in an effort to fathom their political misjudgment. Banned by the French government in June, the Maoists regrouped later that year as the Gauche prolétarienne. The masthead of their broadsheet, *La Cause du Peuple*, was adorned with an image of Mao on one side and a hammer and sickle below it—emblems of unwavering ideological rectitude. Yet, on occasion their ideological dogmatism was offset by the emancipatory spirit of May.

In the spring of 1970 the group pulled off one of its biggest publicity coups, a daring daytime raid on the fashionable Right Bank gourmet food boutique Fauchon. At 1:30 p.m., twenty GP activists, equipped with large plastic sacks, burst through the doors and "liberated" stores of gourmet foodstuffs: caviar, foie gras, champagne, cheeses, and so forth. Meanwhile, fifty *lycée* supporters waited outside to ensure that the GP militants had unimpeded access to the local metro station. Then, switching to Robin Hood mode, the activists proceeded to distribute their spoils in Ivry, an impoverished African quarter, where, according to one observer, the locals were allowed to compare firsthand the relative merits of Russian and Iranian caviar. GP militants alerted newspaper reporters to the impending giveaway, thereby attracting enormous media attention to their cause. In the alternative press, they were lionized as heroes. Even the mainstream press could not help but applaud the Maoists' selflessness. Their actions served to highlight the appalling gap in advanced industrial societies between luxury and squalor.

In the course of the raid, Frédérique Delange, one of the GP militants, had been apprehended by knife-wielding Fauchon employees. As word of her arrest spread, a campaign for her release ensued. Public figures and celebrities far and wide began agitating for her. At one point Rolling Stones lead singer Mick Jagger issued a statement supporting her, to no avail. The French court handed down a draconian thirteen-month prison sentence.

Nevertheless, as a result of the Fauchon raid, combined with the overwrought governmental response, the Gauche prolétarienne, which consisted of no more than a few dozen militants, had suddenly become a household name. French public opinion shifted dramatically in the Maoists' favor. In a classic reversal, the forces of law and order were perceived as the oppressors and the Gauche prolétarienne's Robin Hood revolutionaries were viewed as the oppressed. GP activists such as Frédérique Delange were, after all, the daughters and sons of the French middle classes. By this point the fear of anarchy the May events unleashed had passed. Bourgeois France was justly up in arms over the fact that Interior Minister Raymond Marcellin and company had willfully incarcerated their "children" and then exulted about it during hastily conceived press conferences. Journalist Françoise Giroud commented in *L'Express*: "Who is placing our democracy in peril? Disorganized children who dream of a just world, among whom a few cross the line to deeds they have been taught about in class or in catechism? Or those who give to the social order such odious aspects that they end by mobilizing against it persons who are no more than children?"[31]

More arrests followed. In March 1970 Marcellin had brought charges against the GP leadership for endangering public safety. Without warning, entire print runs of *La Cause du Peuple* were arbitrarily confiscated by the police. On March 22 *La Cause du Peuple* editor Jean-Pierre Le Dantec was apprehended in a police raid and dispatched to La Santé Prison. Once again, the GP was making headlines and gaining droves of sympathizers. At the time, François Mitterrand publicly denounced this series of legally dubious arrests and seizures: "Without prejudging the content of the articles that have appeared in *La Cause du Peuple,* I approve neither of the judicial procedure that has been used against the authors, nor of the preventive arrests of Le Dantec and [Michel] Le Bris, nor of the conception of common law that has been applied to them."[32]

Marcellin and Prime Minister Pompidou foolishly pressed ahead. On April 30 a sweeping and ill-conceived "antiriot" law that the

[31] Cited in *Génération,* by Hamon and Rotman, 2:172.
[32] See the account in Bourseiller's *Maoïstes,* 128.

government had proposed was passed by the National Assembly. It criminalized organizations whose rank and file were involved in public disturbances, thereby inculpating nonparticipants. That day Le Dantec's successor as editor of *La Cause du Peuple*, Michel Le Bris, was arrested.[33] Despite having committed no identifiable crimes, the Gauche prolétarienne had become the target of a massive and systematic wave of government repression. The harsh prison sentences meted out to the Gauche prolétarienne leadership were the coup de grâce: Le Dantec was sentenced to one year in prison; Le Bris received an eight-month sentence. Finally, in what was tantamount to an open declaration of war, on May 27 Marcellin announced that the Gauche prolétarienne had been banned outright. But his attempt to employ state power to forcibly repress a handful of student militants would backfire egregiously.

The Gauche prolétarienne leadership convened an emergency meeting. They quickly resolved to approach Sartre to see if he would become *La Cause du Peuple*'s titular editor. After all, Sartre had perennially supported the persecuted and downtrodden. Since the May revolt, he had consistently backed student causes. Best of all, by installing Sartre as editor, they would be calling the government's bluff. It was one thing to arrest a handful of unheralded normalien twenty-somethings. It would be something else entirely to arrest a world-famous writer and Nobel laureate.

Sartre accepted the invitation without hesitation, daring Marcellin to arrest him. He immediately took to the airwaves of Radio Luxembourg to make his case. He pointed out that, as the *La Cause du Peuple*'s new director, he bore as much responsibility as his predecessors, Le Dantec and Le Bris. His intention was to make the interior minister and his accomplices appear as hypocrites and cowards, and thereby to discredit the government. Bold when it came to arresting students, they wilted when it came to acting against a literary celebrity of Sartre's stature.

Sartre was ambivalent about how much of the Gauche prolétarienne's ideological program he should endorse. He initially distributed a press release claiming that by assuming the post of editor, "I affirm my

---

[33] Ibid., 124.

solidarity with all of the [Gauche prolétarienne] actions that . . . will express the violence that really exists today among the masses in order to underline its revolutionary character."[34] A few days later, however, the philosopher decided to hedge his bets. Instead of offering his blanket support for the Maoists' "actions," he more cautiously affirmed his solidarity with their political articles.

Following the arrest of the Gauche prolétarienne leaders, Sartre immediately upped the ante, convening a rally on their behalf at the Mutualité. Along with Simone de Beauvoir and Michel Leiris, he formed the Association of the Friends of *La Cause du Peuple*. More ominously, a shadowy GP "military wing" began to emerge: the self-styled Nouvelle résistance populaire. The name played on the Maoist belief that French society was under the thumb of an "occupation" government; the Maoists believed that they embodied a new "resistance" movement. Then, following Le Dantec's conviction and sentencing in June, Sartre and de Beauvoir staged a brilliant publicity coup: the high-profile public distribution of the banned broadsheet among the *grands boulevards* of Paris. Marcellin, paralyzed with indecision, failed to lift a finger. In the fall, following the arrest of Alain Geismar, another GP stalwart, Sartre assumed the titular reins of yet another Maoist organ, *Tout!*, as in the May 1968 slogan *"Ce que nous voulons: Tout!"* At this point his public visibility began to rival his profile during the Algerian War protests of ten years earlier.

A turning point in the Maoists' public notoriety occurred in the fall of 1970, just prior to Geismar's trial and sentencing. On September 24 the Rolling Stones were slated to perform at a mammoth outdoor venue, the Palais des Sports at the Porte de Versailles. That afternoon a mutual friend facilitated a meeting between Mick Jagger and the Gauche prolétarienne leader Serge July—future publisher of the French daily *Libération*—at the Stones' Paris residence, the upscale Hôtel Crillon, off the Place de la Concorde. That evening, in the middle of the concert the Stones abruptly halted their performance and invited July to address the audience directly. He stepped to the microphone and delivered a moving plea on behalf of the political prisoners throughout

[34] Hamon and Rotman, *Génération* 2:169.

France—Maoist and non-Maoist alike—who had been unfairly incarcerated by Marcellin. July received a standing ovation. By the end of
the evening, the Gauche prolétarienne could add the name of another
convert to their cause: the Rolling Stones' lead vocalist.[35]

The youthful concertgoers proceeded to turn the affair into a celebration of gauchisme. As Mick Jagger belted out the group's trademark
anthem, "Sympathy for the Devil"—which *Le Monde* described as a
"Black Mass"—one hundred militants managed to break through the
police cordon shouting slogans such as "The music of youth belongs to
the young!" and "Free concerts!" According to France's newspaper of
record, show business had found the gauchistes it deserved.[36]

Despite Sartre and company's wholesale skepticism about the repressive nature of "bourgeois justice," the gauchistes did enjoy one notable judiciary success: at Le Dantec's trial, the judge pointedly refused
to ban *La Cause du Peuple* outright. Thereafter, the Interior Ministry
made continual ham-handed efforts to seize the paper as it was produced and distributed.

Thus began an entirely new chapter of Sartre's storied career as an
engaged intellectual. His biographer aptly summarizes these developments: "For two full years Sartre shared the militant life of his new
Maoist comrades and fully lived a new radicalization of his political
activities, wrote articles, demonstrated, testified, occupied factories."[37]
To be sure, the Maoists exploited Sartre as a "shield" to keep the forces
of repression at bay. For his part, the philosopher fed off their youthful
political enthusiasm to revivify, in the autumn of his life, his persona as
an intellectual activist.[38]

---

[35] See the account in *Le combat des détenus politiques* (Paris: François Maspero, 1970).

[36] *Le Monde,* September 24, 1970, 10.

[37] Cohen-Solal, *Sartre*, 475.

[38] On Sartre's motivations for supporting the Gauche prolétarienne, see the testimony of Henri Leclerc, one of the group's defense lawyers: "It's true that [Sartre] became involved with the Gauche prolétarienne because one sensed he wanted to be 'in
the thick of things'—a result of his permanent fear of repeating the political passivity
he manifested during the occupation. The revolution had arrived, and he wanted to
be part of it." Leclerc, *Combat pour la justice*, 154.

With Sartre's involvement, the GP's public visibility skyrocketed. As one commentator has noted, with Sartre at *La Cause du Peuple*'s helm, "There was no longer a day when the Maoists ceased to be the focal point of newspapers, radio, or even . . . television."[39] Within a brief span of time, nearly the entire Parisian intelligentsia became intoxicated with and fascinated by Maoism. Among writers, artists, and intellectuals, Maoism had become radical chic—the political fashion du jour.

POLITICAL MOTIVATIONS

In 1967, a year after Mao had launched the "Great Proletarian Cultural Revolution," Sartre and Simone de Beauvoir undertook a fact-finding trip to China to examine the momentous political transformations firsthand. They came away disappointed. De Beauvoir explains: "Preventing the emergence of a new privileged class, according the masses genuine power, making a complete person out of each individual—I could only support a program phrased in these terms. Still, I could not accord China the same blind confidence that the Soviet Union raised in so many hearts."[40]

Far from being opportunistic, Sartre's Gauche prolétarienne engagement was motivated by revolutionary conviction. From the outset he made it clear that he had not come to the Maoists' defense on purely civil libertarian grounds. By the same token, he never embraced the Maoist worldview in its entirety. Sartre found the Gauche prolétarienne's ideological dogmatism off-putting—reminiscent of precisely those aspects of communism that he had previously found difficult to bear. After the Maoists lied to him about a protest at the Sacré Coeur Basilica that had gone awry, thus placing the aged philosopher in harm's way, he abruptly resigned—only to return to the Maoist fold soon after. He even went on record criticizing *La Cause du Peuple*'s propagandistic

[39] Bourseiller, *Maoïstes*, 127.

[40] De Beauvoir, *All Said and Done*, 415. See de Beauvoir's earlier, guardedly enthusiastic book on China, *La longue marche: Essai sur la Chine* (Paris: Gallimard, 1957).

slant, going so far as to claim that the bourgeois press, despite its lies, contained more "truth" than the Gauche prolétarienne's daily.[41]

What was it, then, that attracted Sartre to gauchisme in its Maoist incarnation? Above all, Sartre admired the Maoists' revolutionary ardor. In an era when the European working class remained complacent and lethargic, the GP activists were able to preserve a measure of insurrectionary élan that had otherwise vanished. It was certainly nowhere to be found among the French Communists, whose amalgam of bureaucratic rigidity and parliamentary conformism had generated widespread disillusionment among former allies such as students and intellectuals.

In Sartre's later political writings, his analysis of "seriality" stressed the need for an external catalyst to bestir the somnambulant and atomized masses. In *Critique of Dialectical Reason,* Sartre portrayed the dilemma of the "serialized," or inertia-prone, group via the example of a discrete agglomeration of persons waiting for a bus:

> Take a grouping of people in the Place Saint-Germain. They are waiting for a bus at a bus stop in front of the church. . . . These people—who may differ greatly in age, sex, class, and social milieu—realize, within the ordinariness of everyday life, the relation of isolation . . . which is characteristic of residents of the big city. . . . We are concerned here with a plurality of isolations: these people do not care about or speak to each other and, in general, they do not look at each other. . . . The intensity of isolation, as a relation of exteriority between the members of a temporary and contingent gathering, expresses *the degree of massification* of the social ensemble.[42]

For Sartre seriality became a metaphor for the lack of social cohesion among oppositional forces and elements in contemporary French soci-

[41] See the interview with Jean-Edern Hallier, "L'ami du peuple," in *L'Idiot International* (September 1970); English translation in "A Friend of the People," by Sartre, in *Between Existentialism and Marxism,* 287. For the Sacré Coeur episode, see de Beauvoir, *Cérémonie des adieux,* 27–28.

[42] Sartre, *Critique of Dialectical Reason,* 256–57.

ety. Conversely, amid the barren political landscape of Gaullist France, Sartre viewed the Gauche prolétarienne as an unparalleled repository of radical contestation.

The Gauche prolétarienne militants understood themselves as populists rather than vanguardists—another quality that Sartre appreciated. Thereby, they sought to fuse Rousseau and Mao. Like the venerable Jean-Jacques, the Maoists believed that people were intrinsically "good." Their mission was to assist the working class in finding its own voice. Consequently, *Cause du Peuple*'s editorial strategy was *autogestionniste*: the majority of articles were written by and for the workers themselves, along with an occasional ideological editorial push from the Gauche prolétarienne leadership. It was in this spirit that Sartre, in a 1972 interview, avowed that one of the chief reasons he was attracted to the Maoists pertained to their conception of "direct democracy."[43] Increasingly, Sartre came to understand that the history of revolutionary struggle was a history of the betrayal of the masses by its leaders. He believed that by blending in with the masses, "traditional intellectuals" could surmount the self-contradictions of a vocation that made knowledge—which was ideally "universal"—serviceable for the ends of a ruling elite.

On several occasions Sartre paused to clarify in some detail the intellectual basis of his engagement for the Maoist cause. He remained convinced that socialism could not be attained by incremental change (a position that he reaffirmed emphatically in his 1973 article "Elections: A Trap for Fools"), which he associated with "revisionism." Sartre admired the Maoists' unbending commitment to revolutionary struggle.[44] The forces of order never hesitated to use repression to safeguard their interests, as the Pompidou government's rather heavy-handed efforts to shut down *La Cause du Peuple* illustrated well. As Sartre remarked on the occasion of Alain Geismar's arrest and trial in 1970: "*La Cause du Peuple*'s task is to show that the violence inflicted on the people in

[43] Sartre, P. Gavi, and P. Victor, *On a raison de se révolter* (Paris: Gallimard, 1974): "It's your conception of direct democracy that seems to me to be the link between you and me."

[44] Sartre, "Elections: A Trap for Fools," in *Life/Situations*, 198–210.

the name of alleged economic imperatives, the subtle but total violence that [workers] endure in factories here . . . all of that is in reality
a form of slavery. There are no legal means or possibilities for reform
to counter this violence. There is only one solution: *popular violence.*"[45]
In Sartre's eyes, revolutionary violence was a case of *défense légitime*, or
justifiable homicide.

Yet, like many twentieth-century Marxists, Sartre's impassioned
commitment to social justice led him to downplay revolutionism's
ills. The manifold injustices of colonialism, along with his frustrations
with the Soviet model, conditioned Sartre's prodigious sympathies for
third worldism—Cuba, the Congo, Vietnam, and so forth. In his optic,
the "wretched of the earth" (Fanon) appeared as the rightful heirs of
Marxism-Leninism—the revolutionary tradition that, in Sartre's view,
the Soviet Union had openly betrayed. The Gauche prolétarienne's
"ultra," pro-Chinese orientation thereby dovetailed with Sartre's own
radical political leanings during the 1960s. To their credit, the GP militants, through their provocations and symbolic actions, struggled at
every turn to keep the spirit of May alive.

Another one of Maoism's outstanding features, in Sartre's view, was
its distinctly "moral" character. As he declared in the preface to a 1972
collection of Maoist texts, "For the Maoists . . . everywhere that revolutionary violence is born among the masses it is immediately and
profoundly *moral*. This is because the workers, who up until that point
have been objects of capitalist authoritarianism, become the subjects *of
their own history*, if only for a moment."[46] Similarly, during May 1968
Sartre had justified student militancy as a species of "counterviolence,"
"not just occasional counterviolence against the police who provoked
them but against an entire society that oppresses them."[47] Thereby, Sartre reprised a rather questionable—and, it must be said, morally ob-
tuse—position he had first developed in his various texts in support of
third worldism during the 1950s and 1960s. Sartre argued that whereas

[45] Cited in Bourseiller's *Maoïstes*, 158–59; emphasis added.
[46] Sartre, "The Maoists in France," in *Life/Situations*, 169; italics added.
[47] Sartre, "Les Bastilles de Raymond Aron," *Le Nouvel Observateur*, June 19, 1968, 26.

bourgeois violence was repressive, violence on the part of the oppressed constituted a salutary act of self-affirmation.[48] Drawing on the theoretical framework he had developed in *Critique of Dialectical Reason*, Sartre held that underclass violence offered a surefire counterweight to "seriality," or proletarian atomization. It was during such moments of sublime revolutionary upsurge that the working class attained a level of fraternity approximating "class consciousness." In this way, argued Sartre, the proletariat ceased being an object of oppression and, for the first time, became the subject of its own history.

ROBESPIERRE'S GHOST

Sartre's equation of violence with morality—his conviction that violence is regenerative and, as such, a precondition for a reborn humanity—highlights some fundamental problems with his existential phenomenology and with the French revolutionary tradition more generally. Heretofore, Sartre's most unambiguous, as well as troubling, attempt to link violence and morality was his inflammatory preface to Frantz Fanon's *The Wretched of the Earth*.

Sartre wrote the preface at the pinnacle of the Algerian conflict and while Fanon himself, at the height of his capacities, was tragically dying of leukemia. Sartre employed the full range of his considerable rhetorical gifts to vindicate FLN violence as a pivotal act of anticolonial self-affirmation. In terms reminiscent of Hegel's dialectic of master and slave in *Phenomenology of Spirit*, Sartre proposed that for the colonized, the sole path toward self-realization lay in a sanguinary uprising against their oppressors. Having served as the object or target of colonial violence, the native, in Sartre's view, has no choice but to repay his oppressor in kind. Only by annihilating the colonizer, Sartre contended, might the colonized accomplish two worthy ends: free herself from the stultifying psychology of oppression—conducive only to a passive adaptation to colonial circumstances, or "collaboration"—and facilitate her passage to

---

[48] See the essays collected in Sartre's *Colonialism and Neocolonialism*.

fully human status. For Sartre violence on the part of the oppressed was justifiable insofar as it exemplified "counterviolence": violence whose aim is to cast off oppression or domination. Since violence dates from the dawn of history, it would be hypocritical, contended Sartre, for the repressed to forswear such means, distasteful though they may be. It is, he claimed, virtually the only means at their disposal.

For these reasons, in Sartre's view—and as problematic as it may seem in retrospect—violence and rebirth are integrally related. In *The Wretched of the Earth*, Fanon had praised violence as a "cleansing force." Violence emancipated the native, Fanon contended, from his "inferiority complex" and thereby freed him from a mentality of paralysis that was conducive only to "despair and inaction."[49] Echoing Fanon, Sartre declared in his controversial preface: "To shoot down a European is to kill two birds with one stone, to destroy an oppressor and the man he oppresses at the same time: there remain a dead man, and a free man."[50]

At approximately the same time, Sartre had celebrated the Cuban Revolution as an example of "happiness that had been attained by violence." According to Simone de Beauvoir, during his 1960 trip to Cuba Sartre realized the truth of Fanon's claim that "it is only in violence that the oppressed can realize their human status."[51] That the "counterviolence" Sartre had endorsed might metamorphose into a new form of tyranny or oppression was a prospect that the philosopher inexplicably refused to contemplate.

Strangely, Sartre's endorsement of Fanon's arguments abstracted entirely from the political specificity of the Algerian revolt. His infatuation with violence ruled out the prospect that perhaps a negotiated settlement to the conflict might be more conducive to a peaceable and democratic Algerian future. Instead, it was as though Sartre, in a manner consistent with the existential ethics of his early philosophy, had made an a priori moral decision or commitment. His claims have the

[49] Fanon, *Wretched of the Earth*, 73.

[50] Sartre, preface to Fanon's *Wretched of the Earth*. In a 1973 interview, Sartre reaffirmed his belief in the necessity of revolutionary violence, observing that the French Revolution had failed because the Jacobins had refused to kill enough people.

[51] De Beauvoir, *Force of Circumstance*, 503, 606.

quality of a Kantian, "transcendental deduction." It was as though he was trying to legitimate a new categorical imperative appropriate to an age of anticolonial collective struggle—as the German philosopher Ernst Bloch once put it, Bolshevism as a "categorical imperative with revolver in hand."[52] In Sartre's view, negotiations and compromise were distasteful atavisms of bourgeois parliamentarism. Sartre preferred to follow the heady logic of third-world revolutionism through to the very end.

The seeds for Sartre's political radicalism had been sown in *Critique of Dialectical Reason*. There Sartre attributed the problems of class society and social injustice to the phenomenon of scarcity (*rareté*). However, in addition to such historical considerations, there arise, in Sartre's view, adverse circumstances that are endemic to group dynamics, namely the group's ontological tendency to degenerate into "seriality"; its inclination to squander its revolutionary élan and to congeal into something reified and inert—a thing.

Just how wedded Sartre remained to the logic of revolutionism is evident from an examination of the historical examples he employs in *Critique* to illustrate his claims concerning the group's inertial depletion or seriality. He begins with the dawn of the modern revolutionary era, the storming of the Bastille. This violent revolutionary upsurge vis-à-vis a common enemy, in Sartre's view, unites the heretofore centrifugally dispersed group, turning it instead into a "fused group," a "group-in-fusion." For Sartre, the storming of the Bastille exemplified what the writer André Malraux had described in *Man's Hope* as the Apocalypse: "the dissolution of the series into a fused group." As Sartre, quoting an eyewitness account from *L'Ami du Roi*, explains: "By evening Paris was a new city. Regular cannon shots reminded the people to be on their guard. And added to the noise of the cannon there were bells sounding a continuous alarm. The sixty churches where the residents had gathered were overflowing with people. Everyone there was an orator."[53]

Sartre's glowing depiction of the fused group is of a piece with his enduring revolutionary romanticism. In contrast to the serialized

[52] Bloch, *Geist der Utopie*, 242.
[53] Sartre, *Critique of Dialectical Reason*, 357–58.

group, the fused group is engaged, energetic, and heroic. The problem, however, is that in Sartre's social ontology, it becomes extremely difficult, if not impossible, for the fused group to maintain its revolutionary zeal beyond this initial moment of insurrectionary fervor. Existentially and phenomenologically, the group is fated to relapse into serialilty— the lax atomism of the dissociated group.

For the revolutionary project to be maintained, the group must somehow be reenergized. At this point in *Critique* Sartre comes dangerously close to embracing terror as an ideological counterweight to the problems of scarcity and the serialized group. At one juncture Sartre defines terror positively as "common freedom violating necessity."[54] Here, "necessity" assumes the role of a stand-in for scarcity and the "practico-inert"—the irremediable entropic pull of the in-itself, or things. In Sartre's view, terror represents "*justified violence against the practico-inert.*"[55] "The new statute of totalization is Terror," claims Sartre. "Terror is jurisdiction: through the mediation of all, everyone agrees with everyone else that the permanent foundation of every freedom should be the violent negation of necessity, that is to say, that, in everyone, freedom as a common structure is the permanent violence of the individual freedom of alienation."[56] Upon reading these sentences, one would be hard-pressed to disagree with Raymond Aron's verdict that Sartre risks amalgamating a philosophy of human liberation with a philosophy of violence.[57]

To offset the temptations and risks of group depletion, Sartre celebrates the benefits of the revolutionary "pledge," or "oath"—*le*

---

[54] Ibid., 430. For an excellent discussion of this problem in Sartre's work, see Santoni, *Sartre on Violence.*

[55] Sartre, *Critique of Dialectical Reason*, 432; emphasis added.

[56] Ibid., 441.

[57] Raymond Aron, *History and the Dialectic of Violence*, trans. Barry Cooper (New York: Harper and Row, 1973), 160. Following the May uprising, which Aron famously belittled as a "psychodrama," Sartre filed an article with *Le Nouvel Observateur* (June 19, 1968), "Les Bastilles de Raymond Aron," ungenerously suggesting that Aron be deprived of his right to teach, since in his classes he merely recycled old lecture notes dating from the 1930s. See the account of their rivalry in Drake's *Intellectuals and Politics*, 135.

serment. The oath forcibly binds individual members to the group and its goals—on pain of death. As Sartre explains, the oath is "a set of real means (accepted for everyone by all) of establishing in *the group a reign of absolute violence over the members.* . . . To swear is to say, as a common individual: *you must kill me if I secede.*"[58] Here Sartre's belated emulation of the French Resistance (his own activities on behalf of the Resistance were halfhearted and uneventful) surfaces. One can almost imagine the philosopher staring admiringly at Jacques-Louis David's celebrated ode to republican virtue, *The Oath of the Horatii,* conveniently located in the Louvre. It seems that for Sartre almost any act that contributed to the goal of combating scarcity and surmounting oppression qualified as "moral." Hence his disturbing conclusion that "Terror" produces "fraternity." Fraternity, writes Sartre, is "*violence . . . affirming itself as a bond of immanence through positive reciprocities.*"[59]

At the dawn of political Jacobinism, Robespierre famously decreed that under revolutionary circumstances, "terror" was a manifestation of "virtue." The ability to combine the two was, Robespierre believed, the essence of revolutionary government. "Terror," declared Robespierre, "is nothing other than justice, prompt, severe, inflexible; it is therefore an emanation of virtue."[60] The Jacobin leader's lieutenant, Louis-Antoine Saint-Just, celebrated an analagous linkage between "virtue" and "crime."[61] Only were this association maintained could revolutions produce the dramatic and expansive historical tableaux they were destined to engender. Only then could they imprint a permanent and vivid effect on the minds of future generations.

Sartre identified profoundly with this Jacobin lineage and tried to adapt his later political philosophy to suit it. In many respects, he merely transposed the outsize voluntarism of his early philosophy—the

[58] Sartre, *Critique of Dialectical Reason,* 430–31; emphasis added.

[59] Ibid., 43. Sartre goes on to observe: Terror "is the reciprocal translucidity of common individuals . . . ; no 'milieu' is *warmer* than an authoritarian party which is constantly subject to external threats."

[60] Robespierre, "Sur les principes de morale politique qui doivent guider la Convention," in *Ecrits,* 300.

[61] Saint-Just, *Œuvres complètes,* 969: "Nothing resembles virtue more than a great crime."

celebration of the *Pour-Soi,* or "consciousness," in *Being and Nothingness*—
to the collectivist standpoint of the revolutionary class or group in *Critique*.[62] During a 1973 interview, at the height of his activities in support
of the Gauche prolétarienne, he offered the following unflinching endorsement of the Jacobins' sanguinary political legacy:

> In a revolutionary country, when the bourgeoisie has been driven
> from power, those who foment uprisings or conspiracies deserve
> the punishment of death. Not that I would feel the least anger
> toward them. Reactionaries naturally act in their own interest.
> But a revolutionary regime must eliminate a certain number of
> individuals who threaten it; and I see no means but death. One
> can always get out of prison. The revolutionaries of 1793 probably did not kill enough and therefore unintentionally served the
> return to order and then the Restoration.[63]

If Sartre's later philosophical radicalism ran aground with the problem
of the serialized group, the epistemological seeds of this failing may be
traced to the existential phenomenology of *Being and Nothingness*. In
essence, Sartre's philosophical framework was incapable of conceptualizing solidarity or human intersubjectivity. In Sartre's view the Other,
instead of being a fraternal spirit, immediately sets limits upon one's
freedom. In Sartre's optic, intersubjectivity, instead of being a process
of mutual recognition, is inherently adversarial. Thus Sartre cynically
viewed intersubjectivity, à la Kojève—or à la Kojève's Hegel—as an
unremitting struggle unto death.[64] Similarly, for Sartre, the Other is an
antagonistically disposed consciousness—the potential negation of my
existence—that confronts me with the "permanent possibility of being

---

[62] For a comprehensive critique of Sartre's epistemological and political voluntarism, see Merleau-Ponty, "Sartre and Ultra-Bolshevism," in *Adventures of the Dialectic,* 95–202.

[63] Sartre, "On Maoism: An Interview," trans. Robert D'Amico, *Telos* 16 (Fall 1973): 98.

[64] Kojève, *Introduction to the Reading of Hegel,* 7: "To speak of the origin of Self-Consciousness is necessarily to speak of the fight to the death for recognition."

non-human."[65] To quote the oft-cited conclusion of *No Exit:* "L'enfer, c'est les autres" (Hell is other people). Here the problem is that Sartre's social ontology is devoid of a positive sense or conception of human interconnectedness. Little wonder, then, that in *Critique* Sartre's view of the human group founders on the problem of seriality, or group implosion. His combative understanding of intersubjectivity in fact left him with little choice.

"POLITICAL POWER GROWS OUT OF THE BARREL OF A GUN"

Sartre appreciated the fact that, through their actions, the Maoists, who admired the Great Helmsman's maxim "Political power grows out of the barrel of a gun," sought to keep the flame of revolutionism alive.[66] As he observes, "The [Maoist] militants, with their anti-authoritarian *praxis*, appear to be the only group capable of adapting new forms of class struggle in a period of organized capitalism."[67] Sartre also mused that from an autobiographical standpoint, the Maoists' attitudes reminded him of the ethical voluntarism of his early philosophy. He regretted that he had compromised his youthful moralism for the sake of "political realism" during his pro-Moscow, fellow-traveling phase. (This period lasted roughly from the early 1950s until the 1968 Warsaw Pact Soviet invasion of Prague. In *The Ghost of Stalin*, Sartre offered a qualified criticism of the 1956 Soviet invasion of Hungary, one that left room for a future political alliance.) By casting his lot with the GP activists, he felt he had recaptured aspects of the "philosophy of freedom" of his pre-Communist period.[68]

The Maoists appeared to offer Sartre a solution to a dilemma he had been wrestling with for years: what role should the intellectual

[65] Sartre, *Critique of Dialectical Reason*, 697.

[66] Mao's claim, first made at the plenary session of the Sixth Congress of the Central Committee of the Chinese Communist Party in 1938, can be found in *Selected Works* 2:272.

[67] Sartre, "Maoists in France," 171.

[68] See the discussion in Sartre et al., *On a raison de se révolter*, 68.

play in an era of political transition? In his eyes the Leninist vanguard political model had been wholly discredited. Twentieth-century history was littered with instances of leaderships' betrayal of the working class's revolutionary political aspirations: most recently, with the French Communist Party's signing of the Grenelle Accords, which brought the May events crashing to a halt, followed by the Soviets' brutal suppression of the Prague Spring later in the year.[69]

The Gauche prolétarienne had imbibed the populist ethos of the Cultural Revolution: the idea that the Red Guards had risen "spontaneously" to purge a conservative Chinese Communist Party leadership that had become unresponsive to the needs of the masses. In Sartre's view the claim that intellectuals understood the march of history better than the masses had been discredited time and again. In solidarity with his Gauche prolétarienne allies, Sartre came to believe that "truth comes from the people." As he explains, "It is no longer a question of giving ideas to the masses, but of following their movement, going to search them out at their source and expressing them more clearly, if they consent to it. In *Libération* [the independent daily that Sartre had cofounded], for example, I can present an idea which will be both the group's and mine. But I wouldn't dream of writing a book which will determine everything from beginning to end."[70]

Sartre elaborated on these ideas in a 1970 interview, in which he explained that the May events had transformed his appreciation of the intellectual's role. One of the political conclusions he reached was that the May revolt had rendered anachronistic the traditional notion of the intellectual—from Voltaire to Emile Zola to Julien Benda—as the guardian of universal values. The May uprising had demonstrated that the students and workers were fully capable of articulating their own political claims and demands. Moreover, during May the intellectual mandarinate had functioned not as an avant-garde but as a derrière-garde. As Sartre observes, when

[69] For Sartre's analysis of the Soviet invasion of Prague, see "Czechoslovakia: The Socialism That Came in From the Cold," in *Between Existentialism and Marxism*, 84–117. Also see Grémion, *Paris-Prague*.
[70] Sartre, "On Maoism," 100.

May 1968 happened . . . I understood that what the young were putting into question was not just capitalism, imperialism, the system, etc., but those of us who pretended to be against all that as well. We can say that from 1940 to 1968 I was a left-wing intellectual [un intellectuel de gauche] and from 1968 on I became a leftist intellectual [un intellectuel gauchiste]. The difference is one of action. A leftist intellectual is one who realizes that being an intellectual exempts him from nothing. He forsakes his privileges, or tries to, in actions.[71]

In "A Plea for Intellectuals" (1966)—his so-called Tokyo Lectures—Sartre had stressed the contradictory nature of the intellectual's vocation. On the one hand, the intellectual, in good Dreyfusard fashion, seeks to ally herself with the universal values of the good, the just, and the true. Yet, by the same token, the distortions of class society systematically prevent her from actualizing such values.

Circa 1970, Sartre's Maoist involvements caused him to reappraise the intellectual's vocation once again. He concluded that left-wing intellectuals would never resolve the contradiction between their universalistic aspirations and their vocational particularism, which necessitated their loyalty to the status quo. Thus, in the post-May years, he viewed intellectuals as the quintessential embodiment of the Hegelian "unhappy consciousness." Otherwise put, "bad faith"—another quintessential Sartrean epithet—was their essential lot. As a group, intellectuals would never overcome or surmount the ontological contradiction that suffused the essence of their being. Hence, as a caste, intellectuals were "impossible"—just as in Being and Nothingness Sartre had declared that "man" was "impossible," a "useless passion." There, Sartre had defined "human reality" elliptically as "the being which is what it is not and is not what it is." He concluded, with a nihilistic flourish, by observing that "it amounts to the same thing whether one gets drunk or is a leader of nations."[72] Sartre's turn to Marxism was a

[71] Sartre, "Sartre Accuses the Intellectuals of Bad Faith," interview with John Gerassi, New York Times Magazine, October 17, 1971, 118.

[72] Sartre, Being and Nothingness, 797.

way for him to escape the tendential cynicism of his early existential standpoint. In Sartre's view intellectuals were "impossible" insofar as the unbridgeable chasm between their universal pretensions and their class indebtedness meant that they continually dwelled in "bad faith."

Sartre was prone to acute bouts of bourgeois self-hatred. By his own admission, he had been born into a petit-bourgeois social milieu. At the height of his political radicalism, he realized that he could not change his skin. Such feelings resurfaced during his pro-Chinese phase, as Sartre summarily concluded that the traditional vocation of the intellectual as the bearer of universal truth had been rendered obsolete. In Sartre's view, becoming a "leftist intellectual"—an *intellectuel gauchiste* as opposed to an *intellectuel de gauche*—meant bidding adieu to the traditional intellectual and her inadequacies.

Ironically, it was at the height of his pro-Chinese dalliances that Sartre published his most "disengaged" and scholastic work, *The Family Idiot*: an exhaustive, three-volume biographical study of Flaubert. In studying Flaubert, Sartre posed the question, to what extent can we know a man? Sartre employed the "progressive-regressive" method he had utilized earlier in *Critique of Dialectical Reason* in order to evaluate the social and psychological determinants of Flaubert's character. As Sartre explained: "I would like my readers to be able to feel, understand, and know Flaubert's character both as totally individual and totally representative of his times."[73] Nominally, Sartre claimed that he had chosen Flaubert as his subject insofar as the writer's aestheticist conception of the literary vocation was the diametrical opposite of Sartre's own notion of engagement. Yet, was it merely a coincidence that France's greatest twentieth-century writer devoted nearly twenty years of study (Sartre had begun his preliminary sketches for the Flaubert book in the mid-1950s) to France's greatest nineteenth-century writer? Clearly, a profound measure of self-identification was at work in Sartre's choice of Flaubert as his subject. In attempting to decipher the key elements of Flaubert's developmental trajectory, Sartre was simultaneously trying to gain insight into his own life course.

---

[73] Sartre, *Situations,* vol. 9, *Mélanges* (Paris: Editions Galllimard, 1972), 114.

"IT IS RIGHT TO REBEL"

Maoism as political fashion expressed itself in a number of ways. In an effort to capitalize on the general fascination with gauchisme, the prestigious firm of Gallimard, which had been Sartre's publisher since the 1930s, commissioned the philosopher to edit a new series, La France sauvage. Sartre complied with alacrity. The series began with a volume of political conversations among Sartre, Pierre Victor, and Libération journalist Philippe Gavi, On a raison de se révolter (It Is Right to Rebel).[74] Sartre began by recapitulating his own political itinerary: from his studied apoliticism of the 1930s, to his fleeting Resistance activities during the German occupation, to his status as a Communist fellow traveler during the early 1950s, to his gradual disillusionment with orthodox Marxism during the 1960s. Sartre admitted that he had always found the Communists' ideological rigidity distasteful. It sat poorly with his own philosophy of freedom. Their "style," lifeless and dour, which reeked of repression, said it all. Yet, as Sartre observed in retrospect—thereby revealing his own political naïveté—he had always justified his status as a fellow traveler insofar as he viewed the PCF as the sole legitimate representative of the French working classes.[75] How wrong this assumption turned out to be.

Casting one's lot with the Communists offered certain political advantages. The world was neatly compartmentalized into the forces of good and evil: the working class and its representatives on one side versus the bourgeoisie on the other. However, in the aftermath of the May events, as gauchisme took hold of the French political imaginary, the idea of what it meant to be on the Left seemingly went into free

[74] The phrase "It is right to rebel [against reactionaries]" is taken from an open letter Mao wrote at the onset of the Cultural Revolution. Mao's letter is translated in Mao Tse-tung Unrehearsed, ed. Stuart Schram (Harmondsworth: Penguin, 1974), 260–61.

Mao, "A Letter to the Red Guards of Tsinghua University Middle School," in Mao's Selected Works, xx.

[75] See Sartre et al., On a raison de se révolter, 32: "If you put yourself in relation to the largest working class party in France at the time . . . it was because you wanted to enter into contact with the working class."

fall. The revolt's Dionysian aspects—revolution as political struggle and
as festival—suggested that the meaning of socialism had been radically transformed. It could no longer be equated with "socializing the
means of production," a recipe that, to judge by historical experience,
yielded only new forms of repression. The tenor and portent of revolt
had changed dramatically as a new array of radical "cultural" demands
emerged. Feminists, gay rights activists, prisoners, and immigrants all
sought out the limelight of publicity in order to press their demands for
recognition. In 1970 one branch of the Gauche prolétarienne split off to
form Vive la révolution!, abandoning the Maoists' *ouvriériste* orientation
to pursue the demands of libidinal politics full-time.

Though aged, Sartre refused to shy away from these new forms of
revolt. He was a leading spirit behind the formation of Libération, an
alternative press bureau. The name alluded to the gauchiste conviction that there were cogent political parallels between the occupation
years (1940–44) and de Gaulle's quasi-benign eleven-year presidential
dictatorship. Its founders sought to model the daily after a Resistance
organ of the same name that originated in 1941. During its early years,
Libé (as it was known to aficionados) was nothing if not unorthodox.
One commentator has described it: "The paper printed its columns and
headings upside down, perfumed itself with incense when the pope
came to France, left copyright notices off photos, fabricated election
results (Mao: 0.3 percent) and allowed itself to be overrun by the notorious 'Notes from the Compositor.'"[76] The leftists' pronounced—to be
sure, quasi-delusory—identification with the Resistance suffused virtually all their activities. Hence the name of the GP's so-called military
wing, led by Olivier Rolin: the Nouvelle résistance populaire.[77] Sartre
and his fellow gauchistes felt that one could not trust the mainstream
press to report the "truth" about the proliferation of new social struggles that had emerged in the post-May period.[78] They believed that it

[76] Martel, *The Pink and the Black*, 88.
[77] See Rolin's recently published fictionalized account of these years, *Paper Tiger*.
[78] As Simone de Beauvoir explains: "I . . . realized how necessary it was that the
left-wing press, persecuted by those in power, should exist: no one else troubles to give
a truthful, detailed account of the workers' state, their daily life and their struggles.

was essential that such information reach the masses. To jump-start the project financially, Sartre generously donated the entire advance he had received from Gallimard for *On a raison de se révolter,* some thirty thousand francs. Under the leadership of ex-GP militant Serge July, *Libération* grew to become France's major left-wing mass circulation daily.

FROM MAO TO MOSES

One of the strangest subplots of Sartre's Gauche prolétarienne involvement concerns his relationship with Pierre Victor. Victor was the nom de guerre of Benny Lévy: Egyptian-born Jew, political firebrand, and *normalien* who, in May 1968's aftermath, became the Gauche prolétarienne's de facto leader. Among his *confrères,* Victor was perceived as Saint-Just reincarnate: youthful, articulate, vigorous, and possessed of a ruthless political will. According to the testimony of his fellow gauchistes, time and again Victor was willing to push the GP in directions that others feared to tread. Here, one of the ironies is that because Victor lacked French citizenship, he participated in few of the political "actions" he had conceived and masterminded. Arrest would have meant certain deportation.

In general, Sartre famously preferred the company of women to men. In this respect, his relationship with Victor was exceptional. Sartre was seduced by Victor's militancy as well as his ample political charisma.[79] Reflecting on their friendship in a 1977 interview, Sartre commented on Victor's political intelligence, which, he observed, was infinitely superior to that of the Communists he had known. Moreover, Victor displayed a rare willingness to place his own political positions at

---

The *gauchiste* papers do try to tell the workers about what is happening within their own class—a subject that the bourgeois press either ignores or misrepresents"; *All Said and Done,* 443. See also Lallement, *Libé;* and Ian Birchall, "Sartre and Gauchisme," *Journal of European Studies* 19 (1) (1989): 21–53.

[79] See the testimony of Badiou, "Roads to Renegacy," 125–33: "[Victor] was the GP's charismatic leader, and on top of that [he] had been anointed by Sartre. He had a great capacity for intellectual seduction, as well as being very forceful, and the combination captivated a number of activists before seducing Sartre."

risk—a lack of dogmatism that the philosopher found refreshing. Unlike Sartre's other male friends, in conversation Victor also seemed
ready and willing to stray from explicitly political themes, a trait that
Sartre referred to as Victor's "feminine" side.[80] In many respects, Sartre
viewed Victor as the son he never had.

One of the pivotal events that precipitated gauchisme's collapse was
the PLO's attack—viewed around the world in "real time"—at the
1972 Olympic Games, resulting in the deaths of eleven Israeli athletes.
The episode placed Sartre in a difficult position. On the one hand, he
had been a longtime champion of Israel. Among a younger generation
of French Jews, his 1946 book on the Jewish question (*Réflexions sur
la question juive,* translated into English as *Anti-Semite and Jew*) had a
transformative effect as a bold summons to Jewish self-awareness.[81] By
the same token, on previous occasions—most notably at the time of
the Algerian War—Sartre had sought to provide a philosophical justification of terrorism when practiced by the oppressed. Consequently,
Sartre presented a qualified defense of the PLO attacks.

> Those who, by affirming that Israel is a sovereign state, believe
> that the Palestinians have the right to national sovereignty and
> that the Palestinian question is fundamental must recognize that
> the politics of the Israeli [political] establishment is literally in-
> sane and deliberately refuses all possibility of solution to the
> problem. It is therefore politically justifiable to say that a state of
> war exists between Israel and the Palestinians. In this war, the
> only option that is available to the Palestinians is terrorism. It is
> a terrible weapon, but the impoverished and oppressed have no
> other means at their disposal; and French men and women who
> approved of the FLN's terrorism when it was used against the
> French cannot help but approve of, in turn, the Palestinians' ter-
> rorist actions. This abandoned, betrayed, and exiled people can

---

[80] "Pouvoir et liberté: Actualité de Sartre," *Libération,* January 6, 1977, 11; see also
de Beauvoir, *Cérémonie des adieux,* 54.

[81] See Jean-Paul Sartre, *Réflexions sur la question juive* (Paris: Morihien, 1946). See
also Judaken, *Sartre and the Jewish Question.*

only show its courage and the force of its hatred by organizing lethal attacks.[82]

Sartre had based his response in part on the (as it turned out, erroneous) supposition that the Israeli athletes had perished in a hail of gunfire during the German security forces' ill-conceived rescue attempt. He thus assumed that they had been killed by *German* bullets. However, later evidence made it clear that several of the athletes had been murdered in cold blood during the attack by PLO militants. Yet, apart from the particular circumstances surrounding the Israeli athletes' deaths, Sartre had once again overlooked the crucial moral and legal distinction between combatants and noncombatants. Thus, even if one granted for the sake of argument the existence of a "state of war" between Palestinians and Israelis (an assumption that, once made, de facto precluded the prospect of a negotiated settlement), such an avowal would, neither morally nor according to the strictures of international law, underwrite attacks against innocent civilians.

On this occasion Sartre outflanked his Gauche prolétarienne comrades to the left. The GP, proceeding more moderately, pursued a two-pronged approach. On the one hand, it ratcheted up its criticisms of Israel's unjust occupation of the Palestinian lands. On the other hand, its so-called armed wing, the Nouvelle résistance populaire, released a statement pointedly distancing the GP from the Munich massacre. The GP statement specifically contended that an ethic of armed struggle prohibited attacks against innocent civilians. ("The fundamental principle of guerrilla [warfare] is that one only attacks direct enemies of the people. . . . [Hence] one must distinguish between Israelis in general and the army, the police, or the Israeli occupation administration")[83] Conversely, Sartre, who had explored the ethics of violence in his theoretical writings, felt that it would be inconsistent to sanction FLN violence in the case of Algeria while denying the same means to the Palestinians.

---

[82] Sartre, "A propos de Munich," *La Cause du Peuple/J'Accuse* 29, October 15, 1972. See also Auron, *Les juifs de l'extrême gauche*, 236.

[83] Sartre, *La Cause du Peuple*, September 14, 1972.

When the Maoist movement unexpectedly disintegrated circa 1973, Sartre installed Victor as his personal secretary. In doing so, his motivations were both intellectual and practical. On the one hand, Sartre valued Victor as a politically astute interlocutor. By the same token, since Victor's student visa had elapsed, his position with Sartre saved him from having to return to his native Egypt. In 1976, as Victor's immigration status grew precarious, Sartre wrote directly to President Valéry Giscard d'Estaing requesting that he intervene to resolve the problem. Sartre, who had recently gone blind, pleaded that without Victor's assistance he would be unable to finish his work. Giscard obliged, claiming that although he viewed Victor's prior left-wing political dalliances with disdain, the importance of Sartre's being able to complete his work trumped all other considerations.

Victor's growing influence over Sartre began to provoke jealousies among the other member's of Sartre's "family," above all the staff of *Les Temps Modernes* and Simone de Beauvoir. In her affecting portrait of Sartre's final years, *La cérémonie des adieux*, de Beauvoir went so far as to accuse Victor of "le détournement du vieillard," that is, using his undue influence over Sartre to exploit the aging philosopher for his own political ends. The ends in question pertained to Victor's burgeoning interest in orthodox Judaism. Conversely, Sartre's adopted daughter, Arlette Elkaim-Sartre, felt compelled to publish an open letter attesting to the genuineness of Sartre's belated interest in themes pertaining to Jewish messianism in the pages of *Libération*, the French daily that Sartre cofounded.[84]

---

[84] "Polémique: 'La cérémonie des adieux,' open letter to Simone de Beauvoir from Arlette Elkaim-Sartre," *Libération*, December 3, 1981, 26:

> When Sartre and I were alone together, I tried to be his eyes as much as possible. As I did with other interviews of the same period, I therefore read and reread their [Sartre and Lévy's] dialogue to him, repeating word after word as well as the whole text several times, to the point of irritating him, aware that certain phrases of his would be surprising. Sartre added and corrected as he wished. He thought that he would explain himself in greater depth in their future book. I grant that my rereadings didn't achieve the intimacy that one has with one's own text when one reads it oneself, but how could that be helped?

Following the Gauche prolétarienne's implosion, Victor immersed himself in the study of the Talmud. Thereby, Victor, who soon abandoned his nom de guerre for his original name, Benny Lévy, completed a strange intellectual odyssey "from Mao to Moses."[85] Three out of four leaders of the May movement—Daniel Cohn-Bendit, Alain Geismar, and Alain Krivine—had been Jews.[86] For several ex-gauchistes, reconnecting with their long-repressed Jewish origins became a means of providing meaning and orientation once the wave of left-wing revolutionary fervor had subsided. Given the persecutions their families had endured at the hands of the Vichy regime, the former leftists felt they were entitled to recognition, not just as citizens but also as Jews. In this way, several prominent ex-gauchistes metamorphosed from "Jewish radicals" to "radical Jews."

Among left-wing intellectuals, one of the key texts of the Jewish spiritual renaissance was Sartre's *Anti-Semite and Jew*: the philosopher's plea, made in the long shadow cast by the Holocaust, for Jewish self-assertion. Sartre contended that when confronted with anti–Semitism, Jews must refrain from internalizing their would-be persecutors' venomous taunts and insults. Instead, they must all the more emphatically assert and project their identity as Jews. In *The Imaginary Jew*, the philosopher Alain Finkielkraut recalls how Sartre's 1946 essay provided him with a paradigm through which he could think through problem of Jewish authenticity—a problem concerning which French republican intellectual traditions were otherwise silent. As Finkielkraut recalls, "Since I was an admirer of Sartre . . . with what gluttonous pleasure did I avail myself of the vocabulary he bestowed upon my existence. . . . With unimpeachable rigor he told me that I was an

---

[85] See Auron, *Les juifs d'extrême gauche*. See also Friedlander, *Vilna on the Seine*. Toward the end of his life, Lévy wrote a fascinating book—part memoir, part political treatise—on the relationship between politics and religion; see Benny Lévy, *Le meurtre du pasteur: Critique de la vision politique du monde* (Paris: Grasset/Verdier, 2002). For a discussion, see Alexis Lacroix, "Comment passe-t-on de la radicalité politique à l'engagement prophétique: Benny Lévy, de Mao à Moïse," *Le Figaro*, February 14, 2002. See also Judaken, "'To Be or Not to Be French,'" 3–21.

[86] The one exception was Jacques Sauvageot, head of UNEF, or National Association of French Students.

authentic Jew, that I assumed my condition and that courage, even heroism were required. . . . The enchantment of Sartre's prose filled the gap between what I imagined myself to be and the existence I actually led."[87]

Once Victor abandoned left-wing politics, his philosophical allegiances also changed. His interest in Sartre's thought waned. Henceforth he became a disciple of the arch anti-Sartrean Emmanuel Levinas. Whereas the key concept of Levinas's thought is the Other (*l'autrui*), to whom I am (to employ Levinas's idiom) infinitely indebted, in Sartre's philosophy the Other constitutes a permanent threat to the autonomy of the for-itself (Pour-soi). Victor attests:

> I had two great philosophical moments in my life: the first was with Sartre and then Levinas when I abandoned the Left in 1973–75. . . . After a long series of unfruitful attempts to articulate the questions raised by my political experience, including a rereading with Sartre of all his works—after all that, thanks to encountering the works of Levinas, I began to suspect that there was something decisive, something essential, about my existential constitution as a Jew.[88]

Levinas made a deep impression on Victor insofar as "in politics one does not speak very often about the Other; the 'masses,' perhaps, but that's all."[89] In retrospect, Victor felt that he and his fellow revolutionaries had erred by succumbing to an ethos of political messianism—a misguided effort to realize the kingdom of heaven in the here and now. Conversely, the Almighty's dignity lies precisely in its alterity, or transcendence, vis-à-vis the prosaic concerns of creaturely life. Hence, for Victor, Levinas's doctrines served as an important corrective to gauchisme's political excesses. Moreover, in a certain sense, Levinas's notion

---

[87] Finkielkraut, *Imaginary Jew*, 9. See also Judaken, *Sartre and the Jewish Question*.
[88] Lévy, "From Maoism to Talmud," 48–53.
[89] Ibid.

of the Other qua infinite transcendence is a theological refiguring of the French notion of *fraternité*.[90]

HOPE NOW

The controversy over Victor's influence on Sartre was rekindled at the time of the philosopher's death in 1980. A few weeks later, Victor/Lévy published *Hope Now*, a series of interviews in which Sartre, who had been a lifelong atheist, uncharacteristically professed his affinities with Judaism—clearly a result of Victor's influence. In *Hope Now*, Sartre took stock of the fact that his final wager on an ethics of "engagement," his involvement with the Gauche prolétarienne, had foundered. In the end, the demonstrations, strikes, and factory occupations that were a constant feature of post-May political culture had produced few permanent changes. The political elites who had ruled France since the liberation persisted undisturbed. In his final interview, Sartre detected in the Jewish people certain utopian, ethical virtues he had once attributed to the working class. As Sartre comments, "The Jew lives; he has a destiny. The finality towards which every Jew moves is *to reunite humanity.* . . . It is the end that only the Jewish people [know]. . . . It is the beginning of the existence of men for each other."[91] Under Victor's tutelage,

[90] With the important qualification that in Levinas the relationship between Self and Other is one of *asymmetry* rather than symmetry, or *egalité*. One can never fully do justice to the Other's alterity. See Moyn, *Origins of the Other.*

[91] Sartre-Lévy, *Hope Now*, 52. The authenticity of these interviews has been the subbject of a lively controversy among Sartre's "family." Simone de Beauvoir and the staff of *Les Temps Modernes* came to regard Victor's influence on Sartre as nefarious— "le détournement d'un veilliard," the corruption of an old man—as de Beauvoir once put it. For a fair-minded account of this controversy, see Ronald Aronson's lucid introduction to the *Hope Now* interviews. For another helpful discussion of their place in Sartre's oeuvre, see Jean-Philippe Mathy, "Stumbling toward the Truth," a review of Sartre and Lévy's *Hope Now, Cross Currents* 47 (4) (1997): 544–47. As Mathy observes, *Hope Now* "remains a fascinating testimony to the considerable changes that occurred in French thought in the mid-seventies, and to the way the man who had been the most revered incarnation of the postwar oppositional intellectual dealt with the critical left's ideological and political decline." For a discussion of the *Hope Now*

Sartre seemed on the verge of reevaluating several of the key ideas of
his thought—for example, the primacy of politics—and becoming, à la
Levinas, an "ethicist."

By the mid-1970s Sartre had become blind. His entire relationship to
the outside world was mediated by Victor/Lévy. The two planned to
write an ethics together based on Sartre's renewed interest in the concept of fraternity. But Sartre, who, as we have seen, abused his body
with amphetamines during intensive stretches of work, died in April
1980 before the project could be realized. A crowd of fifty thousand
mourners followed his funeral cortege to the Montparnasse Cemetery.
In the end, Sartre concluded that fraternity could no longer be produced
by "politics." From Robespierre to Lenin to Mao, the political dreams
of the Left had all been stillborn. Its new guarantor was ethics. This
was a remarkable reversion to a Camusian standpoint—one that, by the
same token, also showed traces of Victor/Lévy's "Levinasianism."

Since May 1968, Sartre had cast his lot with gauchisme. But following the Gauche prolétarienne's dissolution in 1973, he was bereft of an
ongoing political project. Thereafter, the GP leadership began to take
stock of its errors. Following the May events, the GP activists had gone
far toward demystifying the sins of political vanguardism—Leninism
and its doubles. But they had yet to systematically probe the excesses
and misdeeds of revolutionism in general. Belatedly, the GP militants
realized that political murder in the name of a left-wing cause was no
better than political murder in the name of a right-wing cause. This was
one of the points that the Munich Olympic massacre had driven home.
Suddenly, the fashionable Maoist slogan "Political power grows out of
the barrel of a gun" assumed an entirely new and sinister meaning.

The GP's internal debates revisited the terms of the tempestuous
encounter between Sartre and Camus during the early 1950s. Whereas
Sartre had wagered on the promises of communism and sought to

<hr>

interviews as they relate to Sartre's earlier "Reflections on the Jewish Question," see
Judaken, Sartre and the Jewish Question, chapter 7, "Sartre's Final Reflections: Intellec-
tual Politics and the Jewish Question." See also the symposium on Hope Now in Sartre
Studies International 4 (2) (1998).

subordinate individual morality to this end, Camus refused to embrace a perspective that sacrificed fundamental ethical precepts to an uncertain utopian political future. However, by the mid-1970s, there were virtually no "Sartreans" left. Nearly everyone had become a Camusian, championing the priority of ethics over politics.[92] In France the hour of the "antitotalitarian moment" had sounded, appropriately heralded by, Alexander Solzhenitsyn's April 1975 appearance on the popular literary talk show *Apostrophes*. Solzhenitsyn's breakthrough book *The Gulag Archipelago* had recently been translated into French. Among French intellectuals, the Soviet dissident was widely feted as "the Dante of our time."[93]

Sartre, too, climbed aboard the antitotalitarian bandwagon, appearing with Raymond Aron at a news conference at the Elysée Palace in an attempt to call attention to the desperate plight of the Vietnamese boat people, who were fleeing persecution at the hands of the recently victorious Communist government. In January 1980, just a few months before his death, Sartre took to the airwaves of Europe I Radio to champion the cause of the Soviet dissident Andrei Sakharov, who was living in internal exile. On the same broadcast Sartre launched an appeal for a boycott of the summer Olympic Games, which were scheduled to take place that year in Moscow.

In the eyes of many observers, the Sartre–Aron initiative symbolized a turning point in the development of French political culture. Ideological concerns had lost their primacy. The Left-Right division that had structured French politics since the Revolution had seemingly

[92] For an excellent account of the Sartre-Camus debate, see Aronson, *Camus and Sartre*. Aronson observes that during the mid-1970s "the 'New Philosophers' appeared on the scene; former student leftists who were searching for the roots of their past mistakes and the century's revolutionary debacles, they self-consciously followed in Camus' footsteps. With the overthrow of Eastern European and then Soviet Communism by their own citizens . . . Camus' conclusions have now become dominant across the political spectrum" (117–18). See also Christofferson, *French Intellectuals against the Left*.

[93] See Bernard-Henri Lévy, *Barbarie à un visage humain* (Paris: Editions Grasset, 1977), 179. For an excellent discussion of Solzhenitsyn's television appearance and its implications, see Chaplin, *Turning on the Mind*, 150–78.

forfeited its paramountcy. Instead, a new humanitarian sensibility pre-
dominated, symbolized by Bernard Kouchner's Médécins sans frontières (Doctors without Borders) and kindred groups.[94]

In many respects, toward the end of his life Sartre had reprised the
vocation of the universal intellectual. Abandoning the posture of the
political militant, or *L'Ami du Peuple* (the title of Jean-Paul Marat's
newspaper published during the French Revolution), the tenor of Sartre's final political interventions more resembled those of Voltaire or
Zola. Once the excesses and delusions of revolutionism had been exposed, French society reappraised the universal intellectual's merits and
worth. Henceforth, the universal intellectual's moral leadership would
embody an indispensable component of the antitotalitarian struggle.
Toward the end of the 1970s, France reinvented the figure of the democratic intellectual. Sartre, although blind and enfeebled, gamely participated in this moment of reinvention.

The wide-ranging conversations between Sartre and Lévy in *Hope Now*
are important insofar as the interlocutors pause to assess the political
significance of gauchisme in its GP incarnation. One of the leitmotifs
concerned the GP's fascination with revolutionary violence as well as
with the quasi-systematic role this fascination had played in Sartre's
own work since the days of the Algerian War. As we have noted, in
Critique of Dialectical Reason, Sartre, keeping faith with political Jacobinism, had held that revolutionary violence possessed certain regenerative and salvific capacities. By the late 1970s, however, this view had
been morally and historically discredited.

Perhaps the final nail in the coffin of third worldism, as well as revolutionism in general, had been the grisly reports concerning the "killing fields" in Cambodia. From 1975 to 1979, Pol Pot and his henchmen
murdered some 1.7 million of their countrymen. Moreover, the Cam-
bodian Communist elite—Khieu Samphan, Ieng Sary, as well as Pol
Pot himself—had learned the Marxist catechism at the finest Parisian universities during their stint as foreign exchange students in the

---

[94] See the interview with Bernard Kouchner in *Le Nouvel Observateur*, November 11, 1979.

early 1950s. As Pol Pot's most faithful lieutenant, Democratic Kampuchea's head of state Khieu Samphan, explained to a French journalist: "Prime Minister Pol Pot and I were profoundly influenced by the
spirit of French thought: by the Age of Enlightenment, of Rousseau and
Montesquieu."[95] Like the philosophes, the Khmer Rouge, too, were
faced with the problem of how to conceptualize the transition from the
ancien régime to a modern nation state. One of Ieng Sary's closest aides,
Soang Sikoeun, recounted Robespierre's intoxicating influence on the
Khmer Rouge elite as follows: "Robespierre's personality impressed
me. His radicalism influenced me a lot. He was incorruptible and intransigent. . . . If you do something, you must do it right through to the
end. You can't make compromises. That was my personal philosophy,
my personal ideology. You must always be on the side of the Absolute—
no middle way, no compromise. You must never do things by halves."[96]

The Khmer Rouge had been backed by the Chinese Communists
and followed the Cultural Revolution's model of brutally consigning
city dwellers to the countryside for purposes of "political reeducation."
Under the influence of Mao Tse-tung Thought, they had systematically recruited followers who were destitute and uneducated—"poor"
and "blank," as the Great Helmsman put it. (As Mao noted, "A sheet
of blank paper carries no burden. The most beautiful characters can be
written on it, the most beautiful pictures painted."[97]) Pol Pot's biographer adumbrates the manifold ideological parallels between the two
revolutionary movements as follows:

The primacy of men over machines; the exaltation of human will
(in China) and "revolutionary consciousness" (in Cambodia); the
pre-eminence of ideology over learning (being "red" rather than

[95] Interview with Khieu Samphan, *Le Monde*, December 31, 1998.

[96] Cited in Eric Weitz's *Century of Genocide: Utopias of Race and Nation* (Princeton:
Princeton University Press, 2003), 147. See also Samantha Power, *Problem from Hell*,
93: "The leaders of the Khmer Rouge, or Red Khmer, had been educated in Paris, studied Maoist thought, and received extensive political and military support from China."

[97] Starr and Dyer, *Post-liberation Works of Mao Tse-tung*, 173; cited in *A Problem from
Hell: America and the Age of Genocide*, by Samantha Power (New York: HarperCollins,
2002), 93.

"expert"); the strategy of using the countryside to surround the city and the need to eliminate the differences between them; the concern to bridge the gulf between mental and manual labor; and the view that revisionism, in the shape of bourgeois thought, grew spontaneously within the Communist movement itself.[98]

With the Khmer Rouge experiment in "peasant communism," the sanguinary legacy of Maoism had come home to roost, and the results were manifestly horrifying.

In discussing these topics, Lévy pursued Sartre with the insatiable zeal of an experienced litigator. At a certain point, the enfeebled philosopher could seemingly absorb no further blows and meekly capitulated. In many respects, for Lévy the dialogue with Sartre was a protracted exercise in self-criticism—a manner of confronting his own troubled political past—and, to be sure, of assuaging his own guilty conscience. As Sartre began speculating about the ethical bases of our common humanity, Lévy rudely reminded him of the redemptory role the philosopher had formerly attributed to revolutionary violence. Sartre, repentant, stated simply: "*I am no longer of that opinion.*"[99] Alluding to the predicament of colonialism, he explained that whereas acts of violence might disrupt a state of enslavement, they were devoid of regenerative properties or capacities. Moreover, he continued, his approbation of violence had been "situational": in the main it pertained to the obdurate stalemate of the Algerian conflict. In light of the intractable dilemmas of colonialism, Sartre could perceive no other solution.

Lévy continued to press. If fraternity is created via the bond of a common enemy, as Sartre had argued in *Critique of Dialectical Reason*, what happens after the enemy has been slain? Do the revolutionists inevitably turn upon each other? Must they unfailingly seek a new enemy?

[98] Short, *Pol Pot*, 300. See also the testimony of Ponchaud, *Cambodia*, 139: "In many respects, [Cambodia's] leaders have followed the Chinese model, as in their return to the land, their will to self-sufficiency, their use of traditional medicine, rigorously egalitarian society, identical positions on questions of foreign policy, and elsewhere."

[99] Sartre and Lévy, *Hope Now*, 92; emphasis added.

Lévy, who dominated the discussions, concluded by suggesting that the "insurrectionary violence" that he and Sartre had endorsed was in fact merely a species of *mob violence*; and that the Jew, who had frequently been the victim of such violence, therefore possessed a unique status qua "witness." Hence, if one wants to undo the evils of revolutionism, Lévy contended, Jewish testimony is indispensable. Sartre could do little more than timorously agree: "I think you are not wrong."[100]

Lévy's disgust with revolutionism was profoundly influenced by the International Left's visceral anti-Zionism in the aftermath of the recent Arab-Israeli wars (the 1967 Six-Day War and the 1973 Yom Kippur War). The controversial UN resolution equating Zionism with racism (it was later repealed) dates from 1975. Given Lévy's new self-understanding as an orthodox Jew, solidarity with the increasingly anti-Zionist International Left had become next to impossible.

Although the *Hope Now* transcript is undoubtedly authentic, there can be no doubt that, throughout the discussions, Lévy led and the frail and blind Sartre followed. Their concluding exchange pertained to the vagaries of hope in an era of sharply diminished political expectations. In Sartre's view the left-wing political parties—both the Communists and the Socialists—were not to be trusted, insofar as they had sacrificed their principles for the sake of electoral success. By this point, gauchisme, too, had collapsed. For thirty years Sartre had wagered politically on the feasibility of socialism as an alternative to capitalism. But now these hopes had been permanently dashed. Since the promises of a secular philosophy of history, as defined by Hegel and Marx, had foundered, Sartre professed his admiration for the Jews as a people that for millennia had lived "metaphysically" rather than "historically." Sartre explains:

What is new [in Judaism] is the kind of relationship this God entered into with men. It was an immediate relationship that the Jews had with what they used to call the Name, that is to say, God. God speaks to the Jew, the Jew hears his word, and the reality to emerge from all this was a first metaphysical link of the Jew

[100] Ibid., 100.

with the Infinite. That, I believe, is the primary definition of the ancient Jew, the man whose entire life is somehow determined, ruled, by his relationship with God. And the whole history of the Jews consists precisely of the primary relationship.[101]

That two of the most significant persons in his life, Lévy and Ar-lette Elkaim-Sartre (his adoptive daughter), were Jews could not help but significantly influence his thinking on such matters. In the end, it was Sartre's "children" who had become for him the repositories of "hope."

[101] Ibid., 104.

CHAPTER 6

Tel Quel in Cultural-Political Hell

> Oh, I tried the Left Bank. At university I used to go with
> people who walked around with issues of *Tel Quel* under
> their arms. I know all that rubbish. You can't even read it.
>
> —Philip Roth, *The Counterlife*

During the 1960s *Tel Quel*, led by consummate literary entrepreneur
Philippe Sollers, rode to notoriety the crest of nearly every passing
intellectual trend: the nouveau roman, structuralism, and poststructuralism. Unsurprisingly, the journal's political loyalties were equally
mercurial. After cultivating a studious apoliticism, it lurched from the
most rigid Stalinist orthodoxy to an equally fervent embrace of Cultural Revolutionary China—an instance of revolutionary romanticism
that culminated in a celebrated 1974 trip to Beijing. As Communist
Party loyalists, the Telquelians "missed out" on May 1968. In a now-
legendary episode, Sollers—whose father, incidentally, was a leading
Bordeaux industrialist—actively denounced the student movement
for its insufficiently proletarian character. Unlike Sartre and Foucault,
the Telquelians shunned the Maoist student groups that, during the
post-May years, were in the process of refashioning the French political landscape by translating the ethos of Cultural Revolution into
an indigenous French idiom—the language of "civil society." Instead,
as literary intellectuals, they were readily seduced by Mao's persona
as both an armchair philosopher—a latter-day philosopher king, as it
were—and a poet. Hence, the Tel Quel group swore allegiance directly
to Beijing. *Dazibaos*—large Chinese wall posters—came to grace the
Tel Quel offices on the fashionable rue Jacob.

An integral part of the *Tel Quel* narrative concerns Julia Kristeva's
rise to prominence from a penniless Bulgarian scholarship student to the

toast of the Left Bank. Unlike Sollers, whose work has found few transatlantic echoes, the story of French Theory's American reception could
not be written without recounting Kristeva's pivotal role. Like other
French intellectuals, she wagered that in an era of third worldism, Chinese communism might succeed where other approaches had failed. In
the end, of course, the Telquelians, like other French leftists, were prop-
erly chastised and disillusioned. They took the extreme step of burning
the bridge to their own cultural revolutionary past by dissolving *Tel
Quel* and inaugurating a new, purely literary organ in its stead: *L'Infini*.
As an act of penance for their prior political missteps—and following
the footsteps of many ex-gauchistes—they, too, would, during the late
1970s, vociferously champion the cause of Eastern European dissidence.

   To be sure, it is an altogether strange tale that to be fully appreciated
must be told in full.

SOLELY ART

In March 1960 a new literary review, defiantly brandishing an adage
by Nietzsche on its masthead, appeared on the Parisian scene: "I want
the world and I want it *as it is* [*tel quel*], and I want it again, eternally; I
cry insatiably: again!—not just for myself alone, but for the entire play
and the entire spectacle; not for the spectacle alone, but fundamentally
for me, since I require the spectacle—for it requires me—and because I
make it necessary."[1] The review was the brainchild of a twenty-three-
year-old *bordelais*, Philippe Sollers (né Joyaux), who, as the cliché goes,
was destined for a brilliant literary career. At the age of twenty, Sollers'
first literary sortie, *Le Défi*, had captured the Fénéon Prize. A year
later his novel *Une solitude curieuse* was greeted with lavish notices by
both the Catholic novelist François Mauriac and the surrealist wun-
derkind-turned-Stalinist Louis Aragon—a very strange combination,
to be sure; and it is doubtful whether these two literary lions, hailing
from opposite ends of the political spectrum, ever agreed on anything
besides Sollers' immense talent. For his part, Sollers, his sights fixed

[1] *Tel Quel* 1 (1960): 1; emphasis added.

from an early age on the glories of literary acclaim, was careful to leave nothing to chance. Aware of the fact that in the hyperpoliticized milieu of Parisian intellectual politics talent and success were only conditionally related, he methodically cultivated the contacts that would place him on the cultural fast track. His reward was the editorship, at a remarkably young age, of *Tel Quel*—an extraordinary expression of confidence on the part of the progressive Catholic publishing house Seuil. Still, the Parisian publishers were constantly on the lookout for the next literary sensation—the new Gide, the next Sartre—and, given Sollers' impressive track record, Seuil's wager on him seemed well placed.

The Nietzsche maxim adorning the masthead was intended as a provocation, for the enterprise of *Tel Quel* was Oedipally directed against the reigning French *maître à penser*, Sartre. Although he would receive the Nobel Prize for Literature following the 1964 publication of *Les mots*, as he approached the age of sixty, Sartre's star had unquestionably begun to fade, and the wars of succession to determine his heir apparent had already commenced. There were of course the embarrassing political missteps of the early 1950s, his period of lockstep pro-Moscow fealty. Moreover, the philosophical existentialism he had championed during the 1940s and 1950s had fallen precipitously out of fashion, soon to be supplanted by purportedly more rigorous structuralist approaches. Still, with his influential 1948 tract *What Is Literature?*—in which, following the travails of war and occupation, Sartre sang the praises of *la littérature engagée* ("If literature is not *everything*, it is worth nothing. This is what I mean by 'commitment'")[2]—the philosopher had established a benchmark for literary endeavor that had become impossible to ignore. And thus it was against Sartre qua apostle of literary activism that Sollers and company took aim in *Tel Quel*'s inaugural issue. Whereas *marxisant* intellectuals like Sartre were obsessed with the imperatives of "changing the world," by invoking Nietzsche's idea of *amor fati*, Sollers sought a return to the decadent aestheticism of an earlier generation—the generation of Proust, Valéry, and Gide. As the journal's editorial staff proclaimed in the first issue (with a sideways glance at Sartre and company), "Ideologues have ruled long enough over expression. . . . It's about time

[2] Sartre, "The Purposes of Writing," in *Between Existentialism and Marxism*, 13–14.

a parting of the ways took place; let us be permitted to focus upon expression itself, its inevitability, and its particular laws."[3]

That Sollers' summons to a "return to literature" *tel quel* could be deemed in the least controversial can be understood only in terms of the "Vichy syndrome" afflicting French political culture. As of the early 1960s, France in many respects had yet to recover psychologically from the "strange defeat" of 1940, in light of which the achievements of republicanism—the only democratic tradition the country had known—had been irreparably tarnished. Hopes for political regeneration following the war had been dashed amid the geopolitical imperatives of the cold war and an inglorious return to parliamentary business as usual. And just when the hexagon seemed to be recovering its political footing during the early 1950s, the legacy of colonialism—another one of the Third Republic's ambiguous bequests—bit back with a vengeance. In 1954 the French army suffered a humiliating defeat at an obscure outpost in northern Indochina: Dien Bien Phu. The same year a major colonial uprising occurred in Algeria, precipitating a civil war in metropolitan France and the end of the Fourth Republic. One of the leading post hoc explanations for the nation's rash and bewildering 1940 collapse in the face of the advancing German armies was "cultural decadence": true to the heritage of art for art's sake, France had become a nation of otherworldly aesthetes, incapable of rising to the challenge of twentieth-century Realpolitik. Such allegations are no doubt grossly exaggerated. Be that as it may, they enjoyed an eerie persistence, fed by France's manifold postwar foreign policy debacles. (Here one might add the 1956 Suez Crisis to the list.) For Sartre's generation, which came of age during the political setbacks of the 1930s (Auden's "low, dishonest decade")—Abyssinia, the Spanish Civil War, Munich, and the Hitler-Stalin pact—a return to belle epoque aestheticism seemed an unconscionable regression. Conversely, for Sollers and his contemporaries, who matured during the rosy glow of 1950s affluence, the political strictures of the *Temps modernes* leftists seemed stifling and oppressive—a step removed from the tyrannies of socialist realism.

[3] "Déclaration," *Tel Quel* 1 (Spring 1960): 3.

Thus, with some justification, *Tel Quel*'s inaugural declaration was perceived as an anti-Sartre manifesto. The manifesto form was, of course, one of the distinguishing features of the European avant-garde. Yet, whereas the avant-garde—Dadaism, futurism, surrealism—adopted it for the purpose of transforming life (in the "Manifesto of Surrealism," André Breton famously declared: "Il faut pratiquer la poésie" [One must practice poetry]), Sollers employed it toward the explicit end of *separating* life and literature. As he asserted in the journal's opening number,

> Whenever thought is subordinated to moral and political impera-
> tives, it has ceased to be what we expect from it: the foundation of
> our presence, its clear and difficult artistic expression; each time
> that thought [is] devalued in this way . . . preaching, whereas it
> suffices to love, literature, ever despised yet victorious, is defended
> with a bad conscience. . . . Today to speak of "literary quality" or
> "a passion for literature" could be just what is needed.[4]

Editions du Seuil editor François Wahl, who in 1974 would ac-company the Telquelians on an ill-advised expedition to the People's Republic of China, provided an apt historical analogy when he com-pared the group's project to the dawn of the *l'art pour l'art* movement one hundred years earlier: "We are entering the Second Empire, and there is going to be a new Parnassus. This new Parnassus must ex-press itself. . . . This new Parnassus will be *Tel Quel*."[5] Wahl's char-acterization suggests parallels between the authoritarian rule of Louis Bonaparte—who, with his 1851 coup d'état, had cruelly put an end to the forty-eighters' republican hopes—and that of France's reigning au-tocrat, Charles de Gaulle. Whereas Sartre had justified writing in terms of engagement, Sollers, the upstart and contrarian, appeared to glorify an aesthetics of disengagement.

Sollers' aestheticism was even reflected in his carefully contrived nom de plume, which derived from combining the Latin words *sollus* and *ars*: "solely art." His presumed model was France's most prestigious

[4] Ibid., 3–4.
[5] Wahl, cited in Faye's *Commencement d'une figure*, 68.

twentieth-century literary organ, the *Nouvelle Revue Française* (NRF). During its thirty-year heyday (1910–40) the NRF had been home to the likes of Proust, Gide, and Malraux, as well as the young Sartre. However, after the fall of France, and at the behest of the German invaders, the fascist scribe Pierre Drieu La Rochelle assumed the directorship, and the NRF came to be viewed as an archetype of spineless collaboration. As such, it was an ambiguous precedent. One of *Tel Quel's* early benefactors, the literary critic Roland Barthes, aptly described its mission in the following terms: "The (straight and narrow) path for a review like yours would then be to see the world as it creates itself *through a literary consciousness,* to consider reality periodically as the raw material of a secret work, to locate yourselves at that very fragile and rather obscure moment when the relation of a real event is about to be apprehended by literary meaning."[6]

Just how controversial Sollers' intransigent defense of literary formalism seemed at the time is well illustrated by the reactions of two contemporaries. Early on, fellow editor Jean-René Huguenin began to distance himself from the review. He feared that by ceding so much ground to questions of language, Sollers risked superficiality, for when viewed self-referentially, literature foreclosed the possibility of communicating higher aims or concerns. In Huguenin's view, Sollers' narrow-minded aestheticism lacked "the sense of the tragic, the taste for risk, wild extravagances, despair."[7] The major risk courted by a journal so conceived was that it threatened to become belletristic. The writer and philosopher Jean-Pierre Faye, who enjoyed a brief, if fitful, tenure on the editorial board, gave voice to the burdensome political imperatives of the times when, referring to the group's inaugural declaration, he observed: "At a time when 'expression' freed from 'political and moral directives' chose to take care of itself alone, the French army was busying itself by occupying Algeria, killing a million people and torturing thousands of others."[8] Viewed from this perspective, the *Tel Quel* enterprise was "untimely" in a decidedly negative sense.

---

[6] Barthes, "Literature Today," 157.

[7] Huguenin, *Journal*, 77.

[8] Faye, cited in Knapp's *French Novelists Speak Out*, 84.

If the NRF represented Sollers' literary touchstone, his social role model seems to have been Stendhal's Julien Sorel: the social climber who ruthlessly claws his way to the top only to lose his soul in the process. If one carefully traces *Tel Quel*'s sinuous intellectual course, it seems fair to say that Sollers perennially operated with one ear to the ground and a finger to the wind. Throughout the journal's tempestuous twenty-two-year history—it ceased publication in 1982, only to be reincarnated, under the more prestigious imprint of NRF publisher Gallimard, as *L'Infini*—there seems to be one constant: Sollers' desperate craving for the intellectual limelight.

FROM THE NOUVEAU ROMAN TO STRUCTURALISM

Tel Quel had staked its reputation on a revival of literary modernism, invoking illustrious predecessors such as Flaubert, Mallarmé, Proust, Kafka, and Joyce as *compagnons de lutte*. But unless the journal could include contemporary representatives of the modernist canon, it courted the risk of antiquarianism, an unacceptable posture for a journal that sought to inherit the mantle of the twentieth-century avant-garde. Sollers and company solved this problem by cultivating the loyalties of Alain Robbe-Grillet, the doyen of the nouveau roman. During the 1950s works such as *The Voyeurs* and *The Erasers*—perhaps best described as "novels of consciousness" on behalf of objects or things—had garnered much critical acclaim. Robbe-Grillet's innovative approach, in which nineteenth-century conventions such as plot and character counted for little, meshed seamlessly with *Tel Quel*'s formalist preoccupations, as well as its distaste for realism. His penchant for formal innovation suited *Tel Quel*'s stress, à la Mallarmé, on the noncommunicative, autonomous character of literary language.

Barthes, who became the foremost critical champion of the nouveau roman, codified these precepts in a landmark essay, "To Write: An Intransitive Verb."[9] He argued (as he had earlier in another major

---

[9] Roland Barthes, "To Write: An Intransitive Verb," in *Language of Criticism and the Sciences of Man*, ed. Macksey and Donato.

statement, *Writing Degree Zero*) that the representational or utilitarian function of language was inferior to its poetic side—the autonomous dimension of "expression" that the Telquelians had celebrated in their inaugural Declaration. Opposing the doctrine of *littérature engagée*, the writer, claimed Barthes, could no longer be "defined in terms of his role or value but only by a certain *awareness of language*."[10] Nor was it difficult to discern that Robbe-Grillet's literary techniques—the celebrated *mise en abîme*, or conscious suspension of meaning, his embrace of a depersonalized approach to writing that rejected psychology—were diametrically opposed to Sartre's demonstrative and at times plodding *romans à thèse*. In *Tel Quel*'s generational struggle against *Temps modernes* orthodoxy, Robbe-Grillet and his fellow *nouveau romanciers* were ideal allies. As one critic aptly notes: "By disengaging from politics by means of language *Tel Quel* rejected history itself, a history created not by them but by their elders—the generation of Sartre and Aragon—and in which they had been thrust."[11]

In 1961 Foucault published *Madness and Civilization*. In retrospect, Sollers viewed its appearance as one of the decade's most important publishing events.[12] Toward the end of the book Foucault praised the "great refusal" of four *poètes maudits*: Hölderlin, Nerval, Nietzsche, and Artaud. The lives of all four had ended in madness. Their writing gave

[10] Barthes, *Criticism and Truth*, 64.

[11] Marx-Scouras, *Cultural Politics of* Tel Quel, 39–40. Ironically, at a later point Robbe-Grillet himself challenged the formalist interpretations of the nouveau roman that had been proffered by the likes of Barthes and the Telquelians. He insisted that the "objective realism" he had cultivated in *In the Labyrinth* and other works represented his own way of coming to terms with the historical traumas of the previous decade: war, political collapse, occupation, and collaboration. Yet, by the time he set forth such disclaimers (1984), the nouveau roman's heyday lay twenty years in the past, and few critics bothered to take note.

Already during the 1950s, Jacques Leenhart and Lucien Goldmann offered important political interpretations of Robbe-Grillet's novels. In *Toward a Sociology of Literature*, Goldmann argued that Robbe-Grillet's novels—in which things took precedence over persons—addressed questions of societal reification. In a later work, Robbe-Grillet himself challenged the apolitical interpretations of his work; see Alain Robbe-Grillet, *Le miroir qui vient* (Paris: Editions de Minuit, 1984).

[12] Philippe Sollers, "De *Tel Quel* à *L'Infini*," *Autrement* 69 (April 1985): 8.

voice to what Foucault lauded as *"the sovereign enterprise of unreason . . .*
forever irreducible to those alienations that can be cured" by the co-
ercive methods of modern psychiatry.[13] To this pantheon of execrated
poets, Foucault would soon add the names of the Marquis de Sade and
his late admirer Georges Bataille (1897–1962).

Under Foucault's influence, the Telquelians began abruptly to distance themselves from the ethereal joys of art for art's sake—the "pleasures of the text" (Barthes)—and to focus instead on questions of lived
experience. They ceased to view textuality as an end in itself and began
to address the role the literary imaginary might play in overturning the
deadening and familiar routines of everyday life.

It would prove very difficult, if not impossible, to reconcile this
new focus on the dynamics of "transgression"—which mandated acts
of cultural rebellion reminiscent of surrealism—with the literary pur-
ism of the journal's initial phase. Whereas transgression wishes to have
a transformative effect, aestheticism is more than happy to leave the
world as it is—"tel quel." This situation provided a compelling reason
to sever connections to the *nouveau romanciers*, whose achievements
had propelled Sollers and others to intellectual celebrity.

In the early 1960s a revolutionary theoretical paradigm, structuralism, began to conquer the Parisian intellectual scene. In its wake,
other philosophical approaches—Sartre's existential Marxism, most
notably—seemed tame and outmoded. Structuralism's origins go back
to Ferdinand de Saussure's *Course in General Linguistics*, first published in
1916. Saussure argued that language was determined by pairs of binary
oppositions and that signs or words were fundamentally arbitrary; they
existed, contended Saussure, primarily in relation to other words rather
than in a necessary relation to the things they denominated. By distinguishing between *langue* and *parole*—between the structural invariants
of language as opposed to their variable and contingent embodiment
in individual speech acts—Saussure's structural linguistics appeared to
provide the basis for a genuinely scientific study of language.

[13] Foucault, *Madness and Civilization*, 278; emphasis added.

By the same token, his approach occluded the equally important dia-chronic or historical dimension of language. Ultimately, the neglect of diachrony or history—in structuralist parlance, the realm of "events"—would prove to be structuralism's Achilles' heel, for if structuralism's beloved invariants were, as the paradigm claimed, all-determinant, then it became impossible to account for the advent of anything new. According to the structuralist catechism, a speech act, a poem, and a revolution were, in essence, exemplifications of preordained structural constants. The specificity of "events" remained well-nigh inaccessible.

In the postwar period, Saussure's paradigm captured the imagina-tion of a new generation of scholars in the human sciences. In *The Elementary Structures of Kinship,* Claude Lévi-Strauss relied on it to show that kinship systems, too, were governed by unchanging binary op-positions. He went on to make similar claims about the organization of primitive myths. Renegade Freudian Jacques Lacan, also following Saussure's lead, famously declared that "the unconscious is structured like a language." His trademark distinction between the "imaginary" and "symbolic" dimensions of selfhood was equally indebted to Sau-ssure's influential formulations. In *Reading Capital,* Louis Althusser relied on structuralist concepts to reestablish Marxism's claims to scien-tificity in order to keep the rival paradigm of Marxist humanism at bay.

However, during the 1960s structuralism's most celebrated practi-tioner was *Tel Quel* ally and occasional contributor Michel Foucault. In *The Order of Things* and *The Archaeology of Knowledge,* Foucault sought to delineate the geological constants, or "epistemes," underlying the tran-sient, phenomenal manifestations of human thought. In such works he claimed to be searching for the structural homologies or isomorphisms that subtended the manifest practices of the human sciences. In this way Foucault, in a classically structuralist manner, sought out "the positive unconscious of knowledge: a level that eludes the consciousness of the scientist and yet is part of scientific discourse," for unbeknownst to themselves, "naturalists, economists, and grammarians employed the same rules to the objects proper to their own study, to form concepts and build their theories."[14] Within a few years of *Tel Quel*'s inception,

[14] Foucault, *Order of Things,* xi.

structuralism had penetrated virtually every discipline in the humanities and social sciences.

Sollers realized that structuralist methods were the wave of the future and abruptly severed ties to the nouveau roman authors. By the fall of 1964, the names of Robbe-Grillet and his literary *confrères* permanently disappeared from *Tel Quel*'s pages. As Sollers observed: "The ideology of all of these [new novel] productions is, in reality, highly *conventional, psychological, positivist, or technocratic.* Above all, it serves to conceal the genuine *theoretical* revolutions that occurred between the 1920s and the 1940s."[15] By casting their lot with the structuralist juggernaut, Sollers and company succeeded in remaining au courant at a time when the nouveau roman's star had begun to wane and the "theory" vogue held uncontested sway over Left Bank intellectuals.[16]

Via this cunning act of strategic repositioning, Sollers was able to achieve several ends at once. He managed to extricate the journal from the literary ghetto, a maneuver that in light of the decade's impending political tremors, seems to have been especially clairvoyant. In keeping with the changed tenor of the zeitgeist, Sollers and company now excoriated literature as an expression of bourgeois ideology. It remained confined "within the reductionist limits of the concept of 'belles lettres,' that offspring of middle class liberalism."[17]

In pursuing this course, he dutifully followed structuralism's lead. Lacan had characterized the formation of subjectivity via the symbolic stage as a departure from the imaginary, or primary narcissism. The

[15] Philippe Sollers, "Réponses," *Tel Quel* 43 (Fall 1970): 71–76; emphasis added.

[16] For an account of the Sollers-decreed editorial shuffle, see Huguenin, *Journal.* See also Forest, *Histoire de* Tel Quel, 174–76.

[17] Felman, *Writing and Madness*, 15. See the characterization of Tel Quel's reliance on Althusser and structuralism in ffrench, *Time of Theory*:

In *Tel Quel* the Althusserian conception of ideology soon began to reveal fundamental flaws. . . . This can be seen as a critique of structuralism by a more dynamic theory of its energetic basis. . . . Althusser's ideology was essentially a structural apparatus which interpellated or imposed itself on the subject. . . . A conception of subjectivity, process, and language was left out of the question. At the beginning of the 1970s . . . Kristeva and [Jean-Louis] Baudry . . . developed a notion of ideology as inscribed in signifying practice and in the constitutive development of subjectivity. (115)

imaginary is preceded by the mirror stage, which occurs when the infant is between six and eight months old. At this point the child emerges from a blurred and inchoate sense of self, which Lacan refers to as "the body in pieces," to accede to a more unified ego.[18] For Lacan, by socialization through language, the primal self is reconstituted via a network of preexisting symbols that shape its destiny in ways that are well-nigh permanent and unalterable. As one commentator has remarked: "Caught up in the Symbolic, where he is simply represented, obliged to translate himself through the intermediary of a Discourse, the subject will become *lost, lured away from himself,* and will shape himself in accordance with the Other's look. Identification with various ideals and rationalizing discourse upon oneself are so many forms in which *the subject becomes fixed and betrays himself.*"[19] Similarly, Althusser had described bourgeois thought, which deviated from the scientific correctness of Marxist theory, as a discursive mystification akin to the Lacanian imaginary realm: a type of symptom formation (Freud) that represented an ideological distortion of deeper, "structural," unconscious truths. Via recourse to the same structuralist methods and procedures, Sollers believed that literature could now be analyzed as the vehicle whereby the bourgeois self was ideologically synthesized and fashioned.

Henceforth, Sollers would view the institution of literature as a type of disciplinary mechanism akin to the panoptic practices Foucault analyzed during the 1970s. Sollers claimed that literature served as "a means of instituting a permanent conditioning that goes much further

[18] See the discussion in Roudinesco, *Jacques Lacan,* 111: "The so-called mirror ordeal is a rite of passage that takes place between the ages of six and eight months. It allows the infant to recognize itself and to unify its ego in space. The experience thus represents a transition from the specular to the imaginary and then from the imaginary to the symbolic. . . . The mirror stage in the Lacanian sense is a matrix foreshadowing the evolution of the ego as imaginary."

[19] See the explanation of this point in Lacan by Lemaire, *Jacques Lacan,* 178. Lemaire continues: "The symbolic . . . is the cause of human alienation. . . . Alienation is the fact of giving up a part of oneself to another. The alienated man lives outside himself, *a prisoner of the signifier,* a prisoner of his ego's image or of the image of the ideal. He lives by the other's gaze upon him and here is unaware of this. Misrecognition is the parallel to the imaginary lived experience" (176; emphasis added).

than the book market alone. The novel is the way this society speaks to itself, the way the individual must live himself in order to be accepted there."[20] Moreover, by riding the structuralist wave, the Telquelians were able to secure the collaboration of a talented, up-and-coming generation of "theorists": Barthes, Foucault, Jacques Derrida, Gérard Genette, and Tzvetan Todorov.[21] Thereby, Sollers and company succeeded in reaching out to an important new constituency: knowledge-hungry Latin Quarter students, whose purchasing power would soon drive sales to record levels.[22]

Tel Quel's structuralism-inspired "theory" vogue raised the journal's profile to unprecedented heights. Following Derrida's lead, the buzz-word of the moment became "writing," or *écriture*. Just as Lévi-Strauss had claimed to unlock the "code" that revealed the transhistorical verities of human culture, the Telquelians believed that "textuality" or "writing" was the key to understanding the historical present. After all, what was society, reasoned Sollers and company, if not an instance of objectified writing or externalized textuality?

Critics argued that the Telquelians had succumbed to a peculiar (albeit, characteristically French) genre of linguistic idealism: a belief in the primacy of the "text" vis-à-vis the "real." According to Saussure's conception of language, words were related primarily to other words rather than "things." Moreover, the signifier's relation to the signified—the concept or idea it designated—was entirely arbitrary. Hence, "reality" as such remained forever unreachable. Thus, in "The Novel and the Experience of Limits," Sollers claimed that the real "is manifested nowhere else but in a language . . . a society's language and myths are what it decides to take as reality."[23] Similarly, in *Ecrits* (1966), Lacan, amalgamating Saussure and Freud, would declare: "*It is the world of words*

[20] Sollers, "The Novel and the Experience of Limits," in *Writing and the Experience of Limits*, 186–87.

[21] Todorov and Genette would part company with *Tel Quel* circa 1968, as the journal embarked on its phase of "theoretical terrorism"—the ill-fated alliance with PCF Stalinism—in order to found the more scholarly *Poétique*.

[22] For a detailed account of *Tel Quel*'s vacillating publishing success, see Kauppi, *Tel Quel*.

[23] Sollers, "The Novel and the Experience of Limits," 194.

that creates the world of things."[24] And in "To Write: An Intransitive Verb,"
Barthes celebrated the new epistemological orthodoxy by avowing: "*It
is language which teaches the definition of man, not the contrary.*"[25] Sollers and
company failed to realize that the new religion of textuality probably
revealed more about the literary habitudes and predispositions of Left
Bank intellectuals than it did about the nature of reality per se.

Tel Quel's makeover as an organ of high structuralism was by no
means greeted with universal acclaim. At a 1963 conference titled "New
Literature," where the break with the nouveau roman was consummated, a journalist from *Le Monde* interrupted Sollers' peroration, "The
Logic of Fiction," to inquire pointedly if Sollers had any professional
philosophical training.[26] Increasingly, the journal was perceived as gra-
tuitously inaccessible and *illisible*—"unreadable"—which its champions
interpreted as a mark of distinction. Detractors openly accused Sollers
and others of practicing "theoretical terrorism": raising "theory," or *Tel
Quel*'s version thereof, to the level of entrenched dogma and then proceeding to excommunicate or condemn rivals who embraced different
positions or approaches. At one point even a staunch ally like Foucault
was compelled to voice his extreme skepticism: "The whole relentless
theorization of writing [*écriture*] which we saw in the 1960s was doubtless
only a swansong. Through it, the writer was fighting for the preservation of his political privilege."[27] Foucault felt strongly that by elevating
textuality to a position of unquestioned epistemological supremacy, one
lost the capacity to conceptualize reality, or "events." From this perspective, the workings of power, which were hardly reducible to the
effects of "textuality" or discourse, remained indiscernible. In the eyes
of critics, the Telquelians and their allies had succumbed to a narcissistic delusion: they had merely projected their prior methods of intellectual training—the quintessentially French doctrine of *explication de*

[24] Lacan, *Ecrits*, 65; emphasis added.

[25] Barthes, "To Write: An Intransitive Verb," in *Language of Criticism*, 135; emphasis added.

[26] Forest, *Histoire de* Tel Quel, 207.

[27] Foucault, "Truth and Power," in *Power/Knowledge*, 127. For a discussion of *Tel Quel*'s "theoretical terrorism," see Forest, *L'Histoire de* Tel Quel, 299–303 ("Le théoricisme terroriste de *Tel Quel*").

texte—onto the world as a whole. The obsessive focus on questions of textuality and signification is undoubtedly one of the key reasons behind *Tel Quel*'s failure to seriously engage in politics and its brusque dismissal of the May revolt. As one sympathetic observer notes, for the Telquelians the revolution had more to do with developments in signifying practice than with what was happening in the streets.[28]

"JULIA COMES TO PARIS"

Chapter 35 of François Dosse's definitive two-volume *History of Structuralism* is entitled "1966: Annum Mirabile—Julia Comes to Paris." The "Julia" in question is of course Julia Kristeva. As Dosse's chapter title suggests, in French intellectual lore, Kristeva's arrival in Paris from her native Bulgaria has acquired an aura akin to the Second Coming. The beneficiary of de Gaulle's concept of a "Europe stretching from the Atlantic to the Urals," in 1965 she received a French scholarship to complete a dissertation on the *nouveau roman*. She arrived in Paris on Christmas Eve with five dollars to her name. Since, however, the stipend could not be activated for two months, she was forced to rely on her wits and the proverbial "kindness of strangers" to survive. As she commented to an interviewer, "I'll spare you the peripeties of the plot."[29]

Kristeva had planned to write her thesis under the direction of sociologist of literature Lucien Goldmann, but she soon realized that in Paris the intellectual constellation had radically shifted. The structuralist vogue meant that sociology, perennially derided by the Telquelians as "sociologism," was "out" and "textuality" was "in." Kristeva shifted her allegiances to Roland Barthes, who at times seemed to learn as much from her as she from him. Thereafter, she joined Claude Lévi-Strauss's celebrated anthropology laboratory and participated in Lacan's legendary "seminar," which had recently moved from the Ecole

---

[28] See Ffrench, *Time of Theory,* 119: "The role of *Tel Quel* in the events of 1968 is minimal. The revolution of the review at this stage is theoretical and textual, not in the streets."

[29] Kristeva, *Interviews,* 49.

normale to the Sorbonne. (It seems that in the mid-1970s, Kristeva was also analyzed by Lacan.) The die was cast.

The timing of her arrival could not have been more propitious. At the precise moment that structuralism consolidated its theoretical hold over Parisian intellectuals, its limitations were keenly felt: an Apollonian predilection for system, precision, logic, and grids; a correlative neglect of playfulness, polyvalence, and the gratuitous gesture—the values of alternative French cultural traditions, for example, Dada and surrealism—that the student generation was about to turn against master thinkers of all stripes.

Kristeva arrived in Paris just in time to participate in the next major paradigm change of the intellectual grand game: the transition from structuralism to poststructuralism. Her Eastern European intellectual background outfitted her perfectly to become, at the tender age of twenty-four, a major player. Fluent in Russian, schooled in the tradition of Russian formalism, she was also well versed in the theories of the Russian literary critic Mikhail Bakhtin. In pathbreaking studies of Rabelais and Dostoyevsky, Bakhtin had uncovered the hitherto neglected dialogic dimension of literary texts: the ways in which great literary texts spoke in a plethora of often contradictory voices. Bakhtin demonstrated how novels such as *Gargantua and Pantagruel* and *Crime and Punishment* were characterized by an irreducible discursive polyphony, thus belying considerations of authorial cohesion and narrative unity so dear to traditionally minded literary critics. (One thinks, for example, of the grand inquisitor episode of the *Brothers Karamazov*, where Ivan and Alyosha memorably debate to a standoff how a fallen humanity might react to the Second Coming.) Bakhtin also showed that they stood in a dialogic relationship to previous literary works and traditions. (One thinks, for example, of Cervantes' immortal pastiche of the novels of chivalry in *Don Quixote*.) Thereby, he was able to add a diachronic and historical dimension to literary studies, offsetting one of formalism's greatest deficiencies. In opposition to Western scientific discourse based on the repressive precepts of closure, totality, finitude, and structural invariants, Bakhtin showed how literary texts, conversely, were inherently polyvalent, decentered, and joyous.

In a Soviet context, Bakhtin's work effected the "dissident" function of undermining the Communist Party's claims to univocal truth, in whose name it proceeded to implement an uncompromising dictatorship. In 1960s France, conversely, although the political stakes of Bakhtin's work were minimal, the epistemological stakes were considerable. His dialogic approach to literature was viewed as providing ideal conceptual leverage to overturn structuralism's austere, anti-Dionysian rigidities. Kristeva coined the term "intertextuality" to convey Bakhtin's idea that texts are "constructed as a mosaic of quotations; any text is the absorption and transformation of another [text]."[30]

Thus, Kristeva sounded the poststructuralist clarion against the classifications and exclusions of traditional linguistics, which, she claimed, served only to buttress reigning "social codes." At a later point, the poststructuralist assault on the occlusions and constraints of "Western metaphysics"—with structuralism viewed as that paradigm's latest incarnation—would fuse with Foucault's attempt to unmask the discursive and epistemological origins of "power." In *Revolution in Poetic Language* (1974), Kristeva mocked the rigidities of structuralist linguistics as the lifeless constructs of "archivists, archaeologists, and necrophiliacs." "These static thoughts," she continued, "products of a leisurely cogitation removed from historical turmoil, persist in seeking the truth of language by formalizing utterances that hang in midair and . . . listening to the narrative of a sleeping body: a body in repose, withdrawn from its socio-historical imbrications, removed from direct experience."[31] By pulverizing structuralism's obsession with integral wholeness and formal constraint, intertexuality—the dialogic interplay between texts— would expose linguistics to the intoxications of infinite play.

The basic problem confronting poststructuralist linguistics can be rephrased as follows: insofar as the "logocentric" biases of all intellection mandate the systematic repression of *jouissance*, otherness, and difference, would it be possible to conceive of a new theoretical paradigm that would somehow do justice to these heretofore marginalized

[30] Kristeva, *Kristeva Reader*, 37.
[31] Kristeva, *Revolution in Poetic Language*, 13.

and excluded elements? Kristeva's solution was a linguistic approach she baptized as *semanalysis*. An eclectic admixture of Saussure, Lacan, Freud, Mallarmé, gynocentric feminism, and "body politics," semanalysis was Kristeva's specific contribution to the voguish dismantling of inherited theoretical paradigms and discursive regimes.

Perhaps semanalysis's weakness was its uncritical acceptance of Lacanian drive theory. According to Lacan, the passage from the imaginary to the symbolic realm signifies the transition from primary narcissism to a potentially conformist internalization of the values of "civilization." Here Lacan's ideas parallel Freud's narrative in *Totem and Taboo* of the way the primal horde is subjected to the renunciations imposed by the "law of the father." In Freud's parable, the guilt that is internalized following the brothers' slaying of the primal father corresponds to the formation of the social superego—the introjection of the basic instinctual restraints civilization imposes. Lacan, however, grafting the findings of Saussurean structural linguistics to this powerful Freudian myth, describes the ontogenetic shift from primary narcissism to the symbolic realm (a condition that, for Lacan, is coincident with the acquisition of language) in terms of the child's subjection to the "name [or the 'no'] of the father" (le "nom" du père)—the so-called law of the phallus (the threat of castration), with all its attendant sanctions and repressions. Whereas Freud firmly endorsed the maturity of the rational ego, capable of navigating between the regressive lures of the drives and temptations of social conformity, implicit in Lacan's account of ontogenesis is a highly un-Freudian depiction of the imaginary qua repository of primary narcissism. Lacan's theory of mental topography portrays the imaginary as a prelinguistic sphere of untrammeled gratification that we abandon (although never completely) upon our passage to the misapprehensions (*misprisions*) of the symbolic realm. Ultimately, for Lacan, the symbolic threatens to congeal into a dimension of unmitigated social conformity. The conceptions of self that are formed via language and socialization are largely those of convention.[32]

---

[32] For some of the differences between Freudian and Lacanian drive theory, see Joel Whitebook, *Perversion and Utopia: Studies in Psychoanalysis and Critical Theory*

Lacan's approach also seemed to rule out all prospects for meaningful political change. He denigrated language, self, and society as spheres that are ontogenetically predicated on logics of misrecognition. According to Lacan, insofar as the self is shaped by language as determined by the draconian "name of the father," it is little more than an illusory effect of dominant social codes. In this respect his views harmonized fully with the reigning structuralist credo. Any attempt to transcend the "code" is deemed ontologically futile, insofar as the linguistic means enlisted are "always already" contaminated by language's mandates, restrictions, and exclusions. As Lacan condescendingly informed the sixty-eighters, many of whom were his students: "What you aspire to as revolutionaries is a Master. You will have him."[33] By this injunction he meant that their attempts to revolutionize the existing social order could result only in the creation of one that was equally repressive.[34] According to his conception of the relationship between the imaginary and the symbolic spheres, no other outcomes are possible. As soon as one submits to the "law of the phallus" and to the symbolic/patriarchal constitutions of the self that such acts of submission entail, the die is cast. In this way, Lacan ruled out the prospect that social authority could be rationally challenged.

Since Lacan and his followers dismissed "rational" means of challenging social authority, the only remaining prospects for contesting domination derived, of necessity, from unconscious and libidinal sources. Kristeva's semanalysis fitted squarely within this Lacanian scheme. In *Revolution in Poetic Language* and other works, her major conceptual innovation was the distinction between the semiotic and symbolic realms—a variation on the Lacanian opposition between the imaginary and the symbolic.

Though the semiotic sphere was, like the Freudian unconscious, "prerational," it was not devoid of meaning or signification. Relying

---

(Cambridge, MA: MIT Press, 1996). For an insightful (and more sympathetic) reading of Lacan, see Carolyn Dean, *The Self and Its Pleasure: Bataille, Lacan, and the History of the Decentered Subject* (Ithaca, NY: Cornell University Press, 1992). For a broader appreciation of Lacan's role in postwar French intellectual culture, see Jay, *Downcast Eyes*.

[33] See Lacan, *Television*, cited in Dosse's *History of Structuralism* 2:150.

[34] On this point, see Starr, *Logics of Failed Revolt*.

on insights from object relations psychology concerning nonverbal communication between mother and infant, Kristeva suggested that the semiotic represented a type of pre-Oedipal "body language." Instead of employing "words" or "signs," it communicated wordlessly via rhythms, sounds, and drives. Kristeva sought to provide the semiotic with a dignified philosophical pedigree by tracing its origins back to a Platonic coinage in the *Timaeus,* the *chora,* which the philosopher describes elliptically as "an invisible and formless being which receives all things and in some mysterious way partakes of the intelligible, and is most incomprehensible."[35] In Kristeva's optic, one of the semiotic chora's primary virtues is that, as a prelinguistic phenomenon, it is able to circumvent the repressions and distortions of the symbolic realm.

In *Revolution in Poetic Language* Kristeva described the chora's role as follows:

> Neither model nor copy, the *chora* precedes and underlies figuration and thus specularization [the Lacanian imaginary], and is analogous only to vocal or kinetic rhythm. . . . The theory of the subject proposed by the theory of the unconscious will allow us to read in this rhythmic space, which has no thesis and no position, the process by which significance is constituted. Plato himself leads us to such a process when he calls this receptacle or *chora* nourishing and maternal, not yet unified in an ordered whole because deity is absent from it. Though deprived of unity, identity or deity, the *chora* is nevertheless subject to a regulating process, which is different from that of Symbolic law but nevertheless effectuates discontinuities by temporarily articulating them and then starting over, again and again.[36]

Kristeva highlights the affinities between the pre-Oedipal semiotic and Freud's "death drive" when she observes, "The mother's body is therefore what mediates the Symbolic law organizing social relations and

---

[35] *Timaeus,* in *The Collected Dialogues of Plato,* ed. Edith Hamilton and Huntington Cairns (Princeton, NJ: Princeton University Press, 2005), 1176.

[36] Kristeva, *Kristeva Reader,* 94.

becomes the ordering principle of the semiotic *chora*, which is on the path of *destruction, aggressivity, and death.*[37] It seems that by shunning the symbolic as a figure for "language," "phallocentrism," and "civilization," Kristeva's semiotic openly courts the risks of ontogenetic regression—"psychosis" and even death. But this is a risk that Kristeva and her disciples are apparently willing to take.[38]

In keeping with reigning intellectual trends, Kristeva sought to endow the semiotic chora with a prominent "deconstructive" dimension. One of the chora's primary virtues is that it remains inimical to the synthesizing proclivities of the transcendental subject in all its repressive modalities. The chora is "signification without a subject," the declared foe of Western metaphysics and its train of incurable logocentric prejudices. It threatens to explode the linear time of history qua "progress" in the name of a new, nonlinear, "maternal" temporality. According to Kristeva, the chora represents a series of "ruptures and articulations (rhythm) [that] precede evidence, verisimilitude, spatiality and temporality"— that is, the encumbrances of the symbolic sphere.

However, at this point a performative contradiction besets Kristeva's semanalytic enterprise, for despite her Lacanian diatribes against the deficiencies of the symbolic, Kristeva has no means at her disposal to convey her critique *other than with language itself,* the means provided by that selfsame symbolic sphere upon which she heaps so much opprobrium in *Revolution in Poetic Language* and other works. Instead of allowing the mute maternal significations of "drives, rhythms, and sounds" to proliferate freely, Kristeva inscribes them in discourse, thereby violating her own Lacanian prescriptions (although elsewhere Kristeva appeals to an altered, gender-based approach to language whose aim is to transcend the limitations of the Lacanian symbolic realm).

[37] Ibid., 95; emphasis added.
[38] In this respect, Kristeva's approach can be compared fruitfully with the parallel views of the death instinct (*Todestrieb*) in the work of Herbert Marcuse and Norman O. Brown. See Marcuse, *Eros and Civilization: A Philosophical Inquiry into Freud* (New York: Vintage Books, 1955), and Brown, *Life against Death: The Psychoanalytic Meaning of History* (New York: Vintage Books, 1959).

Another one of semanalysis's peculiarities pertains to Kristeva's efforts to yoke the twentieth-century avant-garde to the ends of political revolution—more specifically, to Bolshevism. She argues that, like the semiotic disruptions of maternal "body language" (the chora), the syntagmatic radicalism of canonical modernism harbors the capacity to pulverize signification, thereby disrupting the logocentric constraints of the symbolic sphere: Comrade Mallarmé meets Comrade Lenin. The writing of Mallarmé, Joyce, Artaud, and Céline embraces *autonomous signification*: signifiers become detached from real-world references, and the free play of signification takes precedence over literature's more traditional narrative and representational capacities. In *Revolution in Poetic Language* Kristeva argues that despite the repressive nature of signifying practice under capitalism, certain privileged avant-garde literary texts—Joyce and Mallarmé, for example—are able to accede to the promised land of the semiotic chora. By doing so, they are able to set off "explosions . . . within the social field," although it remains vague exactly how those explosions function and what political effects they might have. Such texts embody the principle of "unstoppable breakthrough." The end result, Kristeva concludes, is that "the signifying process joins the social revolution."[39]

Well-meaning critics have identified a number of deep-seated problems with Kristeva's approach. It seems that her understanding of literary history relies on an untenable dichotomy between "modernism" and "realism": whereas she lavishes infinite praise on modernism, she views realism as retrograde. This antithesis ends up consigning vast chapters of literary history—classical drama, the epistolary novel, realism, and naturalism—to aesthetic and political irrelevance. Moreover, literary modernism's advances in formal innovation are offset by communication deficits. High-modernist texts increasingly appeal to a circumscribed group of like-minded writers and critics—a fact that helps account for widespread disenchantment with high modernism in the post–World War II period. Nor has modernism proved any more immune than the texts of the realist canon to the perils

---

[39] Kristeva, *Kristeva Reader*, 122 and 112, and *Revolution in Poetic Language*, 104.

of academic "embalmment"—that is, to becoming grist for "seminar literature."[40]

The parallel Kristeva seeks to draw between the revolution in "signifying practice" associated with the names of Joyce and Mallarmé, on the one hand, and the energies of political revolution associated with Lenin and Mao, on the other, seems misplaced and naive. To begin with, it rests on a category mistake concerning the different functions of poetic and political language. Poetic language defamiliarizes the everyday to provoke new ways of seeing. Thereby, it enhances the variety and richness of lived experience. As such, one of its virtues is that it brackets the considerations of "common sense" that prevail in everyday life. Conversely, political language, even when it is "revolutionary," relies on the virtues of generalizable communication. It seeks to convince by advancing arguments or positions that provide a more plausible interpretation of political reality. In the modern period, it must observe the linguistic *règles de jeu* associated with narratives of justice or fairness. Even Leninism, Kristeva's touchstone for the virtues of revolutionism, pays obeisance to such norms. In the case of poetic language, adherence to such real-world norms and constraints would simply prove fatal, as the example of socialist realism well demonstrates. Exactly how these two mutually opposed discourses would ultimately join forces to produce the revolutionary upheaval Kristeva desires is something she never explains.

Moreover, historically, modernism flourished under precisely those democratic polities that Kristeva, the apostle of revolutionism, would prefer to see relegated to the dustbin of history. Unlike earlier societies in which art was chained to a variety of extraneous religious and

[40] In certain respects, Kristeva's position on modernism parallels that of Theodor Adorno in *Aesthetic Theory* and other works. However, in later works such as "The Aging of New Music" and "Transparencies on Film," Adorno expressed second thoughts about the intrinsically critical nature of high modernism. He sensed that it, too, was exposed to conformist tendencies. He also seemed to realize that the public was not composed merely of "cultural dopes" but was indeed more capable of making critical judgments and thinking for itself than he had imagined. See Adorno, "Transparencies on Film," in *Culture Industry*, 178–87. For "The Aging of New Music," see *Essays on Music*, ed. Richard Lepperts (Berkeley: University of California Press, 2002), 181–203.

political ends, democratic polities have offered leeway for art to explore the full range of and capacity for formal innovation. Under revolutionary regimes, conversely, the practitioners of literary modernism have been consigned either to silence or to camps. Strangely, Kristeva directly polemicizes against the social conditions that have allowed the radical aesthetic doctrines she values to flourish.

One final aspect of Kristeva's theory of poetic revolution bears comment: her claim that, unbeknownst to themselves, the representatives of literary modernism function as emissaries of the semiotic chora—the prelinguistic, maternal sphere of pulsions, rhythms, and sounds. Because of its feminist implications, her object relations–derived theory of the semiotic would serve as a bridge to the women's movements that blossomed throughout France and the United States during the 1970s. Yet, often, those who sought to appropriate her theories for feminist ends were deeply troubled by the fact that, strangely, the poets and writers who best exemplified the virtues of "semiotic" communication were *men*. Paradoxically, though it might have taken a woman like Kristeva to account for the repressed maternal dimension of language, in her scheme women seem constitutionally ill suited to becoming revolutionary poets. Thus, whereas the semiotic is a sphere of maternal value, the symbolic, or language, is the well-nigh exclusive preserve of men.

In this view, feminist politics seemed consigned in advance to futility—and how could it not? Once women enter the realm of the symbolic, they become hostages to the Lacanian "name of the father" (nom/non du père). They enter into a fateful compromise with the "masculinist" values of representation, meaning, and reason. Kristeva's doctrines present fellow women with an impossible choice. They may enter the realm of discourse—the terrain of phallocentric "social codes"—at the expense of their femininity, or they can reject such compromise at the cost of succumbing to hysteria or suicide. As Kristeva observes: "If no paternal 'legitimation' comes along to dam up the inexhaustible non-symbolized impulse, [woman] collapses into psychosis or suicide. . . . As soon as she speaks the discourse of the community, a woman becomes a Phallus."[41]

[41] Kristeva, *About Chinese Women*, 41; Julia Kristeva, "Sujet dans le langage et pratique politique," in *Psychanalyse et politique* (Paris: Verdiglione, 1974), 6.

Kristeva's relation to feminism has always been something of a puzzle. Along with Luce Irigaray and Hélène Cixous, she is customarily viewed as belonging to the Holy Trinity of French feminist theorists. Whereas an initial generation of postwar feminists, best represented by Simone de Beauvoir's classic *The Second Sex*, set their sights on the goal of women's equality, a second generation of "gynocentric" feminists avidly celebrated women's "difference." Rejecting the reformist goals of female social equality, radical feminists regarded the values of femininity—maternity, nurturing, and affectivity—as ends in themselves.

"Second wave" French feminists were profoundly marked by Derrida's deconstructionist critique of "phallogocentrism," the idea that Western thought has been irreparably distorted by "rationalist" and "masculine" biases—a preference for sameness over difference, unity over multiplicity, and presence over absence, as well as the attributes of masculinity over those of femininity. However, as a number of critics have pointed out, the theoretical outcome of deconstructive feminism has been paradoxical and ironic: by naively glorifying femininity in terms that would make "first wave" feminists blush, a movement originally inspired by the rallying cry of "difference" has turned into a new "essentialism." Moreover, by arrogantly shunning the less flashy, egalitarian agenda of first-wave feminists, academic feminists seem guilty of elitist indifference vis-à-vis the plight of their less privileged comrades. Kristeva has openly dismissed the goals of egalitarian feminism with characteristic gauchiste contempt: "Feminism may constitute merely a demand for the most vigorous rationalization of capitalism."[42] Thus, in the words of Nancy Fraser, for want of sisterly solidarity, "the writing of deconstructive and psychoanalytic French feminists, with its technical character and unfamiliar vocabulary, has . . . [substituted] a discourse of professional legitimation."[43]

Kristeva's feminism is difficult to situate. Although she seems to accept the epistemological terms of gynocentric feminism, which stress

[42] Kristeva, *Interviews*, 101.
[43] Nancy Fraser, introduction to *Revaluing French Feminism*, ed. Nancy Fraser and Sandra Bartky (Bloomington: Indiana University Press, 1992), 2.

the prerogatives of women's "difference," in a series of controversial published remarks, she has gone out of her way to distance herself from feminism in almost all of its contemporary political incarnations.

One of Kristeva's central feminist insights concerns the "maternal function." Whereas avant-garde poets undermine the phallogocentric imperatives of the symbolic by virtue of their art, women, it seems, achieve the same end by virtue of giving birth. "Real female innovation . . . will only come about when maternity, female creation and the link between them are better understood," observes Kristeva.[44] "By giving birth, the woman enters into contact with her mother; she becomes, she is her own mother; they are the same continuity differentiating itself. She thus actualizes the homosexual facet of motherhood, through which a woman is simultaneously closer to her instinctual memory, more open to her own psychosis, and consequently, more negatory of the social, symbolic bond."[45]

In "Women's Time", an essay written in 1975, while she was pregnant, Kristeva claims that maternity presages a "new ethic," a "herethics" (heréthique), "the slow, difficult and delightful apprenticeship in attentiveness, gentleness and forgetting oneself . . . a creation, in the strong sense of the term."[46]

But as feminist critics have pointed out, by narrowly associating the ends of feminism with maternity, Kristeva risks setting the women's movement back by decades. In truth, her "maternal" framework threatens to consign women to the locus of subjection with which patriarchy feels most comfortable. In the apt words of one feminist critic: "Kristeva still believes that men create the world of power and representation; women create babies."[47] Ironically, whereas first-wave feminists like Simone de Beauvoir viewed motherhood as the enemy of women's autonomy, during the 1970s and 1980s second-wave feminists came to regard it as the apex of women's fulfillment.

[44] Kristeva, *Kristeva Reader*, 298.
[45] Kristeva, *Portable Kristeva*, 303.
[46] Kristeva, *Kristeva Reader*, 206.
[47] Ann Rosalind Jones, "Julia Kristeva on Femininity: The Limits of a Semiotic Politics," *Feminist Review* 18 (November 1984): 63.

The rhetoric of maternity that Kristeva embraced during the 1970s was an essentialist discourse that dealt in the eternal verities of femininity. As such, it was at odds with the deconstructionist epistemological standpoint she had adopted earlier to counter the reifications of structuralist linguistics. To redress this contradiction—but also in response to a series of disastrous left-wing political commitments that we will examine shortly—Kristeva soon began to distance herself concertedly from all manner of feminist politics. Thus, whereas other representatives of the French feminist "Holy Trinity," Irigaray and Cixous, employed the deconstructionist critique of phallogocentrism in order to arrive at a positive, "gynocentric" definition of femininity (stressing the prerogatives of lesbianism, women's writing, women's bodies, and so forth, all of which purportedly assumed a "heterogeneous" modality at odds with the "despotism of Western reason"), Kristeva became convinced that *any* attempt to define women risked succumbing to the logocentric tyrannies of the symbolic order. Thereby, she expressed solidarity with Lacan's provocative dictum *"There is no such thing as Woman."*[48] She proceeded to gloss Lacan's witticism as follows: "Indeed, [woman] does not exist with a capital 'W,' possessor of some mythical unity—a supreme power."[49]

Consequently, in Kristeva's view, feminist politics can be only resoundingly *negative*. It must "reject everything finite, definite, structured, loaded with meaning in the existing state of society. Such an attitude places women on the side of the explosion of social codes: with revolutionary moments."[50] But the idea that there can be no middle ground between the twin extremes of women's "nonexistence," on the one hand, and their "mythical, supreme unity," on the other, leaves us with a false choice. Insofar as Kristeva's deconstructive feminism rejects all attempts at women's self-definition as epistemologically retrograde,

[48] Jacques Lacan, "Dieu et la jouissance de la femme," in *Encore* (Paris: Editions du Seuil, 1975), 68; emphasis added.

[49] Kristeva, *Kristeva Reader*, 205.

[50] Julia Kristeva, "Oscillation between Power and Denial," in *New French Feminisms*, ed. Elaine Marks and Isabelle de Courtivron (New York: Schocken Books, 1980), 166.

it risks consigning women politically to a condition of permanent marginality.

In a controversial 1974 interview, "La femme, ce n'est jamais 'ça'" ("Woman Is Never What We Say"), Kristeva declared:

> A woman can never *be*, for a woman is precisely that which shuns *being*. So women's practice can only be negative; it remains at odds with what exists. All it can say is, "That's not it" and "That's still not it." In my view, "woman" is something that cannot be represented or verbalized; "woman" remains outside the realm of classifications and ideologies. . . . What makes my work the work of a woman is that I pay close attention to the element of avant-garde practice that *eradicates identity* (including sexual identity).[51]

According to Kristeva, all positive conceptions of identity court the risk of solidifying into "totalitarianism." But this conclusion relies on a tenuous and indemonstrable link between "avant-garde practice" and an idiosyncratic deconstructionist notion of female identity qua *nonidentity*. Feminist activists have emphatically rejoined that an epistemological approach such as Kristeva's that flatly rebuffs questions of women's identity jeopardizes the very idea of "agency," to the point where the day-to-day struggles of movement activists become virtually meaningless.

THE MISALLIANCE WITH COMMUNISM

Having scorned the "pleasures of the text" for the rigors of "theory," by the mid-1960s the Telquelians sensed that the political winds in France were about to shift. In 1965 de Gaulle was reelected to a second term by a wide margin, suggesting that prospects for meaningful intrasystemic political change were dim. That year saw the first large-scale U.S. bombing attacks against North Vietnam. The concomitant troop buildup and military escalation provoked worldwide student demonstrations. In December 1966 a throng of two hundred thousand

[51] Kristeva, *Interviews*, 98; emphasis added.

French students participated in one such protest at Place de la Bastille. More violent and larger confrontations would follow. Moreover, as we have seen, in France university conditions failed to keep pace with rapidly expanding enrollments and students' rising career expectations. Classrooms were perilously overcrowded, professors inaccessible, and the road to a degree was mined with needless bureaucratic hurdles. Anachronistic and draconian dormitory regulations did very little to ease students' frustrations. In many respects the Latin Quarter was a political-libidinal time bomb waiting to explode.

Although *Tel Quel* had originally defined itself in opposition to the existentialist summons to engagement, it now risked being left behind by the political tumult of the day. Once again, Sollers hastily decided to pursue a radical editorial volte-face. Otherwise, *Tel Quel*, the review that prided itself on being avant-garde, risked finding itself permanently in the *derrière garde*.

An indication concerning the review's new direction came in a 1966 letter from *Tel Quel* editorial secretary Marcelin Pleynet to Sollers, in which Pleynet articulated the review's need for a new political "line":

> *Tel Quel*'s politicization must become public and unambiguous; it must be declared in such a way that all so-called apolitical cultural tendencies—that is, tendencies hailing from the Right—will not be published in the review and can no longer invoke the review as an ally. . . . To accomplish this end I am not sure that [an alliance with] China will suffice. In a French context, the [Communist] *Party will always be more efficacious.*[52]

On this occasion Sollers chose maladroitly, casting his lot with the terminally sclerotic PCF. Far from being a match made in heaven, this was decidedly a marriage of convenience from which both parties stood to benefit considerably. Following a series of disastrous policy decisions (including early support for the Algerian War), in the mid-1960s the fortunes of the PCF had plummeted. Above all, the party had lost its ability to attract renowned fellow travelers à la Gide,

---

[52] Forest, *Histoire de* Tel Quel, 275; emphasis added.

Malraux, and Sartre, who had provided it with a cultural cachet and intellectual luster that it could never have obtained from its "salt-of-the-earth" rank and file.[53] Hence, in the course of a pivotal March 1966 plenary meeting at Argenteuil, PCF cadres decided that to enhance its prestige, the party would have to soften its neo-Zhdanovite cultural orientation, which for years had privileged socialist realism. One of the fruits of this "cultural opening" was the strange alliance with *Tel Quel*. Sollers, for his part, would embrace the opportunity with alacrity, declaring, "Writing and revolution go hand in hand, significantly reanimating one another from time to time and developing, as a weapon, a new myth."[54]

Sollers elaborated the group's new Bolshevist political credo in a 1968 manifesto, "Revolution, Here and Now," which opened as follows:

> Any ideological undertaking which does not today present itself in an advanced theoretical form and settles instead for bringing together under eclectic or sentimental headings individual and underpoliticized activities, seems to us *counterrevolutionary*, inasmuch as it fails to recognize the process of the class struggle, which has objectively to be carried on and reactivated. . . . *Marxist-Leninist theory [is] the only revolutionary theory of our time.*[55]

The alliance made for quite a spectacle: Western Europe's most servile, pro-Stalinist Communist party in league with a famously "unreadable" organ of poststructuralist literary theory. Surprisingly, this shotgun marriage would persevere for five years, well into 1971. For the Telquelians, the concordat with the PCF provided a welcome shield against charges of "apoliticism" during an era of exceptional social and political turbulence. But it also offered prospects for the review and its authors to surmount the tidy confines of Left Bank

[53] On this point, see David Caute, *The Fellow Travelers: Intellectual Friends of Communism* (New Haven, CT: Yale University Press, 1984).

[54] Sollers, ed., *Théorie d'ensemble*, 70.

[55] Sollers et al., "Révolution ici maintenant," *Tel Quel* 34 (Summer 1968): 4; emphasis added.

intellectual life and reach out to an entirely new international public. The Communist Party had at its disposal a vast publicity machine that included *L'Humanité*, a major Parisian daily with a circulation of nearly two hundred thousand, as well as a battery of prominent cultural quarterlies and weeklies: *France Nouvelle, Les Lettres Nouvelles, La Nouvelle Critique,* and *Les Lettres Françaises* (the latter edited by the former surrealist Louis Aragon). In sheer practical terms, the sales and publicity benefits of an alliance with the PCF were potentially massive. As one observer has noted:

> If one stayed close to the Party lines, as did [the novelist] André Stil, a protégé of Aragon, one might win a Stalin Prize for a novel and become the most translated French author in the world, hailed in banner headlines in *l'Humanité*, the object of daily meetings all over France, and covered with gifts. . . . The Communist world was so complete, with its daily and weekly newspapers, its cultural and political magazines, social affairs and rallies, national and international congresses . . . that one could believe it was the whole world.[56]

Conversely, via its alliance with *Tel Quel*, the PCF hoped to secure the loyalty of a new student generation smitten with structuralism, literature, and left-wing politics.

In *The Samurai*, her fictional account of *Tel Quel*'s literary and political heyday, Kristeva portrays the rationale behind the journal's abrupt politicization as follows:

> Hervé [Sollers] wouldn't give up on his idea: there was to be no more literary experiments in ivory towers, there had to be links with the masses. *Now* [*Tel Quel*] was no longer enough; it had to emerge from the Sorbonne. Intellectuals had always been timid radical-socialists; they had nothing to do with literature. A worker at Citroën was more romantic than a prof. And after all, poverty was an explosive force, and the number counted. So

[56] Lottman, *Left Bank*, 251.

why wouldn't *Now* go to Flins [a French Renault factory]? Culture knows no class—the world is full of illiterate aristocrats and stupid bourgeois. But above all, Hervé had a flair for the media. And in 1968, for a short while, the unions were more powerful than television.[57]

Sollers sought to justify *Tel Quel*'s new pro-Moscow, "cultural revolutionary" line by invoking the historical precedents of the Russian formalists Velimir Khlebnikov and Vladimir Mayakovsky and of the surrealists Louis Aragon and Pierre Naville. He was apparently unaware of the disasters, both actual and literary, that their political involvements precipitated. (According to recent archival findings, Mayakovsky's "suicide" was very likely an NKVD [a forerunner of the KGB] execution.) Although Solzhenitsyn's pathbreaking exposé of the Soviet Gulag did not appear until 1973, reliable postwar accounts by Victor Kravchenko and David Rousset had already documented the camps' sordid existence.[58] Undeterred, *Tel Quel*'s nimble semioticians sought to rationalize their philo-communism by claiming they specialized in the "materialism of the signifier," which presumably represented the extension of the class struggle to the strategically key "semiological plane" (*Semioticians of all countries—unite!*). "It is not possible to bring about an economic and social revolution without, at the same time, on another level, *a symbolic revolution*," Sollers pontificated.[59]

At one point Sollers presented one of his trademark, "unreadable" texts—the novel *H*, which consists of a single sentence—to a proletarian audience. He claimed that the workers had been completely won over by his performance.[60] According to Kristeva's account in "My Memory's Hyperbole," the Telquelians, in a spirit of "entrisme," sought to undermine from within the "bureaucratic deformations of an oppressive [PCF] apparatus" by stealthily importing their own eclectic amalgam

---

[57] Kristeva, *Samurai*, 89.

[58] See Victor Kravchenko, *I Chose Freedom: The Personal and Political Life of a Soviet Official* (New York: Scribner's, 1946); David Rousset, *L'univers concentrationnaire* (Paris: Editions du Pavois, 1946).

[59] Sollers, "Réponses," 76; emphasis added.

[60] Cited in *Cultural Politics of* Tel Quel, by Marx-Scouras, 183.

of materialist dialectics, which she characterized as "a Hegelianism reversed by Lucretius, Mallarmé, and Freud."[61] Sollers, too, later claimed that he and his fellow editors were playing a "double game": they had sought to gain access to the "[PCF] inner sanctum in order to place a bomb inside that would explode everything!"[62] Yet even a charitably disposed biographer (Philippe Forest in *L'Histoire de* Tel Quel) cannot help but observe: "One suspects that Sollers has . . . a posteriori reconstructed the history of this period for the sake of exonerating his compromising 'fellow traveling' during these years."[63]

Sollers may have been a political naïf. But as Max Weber once observed, those who play with the wheel of history get crushed. In Kristeva's case, the alibi of naïveté fails to wash. After all, she hailed from one of Eastern Europe's most repressive Stalinist regimes and had experienced the iron heel of "really existing socialism" firsthand. Among *Tel Quel*'s inner circle, perhaps she alone could have added a crucial dose of political realism. Years later, attempting to defend her conduct at the time, she invoked the expectation that perhaps, "in France, it would be different." After all, "hadn't Althusser . . . taken the toughest (for me, the most 'Stalinist') points of Marxism in order to instill new hope in the French Communist Party and all of French society, the harbinger of a worldwide Marxist spring?"[64]

In "My Memory's Hyperbole" Kristeva observes, "The French Communist Party was, and still remains to a large extent, *the only French party to have a cultural politics.* As a state within a state, having considerable powers of dissemination and propaganda distinct from the traditional circuits saturated with more conventional products, the PCF was the best mouthpiece for experimental literary or theoretical work."[65] In other words, as long as party apparatchiks helped bolster *Tel Quel*'s literary renown by publishing fawning reviews, essays, articles, and interviews, one could safely ignore its repressive internal structure as

[61] Julia Kristeva, "Mémoire," *L'Infini* 1 (1983): 50; English translation: "My Memory's Hyperbole," in *Portable Kristeva*, 16.

[62] Forest, *Histoire de* Tel Quel, 296–97.

[63] Ibid., 297.

[64] Kristeva, "My Memory's Hyperbole," 13–14.

[65] Ibid., 16.

well as the horrific crimes perpetrated in the name of the Communist "idea." Another *Tel Quel* sympathizer has tried to justify this unholy cultural political alliance by claiming that "the Communist Party was the only genuinely organized force on the Left, the only party calling itself revolutionary, and also the only party far from uninterested in cultural questions. Thus, in the France of 1967, if a political debate was to bring writers together, it could take place only [through the Communists]."[66]

But even were one to accept for the sake of argument the pro-Communist apologias of Kristeva and company, in the aftermath of 1968, such hollow self-justifications lose all plausibility, for this was the year that communism's dictatorial core reemerged in all its hideousness. Here one might start with the PCF's ignominious role in helping to squelch the worker–student protests of May 1968. At the helm of one of France's largest trade unions, the Confédération générale du travail (CGT), and sensing an opportunity to enhance their respectability as a mainstream political party, the PCF struck an eleventh-hour bargain with the Gaullist government, thereby putting an end to an immensely popular general strike. If one ever needed graphic evidence of the PCF's fundamentally conservative, "counterrevolutionary" nature, here it was for all to behold.

In truth, were one genuinely interested in advancing the interests of the French working classes, the PCF would be the last organ to which one might turn. Time and again, at Moscow's behest, European Communist parties have sold short rank-and-file interests for the sake of their own bureaucratic and political advancement. The Grenelle Accords were merely an extreme instance of this historically well-documented phenomenon.[67]

At this point, a word should be added about *Tel Quel's* peculiar role during the May 1968 uprising. In principle, the May revolt provided the Telquelians with a golden opportunity to express the courage of their cultural revolutionary convictions. Yet, it so happened that they found

[66] Forest, *Histoire de* Tel Quel, 295.

[67] For a good analysis written by two of the protagonists, see Cohn-Bendit and Cohn-Bendit, *Obsolete Communism*.

themselves on the wrong side of the barricades, having cast their lot with PCF capo Georges Marchais. It was Marchais who, at the height of the May rebellion, calumniated March 22 Movement leader Daniel Cohn-Bendit as little more than a "German anarchist." The implication was clear: Cohn-Bendit, who had been born in France but had opted for German citizenship later in life, was a foreign troublemaker. As a German and a Jew, he was doubly "un-French." Conversely, the major intellectual and literary figures of the day—Sartre, de Beauvoir, Jean Genet, Nathalie Sarraute, and Marguerite Duras—enthusiastically lent their support to the student cause. As a concrete expression of their solidarity with the student activists, on May 18 they gathered to proclaim a new writers' union, the Comité d'action étudiants-écrivains (CAEE). By this time an estimated eight to nine million citizens had joined the strike that students had initiated at two Parisian universities earlier in the month.

The Telquelians, steadfast in their fealty to Moscow, were conspicuous by their absence. At the time, Sollers and company took to parroting the party line in predictably servile fashion. As we have seen, the PCF leadership, mistrustful of any mass action they could not fully control, and claiming that the May demonstrations represented a trap that had been set for French working classes by the bourgeoisie, attempted to deter them from participating. The Telquelians brusquely dismissed the student uprising as "petty bourgeois" adventurism. A genuine revolution, they insisted, could be led only by the Communist Party. At a pivotal meeting of the new writers' union, Sollers publicly reaffirmed his undying loyalty to the PCF, CGT, and the "working masses," piously declaring, "All revolution can only be Marxist-Leninist."[68] A few days later, as the new union was about to embark on a crucial vote, *Tel Quel*'s representatives simply walked out. Thus, during the climactic battles of the May uprising, the Telquelians comfortably watched from the sidelines.

Later that summer Warsaw Pact troops invaded Czechoslovakia, brutally quashing the Czech experiment in "socialism with a human face."

---

[68] The account derives from the testimony of the philosopher and *Tel Quel* intimate Jean-Joseph Goux. Cited in Forest's *Histoire de* Tel Quel, 329.

The Soviet occupation of Czechoslovakia represented an important turning point in the history of communism. Thereafter, illusions about the prospect of reforming Communist regimes from within were permanently dashed. Leading French intellectuals—including, in a strongly worded statement, the members of CAEE (the new writers' union that Sollers and company had scorned back in May)—rallied to denounce the Soviet invasion. The Telquelians, for their part, felt it would be "politically inopportune" to condemn the Warsaw Pact action. Any such criticism would play directly into the hands of the bourgeoisie.

In the eyes of its detractors, *Tel Quel*'s refusal to take a firm position against Soviet aggression disqualified all that the journal claimed to stand for. Derrida recalled a memorable dinner at the house of the writer and memoirist Paule Thevenin, where the host began to rail volubly against the Soviets' brutality vis-à-vis the plucky but defenseless Czechs. According to Derrida, the Telquelians merely sat around in silence, staring deeply into their dinner plates.[69]

A September 1968 letter from Sollers to fellow Telquelian Jacques Henric summarizes the journal's official position at the time: "No point in telling you that you should not count on me, even for a second, to disarm the Red Army (not to speak of the Bulgarian tanks, for which I even feel a guilty affection). I find the stench of sordidly self-interested humanism [that is, the critics of the Soviet invasion] that's making the rounds around here exasperating."[70] Following *Tel Quel*'s break with the PCF three years hence, Sollers would justify the review's support of the Warsaw Pact invasion by claiming that to denounce the Soviet incursion would have played directly into the hands of the political Right.[71]

SINOPHILIA

In the eyes of most French intellectuals, the PCF's 1968 blunders—denouncing the May movement and then, three months later, claiming

[69] Ibid., 333.
[70] Ibid.
[71] Sollers, "Positions du mouvement de juin 71," 136.

implausibly that the Soviet invasion of Czechoslovakia was necessary in order to crush a budding "counterrevolution"—left official communism essentially discredited. However, the Telquelians' romance with Bolshevism lasted until 1971, when they sensed another shift in the political zeitgeist: the "wind from the East" emanating from China's Great Proletarian Cultural Revolution.

Although the Telquelians viewed themselves as a cultural revolutionary vanguard, in the case of Maoism, too, they arrived at the station once the train had already departed. By the early 1970s, when Sollers and company jumped on the pro-Chinese bandwagon, the student Left had largely abandoned its dogmatic, ideological phase. Instead, the ex-sixty-eighters had focused their energies on a series of more productive social concerns, centering around "questions of everyday life."[72] Inspired by Solzhenitsyn, a group of ex-Maoists, led by New Philosophers Christian Jambet and André Glucksmann, were in the process of formulating a pathbreaking critique of Communist tyranny. Within the span of a few years, the former student revolutionaries had transformed themselves into impassioned advocates of human rights.

Not so the Telquelians. Desperately seeking to swim with the political tide, they found themselves swept helplessly downstream. Their enthusiasm for China had been kindled by Italian Communist Party member Maria-Antonietta Macciocchi's travel narrative, *Daily Life in Revolutionary China*. For Macciocchi, who would soon join *Tel Quel's* editorial staff, China was "the most astounding political laboratory in the world," a place where morality suffused politics and where "politics means sacrifice, courage, altruism, modesty and thrift." In China, "a people is marching with a light step toward the future. This people may be the incarnation of the new civilization of the world. China has made an unprecedented leap into history."[73] Macciocchi's book became a *succès de scandale* when, in 1971, the PCF tried maladroitly to ban it from its annual festival. This maneuver spawned a fierce debate

---

[72] For documentation of this turnabout, see Hamon and Rotman, *Génération*.

[73] Maria-Antonietta Macciocchi, *Daily Life in Revolutionary China* (New York: Monthly Review Press, 1972), 107, 466.

among journalists and intellectuals, turning the book's reception into a referendum on PCF censorship.

Sollers and company were convinced that the Cultural Revolution was tailor-made for semiologists like themselves. At last, they reasoned, here was a revolution that placed cultural themes front and center. As Lin Biao remarked at the height of the Cultural Revolution, "If the proletariat does not occupy the positions in literature and art, the bourgeoisie certainly will."[74] In *Tel Quel*'s view, whereas earlier revolutions had stressed the primacy of economic and political questions, the Chinese case was clearly different; at issue was a veritable "revolution in signifying practice." As one sympathetic critic explains:

> Mao's brand of Marxism was more appealing [than the PCF's] because it was more "cultural." Mao accorded tremendous importance to the "cultural" revolution, which *Tel Quel* equated with its own "textual" revolution, its work in the signifier. Furthermore . . . Mao appeared to emphasize ideology over politics, thereby giving the Telquelians the impression that, in China, writers and artists had a leading role to play.[75]

In no uncertain terms, the Cultural Revolution permitted the Telquelians to indulge their "cultural commissar" fantasies better than the more staid and traditional cultural politics of the PCF, where culture was still essentially viewed in line with the tenets of Marxist orthodoxy: subaltern and derivative vis-à-vis the material base.

The Telquelians were conned and seduced by the literary pretensions of the Great Helmsman himself. The fact that Mao was something of a poet and a philosopher cinched matters in their eyes. How could one fail to identify with a revolution that was being fashioned by a like-minded fellow aesthete? *Tel Quel*'s fall 1971 issue boldly announced the journal's new political line: "Down with dogmatism, empiricism, opportunism, revisionism! . . . Down with the corrupt bourgeoisie! Down with filthy revisionism! Down with the binarism of the superpowers! Long live

[74] Cited in Franz and Chang's *Taiping Rebellion* 3:767.
[75] Marx-Scouras, *Cultural Politics of* Tel Quel, 172.

revolutionary China! *Long live the thought of Mao Zedong.*"[76] In "Sur la contradiction," Sollers' own programmatic statement, the journal's editor-in-chief showered praise on Mao's "Four Essays on Philosophy," claiming that "in relationship to the works of Marx, Engels, and Lenin, [these texts] constitute a considerable and completely original 'leap forward' in materialist dialectics."[77] He viewed the Cultural Revolution as the "greatest historical event of our time."[78]

As testimony to the journal's new ideological orientation, Sollers and company outfitted the *Tel Quel* offices, situated on the rue Jacob in Paris's fashionable Saint-Germain District, from floor to ceiling with *dazibaos*—Chinese wall posters commonly used to spread political propaganda. Large-font ideograms—Chinese pictorial writing—graced the journal's cover. According to intimates, Sollers sought nothing less than to turn the *Tel Quel* editorial bureau into a Tiananmen Square in miniature. As proof of the depths of his newly acquired pro-Chinese convictions, Sollers began sporting Maoist dress. As one observer notes:

> A complete staging of the new "radical discourse" occurred through a change of wardrobe. For Sollers, the self-proclaimed representative of the hero, Mao, who had been canonized by the revolution, it was a matter of showing the others that he himself submitted to this ideology in order to be able to subjugate the others. . . . Membership in the revolutionary group had to be proven constantly, either through a mode of dress . . . or by referring to texts by Chinese. Sollers was a chameleon who changed intellectual clothing depending on the terrain.[79]

At this point, many of Sollers' fellow editors had become unspeakably frustrated with his unpredictable theoretical and political shifts. Yet, in many cases their intellectual reputations had become so inextricably tied to *Tel Quel*'s renown that to have broken with the review

[76] "Déclaration sur l'hégémonie idéologique bourgeoise révisionnisme," *Tel Quel* 47 (Fall 1971): 135.

[77] Sollers, "Sur la contradiction," *Tel Quel* 45 (1971): 4.

[78] Sollers, "Positions du mouvement de juin 71," 134.

[79] Kauppi, *Making of an Avant-Garde*, 332.

would have been tantamount to literary suicide. The directors at Seuil, too, began to view their prodigal literary son as something of a loose cannon. By the same token, the review's pro-Chinese turn had resulted in dramatically increased sales figures, depriving them of the financial leverage needed to rein in their mercurial editor-in-chief. Whereas the journal's peak sales during its 1960s structuralist, pro-PCF phase had never exceeded twelve thousand copies, the two special issues on China, both of which appeared in 1972, sold upwards of twenty-five thousand copies. By abandoning the PCF and shifting the journal's ideological allegiances eastward, *Tel Quel* had astutely reinvented itself in a manner that conformed with the heady, pro-Chinese political ethos of the post-May period. Whereas at the time of the May revolt, the review's political line had dismissed the student uprising as a petty-bourgeois affair that merely served to divert energy and attention from the proletarian cause, in the fall 1972 issue Sollers and his fellows editors proclaimed, "The organization of the student masses and their struggle, beginning with the specific conditions of their work and of their place within . . . the capitalist system, [and] as an integral part of the struggle of the popular masses—here is a topical problem that goes well beyond the scope of youth or intellectuals alone to involve all ideological and political struggles in France."[80] The review's student-readership quotient escalated proportionally. Needless to say, the publicity generated by the fallout surrounding the Macciocchi affair had proved invaluable.

Tel Quel's editors reevaluated the entire course of Chinese history vis-à-vis the West and its failings and came up with some impressive discoveries. In one article Sollers concluded that the dialectic had been invented by ancient Chinese philosophy.[81] At this point the journal's political antipathy vis-à-vis Trotskyism—whose French representatives had generally been quite supportive of the May revolt—stiffened. In his writings Trotsky had generally belittled the prospects of Chinese communism. Since industrialization in China remained in its infancy, the Chinese proletariat was inchoate, claimed Trotsky. Consequently, the former head of the Red Army vigorously resisted Mao's contention

---

[80] "Le mouvement étudiant," *Tel Quel* 50 (Fall 1972): 124.
[81] Sollers, "Sur la contradiction," 10.

that in China the long-oppressed peasantry could serve as the carrier of revolution. Sollers and company belittled this standpoint—which maintained that a group could never transcend its ascribed social function—as Trotsky's "sociologism."

In "Sur la contradiction" (1971), Sollers tried to show how Mao's conception of "unequal development" had revamped inherited notions of dialectical materialism. Whereas a vulgar conception of dialectics mandated that history always proceed according to a necessary and implacable sequence (for example, feudalism, capitalism, and communism), Mao's notion of contradiction showed how, often, base and superstructure remained disjunctive, thereby allowing for new and original permutations in the logic of class struggle. At certain historical junctures, the economy, although pivotal, might cede primacy to cultural and ideological factors. This characterization appeared to accurately describe the May student revolt, which had accorded pride of place to considerations of "everyday life" and "cultural revolution." Thus, from *Tel Quel*'s vantage point, Maoism harbored distinct political advantages, for by stressing the centrality of ideology, it appeared to open up the field to the "revolution in signifying practice," which was after all the Telquelians' forte. In their estimation, one of the Great Proletarian Cultural Revolution's primary achievements was to have opened the door to the radical innovations of a cultural avant-garde. As Sollers claimed in 1971, "There is not an avant-garde writer who is not intimately concerned with the Chinese Revolution." At stake was "a practical, new, and contemporary revolution of language."[82]

To clarify *Tel Quel*'s new theoretical and political line, Sollers penned a programmatic article in the review's landmark 1972 double issue on China (numbers 48–49), "The Philosophical Struggle in Revolutionary China." One of the essay's leitmotifs was a critique of the Soviet slogan, "Two fuse into one," which had been coined at the time of the Sino-Soviet rift in direct opposition to Mao's celebrated utterance, "One divides itself into two" (in "On Contradiction"). Sollers viewed the Soviet assertion as, in essence, a denial of dialectics and of revolutionary Marxism *simpliciter*. In his view, the crux of Marx's

[82] Sollers, "Positions du mouvement de juin 71," 140.

philosophy of history was that society advanced through contradictions: forces versus relations of production, bourgeois versus proletariat, capitalism versus communism. To gainsay the notion of contradiction was tantamount to denying the Marxist interpretation of history. The only conceivable outcome of the Soviet position was "revisionism": the rejection of world revolution in favor of "peaceful coexistence." Sollers went so far as to insinuate that "Two fuse into one" represented a veiled philosophical justification of the new superpower alliance between the Soviet Union and the United States. Sollers and company began soliciting numerous articles from pro-Chinese Sinologists. Editorial policy mandated that only articles that painted a favorable image of contemporary China would be accepted for publication. Conversely, the editors dismissed out of hand as "racist" opinions or views of China that were in any way critical; Sollers and others claimed that "Eurocentric biases" prevented doubters and naysayers from appreciating the intrinsically revolutionary nature of Chinese developments.[83] In *About Chinese Women*, Kristeva, advocating an intransigent cultural relativism, insisted that Chinese and European "souls" were differently constituted, declaring that it was inadmissible to judge Chinese circumstances by European standards.

Since both Sollers and Kristeva knew a smattering of Chinese, the Telquelians reinvented themselves as "China experts." However, early on the limits of their expertise began to show. In *About Chinese Women*, Kristeva maintained that traditional Chinese culture had been "matrilineal," despite the dearth of empirical evidence to support this claim. To the general astonishment of her readers, she suggested that the feudal practice of foot binding testified to women's secret power. It was, she claimed, merely the Chinese analogue to the Western practice of male circumcision. Allegedly, both practices represented a prohibition that secretly conferred "superior political and symbolic knowledge."[84] But as one of Kristeva's most sympathetic American interpreters was shocked into observing, "How is it that Kristeva can argue that circumcision is analogous to foot-binding when girls are in pain for years and crippled

[83] See van der Poel, *Révolution de la pensée*, 86.
[84] Kristeva, *About Chinese Women*, 86.

for life as a result of their 'castration'?"[85] Finally, describing herself as someone who "recognized my own pioneer Komsomol childhood in the little Red Guards, and who owes my cheekbones to some Asian ancestor," Kristeva maintained that her biographical heritage provided her with privileged insight into contemporary Chinese life.[86]

Another *Tel Quel* article, addressing the absence of professional psychiatry in China, offered the following pseudoscientific explanation. The practice of psychiatry was a response to social alienation. However, by virtue of having eliminated private property and competition, the Chinese had succeeded in abolishing alienation. Hence, psychiatry had been rendered socially superfluous.[87] It flourished only in the hyperalienated West. The author's conclusion was eagerly supported by Maria Macciocchi, who, in *Daily Life in Revolutionary China*, confidently declared: "There is not a trace of alienation in China, nor of those neuroses or that inner disintegration of the individual found in parts of the world dominated by consumerism."[88]

In China youthful Red Guards ran amuck sending party elders en masse to the provinces to endure humiliating rituals of "political reeducation." With schools closed for the staging of revolutionary struggle, legions of Chinese youth were encouraged by Mao and his allies to destroy old buildings, temples, and art objects and to admonish teachers, school administrators, party officials, and parents for their lack of revolutionary zeal. From his base of operations in the Latin Quarter, Sollers decided he would initiate a cultural revolution of his own. Sollers concluded, in good Jacobin fashion, that certain elements on the *Tel Quel* editorial board were politically untrustworthy. He proceeded to purge suspected "revisionists." From this point on, the editorial committee rarely met. On the few occasions when it did convene, it did so only to enact the director's (that is, Sollers') bidding. In accordance with the Maoist adage "One divides itself into two," the Telquelians simultaneously began publishing a polemical broadsheet, the *Bulletin*

[85] Oliver, *Reading Kristeva*, 110.

[86] Kristeva, *About Chinese Women*, 12.

[87] Giovanni Gervis, "Notes sur la psychiatrie en Chine," *Tel Quel* 50 (Summer 1972): 96.

[88] Macciocchi, *Daily Life in Revolutionary China*, 372.

du Mouvement de Juin 71 (after the date of their historic break with the
PCF, but also an allusion to Castro's 26 of July Movement, commemo-
rating his failed 1953 assault on the Moncada Barracks), essentially for
the purpose of settling political scores.

In later years, the Telquelians proffered a series of implausible rationalizations to justify their pro-Chinese folly. At one point they claimed
that, as a form of political radicalism, their Maoism had managed to
keep the banner of 1968 aloft. But the May revolt's spirit, although difficult to encapsulate, had been libertarian, Dionysian, and antiauthoritarian—in short, it was the diametrical antithesis of Chinese political
dogmatics cum sloganeering that attracted Sollers and company.[89] The
Telquelians also maintained that, at the time, their interest in China
had been predominantly literary and cultural rather than "political."
But the key editorial manifestos from this period—for example, "Positions of the June '71 Movement" and "Mao contra Confucius"—show
that at nearly every turn, the group dutifully towed the party line as
prescribed by Beijing. Later on, Sollers claimed that Maoism was a necessary rite of passage on the road to rediscovering a politics of human
rights. As such, it was an important way station in the struggle against
the PCF's unbending Stalinism. And although this contention, strange
as it may sound, might hold water in the case of the New Philosophers,
the Telquelians' ideological vehemence would seem to place them in a
different camp altogether. During the early 1970s, Sollers and company
merely traded in one set of totalitarian political allegiances—namely,
Stalinism—for another—that is, Maoism.
    Jonathan Spence has described the Cultural Revolution's sanguinary
gist as follows:

> With the euphoria, fear, excitement, and tension that gripped
> the country, violence grew apace. Thousands of intellectuals and

[89] This interpretation is confirmed by van der Poel in *Révolution de la pensée*: "Le
problème du maoïsme de Tel Quel . . . a peu en commun, finalement, avec le militantisme de *La Gauche Prolétarienne* ou le tiers-mondisme du Seuil." (The problem is
that Tel Quel's Maoism ultimately has little in common with the militantism of the
Gauche Prolétarienne or the third worldism of [Editions du] Seuil.)

others were beaten to death or died of their injuries. Countless others committed suicide. . . . Many of the suicides killed themselves only after futile attempts to avoid Red Guard harassment by destroying their own libraries and art collections. Thousands more were imprisoned, often in solitary confinement, for years. Millions were relocated to purify themselves through labor in the countryside.[90]

Should the Telquelians have known better? Was enough critical information concerning the institutionalized political chaos Mao had unleashed available at the time to have facilitated a more nuanced assessment of Chinese developments? Or were the Telquelians, like other contemporary Sinophiles, merely the victims of a polished and well-orchestrated Chinese campaign of disinformation?

Although reliable information concerning events in China was somewhat difficult to come by, an examination of the contemporary literature shows that critical reports were in fact readily available. By 1971 certainly—five years after Mao had initiated the Cultural Revolution and the same year the Telquelians leaped enthusiastically on the pro-Chinese bandwagon—enough critical literature had been amassed to raise serious doubts among many French leftists concerning matters Chinese.

In fact, that year two events transpired that combined to seriously diminish the French Left's Maoist political sympathies. In late 1971 confused bulletins emanating from China reported the death of Lin Biao, the head of the People's Liberation Army and the figure Sinologists viewed as Chairman Mao's most likely political heir. At first, Chinese authorities claimed that Lin had died in a plane crash in Outer Mongolia. Although to this day the events surrounding his death remain murky, the most likely scenario suggests that Lin died attempting to flee the country following an unsuccessful coup attempt. In any event, Lin's death and the mysterious circumstances surrounding it had, in the eyes of many, permanently tarnished the Cultural Revolution's luster.

The second event was the publication of Belgian Sinologist Simon Leys's groundbreaking book, *The Chairman's New Clothes*. Leys's study

[90] Spence, *Search for Modern China*, 575.

contained the first detailed account of the Cultural Revolution's notorious political excesses: the vicious Red Guard assaults on party officials, writers, professors, and, more generally, anyone suspected of
harboring "bourgeois" or "counterrevolutionary" views. The Cultural Revolution had degenerated into a vehicle for settling political
scores as well as a means of political self-advancement for revolutionary youth. By 1967, as the political chaos in China threatened to spin
wholly out of control, raising the specter of total chaos, the People's
Liberation Army had to be summoned to cool the Red Guard's revolutionary ardor.[91]

Leys's book was widely vilified by the French press, especially
France's newspaper of record, *Le Monde*.[92] Leys was the messenger bearing news that no one on the French Left wanted to hear, for according
to the twisted political logic of the day, to be critical of Mao's China
meant being pro-American and thus implicitly sanctioning imperialism, nuclear brinkmanship, and the war in Vietnam. One of the few
organs that endorsed Leys's criticisms of Red Guard zealotry was the
Left-Catholic journal *L'Esprit*. *L'Esprit* also published critical articles by
the French Sinologist Paul Bady, who, in no uncertain terms, adjudged
the Cultural Revolution a "hecatomb."[93] Thus, reliable critical views
of Chinese developments were readily available for anyone who cared
to seek them out.

In 1974 Leys published his second exposé of political persecution in
China, *Chinese Shadows*. By this time the French Left had long abandoned its uncritical Sinophilia. Gradually, the French press, too, came
around to accepting the dissenting perspectives that Leys and others advanced. It was now left to the Telquelians alone to hold aloft the banner
of pro-Chinese ideological purity. They gleefully fulfilled their role
as ideological dupes, undertaking a highly publicized, all-expenses-

[91] For a good summary of the Cultural Revolution, see ibid., 565–86.
[92] For a good account, see van der Poel's *Révolution de la pensée*.
[93] Paul Bady, "La révolution dans l'enseignement en Chine," *L'Esprit* 399 (January
1971): 73–88 and "La révolution culturelle en Chine (II), le degré zéro de la culture
bourgeoise," *L'Esprit* 401 (March 1971): 505–23.

paid junket to the People's Republic of China—a classic instance of "revolutionary tourism."[94]

The visit was orchestrated from dawn to dusk by the authorities of the People's Republic of China. The Telquelians were shown model schools, model factories, and model publishing houses—the time-honored Potemkin village routine. Kept on a tight leash by their Chinese handlers, they were strictly barred from speaking with dissidents. At one point, they visited a Peking publisher that displayed a banner welcoming the group by name. Sollers naively interpreted this as an indication that *Tel Quel*'s reputation had spread thousands of miles to the Middle Kingdom's capital. He hardly suspected that the banner, like almost everything else on the tour, was a government put-up. The quid pro quo for the royal treatment the Telquelians received was the understanding that upon their return to Paris, the revolutionary tourists—Sollers, Kristeva, Pleynet, Barthes, and François Wahl—would keep all political doubts and second thoughts strictly to themselves. Sollers and company rigidly adhered to the bargain, continuing to publish supportive articles and travel memoirs in praise of the social achievements of the People's Republic under Chairman Mao's providential guidance. As Barthes wrote in *Le Monde*:

> Mao's calligraphy, reproduced at every turn (a factory hall, a park, a bridge), marks Chinese space with a lyrical and elegant jetéok: admirable art, omnipresent, more convincing to us than the hagiography that comes from afar. . . . A people (that in twenty-five years has already constructed an admirable nation) travels, labors, drinks its tea or practices gymnastics alone: without theater, without noise, without posing—in sum, without hysteria.[95]

[94] For an important (if denunciatory) study of "revolutionary tourism," see Hollander, *Political Pilgrims*. Although Hollander includes a brief discussion of Kristeva's *About Chinese Women*, he otherwise inexplicably neglects the *Tel Quel*'s pro-Chinese phase. See also Hourmant, *Au pays de l'avenir radieuse*.

[95] Barthes, "Alors, la Chine, " *Le Monde*, May 24, 1974; in a more skeptical vein, Barthes was frustrated at the inscrutability of Chinese practices and habitudes—the semiotic impenetrability of Chinese culture—and speculated that the interpretive

Upon their return, the Telquelians demonstrated a special fondness for the "anti-Confucius, anti–Lin Biao" purges following Lin's ill-fated 1971 effort to flee. In Kristeva's view, this campaign demonstrated a "deepening" of the Cultural Revolution, an important step toward the realization of "Chinese Socialism."[96] In her estimation, Chinese communism's uniqueness was that it struggled not only to overturn the existing means of production, but also to definitively transform relations between the sexes. As she explained in *About Chinese Women*, to understand contemporary China, one must position oneself at the site of monotheistic capitalism's disintegration. But where, precisely? Since May 1968 a variety of new ideological loci emerged, but many of these sites mimiced the shortcomings and flaws of the old dogmatisms on the "left" or "right." We are left with what Kristeva, alluding to Dostoevsky, calls "the Underground": the locus of a pure and unassimilable otherness or difference. The Underground's inhabitants, as Kristeva describes them, are "those who aren't yet organized, who in their impossible utopian 'dadaist' approach to politics provoke only laughter." In her view, China is a figure of such otherness. It is a symbol of "all that monotheistic capitalism has crushed in order to make itself everywhere identical and impermeable to crisis."[97]

In this way, China's attractions were no longer "political" in the conventional sense. Increasingly, Chinese communism ceased to exist or have meaning on the plane of the real. Instead, Kristeva and others employed it as a projection screen for the textual concerns ("otherness," "difference," "polyvalence") that had animated their theoretical project throughout the 1960s and 1970s.

For the Telquelians, one of the Cultural Revolution's main advantages lay in the fact that it offered an opportunity for intellectuals and artists to fulfill their historically prescribed role as a revolutionary vanguard. Yet, one critic appositely observes:

---

failures suggested the "death of hermeneutics." See the useful discussion in Eric Hayot's *Chinese Dreams: Pound, Brecht*, Tel Quel (Ann Arbor: University of Michigan Press, 2003), 131–33.

[96] Kristeva, "Les chinoises à 'contre-courant,'" *Tel Quel* 59 (Fall 1974): 29.

[97] Kristeva, *About Chinese Women*, 13–14.

In few societies in our times . . . have intellectuals (and artists) been more harshly treated, humiliated, and deprived of autonomy than in China under Mao, especially during and after the Cultural Revolution. . . . Intellectuals and artists of various kinds were silenced, imprisoned, tortured and made to perform menial labor. Writers allowed to publish were forced into the straitjacket of the most primitive forms of socialist realism; books were literally destroyed . . . as were many monuments and works of art. Book shops stood empty but for the worst of Mao, Stalin, Kim Il Sung, and Enver Hoxha; in the National Library at Peking, all traces of the twentieth-century literary and historical works that do not conform to Maoist orthodoxy have simply vanished.[98]

In *Chinese Shadows*, Leys refers to the Cultural Revolution as the "death warrant of Chinese intellectual life."[99] Sadly, it was a death warrant co-signed by fellow-traveling Western intellectuals.

Although the vast majority of Parisian intellectuals had long since jettisoned their pro-Maoist infatuations, the *Tel Quel* loyalists hung on until the bitter end. Only with the Great Helmsman's death in 1976 and the ensuing campaign to liquidate the Gang of Four would they definitively abandon their pro-Chinese pipe dreams.

Thereafter, Sollers and company quickly boarded the antitotalitarianism bandwagon. *Tel Quel* opened its pages to the New Philosophers, and a close intellectual collaboration developed between Sollers and Bernard-Henri Lévy.[100] Sollers penned a fulsome review of *Barbarism with a Human Face* in *Le Monde*, praising Lévy's ability to reconcile philosophy with literature and extolling the reemergence, for the first time since May 1968, of a "grand romantic style."[101] In a similar vein Sollers lionized *nouveau philosophe* André Glucksmann as "one of the most

[98] Hollander, *Political Pilgrims*, 331.

[99] Leys, *Chinese Shadows*, 129.

[100] See Bernard-Henri Lévy, "La preuve du pudding," *Tel Quel* 77 (Fall 1978): 25–35; and Bernard-Henri Lévy, "C'est la guerre," interview with Philippe Sollers, *Tel Quel* 82 (Winter 1979): 19–28.

[101] Sollers, review of *La barbarie à visage humain*, *Le Monde*, May 5, 1977.

brilliant contemporary French philosophers."[102] But as critics pointed out, neither Lévy nor Sollers could be bothered with an in-depth, empirical analysis of totalitarianism as a form of political rule. Instead, by celebrating dissidence, both writers contented themselves with a facile and media-friendly form of hero worship. One could not help but sense that in exalting dissident literati and nonconformist writing, the *Tel Quel* group was simultaneously exalting itself.

Tel Quel acolytes felt betrayed by the journal's unmistakable shift to the right. The political volte-face was confirmed in 1977, the year the Telquelians published a triple issue on the United States that included contributions from John Ashbery, Allen Ginsberg, and Philip Roth. After their disappointing encounters with the evils of communism, the Telquelians projected their utopian longings for "heterogeneity" and "otherness" onto the New World. (Ten years earlier, in a gesture of principled anti-imperialism, Kristeva had pointedly refused an invitation to lecture at American universities.)[103] As Kristeva remarked in "Why the United States?": "In America, it seems to me that opposition to constraint is . . . *polyvalent* in a way that undermines the Law without attacking it head on."[104] In *Tel Quel's* view Americans excelled in the "nonverbal arts": modern dance, action painting, and happenings. As Kristeva commented (with a dash of Gallic condescension): "They don't have a verbal, that is to say, conscious and analytical . . . connection to what they are doing. . . . There is no great American literature today, apart from a few exceptions, which are of English origins."[105] Alluding to Freud, she observed that America was the land where "'it' [ça] doesn't speak." "It"—a figure for "the unconscious"—needed European intellectuals to speak for it.

By the time the much anticipated 1978 French legislative elections rolled around—the Common Front between the Socialists and Communists was poised for success, until the Communists abandoned the coalition at the eleventh hour—*Tel Quel's* political course had come

[102] Sollers, "La révolution impossible," *Le Monde,* May 13, 1977.
[103] Forest, *Histoire de* Tel Quel, 271.
[104] Kristeva, "Why the United States?" in *Kristeva Reader,* 274.
[105] Ibid., 275, 276.

full circle. Sollers openly announced he was supporting President Valéry Giscard d'Estaing's Union for French Democracy, claiming, "It seems obvious to me that a liberal like Giscard is more left-wing than the [PCF]."[106]

The journal's new rapprochement with the ethos of Central European dissidence was proclaimed in one of Kristeva's programmatic essays, "A New Type of Intellectual: The Dissident."[107] Afflicted by selective remembrance, the Telquelians claimed that the dissident movement was in fact a confirmation of their own intellectual itinerary and legacy. Kristeva and company argued that since most of the dissidents were *literary* figures, this suggested unmistakable affinities with *Tel Quel*'s original project of preserving literature from the perils of Sartrean "engagement." In fact, for a period of ten years the Telquelians had abandoned belles lettres to strike up alliances with two regimes where to defend art for art's sake was tantamount to crimes against the state.

AFTER THE REVOLUTION

In the late 1970s Kristeva became a practicing analyst. Thereafter, she inexplicably burned her bridges to fellow feminists. When pressed to define her relationship to the women's movement, she rashly rejected the concept of gender: "I would emphasize not the notion of gender, but the notion of *singularity*. . . . We must . . . work at the level of *individuals* . . . trying to maximize singularities."[108] Reeling from her earlier political setbacks, Kristeva foreswore politics *simpliciter* as a totalitarian realm that inexorably sacrificed individuals to the repressions of the collective superego. "We must not try to propose global models," she explained. "Of the political there is already too much."[109] She

---

[106] Sollers, "Gauche, droite . . . ," in *La droite aujourd'hui*, ed. J-P Apparu (Paris: Michel Albin, 1979), 339.

[107] Kristeva, "A New Type of Intellectual: The Dissident," in *Kristeva Reader*, 293.

[108] Kristeva, *Interviews*, 42, 43; emphasis added.

[109] Ibid., 42.

recommended that, instead of striving for political solutions, everyone who can afford it enter psychoanalysis.

In *New Maladies of the Soul*, a book inspired by her psychoanalytic practice, Kristeva lamented the narcissistic emptiness of the modern self. Once the rich, archaic imagery of mythology and religion had disappeared, all that remained to replace it were shallow, one-dimensional images derived from the sphere of mass culture: television, film, and cyberspace. We have all become "extraterrestrials," she claimed, hopelessly alienated from our drives and affects. We seek to relieve this sense of loss through the use of narcotics and alcohol, but such remedies prove temporary and artificial. Love and art are the only solutions. Psychoanalysis alone furnishes us with a means of self-recovery. Insofar as it teaches us to embrace the "otherness" within ourselves, it also provides the only basis for ethics and politics.

However, reflecting poststructuralism's endemic suspicion of "meaning," her conception of psychoanalysis turns out to be an emphatically negative one: "The task is not to make an interpretive summa in the name of a system of truths. . . . The task is, instead, to record the crisis of modern interpretive systems . . . to affirm that this crisis is inherent in the symbolic function itself and to perceive as 'symptoms' all constructions, including totalizing interpretations which try to deny this crisis."[110]

In *Powers of Horror* Kristeva, who had once endeared herself to second-wave feminists by lauding the virtues of womb and "maternal instinct," undertook another surprising reversal. She declared that it was *patriarchy*, not maternity, that was responsible for higher cultural achievement: "I think that culture—in particular Occidental culture, which is founded on patriarchy and expressed in the great religions . . . [of] Judaism and Christianity, has produced profoundly true visions of the human being as the symbolic being. . . . So if one says it's patriarchy which produces that, *long live patriarchy*."[111]

In *Black Sun*, a work on female depression, she argued that women are especially prone to melancholia. For men it is natural to identify

[110] Kristeva, *Kristeva Reader*, 319.
[111] Kristeva, *Powers of Horror*, 143–44; emphasis added.

with the father, leading to the abandonment of primary narcissism and a successful resolution of the Oedipal conflict. Women, conversely, are confronted with a distasteful "double-bind." They can identify with the father, thereby entering into the symbolic (the realm of language and "patriarchy"), but at the cost of relinquishing the maternal bond, and thus an indispensable part of themselves qua women. Alternatively, women can reject the paternal-symbolic order, shunning individuation and thereby inviting psychosis or suicide. When confronted with the patently unattractive choices her theories presented for women, she replied, "A woman is caught there, and can't do too much about it."[112] At times, Kristeva openly flirted with the destructive second option: "I see the role of women as a sort of vigilance, a strangeness, an always being on guard and contestatory. In fact, *it's the role of a hysteric*."[113]

In France today the intellectual tide has decisively turned against poststructuralism's brand of epistemological cynicism, the conviction that concrete expressions of identity, truth, or meaning are retrograde theological atavisms, the belief that the only way to avoid the delusions of "sense" and "coherence" is to remain faithful to what Kristeva has called a "negatory" or "nonidentificatory" approach to life and thought. Instead, a new republican intellectual and political consensus has arisen around the imperatives of human rights—a French invention, after all, deriving from the eminently "logocentric" tradition of modern natural law.[114] A sober, moderate, humanist approach has supplanted poststructuralism's latently nihilist negative hermeneutics—a hermeneutics of "absence" rather than "presence." Liberal political philosophers who had been roundly tabooed by the poststructuralist camp—Tocqueville, Camus, and Raymond Aron—have acquired renewed political relevance. Increasingly, the esoteric, "unreadable" approach to theory that was poststructuralism's trademark reeks of anachronism. The rarefied theoretical hairsplitting among philosophical titans that dominated

[112] Kristeva, *About Chinese Women*, 37.

[113] Kristeva, *Interviews*, 46.

[114] See my discussion of this problem in "The French Republican Revival: Reflections on French Singularity," chapter 10 of *The Frankfurt School Revisited* (New York: Routledge, 2006).

Parisian intellectual life during the 1960s has yielded to a more cautious and pragmatic temperament.[115]

In "Julia Kristeva Speaks Out," the former Telquelian has provided a spirited defense of poststructuralism's historical legacy. Those who criticize its "esotericism" have failed to appreciate the important role it played in combating the "identificatory tendencies that have always threatened [civilization]."[116] Her detractors, she claims, are merely defending "corporatist privileges" and the debilities of an "accessible rationalism." Reminiscing about *Tel Quel*'s intellectual heyday, Kristeva waxes nostalgic: it was a "time of serene enthusiasm, a time when I believed we were making a clean break from the archival culture that houses the best of contemporary knowledge and were developing an alchemy of the passions and a radiography of significations. What some people believed . . . to be gratuitous esotericism was merely a terminological . . . loyalty to the critical states we found in an individual, a society, or a text."[117]

One cannot help but be struck by Kristeva's reliance on generalities to prove her point. Her self-vindication operates at a safe remove from concrete institutional, political, and historical questions in whose light alone the plausibility of her claims might be judged. Instead, we are offered a Manichaean opposition between the Telquelians' own "critical" standpoint—their faux-revolutionary "radiography of significations"—and the allegiance to "archival culture" characteristic of everyone else who writes and thinks. In view of the journal's theoretical and political missteps, one wonders whether, apart from a handful of diehards, there is anyone alive who would countenance such transparent apologetics.

It has become fashionable to bemoan the decline of French intellectuals since the death, circa 1980, of master thinkers Barthes, Foucault, Lacan, and Sartre. Critics often invoke structural changes in the French educational system—which has been democratized and is no longer a training ground for privileged elites—as well as the rise of the mass

[115] Mark Lilla, ed., *New French Thought* (Princeton, NJ: Princeton University Press, 1994); Terry Eagleton, *After Theory*.

[116] Kristeva, *Interviews*, 259. Here, by "identificatory tendencies," Kristeva presumably means tendencies that are inimical or hostile to "difference."

[117] Ibid., 261.

media. But it is also the case that in France the intellectual vocation has been irreparably tarnished as a result of political misalliances with "power," the phenomenon against which Julien Benda prophetically warned in *The Treason of the Intellectuals*. One of the supreme ironies of the *Tel Quel* experience is that although the journal was begun as a *machine de guerre* against Sartre, the group ended up repeating all of his political errors—before proceeding on their own to invent some entirely new ones.

CHAPTER 7

Foucault and the Maoists: Biopolitics and Engagement

> *Discipline and Punish* corresponded perfectly to the state of
> mind of a generation that wanted to get the cop and the petty
> bureaucrat "out of its head," and that saw manifestations of
> power everywhere: so much so that Foucault's ideas quickly
> evolved beyond even their author's wishes and became a
> vulgate for those fighting against different forms of social
> control. . . . Never had a philosopher so well echoed the
> ideals and discomforts of a generation: that of '68.
>
> —François Dosse, *History of Structuralism*

Through no fault of his own, Michel Foucault missed out on May
1968. When the explosion erupted, he was hundreds of miles away
teaching philosophy at the University of Tunis. Nonetheless, the May
events had a profound effect on Foucault's intellectual and political trajectory. Foucault himself acknowledged as much, observing that May
was the unanticipated "political opening" that gave him the courage
to investigate the mechanisms of power operating in Western societies
and to "pursue [his] research in the direction of penal theory, prisons,
and disciplines."[1]

Before 1968, Foucault's name was still primarily associated with his
improbable 1966 best seller *The Order of the Things*: the arcane philosophical treatise that famously proclaimed the "death of man." And
although he himself rejected the appellation, Foucault was widely regarded as a "superstar of structuralism," a philosophy that famously

---

[1] Foucault, "Truth and Power," in *Power/Knowledge*, 111.

rejected the powers of reason and human agency to change society for the better. By the early 1970s, conversely, Foucault had become the very embodiment of the militant intellectual. During this period the once shy and reserved philosopher fashioned a new public persona; he began shaving his head, donning horn-rimmed glasses, and sporting a trademark white turtleneck, thus creating the iconic look for which he is best remembered today.

The transformation, however, was more than skin-deep. Foucault's adventures in radical militancy after May 1968—above all, his almost daily interaction with the Maoists who made up the rank and file of the Prison Information Group (GIP)—laid the groundwork for his extremely influential investigations of power during the 1970s. By working shoulder to shoulder with the Gauche prolétarienne activists, Foucault became *"personally involved in his theoretical object of study."*[2] As a result, the Maoist focus on the "practice of everyday life" came to determine the methodology of his two best-known works from this period, *Discipline and Punish* and the *History of Sexuality*. As Jean-Claude Monod observes in *Foucault et la police des conduites*, "As far as prisons were concerned, with Foucault, the practice of contestation preceded the historical theorization [in *Discipline and Punish*]."[3] Fellow Prison Information Group activist Michelle Perrot, editor of *L'impossible prison*, similarly asserts that Foucault's GIP engagement during the early 1970s was decisive for the conception of power he developed in subsequent years.[4] And as Gilles Deleuze notes in a seminal review essay of Foucault's prison book,

> From 1971 to 1973, under Foucault's auspices, GIP functioned
> as a group that tried to combat the resurgence of Marxism and
> the authoritarianism endemic to gauchisme in order to preserve

---

[2] Dosse, *History of Structuralism* 2:249; emphasis added.

[3] Monod, *Foucault et la police*, 75.

[4] Michelle Perrot, "La leçon des ténèbres: Michel Foucault et la prison," *Actes* 54 (Summer 1986); as Perrot observes with reference to GIP, "More than his other books, *Discipline and Punish* is rooted in a historical present in which Michel Foucault is profoundly implicated" (75). See also *L'impossible prison: Recherches sur le système pénitentiaire au XIXe siècle,* ed. Michelle Perrot (Paris: Editions du Seuil, 1980).

a fundamental relationship between prison struggles and other popular struggles. *Discipline and Punish* issued from this political experience. . . . When in 1975 Foucault returned to a theoretical publication [namely, *Discipline and Punish*], to us he seemed to be the first to conceptualize the new understanding of power that we were looking for without knowing either where to find it or how to articulate it. . . . It was as though, finally, something new since Marx had burst forth, another theory, another practice of struggle, another mode of organizing strategies.[5]

Foucault himself hinted at this intellectual genealogy when, in the preface to *Discipline and Punish*, he observed that his conclusions were less informed by history than by contemporary politics. Thus, during these years, the author of *Madness and Civilization* assiduously combined philosophical passion and political activism, in essence leading the life of a committed militant. Although Foucault contributed his name and his support to dozens of causes during this period, he offered his full energies as a philosopher–activist only to the Gauche prolétarienne, thereby bestowing considerable prestige on the infamous banned Maoist organization. Foucault remained in the Maoist orbit until the Gauche prolétarienne's precipitous collapse circa 1973. He once observed that GIP was the GP plus "intellectuals."

To highlight the originality of Foucault's ideas and positions, many critics have viewed his intellectual development during the 1970s as a wholly innovative departure vis-à-vis the reigning Marxist approaches. Yet, a closer examination of Foucault's trajectory as a militant reveals his striking proximity to gauchisme—a political approach that was "leftist" yet opposed to the dogmatic assertions of Marxist orthodoxy. As one commentator has appositely noted: "Taking gauchiste orthodoxy as his point of departure—more specifically, political slogans borrowed from the Maoist tribe—Foucault invented a new vision, a new language, which he systematized in *Discipline and Punish*, and which

[5] Gilles Deleuze, "Ecrivain non: Un nouveau cartographe," *Critique* 343 (December 1975): 1208, 1212.

was destined to become a new orthodoxy among politicized laypersons during the second half of the 1970s."[6]

As we have already noted, French intellectuals played only a minor role during the May events. Observing the unfolding revolutionary drama with a mixture of fear and fascination, they were forced to concede that they had been upstaged by the younger generation of student activists. In vain, a few attempted to make their voices heard from the sidelines. Raymond Aron was struck by the fact that all of the protagonists seemed to be playing roles. "I played the role of Tocqueville, which was somewhat silly of course, but others played the role of Saint-Just, Robespierre, or Lenin, which, all things considered, was even more ridiculous."[7]

It is a matter of speculation what kind of role Foucault would have played had he been in Paris. On the one hand, although Foucault was neither a gauchiste nor a Communist at the time, his sympathies were surely with the student radicals who were fighting against the rigid institutions of Gaullist France. Even though he never made any public statements in their support, privately, at least, he expressed an admiration for their courage to defy the Gaullist regime.[8] In the second half of May, Foucault was finally able to return to Paris for a few days. There he witnessed a fifty-thousand-strong student-worker rally at the Charléty Stadium. Later, he told *Nouvel Observateur* editor Jean Daniel: "They [the students] are not making a revolution; they are a revolution."[9]

On the other hand, Foucault seems to have regarded the students with a healthy dose of contempt appropriate for a man of his generation. Born in 1926, Foucault was not a *soixante-huitard* (sixty-eighter). As an adolescent in the 1940s, the formative events in his life were World War II and the German occupation, not the cold war and

[6] Gerard Mauger, "Un nouveau militantisme," *Sociétés et Représentations* (November 1996): 55.

[7] Raymond Aron, *La révolution introuvable: Réflexions sur les événements de mai* (Paris: Fayard, 1968), 33.

[8] Macey, *Lives of Michel Foucault,* 206–7.

[9] Quoted in Eribon's *Michel Foucault,* 192.

decolonization. Although his family remained largely uninvolved in the politics of the occupation and its aftermath, and although Foucault himself spent most of this period studying diligently for his exams, his daily life, like that of every French citizen, was inevitably structured by the war. While preparing for the entrance exam to the Ecole normale supérieure, for example, Foucault was once forced to evacuate his family home in Poitiers to avoid the Allied bombing campaigns; his family home was damaged during the raids but not destroyed.[10]

Perhaps there was something more significant than the generation gap that kept Foucault from identifying fully with the student militants. Like the leaders of the Union des jeunesses communistes marxistes-léninistes (UJC-ML) who formed the political nucleus of the Gauche prolétarienne, Foucault was a product of France's most elite institutions and knew little of the "poverty of student life"—to cite the title of Mustapha Khayati's influential Situationist tract—which fueled the 1968 student rebellion. In fact, throughout much of the 1950s and '60s, Foucault was not even in France. Whereas many of his academic peers had taken up positions at campuses that were later known for their political radicalism, such as Nanterre and the University of Strasbourg, upon passing the *agrégation* in 1953, Foucault spent much of his early career fleeing his home country, teaching abroad in Germany, Sweden, Poland, and, finally, Tunisia.

EXILED IN PARADISE: FOUCAULT IN TUNIS

Foucault did not have his first taste of student politics until 1968. However, it was not the French *enragés* but the student radicals in Tunisia who enticed him to political activism. While teaching philosophy in Tunisia in 1967 and 1968, Foucault became involved, unwittingly at first, in the student protests against the authoritarian regime of Habib Bourguiba. A fervent modernizer influenced by the French Jacobin tradition, Bourguiba sought to unite Tunisia under a single political party. One of the linchpins of his secular vision was a new university system

---

[10] Macey, *Lives of Michel Foucault,* 15.

in the Western European mode. Foucault had obtained a teaching position at the flagship campus in Tunis, where, paradoxically, his students were slowly being introduced to new anti-Western ideas. During the 1967 Arab-Israeli war, pro-Palestinian student demonstrations turned against the Bourguiba government, which was widely perceived to be a puppet of the pro-Zionist West. The conflict peaked in the spring of 1968 at the time of American vice president Hubert Humphrey's visit. During the ensuing wave of repression, a number of Foucault's students were viciously beaten and imprisoned.

To Foucault's dismay, these student demonstrations sometimes degenerated into anti-Semitic mobs that burned and looted Jewish homes, shops, and synagogues. A lifelong philo-Semite, Foucault did not hide his abhorrence for the anti-Semitic undertones of the revolt; nor did he deny the legitimacy of the students' struggle against state repression. Foucault was also wary of the Tunisian students' uncritical adoption of popular Marxist slogans. He had resigned from the French Communist Party (in which he was never particularly active) in 1952. The sterile Marxist debates of the 1950s and 1960s, and his own experience living under a Marxist dictatorship in Poland, had "left a rather bad taste in my mouth," Foucault recalled. Despite these reservations, Foucault found himself viscerally drawn to the Tunisian students' cause.

> During those upheavals I was profoundly struck and amazed by those young men and women who exposed themselves to serious risks for the simple fact of having written or distributed a leaflet, or for having incited others to go on strike. Such actions were enough to place at risk one's life, one's freedom, and one's body. And this made a very strong impression on me: for me *it was a true political experience.*[11]

Foucault helped hide students running from the police; he even allowed them the use of his home to print their tracts. In doing so, he knew that he was risking much more than his professor colleagues did back in France. One night, while giving a ride to a student, Foucault

---

[11] Foucault, *Remarks on Marx*, 134; emphasis added.

was pulled over and savagely beaten by the police. He was convinced that he was under surveillance by the secret police and that his personal phone had been tapped.[12]

If risking "one's life, one's freedom, one's body," was the measure of a "true political experience," then it is not surprising that Foucault was disappointed by the May 1968 uprising in Paris. As many commentators have noted, May 1968 was more street theater than revolution. Participants on both sides of the barricades were self-consciously playing roles. Fortunately, they were unwilling to take the political confrontation at hand to a higher level. The barricading of the Latin Quarter during the second week of May was clearly a tribute to the Paris Commune of 1871. Yet no one believed the barricades would hold out against a possible military invasion, and no one in power—with the possible exception of de Gaulle for one brief moment—was seriously planning one. Had movement activists been interested in seizing power after the model of 1848, 1871, or 1917, the students might have laid siege to the Elysée Palace or the National Assembly. Instead, they symbolically chose to occupy the Odéon Theater. As Pierre Goldmann, a "serious" Marxist who had trained in guerrilla warfare in Venezuela prior to 1968, described the point of view of the left-wing hardcore in 1968:

> The students streamed into the streets and the Sorbonne like a twisted and hysterical torrent. In a playful and masturbatory demeanor, they satisfied their desire for history. I was shocked that they always spoke out with such visible jubilance. In place of action they substituted the verb. I was shocked that they called for the empowerment of imagination. Their seizure of power was only an imaginary one.[13]

Foucault expressed his relative disappointment with the May revolt in a 1968 interview with an Italian journalist:

---

[12] On Foucault's experiences during the Tunisian student revolt, see Macey, *Lives of Michel Foucault*, 183–208.

[13] Cited in Régis Debray's tribute to Pierre Goldmann, *Les rendez-vous manqués (pour Pierre Goldmann)* (Paris: Editions du Seuil, 1975), 124. On Pierre Goldmann's life, see Dollé, *L'insoumis*.

When I returned to France in November–December 1968, I was quite surprised and amazed—and rather disappointed—when I compared the situation to what I had seen in Tunisia. The struggles, though marked by violence and intense involvement, had never brought with them the same price, the same sacrifices. There's no comparison between the barricades of the Latin Quarter and the risk of doing fifteen years in prison, as was the case in Tunisia.[14]

Foucault rightly insisted on making the distinction between the Gaullist regime, however authoritarian it might have seemed, and the repressive Bourguiba dictatorship in Tunisia, a distinction that the gauchistes' standard "antifascist" discourse commonly ignored. Clarifying the reasoning underlying his "existential" preference for the Tunisian student movement, Foucault added:

What I mean is this: what on earth is it that can set off in an individual the desire, the capacity, and the possibility of an absolute sacrifice without our being able to recognize or suspect the slightest ambition or desire for power and profit? This is what I saw in Tunisia. The necessity for a struggle was clearly evident there on account of the intolerable nature of certain conditions produced by capitalism, colonialism, and neo-colonialism. In a struggle of this kind, the question of direct, existential, I should say physical commitment was implied immediately.[15]

Despite his distaste for Marxism, Foucault was willing to overlook the Tunisian students' allegiance to the Marxist catechism and identify with the life-or-death, existential nature of their struggle. Thus, whereas Marxism had long since grown academic and sterile in France, "In Tunisia on the contrary, everyone was drawn into Marxism with radical violence and intensity and with a staggeringly powerful thrust. For those young people, Marxism did not represent merely a way of

[14] Foucault, *Remarks on Marx*, 138.
[15] Ibid., 136–37.

analyzing reality; it was also a kind of moral force, an existential act that left one stupefied."[16]

In France, too, at least a handful of radical circles took Marxist theory very seriously in the summer of 1968. Some of these groups tried in vain to steer the student movement from within. The Trotskyist Jeunesse communiste révolutionnaire, a student group that had been instrumental in organizing protests at the Sorbonne, had formed action committees to coordinate activities in the student-controlled areas of the Latin Quarter. As we have seen, the Maoist UJC-ML simply boycotted the "trap" laid for them by the bourgeoisie; only later would they reevaluate their position when the workers' strikes began.[17]

In general, Marxism served as a lingua franca for the entire student movement, not just the political radicals. It was the language the students employed, albeit at times reluctantly, to express their libertarian demands and to articulate their utopian vision of an alternative society. Yet, as Alain Touraine argued in his book on the May revolt, *Le mouvement de mai, ou Le communisme utopique*, there was a critical disjunction between the students' Marxist rhetoric and the true nature of their revolt. In Touraine's view, the May insurrection was less a revolt against capitalism than an uprising against political technocracy. The stakes at issue were less economic than about who had the power to make decisions. In opposition to the technocratic utopian vision of France's economic and political cadres (many of whom were so-called *Enarques*, or graduates of the Ecole nationale d'administration), which reduced all social problems to questions of modernization, adaptation, and integration, during May the students invented a libertarian counterutopia: "utopian communism." As Touraine aptly observes, "The message of the technocrats who controlled society was *adapt yourself*, to which the May movement countered *express yourself*."[18] Just as in the nineteenth century the Industrial Revolution marked the entry of "work" into

[16] Ibid., 135.

[17] See Christophe Bourseiller, "De mai à décembre 1968: Le rendez-vous manqué," in *Les Maos*, 89–103.

[18] Alain Touraine, *Le mouvement de mai, ou Le communisme utopique* (Paris: Editions du Seuil, 1972), 11. See also the influential book by Michel de Certeau, *The Practice of Everyday Life*, trans. Steven Rendell (Berkeley: University of California Press, 1984).

the public sphere, May 1968 marked the entrance of "everyday life."[19] Suddenly, hierarchy, consumerism, city planning, gender and sexuality, and the nature of human intimacy became legitimate topics of public discussion and political struggle. Resistance to the colonization of everyday life had become an urgent political imperative. As a metaphor and figure, the idea of cultural revolution was detached from its original Maoist moorings to become the battle cry of a sweeping, grassroots project of social transformation.

Originally, Foucault was unimpressed by the cultural dimension of the May revolt. He had failed to witness firsthand the legendary Sorbonne student commune, which was animated by music, poetry, drugs, graffiti, and radical democracy. He saw nothing of the student occupations and action committees, nor of the spontaneous teach-ins and sit-ins that spread to virtually every town and village across the hexagon. Even if he had witnessed this side of the revolt, it is not clear that he would have regarded the student utopia with the same enthusiasm as his colleagues Claude Lefort, Cornelius Castoriadis, and Henri Lefebvre did, who famously defended their pupils-turned-activists before the university disciplinary courts and humbly allowed themselves to become their followers. Foucault had held a couple of teaching positions in France before 1968, but by most accounts he was not the kind of professor who rubbed shoulders with the students. In his six years as a professor at Clermont-Ferrand, he never lived on-site, preferring the six-hour rail commute from Paris.

Toward the end of May, de Gaulle orchestrated his improbable return to power. He had weathered the storm, but just barely. The regime's manifest vulnerability further radicalized French youth in May's aftermath. On June 1, throughout the streets of Paris, thousands of students chanted "May '68 is only the beginning. We must continue the struggle!"[20] In the months that followed, the student movement forgot

[19] Discussion with Alain Touraine in "Itinéraires intellectuels des années 1970," *Revue Française d'Histoire des Idées Politiques* 2 (1995): 392–400.

[20] BDIC, *Mai 68: Materiaux pour l'histoire de notre temps* (Paris: Bibliothèque de documentation internationale contemporaine, 1988), 299.

about the "poverty of student life," setting their sights instead on the next "May." The editors of *Cahiers de Mai*, one of the first new student publications to emerge in the post-May period, summarized the predominant student attitude as follows:

> Should we now feel only bitterness and deception? An extraordinary new *époque* has just announced itself in France and Europe more broadly. We can see now that a socialist revolution in a highly industrialized society—the conditions hoped for by Marx in other words—is under way. The revolution will transform the face of socialism in the world. During the events of May, the revolutionary fermentation in France produced surprising and unprecedented results. Without haste we must recognize, study, and understand them. They hold a treasure of knowledge and resources for the working-class movement in France and abroad. [May 1968] is a war chest for the battles to come.[21]

The "revolution of everyday life" was never entirely suppressed. It continued to survive and prosper within certain elements of the radical student milieu. In the years that followed, as the dream of a political revolution gradually faded, its energy and ideas reemerged in the new social movements of the early 1970s. Yet, for the most part, Foucault missed out on this "revolution," too, even though it was taking place all around him.

THE EXILE'S RETURN

Following May 1968, Foucault was eager to return to France. Unnerved by the pressures and anxieties of living in an authoritarian state and intrigued by the new wave of contestation in France, he abandoned his plans to purchase a beachfront home in Tunisia and accepted an offer to head the philosophy department at the newly created "experimental" University at Vincennes. A direct response by the Ministry of

---

[21] "Ce qu'on cherche à nous faire oublier," *Cahiers de Mai* 1 (June 15, 1968): 3.

Education to the sixty-eighters' demands for university reform, Vincennes was a radical experiment in antiauthoritarian education. Professors were elected by their peers and evaluated by their students, rather than by deans or administrators. The curriculum was resolutely interdisciplinary. Perhaps most radical of all, the university was open to candidates from all backgrounds, not just those who had completed the *baccalauréat*. As René Schérer, one of the first professors elected to the philosophy department, explains: "Vincennes was the 'outside' entering the university and, simultaneously, the university opening itself to the outside."[22]

Predictably, and in accordance with the ministry's plan to relocate the most instransigent political activists at a remove from central Paris, Vincennes immediately attracted the most radical factions of the French Left. Foucault played a pivotal role, recruiting *gauchistes* of all stripes for the philosophy department.

Ironically, Foucault had been a politically uncontroversial choice to head the new philosophy department. Since the enormously successful publication of *The Order of Things* in 1966, his reputation had grown steadily; hence, his philosophical credentials were never in doubt. More important for his appointment, at the time of the May events Foucault had been absent. Nor had he spoken publicly about his political involvements with the Tunisian student movements. Yet although his absence in May 1968 made him a safe choice to head the Vincennes philosophy department, it also meant that he would have to establish his revolutionary bona fides among his colleagues and students.

Foucault wasted little time. In January 1969, during the first of many campus battles, he had his first lesson in street fighting. With a small group of Vincennes professors, including his partner, Daniel Defert, he helped mount an occupation of one of Vincennes' main buildings. When the riot police arrived with truncheons and tear-gas grenades to evacuate the protesters, Foucault was among the very last to leave.

[22] René Schérer, *Hospitalités* (Paris: Anthropos, 2004), 95–96. For more on Vincennes, see Charles Soulié, "Le destin d'une institution d'avant-garde: Histoire du département de philosophie de Paris VIII," *Histoire de l'Education* 77 (January 1998): 47–69.

Fearless, he retreated up the staircase, barricading the way behind him and hurling down random objects. As Defert later recalled, Foucault thoroughly enjoyed himself that evening: "[Foucault] was no doubt experiencing a definitely Nietzschean 'joy in destruction.'"[23]

The events that sparked this clash remain complicated and confusing. The decision to occupy the university building was made in response to the arrests of dozens of activists at the Sorbonne who had been protesting inadequate financial support.

For Foucault and the protesting students, however, the specific cause was merely a pretext. They had planned to disrupt the new university long before it had opened its doors. After this initial battle, a permanent police presence was established on the campus. Yet order was never really restored. Daily protests and riots regularly interrupted classes and the administrative functions of the university. Books disappeared from the library, and buildings and facilities were blighted by vandalism.

Although plagued by political and ideological factionalism, ultimately the Gauche prolétarienne managed to seize control of the philosophy department and make its presence known across the Vincennes campus. Libertarians and cultural revolutionaries the Gauche prolétarienne militants were not. In the fall of 1968, they articulated their ultimate aims unambiguously in their newly established daily, *La Cause du Peuple*: "The central and supreme goal of the revolution is the conquest of power by armed struggle. . . . This revolutionary principle of Marxism-Leninism is valid everywhere—in China as in other countries."[24]

Although the GP leaders had missed the boat in May, by the fall of 1968 they had begun to read the changing political situation correctly. Whereas prior to May 1968, the UJC-ML (the Gauche prolétarienne's forerunner) held that the primary goal of student radicals should be the formation of a revolutionary student-worker avant-garde, they now argued that the task of the student militants was not to lead or ally themselves with the workers, but to *immerse* themselves in their struggles. In the wake of the May uprising, the GP's *ouvrièriste* message and its model of revolutionary discipline struck a chord with young activists

[23] Cited in Macey's *Lives of Michel Foucault*, 226.
[24] "De nouveau le combat!" *La Cause du Peuple* 1 (November 1968): 2.

who were disenchanted with the established Left, disheartened by the May revolt's failure, and yet still intoxicated with the allure of political militancy. Their ranks quickly swelled. France's intellectuals and cultural elites added their support. Maoism's prestige quickly blossomed.

Foucault was profoundly impressed by the *gépistes*, or GP members, who seemed to embody the same "ultra" qualities he had admired in his Tunisian students.[25] In a letter to Daniel Defert written a few months after the Cultural Revolution's onset, Foucault admitted he was "very much inspired by what is happening in China" (Je suis bien passioné par ce qui se passe en Chine).[26] Above all, he was drawn to the Maoists' unique approach to militancy. Although the UJC-ML had been late to join the May movement, it was one of the few student groups that continued to agitate throughout June and July—as though May had never ended. Abandoning the Latin Quarter, the Maoists focused their attention on the politically volatile factories on the outskirts of Paris, where the workers had refused to accept the terms of reconciliation Prime Minister Pompidou offered. Even after the group disbanded, the UJC-ML *établis* remained in the automobile plants in and around Paris, functioning as autonomous *groupes de bases,* or grassroots groups. As student activism moved "from the amphitheaters to the factories" (to quote the title of a well-known book on the établis), these Maoist cells seemed to embody new possibilities for decentralized, local resistance.[27]

The Maoists' model of revolutionary action quickly became known as *spontanéisme* (spontaneity), a term that was originally applied to the Gauche prolétarienne by its Marxist-Leninists critics. Whereas following May, Marxist-Leninist groups such as the Trotskyists sought to establish a new revolutionary party, the Maoists favored "direct action." Inspired by the Cultural Revolution, they sought to efface all traces of social distinction: between the "intellectuals" and the "people," as well as between the students and workers. Spontanéisme translated into a kind of philosophical pragmatism. Its proponents rejected a priori

[25] Miller, *Passion of Michel Foucault*, 177.
[26] Cited in Foucault's *Dits et écrits* 1:59.
[27] Dressen, *De l'amphi à l'établi*.

theorizing. Instead, theory was supposed to exist in a dialectical relationship with practice. Ideally, it would emerge from engagement with
the struggles of the people; otherwise, it remained of secondary importance and provisional. The Maoists placed their faith in the people's
capacities to continually adapt their struggles to new situations.

The GP came to view the Cultural Revolution not as a blueprint for
revolution, but as proof that no such blueprints existed. Increasingly,
the "real" China ceased to matter. What counted was, according to a
Maoist saying, the "China in our heads" (la Chine dans nos têtes). The
crucial lesson they claimed to have learned from Mao's example was
that each people was essentially different; hence each nation needed to
carve out its own path to socialism. Just as Mao had broken with the
Soviet Union to help China discover its own path, the French people
would have to forge their own way toward socialism. It was not the
model of Chinese socialism per se that the Maoists sought to emulate.
Instead, they aspired to be like Mao, to employ his way of thinking,
"Mao Tse-tung Thought."[28]

Whereas heretofore Foucault had kept a safe distance from the frac-
tious French Marxist circles, in spontanéisme he found a means of entering the arena of radical politics and a Marxist philosophy he could
abide. Without mentioning the Maoists by name, Foucault expressed
his admiration for spontanéisme to a Japanese audience during a talk at
Keio University in 1970. Despite the fact that this new form of Marxism
had been formulated by students and intellectuals, it was, in Foucault's
view, "anti-theoretical." He characterized the new political movements
as being "closer to Rosa Luxemburg than to Lenin: they rely more on
the spontaneity of the masses than on theoretical analysis."[29]

As we have seen, political militancy eventually landed dozens of
Maoist activists in French prisons. In May 1970 Interior Minister Raymond Marcellin summarily banned the Gauche prolétarienne. The

[28] This term was borrowed from the ninth congress of the Chinese Communist
Party in 1969, where it was coined to replace the term "Maoism" as part of an attempt
to put more distance between the Chinese Communist Party's revolutionary philosophy and the person of Mao Tse-tung. See Pierre Masset, L'empereur Mao: Essai sur le
maoïsme (Paris: Éditions Lethielleux, 1979), 287.

[29] Foucault, Dits et écrits 1:1140.

government arrested several highly placed GP militants, under a new antiriot act that made leaders of a political organization legally responsible for any transgressions perpetrated by the rank and file. Other Maoists were arrested for allegedly attempting to "reconstitute a banned organization." Their crime? Continuing to publish and distribute *La Cause du Peuple*. In prison the GP activists made contacts with other student radicals and wasted no time "investigating"—that is, undertaking *enquêtes* of—their new surroundings.

In September 1970 thirty gauchiste prisoners, many of them gépistes, began a hunger strike demanding recognition as "political prisoners," a designation that had been accorded to certain members of the FLN during the Algerian War. According to this precedent, this status would allow them certain rights and privileges: the right to congregate as a group, the right to communicate with fellow gépistes on the outside, and access to the press. Yet, the gauchistes soon realized the unfairness of arguing for their own superior, "political" status vis-à-vis their fellow detainees—an elitist mind-set that flouted the egalitarian spirit of the post-May period. Were common criminals intrinsically inferior to the Maoist political aristocracy? Was not the lot of *all* prisoners similarly unjust? The gauchistes soon realized that by acceding to the mentality that opposed political prisoners to common criminals, they had implicitly accepted a series of ideologically tainted, bourgeois conceptual dualisms: moral and immoral, good and bad, vice and virtue. Very soon the gauchistes' political aim was to coax all inmates to join their strike, since, in a "fascist" judicial system, *all* prisoners are political prisoners.[30]

The initial hunger strike lasted a month and failed to attract public attention. In January 1971 the Maoists tried again. This time, however, they succeeded insofar as they had persuaded dozens of other activists outside the prison walls to join them. Most notably, hunger strikers gathered in the heavily traveled Montparnasse railway station and in a small, adjacent church, the Saint-Bernard Chapel. At this point a

---

[30] See ibid.: "The cultural revolution in its widest sense implies that, at least in a society like ours, you no longer make the division between criminals of common law and political criminals. Common law is politics, it's after all the bourgeois class which, for political reasons and on the basis of its political power, defined what is called common law."

number of influential cultural and intellectual luminaries took note. Actors Yves Montand and Simone Signoret, the philosopher Vladimir Jankélévitch, and the journalist Maurice Clavel dropped by to publicize their solidarity with the strikers. In the National Assembly, future president François Mitterrand spoke eloquently on the strikers' behalf, plausibly accusing Guardian of the Seals René Pleven of having arrested the Maoist leaders merely to settle old political scores. Mitterrand also brought welcome public attention to the lamentable prison conditions the gauchistes had unjustly been forced to endure.[31]

THE EXTENSION OF THE DOMAIN OF STRUGGLE: FOUCAULT AND THE PRISON INFORMATION GROUP (GIP)

Foucault was eager to participate in Maoist activism, but he wanted to do so on his own terms. He noticed how the Gauche prolétarienne had exploited Sartre as its figurehead and spokesperson following the arrest of *La Cause du Peuple*'s editors. Hence, he was reluctant to become just another bit of intellectual window dressing like the other so-called democrats. At the time, Serge July and Pierre Victor—using the semi-ridiculous pro-Chinese pseudonym Jean Tse-toung—had formed the Organisation des prisonniers politiques (OPP), a support group for the imprisoned Maoists who had been orchestrating the hunger strikes. The gépistes dispatched Judith Miller and Jacques-Alain Miller (Lacan's daughter and son-in-law)—Maoist activists who were Foucault's research assistants in the department of philosophy at Vincennes—to persuade the philosopher to abandon his monastic work habits for the sake of political engagement.

But it was Daniel Defert, Foucault's partner and a Gauche prolétarienne militant, who proposed the idea of forming a popular tribunal similar to the one Sartre had established at Lens to investigate prison conditions. Foucault suggested instead calling it an information group.

[31] For Mitterrand's intervention, see Grégory Salle, "Mai 68: A-t-il changé la prison française?" *Critique Internationale* 16 (2002): 183–95.

He was concerned that were a formal commission of inquiry established, its focus and energies would be directed toward the French state and judiciary system. Thereby, it would immediately become enmeshed in traditional, top-down, and juridical conceptions of power. An information group, conversely, would be less handicapped by conventional political preconceptions. It would offer the distinct advantage of addressing the more subtle, capillary modalities of biopower as Foucault had recently conceived them. Conventional approaches to penality typically bypassed the "materiality of punishment": the everyday violence and humiliation, the judges' callousness, the lawyers' indifference, the obstructionist tactics the prison guards' union employed (the group that, in essence, ran the penitentiary system on a daily basis), and the families' helplessness and shame. It was this "material" aspect of punishment, as meticulously documented in GIP's Enquête-Intolérable (Investigation Intolerable) publication series, that revulsed French public opinion and that would soon become an object of intense political debate.

More than anyone else, Foucault was keenly aware of the extent to which information could be a political weapon. By the same token, his new insights about the amorphousness of power led to a correlative skepticism about the traditional French sacralization of the writer's vocation. Henceforth, Foucault no longer wished to be described as a writer and an intellectual, but as a "merchant of political instruments" (un marchand d'instruments politiques).[32]

In this way the Groupe d'information sur les prisons was conceived.

Initially, Foucault thought of GIP as merely one aspect of a more general confrontation with contemporary society's capacity for disciplining individuals via the mechanisms of "power-knowledge." Thus, in the group's initial press release, in addition to prisons, Foucault cited hospitals, psychiatric institutions, universities, and the press and other

[32] See Daniel Defert, "L'émergence d'un nouveau front: Les prisons," in *Le groupe d'information sur les prisons: Archives d'une lutte, 1970–1972,* by Philip Artières et al. (Paris: Editions de L'IMEC, 2003), 323; see also Gérard Mauger, "Un nouveau militantisme," *Sociétés et Représentations* (November 1996): 60, and Mauger, "Un marchand d'instruments politiques: A propos de Michel Foucault," in *Lire les sciences sociales,* by Gérard Mauger and Louis Pinto, vol. 3, *1994–96* (Paris: Hermes Science Publications, 2000), 123–46.

organs of information as parallel sites where expertise and political oppression enjoyed an unwholesome, symbiotic intimacy. But, soon, the focus on prisons acquired an autonomy and momentum all its own.

On February 8, 1971, the author of *Madness and Civilization* held a landmark press conference in front of the Saint-Bernard Chapel, where the hunger strikes had begun only few weeks earlier, to launch GIP. According to the manifesto distributed to the press, the organization's goal was to gather information: "to make known what a prison is: who goes there, how, and why, what happens there, what the lives of prisoners are like, and at the same time, what the lives of the guards are like, what the buildings are like, the food, the hygiene, how the prison functions internally, the medical facilities, the workshops; how one gets out of prison and what it means in our society to be an ex-con."[33]

Foucault and GIP thus launched Enquête-Intolérable. This sobriquet was an allusion to the unbearable nature of French prison conditions. Unlike the United States, in France outsiders were by law forbidden to set foot in prisons. Hence, to the world outside, the prison's real nature was shrouded in secrecy. The GIP activists circumvented the on-site ban by interviewing former inmates, prison employees, guards, and detainees' relatives. Since family members possessed visitation rights, they had seen the prisons from the inside. Foucault and his fellow militants sifted through hundreds of questionnaires, analyzing the prisoners' grievances, their relatives' complaints, as well as those of prison guards.

One of their more interesting findings concerned the class biases of French prison life. One investigation found that whereas 80 percent of the bourgeois prisoners benefited from furloughs, only 32 percent of the working-class inmates enjoyed such privileges. Similarly, 90 percent of the bourgeois inmates received parole or early release in comparison with 33 percent of the working-class prisoners.[34] The French

---

[33] Foucault, *Dits et écrits* 2:1043.

[34] See Christophe Soulié, "Années 70: Contestation de la prison; Information est une arme," *Raison Présente* 130 (1999): 25; Grégory Salle, "Mettre la prison à l'épreuve: Le GIP en guerre contre l'"Intolérable,'" *Cultures et Conflits* 55 (2004): 71–96; see also Philippe Artières, Pierre Lascoumes, and Grégory Salle, "Prison et résistances politiques: Le grondement de la bataille," *Cultures et Conflits* 55 (2004): 5–14.

working class endured a kind of triple jeopardy: (1) their illegalities were more closely monitored; (2) they were more readily imprisoned; and (3) once incarcerated, it became more difficult for them to leave.

The results were published in a series of widely distributed pamphlets over the ensuing year and a half. During this time Foucault committed himself body and soul to GIP. His apartment at 285, rue de Vaugirard became the organization's de facto headquarters. Foucault was involved in every one of the group's activities, from the publication of its press releases to addressing envelopes and making phone calls.

Despite GIP's purportedly modest goal of exposing the unbearable conditions of French prisons, Foucault's investigations, like the Maoist enquêtes, ultimately had a more radical political aim. The point was not to *reform* the penal system, but *to call into question its very foundations.* When he introduced GIP to the French public at a February 1971 press conference, Foucault explained that the struggle against the penal system involved not only prisoners but every member of contemporary French society. As he put it, "None of us can be sure of avoiding prison. This is truer today than it has ever been. . . . They tell us that the prisons are overpopulated. But what if, instead, the population is overimprisoned?"[35] Instead of "organizing" the prisoners and prison

---

[35] Foucault, *Dits et écrits* 2:1042. In "The Red Guards of Paris: French Student Maoism of the 1960s," *History of European Ideas* 4 (31) (2005): 472–90, Julian Bourg shows how GIP's enquêtes paradoxically paved the way for a revivification of French civil society:

> French Maoist uses of the strategy of the investigation [contributed] unintentionally to an invigoration of civil-social practices. The *Gauche prolétarienne* found itself faced with, not a singular mobilizing working class, but a myriad of social groups: feminists, gay liberationists, high school students, soldiers, immigrants, early ecologists, and so forth. . . . The Maoist method of investigation ran up against the inconvenient fact that the New Left was composed of disparate interests with vaguely commensurate, and sometimes conflicting, liberationist goals. The most noteworthy example of where the Maoist investigation led was the *Groupe d'information sur les prisons*, formed in February 1971 under the inspirational presence of Michel Foucault. Organized on the fringes of the *Gauche prolétarienne*, the prison information group pointed the investigation in new directions, distributing surveys and publicizing information to the general public about the "intolerable"

workers formally as unions and political parties had traditionally done, the GIP sought, in the spirit of Maoist populism, to empower them so that they would be capable of organizing their own resistance to the penal system.

When he assumed the leadership of GIP, Foucault worked carefully to distinguish himself from the model of the universal intellectual as embodied by Sartre. Whereas the universal intellectual embraced a timeless set of transcendent human values, Foucault proposed a new model of engagement: the "specific intellectual."[36] The specific intellectual refuses to stand outside of the webs of power that suffuse modern society. Instead, she tries to work strategically within them. Like the Maoist établi, the specific intellectual fights power by channeling the "local knowledge" of the people who are in direct contact with that power. As Foucault explains, "The masses don't need him [the intellectual] to gain knowledge: they know perfectly well, without illusion; they know far better than he and they are certainly capable of expressing themselves."[37] In Foucault's view, those who set themselves up as repositories of a higher-order theoretical truth, as the masses' spokespersons or representatives, are an integral component of a disciplinary society that works to maintain them in a condition of dependency or bondage. They are in essence agents of the system of power. The intellectual's role is "no longer to place himself 'somewhat ahead and to the side' in order to express the stifled truth of the collectivity; rather, it is to struggle against the forms of power that transform him into its object and instrument in the sphere of 'knowledge,' 'truth,' 'consciousness,' and 'discourse.'"[38]

----

conditions in French prisons. . . . Investigations yielded information, and information itself was a weapon to be used tactically in struggle. . . . The *Groupe d'information sur les prisons* contributed to the radical shift in 1970s French cultural politics, from Marxism to post-Marxism.

[36] Foucault, "Truth and Power," in *Power/Knowledge*, 109–33.

[37] Michel Foucault and Gilles Deleuze, "Intellectuals and Power," in *Foucault Live: Collected Interviews, 1961–1984,* ed. Sylvère Lotringer (New York: Semiotexte, 1994), 75.

[38] Ibid.

Foucault's new conception of engagement was part of a broader transformation of his intellectual trajectory; one might justly describe it as an "epistemological break." In part, the change had been facilitated by the events of May 1968. Yet, to an even greater extent, it was indebted to the gauchiste milieus that flourished in the post-May period.

When *The Order of Things* appeared, the mainstream press seized on Foucault's celebrated adage concerning the "death of man" as a major cause for concern. Foucault had reiterated this thesis, in a manner shorn of nuance, in a 1966 interview, boldly declaiming: "Our task is to free ourselves definitively from humanism. It is in this sense that my work is political, insofar as, in both the East and the West, all regimes purvey their shoddy wares under the humanist banner."[39] One logical conclusion that political activists drew from Foucault's declaration was that all attempts at political change were condemned in advance to futility. If the paradigm of the subject was in fact obsolete, what forces could be relied on to effectuate political change?

Writing in *Le Figaro*, the novelist François Mauriac—one of Sartre's long-standing foes—declared that Foucault's structuralist antihumanism had succeeded in rendering Sartre's approach more sympathetic.[40] Sartre's own journal, *Les Temps Modernes*, followed suit, publishing a review essay titled "The Cultural Relativism of Michel Foucault."[41] But for Foucault, perhaps the ultimate indignity derived from a now-famous scene in Jean-Luc Godard's cult political classic *La Chinoise*. At one point, the "pro-Chinese" heroine, Véronique (played by Anna Wiazemsky), hurls a battery of rotten tomatoes at the book *The Order of Things*, since Foucault's inflexible structuralism seemed to deny prospects for revolutionary political change.

By the same token, the journalist Maurice Clavel recounts his arrival in Paris amid the disorder and chaos of the May student revolt, reflecting that Foucault's controversial dictum had proven correct after all.

[39] Foucault, interview with Madeleine Chapsal, *La Quinzaine Littéraire* 16 (5) (May 1966): 15.

[40] François Mauriac, "Bloc-Notes," *Le Figaro*, September 15, 1966.

[41] Michel Amiot, "Le relativisme culturel de Michel Foucault," *Les Temps Modernes* (January 1967).

Did *The Order of Things* not prophesy "the geological breakdown of our humanist culture such as it came to pass during May '68"?[42]

In the early 1970s Foucault definitively abandoned the "archaeological" method on which his reputation as a thinker had been predicated. In *The Order of Things* he had treated the discourses of the human sciences as autonomous spheres—"epistemes"—that could be studied exclusively in terms of their internal logics: in light of the rules that determine the limits of what can and cannot be said. The archaeological approach, with its inordinate focus on language and discourse, lacked a critical element necessary to link Foucault's theory to the revolutionary activity of the gauchistes: insight into the practical functioning of power at the "corpuscular" level of everyday life. In retrospect, Foucault would belittle *The Order of Things* and *The Archaeology of Knowledge* as "formal exercises" that occupied a "marginal" position within his oeuvre. He regretted that these two texts failed to address the newer, more explicitly political themes that concerned him, themes that pertained to questions of power and resistance.[43]

Foucault's identification with Maoist populism brought certain anti-intellectual tendencies in his persona to the fore. He admitted that he viewed his political engagement on behalf of GIP as a "veritable deliverance from the lethargy I am experiencing with regard to literary pursuits."[44] Adherence to the Maoist "mass line" entailed a celebration of the people's pristine, incorruptible good sense. Intellectuals, conversely, were disparaged as an alien element. Rousseau, in his second *Discourse,* had argued that "sophistication" risked corrupting the people's healthy common sense. For similar reasons, Foucault began to wonder whether, in addition to the universal intellectual's obsolescence, "writing" itself had not been surpassed as a form of contestation. After all, had not the Maoists shown that the time had come for struggle to express itself directly in the form of revolutionary action, forgoing the mediating function of the verb? If in fact intellectuals of the classical stamp *interfered* with the attainment of political consciousness,

---

[42] Maurice Clavel, *Ce que je crois* (Paris: Editions Grasset, 1975), 140.

[43] See Eribon, *Insult and the Making of the Gay Self,* 259–60.

[44] Foucault, *Dits et écrits* 1:51.

could not one say the same of "textuality," the intellectual's preferred mode of expression? At one point Foucault frankly avowed that he far preferred his practical work on behalf of GIP "to university banter and the scribbling of books."[45]

In working with GIP, Foucault sought to return to the problems raised in his first major work, *Madness and Civilization*, a book that radically challenged inherited ideas about societal normalcy. In *The Order of Things* and *The Archaeology of Knowledge*, the themes of power and resistance were largely absent. In retrospect, Foucault would fault himself for having been overly preoccupied during his so-called archaeological phase with the realm of language or discursiveness, a bias that was characteristic of structuralism in general. By the same token, by his own admission he had undervalued the *practical effects of power*: its finite, concrete, and molecular operations on the plane of everyday life.[46] In *Madness and Civilization*, these thematics had surfaced—albeit obliquely—via Foucault's attempt to evaluate a society by examining the modalities with which it distinguished the "normal" from the "pathological": who was included vis-à-vis who was excluded, the center from the periphery, and so forth. In this context Foucault felt compelled to resuscitate and recover what he referred to as the "sovereign enterprise of unreason" that, since the Enlightenment, had been ghettoized, interned, and silenced. Years later he was heartened by the enthusiastic reception of the book among a new generation of militants in the post-May period. For example, Deleuze and Guatarri's *Anti-Oedipus*, written in the spirit of "anti-psychiatry" and destined to become one of the most influential expressions of the post-May critique of the repressive nature of technocratic expertise, was inordinately indebted to Foucault's démarche in *Madness and Civilization*. At Deleuze's insistence, Foucault composed the preface.

[45] "Le grand enfermement," in *Dits et écrits* 1:301; see also "Folie, littérature, et société," in *Dits et écrits* 2:115.

[46] See Foucault, "Truth and Power," 114: "I don't think I was the first to pose the question [of power]. On the contrary, I'm struck by the difficulty I had in formulating it. When I think back now, I ask myself what else it was that I was talking about, in *Madness and Civilization* or *The Birth of the Clinic,* but power? Yet I'm perfectly aware that I scarcely ever used the word and never had such a field of analyses at my disposal."

Reflecting back on this early period in his thought, Foucault recalled
the conceptual and political impasse of the predominant approaches to
power. Among orthodox Marxists, power was still understood primarily in economic terms: as a function of class standing or ownership
of the means of production. To be sure, Althusser's 1970 essay "Ideological State Apparatuses," which first appeared in the PCF theoretical
organ *La Pensée*, had belatedly argued for the semiautonomous influence of politics and culture.[47] Among liberals and conservatives, power
was typically viewed according to the modern natural law or juridical
model: as a function of rights and constitutions. Yet, both approaches
proceeded on a plane of theoretical abstraction that often masked and
obscured power's concrete, phenomenological, everyday efficacy. Both
standpoints viewed power as something negative—the embodiment of
restrictions or limitations—rather than as a productive force capable of
fabricating the docile bodies and pliable selves that, ultimately, revealed
power's authentic societal nature.

In a later interview, Foucault described the muted reception of *Madness and Civilization* as follows: "What I myself tried to do in this domain was met with a great silence among the French intellectual Left."
It was only because of the political opening the May events created,
Foucault continued, "that, in spite of the Marxist tradition and the
PCF, all of these questions came to assume their political significance,
with a sharpness that I had never envisaged, showing how timid and
hesitant those early books of mine had still been."[48]

Thus, during the early 1970s, among French intellectuals hospitals,
prisons, asylums, and psychiatric institutions began to take on an entirely new political import and meaning. Among the gauchistes, the notion of political contestation was reconceived and reformulated. Class
ceased to be the alpha and omega of political struggle. Instead, as an

[47] Althusser, "Idéologie et appareils idéologiques d'état (notes pour une recherche)," *La Pensée* 151 (1970): 3–38.

[48] Foucault, "Truth and Power," 111. As Foucault later observed: "It is certain that
without May '68, I never would have done what I did with regard to the prison, delinquency, sexuality. In the earlier climate, it would not have been possible"; "Conversation avec Michel Foucault," in *Dits et écrits* 4:81.

outgrowth of the GIP experience, the populist idea took hold that the proper end of politics was to give those who were deprived of the right to speak—"les exclus"—a voice. The new goal of political activism was to create a space for those who had been systematically marginalized and excluded to speak out, and to do so in a way that proved impossible when their champions had been political parties, unions, and "prophetic intellectuals" who presumed to speak in their name.

At one point during this period, Foucault is alleged to have remarked to Deleuze: "We have to free ourselves from the errors of Freudian-Marxism." Deleuze responded: "All right: I'll take care of Freud, you take care of Marx."[49]

The extension of "the political" that flourished in the post-May period among leftist groups such as the Gauche prolétarienne disconcerted traditional Marxists, for whom the proletariat was the privileged and exclusive bearer of class consciousness. In the eyes of orthodox Marxists, the unpardonable heresy the gauchistes had committed was to have afforded equal consideration to the lumpenproletariat, who, according to the tenets of the Marxist catechism, were incapable of acceding to proper political consciousness.

As Foucault noted at the time, "After May '68, when the problem of [government] repression and judicial prosecution became increasingly acute, it shocked me and rekindled a memory . . . : [It suggested] we were returning to a generalized confinement that already existed in the seventeenth century: a police force with unlimited discretionary powers. . . . Today . . . one is returning to a sort of generalized, undifferentiated confinement."[50]

In Foucault's view a new method of historical analysis was needed which would permit one to analyze the evolution of the human sciences through their "microeffects" on subjectivity. Foucault outlined his new approach in "Nietzsche, Genealogy, History." Taking his bearings from Nietzsche's On the Genealogy of Morals, Foucault defined the task of the genealogist as a critical enterprise that demystifies humanist ideals and their correlative institutional manifestations by tracing them

[49] Foucault, Dits et écrits 1:55.
[50] Foucault, "Grand enfermement," ibid. 2:308.

back to specific historical assertions of the "will to power." This approach sought out the "origins" of those ideals not in the lofty formulations of Enlightenment philosophes but in the everyday vicissitudes of historical practice. In this way, the method of genealogy confuted the humanist standpoint of self-described universal intellectuals. The skills of the specific intellectual, conversely, "required patience and a knowledge of detail and . . . depend[ed] on a vast accumulation of source material. . . . [It] demands relentless erudition."[51]

This characterization faithfully describes the way Foucault envisioned his work with GIP. In a roundtable discussion published in the countercultural magazine *Actuel*, Foucault explained the Nietzschean impetus underlying GIP's practical struggles and aims. Just as in *On the Genealogy of Morals* Nietzsche had effected a transvaluation of the Christian ideals of "noble" and "base"—prior to Christianity, "noble" connoted the uninhibited exercise of power and rank; conversely, with Christianity's rise, the meek and demure were deemed noble and the powerful were viewed as morally "base"—Foucault argued that a similar exercise in transvaluation was required for the predominant approaches to "guilt" and "innocence."

> The ultimate goal of its [GIP's] interventions was not to extend the visiting rights of prisoners to thirty minutes or to procure flush toilets for the cells, but to question the social and moral distinction between the innocent and the guilty. . . . Confronted by this penal system, the humanist would say: "The guilty are guilty and the innocent are innocent. Nevertheless, the convict is a man like any other and society must respect what is human in him: consequently, flush toilets!" Our action, on the contrary, isn't concerned with the soul or the man behind the convict, but it seeks to obliterate the deep division that lies between innocence and guilt.[52]

[51] Foucault, "Nietzsche, Genealogy, History," in *Foucault Reader*, ed. Paul Rabinow (New York: Panthcon, 1984), 140.
[52] Foucault, "Revolutionary Action: 'Until Now,'" in *Language, Counter-Memory, Practice*, ed. Donald F. Bouchard (Ithaca, NY: Cornell University Press, 1977), 227.

Less than five months after the press conference at Saint-Bernard Chapel, GIP published its first pamphlet, *Enquête dans vingt prisons* (Investigation in Twenty Prisons). Although *Enquête* contained no statistical information, it did include two completed questionnaires and a selection of representative answers.[53] In his introduction to the forty-eight-page booklet, Foucault reaffirmed that the investigations were not designed to ameliorate or soften a manifestly oppressive institution, to make what was unacceptable palatable. Instead, GIP's investigations were designed to expose the deceptions of a "carceral society." It would confront that society at those junctures where it acted in the name of "efficiency," "right," and "the norm." Rehearsing the Maoists' "populist" line, Foucault continued:

These investigations are not being made by a group of technicians working from the outside; the investigators [namely, the prisoners] are the ones who are being investigated. It is up to them to begin to speak, to bring down the barriers, to express what is intolerable, and to tolerate it no longer. It is up to them to take responsibility for the struggle which will prevent oppression from being exercised.[54]

In the year and a half that followed, Foucault and GIP produced three more pamphlets. Their investigations encompassed issues ranging from the mundane procedures for censoring prisoners' mail to heart-rending descriptions of widespread prisoner suicides (in 1973 alone forty-three suicides were documented).

In February 1971, even as Foucault was announcing the creation of GIP, the aforementioned hunger strikes were beginning to place massive, unwelcome pressure on the Pompidou government. To bring the first wave of strikes to an end, the authorities conceded new privileges to dozens of prisoners: more liberal visitation rights, unlimited access to newspapers and radio (both of which had previously been forbidden), and so forth. In response to an ensuing wave of strikes, the

---

[53] Artières et al., *Groupe d'information sur les prisons*, 80–81.
[54] Ibid.

government agreed to additional concessions: the maximum period of solitary confinement was reduced from ninety to forty-five days, the censoring of prisoners' mail was eliminated, and regulations governing furloughs were liberalized.[55] A new government commission was established to ensure that in each French prison punishments were being fairly and equitably administered. Previously, prisons had been sites of law-free surveillance; oversight had been virtually nonexistent.

Through the GIP enquêtes, it came to light that at Toul the regional director had explicitly instructed the medical staff not to treat sick or injured prisoners. According to the prison psychiatrist, Dr. Edith Rose, it was common practice for inmates to be bound hand and foot and left to lie motionless for days at a time. Prisoners were regularly treated sadistically. They were arbitrarily denied the most minimal amusements and pleasures: a soccer ball during exercise period; their daily ration of five or six cigarettes. Dr. Rose told of prisoners emerging from up to a year of solitary confinement with severe mental disorders. Her chilling indictment of the prison system was published in a special issue of the Maoist organ, La Cause du Peuple (December 18, 1971). She copied her brief to President Pompidou and Guardian of the Seals René Pleven. When government authorities sought to undermine her credibility, Foucault rose eloquently to her defense in the pages of Libération.[56] For him, Dr. Rose was the archetype of the new breed of "specific intellectual": purveyor of concrete information and stubborn truths rather than vacuous, ineffectual ideals.

GIP's 1971 enquête on prison suicides had an especially profound and widespread impact. As a result of the group's efforts, within a few months the inhumane and degrading conditions of French prison life became front-page news.[57]

---

[55] See Salle, "Mai 68," 9–10.

[56] See Foucault, "Le discours de Toul," in Agence de Presse Libération, bulletin no. 12, January 9, 1972 (reprinted in Dits et écrits 1:1104–1106).

[57] See GIP, Suicides de prison (Paris: Editions Champs Libre, 1972). Daniel Defert recounts that following GIP's investigations into unreported suicides in French prisons, the story appeared on page 1 of France Soir, n.d.; Defert, "Emergence d'un nouveau front," 324.

Over the ensuing eighteen months, uprisings and hunger strikes erupted throughout the French penitentiary system. Major disturbances occurred at Lyon, Poissy, Grenoble, Draguignan, Nancy, and Nîmes. All told, thirty-five prisons experienced significant upheavals. Given the prisoners' isolation, the humiliating disciplinary procedures and techniques of surveillance to which they were regularly subjected, as well as the arbitrary cultural deprivations, outright rebellion was quite likely the inmates' only recourse. In many cases the upheavals were indirectly traceable to GIP's efforts to galvanize the inmates' political consciousness and enhance their capacities for self-organization.

"LET IT BLEED": THE YEAR OF THE INTERNATIONAL PRISON REVOLT

During the 1970s, the international political conjuncture was favorable to a reexamination of the prison's political and social function. In the mid-1960s, the Swedish prison reform organization KRUM (National Association for the Humanization of Prison Life) pioneered the tactic of hunger strikes and work stoppages to galvanize public opinion concerning prison conditions. Their methods proved successful in gaining concessions from the Swedish government, including the unrestricted access to mail and regular conjugal visits.

However, of even greater significance for GIP was the Italian leftist group Lotta Continua, many of whose militants and sympathizers had been imprisoned during the late 1960s as a result of their political activism. Upon discovering that the majority of the prison population consisted of unemployed youth, petty criminals, and members of the underclass, Lotta Continua developed a theory of the sub- or lumpenproletariat as a complementary or supplemental revolutionary force. As a result, the group began to shift its organizing strategy from factories to the so-called popular districts, or slums, of major cities. Along with other representatives of the Italian non-Communist Left, Lotta Continua developed a concept of the social factory—an idea that had important parallels with the theories of French Far Left groups such as Arguments, Socialisme ou barbarie, and the Situationist International.

According to this notion, under conditions of late capitalism, domination was no longer exclusively confined to the workplace. Instead, it had spread to include manifold aspects of everyday life: leisure time, patterns of consumption, urban planning, and higher education. These developments suggested that political contestation was no longer the prerogative of the proletariat alone. It equally concerned other socially marginalized groups—the subproletariat, or *i dannati della terra* (the wretched of the earth)—who, in theory, had become the industrial proletariat's natural allies. As one important Lotta Continua pamphlet concluded: the prison struggles "will give birth to a general political program that will encompass the entire world: emancipation from the bourgeoisie's manipulation of delinquency so that 'delinquents' might also find their path to revolution alongside the proletariat."[58]

All of these ideas would have a pronounced impact on GIP's expanded conception of contestation and political militancy. In 1971 GIP militants Daniel Defert and Jacques Donzelot traveled to Italy to consult with Lotta Continua activists about the prisoners' rights movement, organizing strategies, and related issues.[59] Between 1969 and 1972 Italy experienced a massive wave of prison uprisings; Turin, Monza, Trevise, Genoa, San Vittore, and Trieste all underwent major revolts.

But it was the American Black Panther movement that undoubtedly had the most significant impact on GIP's understanding of the political nature of incarceration. Beginning in 1968, Foucault read the Panthers' political writings assiduously. He praised them for "having developed a strategic analysis freed from the Marxist theory of society."[60] During the late 1960s and early 1970s, police repression—in essence, a series of political murders—had decimated the Panther leadership. In 1969 Mark Clark and Fred Hampton, the founder of the Panthers' Illinois chapter, were killed in bed during a sanguinary predawn police raid. At the confrontation's outset, the police reportedly fired off some ninety

[58] Lotta Continua, *Liberare tutti i dannati della terra* (Rome: Edizioni di Lotta Continua, 1972), 14–17.

[59] A few years later, Donzelot would publish an important book that was methodologically inspired by his work with GIP, *The Policing of Families*, trans. Robert Hurley (New York: Pantheon, 1979).

[60] Foucault, *Dits et écrits* 1:44.

unanswered rounds. An informant had provided the police with the floor plan of the Panthers' residence. An independent inquiry undertaken by civil rights activist Roy Wilkins and former attorney general Ramsey Clark concluded that Clark and Hampton had been murdered without provocation and that their civil rights had been egregiously violated.[61]

In August 1971 Black Panther leader George Jackson was gunned down, putatively during the course of an escape attempt, in California's San Quentin Prison. Jackson had been imprisoned twelve years earlier for a gas-station robbery that he denied having committed, in which a mere $70 was taken. He was initially sentenced to a year in prison. But because he was an unbowed, charismatic, and politically savvy African American, his annual parole requests were routinely denied. A year earlier, Jackson's seventeen-year-old brother, Jonathan, was one of four people slain in the course of a hostage-taking incident at the Marin County courthouse.

Under the Gallimard imprint, GIP published a pamphlet devoted to Jackson's case, L'assassinat de George Jackson, which featured a moving preface by the writer and Panther advocate Jean Genet. (GIP's original publisher, the anarchist-oriented Champ libre, severed all ties once it realized that GIP was staffed and run by Maoists.) Genet, the author of A Thief's Journal (1949), had spent many years in French prisons and was thus a natural GIP ally. While working with GIP, Genet told Foucault about the humiliation he had suffered in prison when a Communist prisoner refused to be shackled to him because Genet was a common criminal rather than a "political prisoner" like himself. Genet was openly gay. During the early 1950s, one of his films, Un chant d'amour, had been banned in the United States due to its frank portrayals of homosexual themes.[62] Genet identified with the Panthers as charismatic militants who had the courage to rise up and defend oppressed African Americans, but also as a group whose leaders possessed a rare capacity

[61] See Roy Wilkins and Ramsey Clark, Search and Destroy: A Report by the Commission of Inquiry into the Black Panthers and the Police (New York: Metropolitan Applied Research Center, 1973).

[62] See Edward de Grazia, "An Interview with Jean Genet," Cardozo Studies in Law and Literature 2 (5) (Autumn 1993): 307–24.

for lucid prose and a knack for *le mot juste*. Genet was especially impressed by Eldridge Cleaver's searing memoir, *Soul on Ice*, a best seller that had been translated into French in 1969.

In 1970 Genet toured the United States to publicize and raise money on behalf of the Panther cause. Reflecting on the Panthers' ideological proximity to Marxism, Genet remarked that Americans could little stomach a "red ideology in a Black skin."[63] All told, he spoke at fifteen universities. For a period of three months, he lived in Panther safe houses. In New Haven, speaking on behalf of imprisoned Panther cofounder Bobby Seale, Genet attracted a crowd of twenty-five thousand. The following year, he penned the introduction to George Jackson's prison letters, *Soledad Brother,* an impassioned *cri de coeur* written from within the belly of the beast. Commenting on Jackson's death, which he viewed as a political murder, Genet observed: "The word 'criminal,' applied to blacks by the whites, is devoid of meaning. For the whites, all the blacks are criminals because they are black, which is another way of saying that in a society dominated by whites, no black can be a criminal."[64] In Genet's view, to explain African American criminality via recourse to the customary juridical lexicon of law and penality— in essence, the ideological window dressing of state-sanctioned racial discrimination—remained woefully myopic. Instead, only a *political* approach to the problem, one that included an in-depth understanding of the institutionalized racism that suffused American life, stood a chance of apprehending the true nature of the dilemma at issue.

Remarkably, the Panthers, who traded on black machismo and otherwise scorned white support, embraced Genet as one of their own, despite his avowed homosexuality and despite the fact that, at one point, Genet fell in love with the Panthers' charismatic national chief of staff, David Hilliard. The Panthers' familiarity with Genet led them to reassess their earlier, homophobic attitudes and dispositions.

Prior to meeting Genet, "faggot" had been one of the group's standard terms of derision. Conversely, shortly after Genet returned to

---

[63] Cited in Edmund White's *Jean Genet: A Biography* (New York: Vintage, 1994), 522.

[64] Jean Genet, preface to *L'assassinat de George Jackson* (Paris: Gallimard, 1971).

France, Panther cofounder Huey Newton, who at the time was imprisoned on a soon-to-be dismissed murder charge, published a position paper, "The Woman's Liberation and Gay Liberation Movements." Newton reminded his readers that homosexuals, too, were an oppressed minority—perhaps the "most oppressed." As a matter of principle, Newton continued, all people should have the freedom to use their bodies in whatever way they deemed fit. The Panther minister of defense concluded by calling attention to the fact that in the emancipatory struggles to come, both gays and women represented potentially valuable allies: "When we have revolutionary conferences, rallies, and demonstrations, there should be full participation of the gay liberation movement and the women's liberation movement."[65]

Newton's declarations in support of homosexuals had an important transatlantic ripple effect. Shortly after his position paper on gay liberation and feminism had begun to circulate, French gauchistes associated with the Maoist organ *Tout!* began exploring in earnest questions bearing on sexuality and identity politics. Initially, many of the gauchistes doubted whether these themes were the proper concerns of a movement such as theirs, which had revolutionary political aspirations. In the eyes of many French activists, Newton's endorsement of homosexual liberation basically settled the matter. *Tout!*'s sister publication, *Vive la révolution!*, edited by Roland Castro, translated Newton's manifesto in its entirety.[66] Such was the degree of international esteem that the Panther leaders enjoyed, especially in France.

In September 1971, only a month after Jackson's death, New York State's infamous Attica Prison uprising occurred. More than forty inmates and guards perished when one thousand state police and national guardsmen stormed the prison. In 2000 relatives of those who were slain were awarded an $8 million court settlement. In its publications, GIP sought to publicize the international dimension of all these prison-related events.

[65] See Huey Newton, "The Woman's Liberation and Gay Liberation Movements: August 15, 1970," in *To Die for the People: The Writings of Huey P. Newton* (New York: Random House, 1972): 153.

[66] Hamon and Rotman, *Génération* 2:231.

In France the most serious unrest occurred in December 1971 in the eastern city of Toul as a result of Minister Pleven's decision to forbid the customary receipt of Christmas parcels in response to an escape attempt at the neighboring Clairvaux Prison. The older convicts immediately barricaded themselves in the prison workshop and began destroying equipment. Younger inmates set fire to the library. Prisoners hurled furniture, bedding, and dishes from the prison windows. They succeeded in gaining complete control of one of the prison's four cell blocks. One of the younger inmates scribbled on the door of the prison's chapel: "We respect those who treat us with humanity." Yet, at no time during the uprising did the prisoners attempt to seize hostages. During the ensuing negotiations, the inmates requested improved dental care, warm showers, and a general amelioration of prison conditions. Their central demand, that the warden be replaced, went unmet.[67]

The unprecedented disruptions at Toul and other prison facilities received massive media attention. They unsettled the nation and spurred the government to overhaul the penal system. In what was undoubtedly GIP's greatest triumph, reforms were enacted to eliminate aspects of prison life that entailed the prisoners' moral stigmatization. The notion that the prisoners' character was somehow "malformed" was jettisoned, as was the idea of "deviance" in general.[68] Pressure from GIP resulted in the passage of an April 1972 law that voided convictions based primarily on a defendant's criminal record and police files. Foucault perceived such dossiers as an expression of the insidious workings of "power-knowledge."[69] Henceforth, punishment would focus on the crime rather than on the criminal. Following Giscard d'Estaing's election in 1974, a cabinet-level post to monitor prison conditions was created.

In April 1972 Foucault traveled to upstate New York to tour the Attica penitentiary. A year later, he published an interview detailing his impressions. Since in France prisons were "closed sites," the Attica visit was Foucault's first experience inside a prison. Above all, he was struck by the prison's "industrial" facade and layout. He described the facility

[67] Ibid., 379.
[68] See Monod, *Foucault et la police des conduites*, 90–91.
[69] Foucault, *Dits et écrits* 1:57.

as an "immense machine," a giant maw charged with breaking down and eliminating socially unpalatable elements, something it apparently did with exceptional proficiency. Prison authorities claimed they had granted him full access to the penitentiary's four cell blocks. Only later did Foucault learn they had concealed from him the existence of a fifth cell block: the prison's psychiatric ward.[70]

ARISE YE WRETCHED OF THE EARTH: LUMPENPROLETARIANS OF THE WORLD UNITE!

Despite his self-effacing rhetoric and objections to so-called universal intellectuals, Foucault gleaned a number of fundamental "Maoists truths" from his two-year enquête concerning the nature of the French penal system. Reform, Foucault confidently asserted, was not what the people wanted. As he explained in an interview with Gilles Deleuze: "It is not simply the idea of better and more equitable forms of justice that underlies the people's hatred of the judicial system, of judges, courts, and prisons, but—aside from this and before anything else—the singular perception that power is always exercised at the expense of the people."[71]

But if the people remained unconcerned with *reforming* the penal institution, then how exactly might one describe their demands? In his debate with Maoist leader Pierre Victor on the subject of popular justice, Foucault provided his clearest response. Whereas Victor, following the practices of the Cultural Revolution, advocated the creation of people's tribunals to effectuate summary justice, Foucault countered that people's courts were an expression of retrograde, bourgeois legality. The very idea of a court, he insisted, was a construct of bourgeois society whose function was "to ensnare it [popular justice], to control it, and to strangle it, by re-inscribing it within institutions which are typical of a state apparatus."[72] Ultimately, such courts gave voice to a

---

[70] Ibid., 1395.

[71] Foucault and Deleuze, "Intellectuals and Power," 77.

[72] Foucault, "On Popular Justice," 1.

petty-bourgeois mentality that served to defuse and tame the people's healthy and innate revolutionary instincts. As Foucault explains:

> The people's court during the Revolution . . . had a very precise social basis: it represented a social group which stood between the bourgeoisie in power and the common people of Paris [la plèbe]. This was a petty bourgeoisie composed of small property owners, tradesmen, artisans. This group took up a position as intermediary and organized a court which functioned as a mediator. . . . So it is clear that it had reoccupied the position of the judicial institution just as it had functioned under the ancien régime. Where there had originally been the masses exacting retribution against those who where their enemies, there was now substituted the operation of a court and of a great deal of its ideology.[73]

In opposition to the Cultural Revolution's model of popular tribunals endorsed by Victor, Foucault suggested a stark alternative: the September massacres of 1792, when the revolutionaries executed hundreds of helpless prisoners out of fear that they might turn counterrevolutionary.

In a debate with Noam Chomsky later that year before a Dutch television audience, Foucault presented a Nietzschean unmasking of justice, which he criticized as "an idea invented and put into practice in different societies as an instrument of a particular political or economic power." "It is clear," Foucault continued, "that we live under a dictatorial class regime, under a class power that imposes itself with violence, even when the instruments of this violence are institutional and constitutional." The philosopher concluded: when the proletariat triumphs, "it will exert a power that is violent, dictatorial, and even bloody over the class it has supplanted." He added, somewhat naively: "I don't know what objection one can make against this."[74] In Foucault's estimation, the people wanted—and deserved to

---

[73] Ibid., 3–4.

[74] Foucault, "De la nature humaine: Justice contre pouvoir," in *Dits et écrits* 1:1363, 1371.

have—blood! Foucault fundamentally agreed with Nietzsche's insight in *On the Genealogy of Morals* that the hallmark of the civilizing process is the progressive sublimation of cruelty. Yet, whereas the bourgeoisie lauded this development as a vindication of its values and morality—as a testament to "civilization" and "progress"—Nietzsche and Foucault criticized it as a mechanism of "normalization." It stripped individuals of their instinctual vitality, thereby transforming them into servile and conformist beings—the compliant executors of bourgeois moral and legal codes.

Foucault's championing of the September massacres as a model of people's justice was more than a passing aside. Instead, it was part of what one might describe as a rearguard effort to preserve the idea of revolutionism in an era in which the proletariat seemed perfectly content with piecemeal economic gains and the comforts of upward social mobility. Faced with this dilemma, many apostles of revolutionary struggle, like Sartre, Régis Debray, and Herbert Marcuse, had flirted with third worldism. If the working classes in advanced industrial societies seemed uninterested in revolution, in an era of decolonization perhaps the "wretched of the earth" would set in motion global capitalism's downfall.

Foucault, conversely, placed his wager on late capitalism's "human waste": the lumpenproletariat, or underclass. He opted for this route in part under the influence of Georges Bataille's theory of *la part maudite,* or "the accursed share." In Bataille's view, all societies engage in forms of sacrifice or expenditure in order to rid themselves of unwanted elements or components. By the same token, such practices lend these execrated strata or groups an inverted nobility. By dint of their status as outcasts, they manage to resist the normalizing compulsions of bourgeois socialization. In "The Notion of Expenditure," Bataille—in a manner similar to Foucault's glorification of the September massacres—celebrated the massive bloodletting that would occur when the salt of the earth rose up to slay or lay low their reviled oppressors. According to Bataille, the "masters and exploiters" bear responsibility for creating "contemptuous forms that exclude human nature—causing this nature to exist at the limits of the earth, in other words in mud." Hence, "a simple law of reciprocity requires that they be condemned . . . to the

Great Night in which their beautiful phrases will be drowned out by
death screams in riots. That is the bloody hope that . . . sums up the
insubordinate content that is class struggle."[75]

Foucault lamented that the French working class had readily imbibed
bourgeois morality. When the Maoists had tried to hawk at factory gates
the issue of *Tout!* treating homosexual liberation, they were given the
cold shoulder—or worse. From an ethical standpoint, it was clear that
French workers, in their attitudes toward family structure and sexuality,
had become "embourgeoisified." As Foucault lamented in an interview:
"The proletariat has been thoroughly imbued with bourgeois ideology
concerning morality and legality, concerning theft and crime."[76] In the
post-May period, the notion of "extending the domain of struggle" (extension du domaine de la lutte)—applying the methods of contestation
that had been learned during the May uprising to domains of everyday
life that lay outside of the workplace—had become popular. By advocating the cause of those who were social outcasts—prisoners, the mentally
ill, immigrants, the unemployed, and so forth—Foucault stamped his
own interpretation on this post-May adage.

In Foucault's view, prisons were by no means the only social institution that exercised power at the expense of the people. Prison was
simply the institution where power was most evident. The institutional
structure of bourgeois society was saturated with power, thoroughly
suffused with carceral practices and disciplinary techniques. "The
courts, the prisons, the hospitals, the psychiatric wards, workers' health
care, the universities, the media: throughout all of these institutions
and under various masks, there is an oppression at work," Foucault
proclaimed, "that is fundamentally political."[77] As he once quipped, the
prison "begins well outside of its gates. From the moment you leave
your house!"[78] Prisons helped facilitate the illusion that society's disciplinary mechanisms were confined to this single, institutional locus. In

[75] Georges Bataille, "The Notion of Expenditure," in *Visions of Excess: Selected
Writings*, trans. Allan Stoekl (Minneapolis: University of Minnesota Press, 1986), 179.

[76] Foucault, "On Attica," in *Foucault Live*, 117.

[77] Foucault, preface to *Enquête dans vingt prisons*, in *Dits et écrits* 1:1063.

[78] Foucault, "La prison partout," *Dits et écrits* 1:1062.

reality, however, they represented merely one concentrated instance of what Foucault at times referred to as the "carceral society."

Building on this metaphor, in the early 1970s Foucault sought to conceptualize anew the inner workings and machinations of power. In *The History of Sexuality,* his most developed elaboration of this new approach, and probably his best known, Foucault began by challenging the "juridical" conception of power: power conceived as a "negative" limitation restricting our freedom. In Foucault's view, when it came to power, we still had not, metaphorically speaking, cut off the king's head, for power is not "something that is acquired, seized, or shared"; nor does it emanate from a single source.[79] Furthermore, "relations of power are not in superstructural positions, with merely a role of prohibition or accompaniment; they have a directly productive role, wherever they come into play."[80] When power is conceived as productive, decentralized, anonymous, and ubiquitous, the traditional boundaries of the political dissolve; the focus of analysis then becomes *society as a whole* rather than "politics" in the narrow juridical sense. Resistance, too, must be entirely reconceptualized. One can no longer proceed as before, simply by opposing the state. Insofar as the disciplinary mechanisms of the "state"—whose innate propensity toward control and domination Foucault redefines qua "governmentality"—are omnipresent, resistance, too, must take place everywhere. In other words, "local action" is called for in every instance and on all fronts.

As distant from traditional Marxism as Foucault's new approach to understanding power and resistance may seem, parts of it jibed perfectly with the gauchistes' militant *ouvrièrisme*. In Foucault's view, the struggle against power's omnipresence—its manifestations in prisons, hospitals, psychiatric wards, and universities—ultimately coincided with the proletariat's struggle against bourgeois society, for one of power's main functions remained to buttress and streamline the capitalist system. In a March 1972 discussion with Gilles Deleuze, Foucault, in a display of impressive rhetorical eloquence, demonstrated this point convincingly:

[79] Michel Foucault, *The History of Sexuality,* trans. Robert Hurley (New York: Vintage Books, 1990), 1:94.
[80] Ibid.

As soon as we struggle against exploitation, the proletariat not only leads the struggle but also defines its targets, its methods, and the places and instruments for confrontation; and to ally oneself with the proletariat is to accept its positions, its ideology, and its motives for combat. This means total identification. But if the fight is directed against power, then all those on whom power is exercised to their detriment, all who find it intolerable, can begin the struggle on their own terrain and on the basis of the proper activity (or passivity). In engaging in a struggle that concerns their own interests, whose objectives they clearly understand and whose methods only they can determine, they enter into a revolutionary process. They naturally enter as allies of the proletariat, because power is exercised the way it is in order to maintain capitalist exploitation. They genuinely serve the cause of the proletariat by fighting in those places where they find themselves oppressed. Women, prisoners, conscripted soldiers, hospital patients, and homosexuals have now begun a specific struggle against the particularized power, the constraints and controls, that are exerted over them. Such struggles are actually involved in the revolutionary movement to the degree that they are radical, uncompromising and nonreformist, and refuse any attempt at arriving at a new disposition of the same power with, at best, a change of masters. And these movements are linked to the revolutionary movement of the proletariat to the extent that they fight against the controls and constraints *which serve the same system of power*.[81]

This notion of power as ubiquitous and its corollary notion of dispersed and local resistance were by no means Foucault's discovery alone. Such precepts were central to the ethos of post-1968 gauchisme. In the aftermath of the May events, the student activists became convinced that there was no such thing as second-order, or lesser, political struggles. The fight for sexual liberation and for freedom of expression in the high schools and universities, the struggles against racism, discrimination, and homophobia—each and every local struggle against

---

[81] Foucault and Deleuze, "Intellectuals and Power," 216; emphasis added.

oppression was central to the fight against late capitalism as an oppressive and totalizing mode of domination. Surveying the landscape of radical politics in 1970, the left-wing activist Jean-Edern Hallier, publisher of the gauchiste organ *L'Idiot Internationale*, aptly summarized the post-May political zeitgeist as follows: "The slogans of May '68 have faded, but they are taking on a new, corrosive meaning, eating away at bourgeois culture. . . . The revolutionary combat on the cultural front, long considered a secondary objective, has become fundamental, at the same time as this front expands."[82]

During May 1968, the students had delayed their support of the workers' movement. The collapse of the Left and the rallying of France's silent majority behind de Gaulle in subsequent months convinced them that this failure had been a grave mistake. Henceforth, bourgeois society needed to be confronted head on. Cultural revolution and the proletariat's struggle against capital needed to reinforce one another.

This situation helps to explain why in the post-May period Mao's notion of a cultural revolution resonated so deeply with student radicals. In traditional Marxist thought, culture had always been regarded as epiphenomenal: a pale reflection of society's socioeconomic base. Mao's doctrine of cultural revolution, conversely, postulated that the arrows of causality linking "base" and "superstructure" could also be reversed. Culture represented an intrinsically legitimate locus of revolutionary struggle. The gauchistes still believed that proletarian revolution was a sine qua non for the creation of a socialist society. They continued to organize in the factories to prepare the workers for this eventuality. On the other hand, following Mao, they also believed that socialism could not be realized without a sweeping transformation of bourgeois values and mores.

May 1968 refocused the students' political energies on problems endemic to French society. In the years leading up to the May revolt, the Left had grown accustomed to the idea that politically significant events always occurred elsewhere—in Eastern Europe, North Africa, Cuba, and Asia. Thus, in the global struggle to topple imperialism, French radicals had been consigned to act as cheerleaders, demonstrating in support of Che, Arafat, Castro, and Ho Chi Minh. A few radicals,

[82] Jean-Edern Hallier, "Éditorial," *L'Idiot Internationale* 1 (December 1970): 3.

such as Régis Debray and Pierre Goldmann, took their commitment a step further by joining their Marxist comrades abroad. However, prior to 1968, no one would have guessed that revolution was possible in France or that the hexagon itself might once again become an epicenter of world revolution. If a few enragés at Nanterre could ignite a revolt that nearly toppled Gaullism, then perhaps it was not unreasonable to "demand the impossible," as a well-known May-era graffito urged. Disenchanted with the traditional Left, disillusioned with the working classes as well as with the reformist orientation of union leaders, in the post-May years many gauchistes felt justified in casting their lot with marginalized elements of society in order to activate heretofore untapped revolutionary potentials. Félix Guattari aptly captured the post-May ethos of "revolutionary pluralism" when he observed: "May '68 taught us to read the writing on the walls; since then we have begun to decipher the graffiti in the prisons, the mental asylums, and now in the public urinals. A 'new scientific spirit' is being born!"[83]

COMING OUT: FOUCAULT AND THE REVOLUTIONARY HOMOSEXUAL ACTION FRONT

The GIP was only one manifestation of the new "scientific spirit" alluded to by Guattari. By 1971 gauchistes and countercultural enthusiasts had begun investigating not only the lives of factory workers, but also the lives of farmers, immigrants, psychiatric patients, women, and homosexuals. In August 1970 the Women's Liberation Movement (MLF) was born, largely out of the same Maoist milieu that had engendered GIP. The MLF immediately began investigations, or enquêtes, bearing on heretofore taboo or repressed themes relevant to women's daily lives. In the post-May years, the transformation of everyday life on the micropolitical level had become the order of the day.

Several months later, France's first homosexual liberation movement, the Front homosexuel d'action révolutionnaire (FHAR), was founded. In their early years, both the MLF and FHAR remained closely allied

[83] Le directeur de publication, "Liminaire," *Recherches* 12 (March 1973): 3.

with Maoist groups like the Gauche prolétarienne, insofar as they shared a kindred revolutionary outlook. As Guy Hocquenghem aptly characterized the emancipatory ethos subtending the founding of the homosexual liberation movement: "If we called ourselves a 'revolutionary homosexual action front,' it was because, for us, what was most essential was not homosexuality but revolutionary action. It was a way of saying not only that a revolutionary could be homosexual too, but that being homosexual might be the best way of being revolutionary."[84]

In 1971 and 1972, while Foucault was investigating prisons, FHAR militants were exploring the lives of homosexuals—not "elite" homosexuals such as André Gide, Jean Cocteau, or Jean Genet, whose celebrity provided them a certain degree of freedom, but anonymous, "everyday" homosexuals who worked in low-income, blue-collar jobs, who inhabited the poor suburbs or slums on the outskirts of Paris, or who grew up in France's immigrant communities. Like GIP, FHAR gathered information through surveys and questionnaires on homosexuals' everyday living and working conditions: the shady bars and late-night cruising spots they frequented, even the prisons and mental institutions where many of them ended up.

Through René Schérer and Guy Hocquenghem, homosexual militants established a visible presence at the University of Vincennes. In 1971 they convened the first university seminar on homosexuality. There were rarely any assigned lectures or readings. Instead, they invited sex-trade workers, transvestites, and transsexuals—none of whom had any connection to the academic world—to lead wide-ranging discussions. Many were recruited from notorious homosexual cruising spots such as the Bois du Boulogne west of Paris and the Saint Denis District.[85]

In its early phase, FHAR sought to align itself with the cause of the proletariat. While the workers waged their struggle on the shop floor, FHAR would mobilize a *"tourbillon des folles"*—"whirlwind of fags" (a play on the stock phrase *tourbillon des feuilles,* or a "whirlwind of leaves")—to lead the assault on bourgeois propriety and mores.[86] But

[84] "Les premières lueurs du Fhar" (interview with Hocquenghem), *Gai Pied Hebdo,* March 12, 1988, 32.

[85] See René Schérer, *Hospitalités* (Paris: Anthropos, 2004).

[86] *Le Fléau Social* 2 (October 1972): 2.

to do so, it would first have to persuade others to "come out" and join their struggle against bourgeois "normalcy." In one of FHAR's earliest calls to arms, militants declared:

> You dare not say it out loud. Perhaps you won't even say it to yourself. We were like you a few months ago. Our Front will be what we make of it together. We want to destroy the family and this society because they have always repressed us. . . . We continue to suffer daily repression, risking interrogation, prison, and beatings, enduring mocking smiles and commiserating gazes. . . . We are for a homosexual Front whose task is to fight and destroy "fascistic sexual normalcy."[87]

Although Foucault sympathized with the new generation of homosexual activists, he maintained a cautious distance from FHAR. He welcomed FHAR's existence, but he feared that the very idea of a positive "gay identity" could turn into an oppressive social construct. In its own way, it could prove as limiting and restrictive as mainstream heterosexual prejudice.

Through most of his life, Foucault's sexuality had been a troublesome issue. During the late 1950s, while serving as cultural attaché in Warsaw, he had been entrapped by the Polish police during a furtive same-sex tryst—his partner had been a government "plant." The incident forced him to leave Warsaw abruptly and return to France. A few years later, he was passed over for a prestigious appointment in the Ministry of Education due to defamatory rumors concerning his sexual preference.[88] Sexual orientation was very likely one of the factors that propelled Foucault to study psychology and psychiatry at a relatively young age. When a brash and uninhibited homosexual culture began to emerge in the early 1970s, Foucault, like many homosexuals of his generation, did not really fit in. Foucault was a homosexual of the Arcadie generation: the secretive, upper-class, genteel, homophile organization founded by Alain Baudry in the 1950s. Like the Matta-

---

[87] FHAR, *Rapport contre la normalité* (Paris: Editions Champ Libre, 1971), 9–11.
[88] Foucault, *Dits et écrits* 1:55.

chine Society in the United States, during the 1950s and 1960s Arcadie provided a discreet, tightly knit community for closeted homosexuals. In 1978 Foucault was the featured speaker at Arcadie's annual gathering. He turned down his speaker's fee (two thousand francs), quipping that no homosexual should be paid to speak to other homosexuals.[89] As his biographer Didier Eribon confirms: "It is obvious that Foucault belonged to the pre-Stonewall, pre–May 1968 generation."[90] Not the least of Foucault's concerns was the consequences that "coming out" might have on his intellectual reputation.[91]

By the same token, Foucault clearly identified with and supported FHAR's thoroughgoing critique of bourgeois "normalcy." He believed that, in his own way, he had been working on a similar critique since *Madness and Civilization*. Whereas in 1961 Foucault's pathbreaking work may have seemed ahead of its time, ten years hence the gauchistes had more than caught up with him. Deleuze and Guattari, the intellectual eminences behind the antipsychiatry movement (a trend that viewed Freudianism and psychiatry in general as inherently repressive), clearly appreciated the significance of Foucault's early attempt to write the history of madness qua the repressed "other" of reason. They relied extensively on Foucault's approach for their 1972 magnum opus *Anti-Oedipus*. Considered the central text of the French antipsychiatry movement, *Anti-Oedipus* is perhaps best understood as a critical response to Lacan's immense influence and, by extension, a critique of the Freudian tradition. (Guattari was a Lacanian analyst who had been psychoanalyzed by Lacan himself.) In a conversation with Pierre Nora, his editor at Editions Gallimard, Foucault described his 1976 book, *The History of Sexuality*, as his own critical rejoinder to Lacan.[92]

[89] Macey, *Lives of Michel Foucault*, 125.

[90] Eribon, *Insult and the Making of the Gay Self*, 300–301.

[91] See Miller, *Passion of Michel Foucault*, 254–57.

[92] Dosse, *History of Structuralism* 2:339. Nora describes Foucault's comportment, upon turning in the manuscript for his *History of Sexuality*, as follows: "I remember him tapping his foot in my office: 'I don't have an idea, my dear Pierre, I have no ideas. After the battle, I come to sexuality, and I have said everything I have to say.' One fine day he brought me a manuscript, saying, 'You will see, the only idea that I had was to beat on Lacan by arguing the opposite of what he says.'"

In the 1950s and 1960s, Lacan's "recovery of Freud" was one of the single most influential currents in French philosophy and human sciences. In his legendary seminar, Lacan relied on structuralist linguistics to translate Freudian concepts from the sphere of biology into the realms of language and culture. By the same token, Lacan continued to rely on Freud's theory of ontogeny or individuation, culminating in the Oedipal stage—a metaphor for the socialization process. "Oedipalization," which represented the successful formation of the ego, was, for Lacan, a linguistic and cultural process rather than a biological one. At the same time, in Lacan's framework, ontogeny and individuation were treated as unproblematic, ahistorical constants. It was on this latter point, above all, that Deleuze and Guattari parted ways with Lacan. They contended that the Oedipal stage, rather than representing a necessary step in human psychological development, was an invention of bourgeois society. As the discourse that aims to understand and guide this process, psychoanalysis was in essence the discursive executor of the bourgeois subject. Hence the polemical title of their opus: *Anti-Oedipus.*

Foucault had long contemplated the idea of writing a history of sexuality—more specifically, a history of *homosexuality,* a subject that was clearly of significant existential import for him and one that he had been exploring indirectly since the late 1950s.[93] Prior to the 1970s, however, he had conceived the project along the same methodological lines as *Madness and Civilization*: as a history of the exclusionary acts that condemned homosexuality to secrecy and shame. But during the mid-1970s, when Foucault finally decided to undertake the project in earnest, conceptions of homosexuality were undergoing a remarkable metamorphosis.

Above all, homosexuals had begun to "come out" en masse. The most celebrated instance occurred in January 1972, when, in an essay entitled "The Revolution of Homosexuals," Guy Hocquenghem came out in the pages of *Le Nouvel Observateur.* Hocquenghem related in frank detail the story of his becoming self-aware as a homosexual—as

[93] See Eribon, *Insult and the Making of the Gay Self,* pt. 3, "Michel Foucault's Heterotopia."

he later acknowledged, "not without a good dose of exhibitionism."[94] Perhaps more than any single event, Hocquenghem's "revolutionary" act—in Pompidou's France, it took considerable courage to openly proclaim one's homosexuality—helped establish the cause of gay liberation firmly in French public consciousness. It also propelled Hocquenghem to instant stardom in Parisian intellectual circles.

That year, Hocquenghem bested Foucault by publishing the first theoretical elaboration of revolutionary homosexuality, *Homosexual Desire*. On the manifesto's opening page, Hocquenghem achieved a theoretical and political watershed by inverting the terms of previous debates over homosexuality. As Hocquenghem wrote: "*The problem is not so much Homosexual Desire as the fear of homosexuality*."[95] In other words, the real question is not what homosexuality is but why society is so fearful of it. Hocquenghem used the term "homosexual paranoia" to describe the prevalent antihomosexual sentiment. (The word "homophobia" had yet to be invented.)[96] After surveying a number of current instances of homosexual paranoia in France—the controversies surrounding the work of Jean Genet, for example—Hocquenghem moved on to challenge the idea propagated by social reformers that society was moving steadily toward the liberalization of attitudes to homosexuality. A cursory glance at the history of homosexual repression in contemporary Europe revealed this idea to be chimerical, Hocquenghem claimed. The incipient tolerance of homosexuality during the twentieth century's early decades had disappeared with the rise of fascism during the 1930s. In the frantic rebuilding of the postwar era, antipathy to homosexuality continued to intensify. In fact, in France homosexuality had not been criminalized until the Vichy era (1940–44). As Hocquenghem convincingly demonstrated, since the 1950s the number of arrests and the severity of punishments had risen steadily.

[94] *Le Nouvel Observateur,* January 10, 1972.

[95] Hocquenghem, *Homosexual Desire*, 49; emphasis added.

[96] On the history of the term "homophobia," see "Homophobie," in *Dictionnaire des cultures gays et lesbiennes*, ed. Didier Eribon (Paris: Larousse, 2003), 225, and Michael Moon's introduction to the 1996 edition of *Homosexual Desire*, 15–16.

Hocquenghem went on to describe how "capitalist society manufactures homosexuals, just as it produces proletarians, constantly defining its own limits."[97] He showed that whereas the Christian West had been perennially hostile toward homosexuality, the contemporary criminological and psychiatric classifications of homosexuality were relatively recent. The term "homosexual" was first coined in the 1860s by the German sex researcher and social reformer Magnus Hirschfeld. With the late nineteenth-century classification of homosexuality as a sickness or disease, "homosexual paranoia" had been transposed from the religious domain and secularized, as it were. With the advent of psychoanalysis, homosexuality became a fixed scientific category. At this point homosexuals began to internalize and display the stereotypical traits that bourgeois society had manufactured for them. As Hocquenghem aptly observes: "We have escaped hellfire in favor of psychological hell."[98]

The motor force behind all of these developments was what Hocquenghem referred to as modern society's "growing imperialism": its inordinate need to control the population and maximize output.[99] In Hocquenghem's view, to ensure the continued reproduction of healthy laborers and consumers, capitalism divided up the plenum of unrestricted libidinal pulsation into "heterosexual" and "homosexual" desire. Heterosexual desire, which is teleologically directed toward procreation, was established as the norm. Homosexual desire became its doppelgänger and foil. By locating homosexual desire in a specific pariah group—"homosexuals"—society succeeded in restricting it. Whereas heretofore homosexual desire had been regarded as a possibility for everyone, modern psychiatry treated it as a pathological manifestation associated with a particular social group. Society required both heterosexuals and homosexuals, but these categories were effectively bourgeois constructs, fictions invented by capitalism in order to impose divisions and restrictions on the infinite flux of desire. In reconstructing the history of homosexuality, Hocquenghem made

[97] Hocquenghem, *Homosexual Desire*, 50.
[98] Ibid., 93.
[99] Ibid., 51.

explicit reference to *Madness and Civilization*. Like Foucault's madman, Hocquenghem's homosexual is little more than a convenient fabrication of modern capitalism.

The emergence of a bold and uninhibited gay subculture, coupled with Hocquenghem's sensational "coming out" and the pathbreaking publication of *Homosexual Desire,* confronted Foucault with a dilemma. The philosopher began to feel that he had been deprived of a project that had long been close to his heart. It became clear to him that the initial breakthrough had already been achieved and that his own contribution would no longer be "audacious." Moreover, as Eribon suggests, he began to take stock of the fact that the approach he had conceived had been essentially misguided. Foucault had intended to "denounce certain prohibitions, to break a certain silence." Yet, by this point, the situation had changed drastically; "people were speaking for themselves everywhere, including in newsmagazines."[100] As Hocquenghem had already written in his "coming out" article in *Le Nouvel Observateur,* "We are all somehow deformed in an area known as sexual desire or love. We must begin to uncover these desires that we have been forced to hide. No one else can do it for us."[101]

"THREE BILLION PERVERTS"

After the publication of *Homosexual Desire,* Hocquenghem suggested to Deleuze and Guattari that they gather a group of researchers for a special issue on "homosexualities" in the journal *Recherches,* a publication of the Centre d'études, de recherches et de formation institutionnelles (CERFI). Deleuze and Guattari eagerly assented and began to assemble a team. Since they had been intellectually and personally close to Foucault during their tenure at Vincennes (in the meantime, the philosopher had left the experimental university for his post at the Collège de France), they immediately asked him to participate. Although initially

[100] Eribon, *Insult and the Making of the Gay Self,* 297.
[101] Hocquenghem, "La révolution des homosexuels," *Le Nouvel Observateur,* January 10, 1972.

intrigued, Foucault gradually lost interest as younger, more assertive, and outspoken homosexuals such as Hocquenghem took over.

Hocquenghem had first become acquainted with Foucault through GIP, which in association with FHAR had launched an investigation into the dubious suicide of Gérard Grandmontagne, a young, openly homosexual prisoner who had been severely beaten by prison guards before dying mysteriously in solitary confinement. To this day it remains unclear whether the cause of death was strangulation or electrocution.[102] (It is noteworthy that *Homosexual Desire* is dedicated to Grandmontagne.)

Six months later, in March 1973, the final result appeared: *Three Billion Perverts: The Great Encyclopedia of Homosexualities.* The special issue consisted mostly of unprecedentedly frank and explicit discussions of topics such as cruising, masturbation, sex in the *cités* (subsidized urban housing projects), and sexual relations among France's North African population. It also included Situationist-inspired homoerotic "recuperations" of children's cartoons.

Noticeably absent from the large volume, however, were the theoretical discourses of *Madness and Civilization, Anti-Oedipus,* and *Homosexual Desire.* Instead, the participants, from the "intellectuals" such as Hocquenghem to the various homosexuals they interviewed, spoke in plain and unadorned language about their own experiences, ideas, and fantasies.

Three Billion Perverts was immediately banned, and Guattari was charged with public obscenity—*outrage contre bonnes mœurs*—an offense that cost him a small fine, but which, strangely, did not seem to adversely affect the journal's financial ties to government ministries. In the end, Foucault's only imprint on the issue was his signature, along with those of Deleuze, Guattari, Sartre, and numerous others.

Foucault's experiences as an activist came to intellectual fruition in *Discipline and Punish,* his magisterial exposé of modern disciplinary mechanisms and practices. To allay the suspicion that his involvement with

---

[102] Jacques Girard, *Le mouvement homosexuel en France, 1945–1981* (Paris: Syros, 1981), 106–7.

GIP might have been a subterfuge to gather material for his forthcoming study, he delayed the book's publication by two years.

In *Discipline and Punish* Foucault's ingenious stratagem was to shift the focus of debate away from the criminal and toward the system of punishment. He understood penality, first and foremost, as a political form. Disciplinary society's goal was to parry and defuse political challenges from below: uprisings and revolts on the part of an assortment of diffuse lumpenproletarian groups—the so-called dangerous classes.[103] This underclass of social outcasts harbored an inchoate, yet robust potential for spontaneous action. In Foucault's view the prison system's political mission was to neutralize that potential by reclassifying these unbowed "primitive rebels" as "criminals" and "misfits." By transposing the debate from the realm of politics to the putatively value-free domains of science, medicine, psychiatry, and genetics, disciplinary society was able to turn a political threat into an "objective" debate about "deviancy" and "social pathology." However, in truth, the prison system was merely a cog in a much larger project of societal "normalization." The "means of correct training" and the microphysics of "carceralism" that Foucault described so vividly in *Discipline and Punish* were also practiced by an array of kindred institutions and organizations: hospitals, schools, asylums, factories, the military, and so forth.

By the same token, historians felt that by treating three centuries of prison life in some three hundred pages, Foucault had covered too much ground too quickly. Inattention to detail and neglect of historical variation made the book more of a lively, speculative essay than a rigorous, well-documented study. A number of scholars pointed out that Foucault's account of the rise of "disciplinary society" was overly linear. They feared he had merely inverted the Enlightenment narrative of progress by substituting a narrative of increasing social control. Efforts to humanize prison life that the revolutionary governments had undertaken in the early 1790s had been reversed during the Napoleonic era and the Restoration. Only belatedly, during the July Monarchy (1830–48), were many of the draconian features of ancien régime

---

[103] See the classic study by Louis Chevalier, *Laboring Classes and Dangerous Classes during the Nineteenth Century*, trans. Frank Jellinek (New York: Howard Fertig, 1973).

penality—the iron collar, branding, the amputation of digits, and so forth—eliminated once and for all.

Commentators also felt that Foucault's portrayal of carceralism's hegemony was far too monolithic. As a result, Foucault's account failed to do justice to a panoply of countervailing tendencies whose combined effect was to make surveillance much less omnipotent than the philosopher claimed. Labor history has convincingly shown how, during the nineteenth century, traditional and modern production methods coexisted. Much the same could be said of prisons. Not only did many atavisms of ancien régime penality persist, but the practical administration of prisons was much more disorganized and haphazard than Foucault led readers to believe. Both the prison system and modern society in general were much less totalizing and seamless than Foucault had portrayed them as being. Often, it was quite easy for individuals, as well as entire social groups, to slip through the cracks. Moreover, the disjunction between the disciplinary intentions of experts and on-the-ground social practices was often cavernous. Thus, Bentham's panopticon, which for Foucault had become emblematic of modern carceralism in general, was rarely built.

Analysts also pointed out that the modern prison, far from being the smooth-running machine Foucault described, remained suffused with traditional ecclesiastical influences. The church continued to play a major role in the moralization of crime, methods of rehabilitation, and various supervisory practices. After all, it was post-Tridentine Catholicism that "condemned rebels of all sorts—witches, libertines, heretics; that originated the theory of guilt that registered and dramatized moral failings. And it was the church that stressed the incurable nature of sin."[104] By criticizing the Bastille as the emblem of autocratic arbitrariness, nineteenth-century republicans such as Victor Hugo and Léon Gambetta were not exactly working to establish a new Gulag. By casting his net so widely, by simplistically holding "bourgeois rationalism" accountable for power's excesses and machinations, was not Foucault willfully blind to French republicanism's emancipatory

---

[104] See Jacques Léonard, "L'historien et le philosophie: A propos de *Surveiller et punir; Naissance de la prison*," *Annales Historiques de la Révolution Française* (1977): 2.

achievements?[105] Was "Liberty, Equality, Fraternity" merely an instance of ideological subterfuge meant to mask and conceal increasingly sophisticated mechanisms of "biopower"?

For these and other reasons, observers felt that Foucault's description of nineteenth-century institutional practice as a massive instance of "normalization" was untenable. By methodologically elevating "carceralism" to the status of an impregnable power, had not Foucault ended up seriously undermining capacities for resistance? By dispersing power in all directions, he paradoxically risked diluting—and, hence, rendering unrecognizable—its core elements and components. No longer exercised by a particular group or class, power circulated amorphously through individuals before recentering itself—but where, exactly? Ultimately, the workings of power seemed vague and nebulous.

Once power is divested of its core, resistance is deprived of its object. Where should one strike? What tactics should one employ? Whom, precisely, should one strive to contest or resist? Once power has been elevated to the level of an all-encompassing "discursive regime," efforts to combat it seem almost pointless. They seem to be "always already" inscribed in "power-knowledge" qua episteme. As omnipresent and strangely anonymous, power seemed to be both everywhere and nowhere. As one commentator aptly concluded, in Foucault's scheme "[power] was irresistible since there was nothing to resist."[106]

Critics also objected to Foucault's continued reliance on "archaeological" concepts and methods that, by definition, banished the "subject"—and, along with it, social actors and oppositional groups—from the philosopher's interpretive framework. As one commentator demurred, "The vocabulary of geometry turns human society into a desert." Thus, instead of highlighting the oppositional potentials of human subjectivity and will, Foucault "speaks about spaces, lines, frameworks, segments, and dispositions."[107] Having belittled prospects for contestation, Foucault's characterization of modern disciplinary practice seemed nightmarish and Kafkaesque. Nowhere in sight were there

[105] See, for example, the important book by Nord, *Republican Moment*.
[106] Dosse, *History of Structuralism* 2:251.
[107] Ibid.

identifiable actors and social groups who might be capable of resisting power's ineluctable maw.

FOUCAULT'S PROGENY: THE NEW PHILOSOPHERS

Despite his vigorous promotion of the idea of "specific intellectuals," Foucault paradoxically discovered—along with many of his erstwhile Maoist allies—that he could not dispense with the idea of universal human rights. At issue was a sweeping realignment of French oppositional political culture: from gauchisme to *droits de l'homme*, one might say. Here, Maoism, in its post-May incarnation, played the unsuspecting role of a way station or transmission belt, weaning intellectuals away from the dogmas of orthodox Marxism and exposing them to an expanded definition of human emancipation. After leftism's implosion, the Eastern European dissident movement arose to capture the imagination of former gauchistes. And in this context, critics of "power" found the idea of human rights indispensable.[108] To have done any less would have been the ultimate in hypocrisy. After all, how could one in good conscience denounce the oppression of "power-knowledge" in the West while turning a blind eye to its repugnant, totalitarian manifestations in the East? Following the publication of Solzhenitsyn's pioneering book on the Soviet Gulag, the "antihumanist" paradigms of structuralism and Marxism were perceived in a new moral light—and found seriously wanting. Both were viewed as "sciences of legitimation" that underwrote oppressive logics of social control.

Thus, during the late 1970s, in what can only be considered a striking political volte-face, Foucault, along with former Maoists such as André Glucksmann and Serge July, became a committed *droit-de-l'hommiste*— a human rights advocate. In 1977, along with Sartre and Glucksmann, Foucault protested a state visit by Soviet president Leonid Brezhnev by staging an alternative public reception for a group of Eastern European dissidents. A year later, along with Bernard Kouchner, the founder of Médecins sans frontières (Doctors without Borders), Foucault helped

[108] The story is best told by Grémion in *Paris-Prague*.

establish A Boat for Vietnam, an organization dedicated to helping Vietnamese refugees fleeing the ravages of left-wing dictatorship.[109] In 1981, when General Wojciech Jaruzelski declared martial law, thereby quashing Solidarity, Poland's nascent independent trade union movement, Foucault successfully lobbied newly elected president François Mitterrand to reverse the government's policy of noninterference.[110]

The alliance with Kouchner and ex-Maoist Glucksmann transformed Foucault into a passionate advocate of humanitarian intervention (*le droit d'ingérence*): the moral imperative to intervene in the domestic affairs of a nation when human rights are being systematically violated. In 1981 Foucault addressed a major conference held in Geneva where these themes were being debated and discussed, with the intention of promoting a new and more vigorous Declaration of Rights of Man and Citizen.[111] Explicitly relying on the human rights idiom of the day, Foucault celebrated the existence of "an international citizenship" requiring individuals to speak out against abuses of power wherever they may occur. "It is the duty of this international citizenship," he continued, "to always bring the testimony of people's suffering to the eyes and ears of governments. . . . The suffering of men must never be a silent residue of policy. It grounds an absolute right to stand up and speak to those who hold power."[112] Foucault went on to praise humanitarian NGOs such as Amnesty International, Terre des hommes, and Kouchner's Médecins du monde as exemplary of the new moral

[109] As a youth, Kouchner had been a member of the Union des jeunesses communistes and was never a Maoist. Nevertheless, his itinerary—from leftism to staunch human rights advocate—is highly representative of the political trajectory Maoists pursued. Kouchner became minister of health under François Mitterrand's presidency (1992–93) (and then again in 2001 under Lionel Jospin) and French foreign minister under Nicolas Sarkozy (2007–). For a brief account of his career, see James Traub, "A Statesman without Borders," *New York Times*, February 3, 2008.

[110] Foucault, "The Moral and Social Experience of the Poles Can No Longer Be Obliterated," in *Power*, ed. James Faubion, trans. Robert Hurley et al. (New York: New Press, 2000), 465–73.

[111] See Foucault, *Dits et écrits* 2:1526. As the editors explain, Foucault sought to "get as many persons as possible to react to this text, with the hope that the result would lead to a new Declaration of the Rights of Man."

[112] Foucault, "Face aux gouvernements, les droits de l'homme," ibid., 1526–27.

standpoint of international citizenship, which, in his view, established
the "right . . . of private individuals to intervene effectively in the order
of international policies and strategies."[113]

Foucault's alliance with the GIP Maoists had sensitized him to the
multiplicity of forms in which domination appeared in modern society.
But the GIP response, for all its bravado and tenacity, had remained
diffuse and ad hoc. Unquestionably, a more systematic and principled
approach to the problem of "power" was needed. Thus, during the late
1970s and under the influence of a changed political zeitgeist, Foucault assumed the guise of a "universal intellectual" and a champion
of democratic values. (His one relapse—and a serious one—was his
defense of the revolution of the mullahs in Iran. Foucault viewed the
popular revolt against the shah as a praiseworthy, indigenous anticolonial insurrection. Once again, a prominent Western intellectual had
been seduced and deceived by the lure of third worldism—albeit, this
time a third worldism draped in religious garb.)[114]

During the late 1970s the so-called New Philosophers articulated
the new humanitarian sensibility. In their front ranks, former Gauche
prolétarienne militants such as Glucksmann, Jean-Paul Dollé, Christian Jambet, Guy Lardreau, and Philippe Nemo figured prominently.
As an ex-GIP leader and activist, Foucault enthusiastically supported
his former colleagues and fellow militants.

For decades left-leaning Parisian intellectuals had sought to separate
Marxism qua doctrine from its various concrete historical deformations, thereby holding out the prospect that the radiant utopian future
guaranteed by historical materialism's founders was still beckoning on
the horizon. The New Philosophers' gambit—which owed more to the
voluble media coverage their books received than to their intellectual
originality (the critique of Marxism they embraced had for the most
part been developed by the Socialism or Barbarism group during the
1950s and 1960s)—was to link communism's manifest political failings

[113] Michel Foucault, *The Essential Foucault*, ed. P. Rabinow and N. Rose (New
York: New Press, 2003), 64–65.
[114] See Janet Afary and Kevin Anderson, *Foucault and the Iranian Revolution* (Chicago: University of Chicago Press, 2005).

to the missteps of Marxist theory. Glucksmann first developed this thesis in his 1975 book, *La cuisinière et le mangeur d'hommes* (The Cook
and the Man-Eater). In Glucksmann's view, Marx was the "chef" who
contrived "recipes" for the theoretical mastery of humanity—recipes
that were implemented by "man-eaters" such as Lenin, Trotsky, Stalin,
and Mao.

Thus, in 1977, when Glucksmann's *Master Thinkers* first appeared,
Foucault published a laudatory review entitled "The Great Rage of
Facts" in the left-wing mass-circulation weekly *Le Nouvel Observateur*.[115]
The imprimatur of France's leading philosopher-intellectual was an unequivocal signal that New Philosophy deserved to be taken seriously by
a broadly educated public. By choosing this title, Foucault, who once
described himself as a "happy positivist," suggested that no amount of
Marxian-inspired theoretical pyrotechnics could change the nature of
the "facts" attesting to communism's abysmal, real-world track record.
(The title was also an unsubtle jibe directed against Althusser, whose
structuralist approach stressed Marxism's unimpugnable theoretical cogency despite any "deviations" that might be found in practice.) In Foucault's view, the stubbornness of "facts" stood as an insuperable obstacle
to the delusional belief that, somehow, a return to Marxist theory in its
original, pristine state could set the world right. Moreover, in *The Gulag
Archipelago*—a book that washed over the Parisian intellectual scene like
a tidal wave—Solzhenitsyn based his case not on sophisticated interpretive paradigms but on stolid and immovable "facts."

Further, the narratives of hardship and deprivation he recounted
consisted of unadorned testimonials by the Gulag's innocent victims:
the "plebs," who fell beneath the radar scope of sophisticated theories like structuralist Marxism. As such, the plebs were doomed to a
"pretheoretical" consciousness; from the standpoint of intellectual sophistication, they had nothing to say. Yet, as Solzhenitsyn had shown,
it was their testimony alone, and not Marxism qua "theory," that had
allowed the truth to unfold and become known. Following the lead of

[115] Foucault, "La grande colère des faits," *Le Nouvel Observateur*, May 9, 1977; reprinted in Sylvie Bouscasse and Denis Bourgeois's *Faut-il brûler les nouveaux philosophes:
Le dossier du "procès"* (Paris: Nouvelles Editions Oswald, 1978).

Glucksmann, who employed the term extensively in *The Cook and the
Man-Eater* and *The Master Thinkers,* in his writings on carceralism Foucault would embrace the notion of the "pleb" as a type of premanipu-
lated existential substrate: the individual in her "sheer being" prior to
logics of modern disciplinary control or "subjectivization."[116] Although
Foucault was wary about turning the "pleb" into a new *fundamentum
inconcussum,* or essence, on numerous occasions he affirmed its status as
a preconceptual, ontic basis of resistance. "There are plebs," Foucault
enthuses, "in bodies, in souls, in individuals, in the proletariat, in the
bourgeoisie . . . everywhere in a diversity of forms and extensions, of
energies and irreducibilities." Whereas it would be an exaggeration to
claim that the pleb *escapes* relations of power, insofar as he or she exists
at power's limits, Foucault continues, the pleb provides an indispensable basis for theorizing the Other of power qua contestation.[117] A good
illustration of the use to which Foucault put the concept occurs in *Discipline and Punish,* where, following Fourier, he celebrates criminality as
a form of transgression or resistance vis-à-vis reigning societal norms.
("It may be," observes Foucault, "that crime constitutes a political instrument that could prove precious for the liberation of our society. . . .
Indeed, will such an emancipation take place without it?")[118] It is in this
context that Foucault urges greater attention to the linkages between
the lower classes and illegality, the reciprocal relationship between the
proletariat and the "urban plebs."[119]

In solidarity with Glucksmann, Foucault held that the totalizing nature of Marxist thought was at the root of the doctrine's historicopoliti-
cal excesses. Unorthodox or reformist currents of Marxism continually
held out the prospect that if only Marx's thought were correctly interpreted, socialist humanity would, at long last, come into its own.
Foucault effusively praises *The Cook and the Man-Eater* as the book that
took the courageous final step in breaking with historical materialism's

[116] Foucault used the expression the "non-proletarianized pleb" as early as "On
Popular Justice: A Discussion with the Maoists" (1972).

[117] Foucault, "Pouvoir et stratégies," in *Dits et écrits* 2:420–21.

[118] Michel Foucault, *Discipline and Punish,* trans. Alan Sheridan (New York: Vintage,
1979), 289.

[119] Ibid., 287.

long train of rationalizations and self-deceptions.[120] Foucault summarizes Glucksmann's position as follows:

> The whole of a certain Left has attempted to explain the Gulag . . .
> in terms of the theory of history, or at least the history of theory.
> Yes, yes, there were massacres; but that was a terrible error. Just
> reread Marx or Lenin, compare them with Stalin, and you will
> see where the latter went wrong. It is obvious that all those deaths
> could only result from a misreading. It was predictable: Stalin-
> ism-error was one of the principal agents behind the return to
> Marxism-truth, to Marxism-text, which we saw in the 1960s. If
> you want to be against Stalin, don't listen to the victims; they will
> only recount their tortures. Reread the theoreticians; they will
> tell you the truth about the true.[121]

The New Philosophers were Foucault's intellectual progeny in another important sense as well. The theoretical basis of their critique of Marxism was Foucault's "power-knowledge" dyad: the idea that knowledge, rather than being something that will set us free as the philosophes had argued, is itself a form of power; the contention that no form of knowledge is disinterested or value free; that, instead, all insight is implicated in the production and maintenance of power relations. Of course, Foucault derived this standpoint from a critical reading of Nietzsche, who had famously unmasked the "will to power" subtending all allegedly impartial claims to knowledge or truth. In *The Master Thinkers*, Glucksmann carried this argument to an implausible extreme, going so far as to suggest that Auschwitz and the Gulag represented the hidden telos of the Western intellectual tradition. The only figures he seemed to exempt from this simplistic, denunciatory litany were Socrates and Rabelais—and Foucault, of course, whose portrayal of the "disciplinary society" as a manifestation of "soft totalitarianism"

[120] See Foucault, "La grande colère des faits," 420–21: "It seems to me that Glucksmann's analysis escapes all these so readily practiced forms of reduction."

[121] Ibid. For an excellent account of the "Solzhenitsyn effect," see Grémion, *Paris-Prague*.

figures prominently in Glucksmann's account. (The East had its Gulag, but the West specialized in "means of correct training.") The problem was that, by shifting their thinking to the strategic plane of "power" and "force," New Philosophers such as Glucksmann abandoned the terrain of reason and philosophical argumentation. Reason was reduced to a manifestation of the will to theoretical mastery—as with Foucault's expression "the will to knowledge" (la volonté à savoir)—and "truth" became merely the ideological window dressing for power relations or "interest."[122] Suffice it to say that once one discounts reason and intellection as inherently repressive, one abandons the only means available to think through the problems of the political and historical present.

Jacques Lacan's theories were another important influence on the New Philosophers. In the post–May period, the idea took hold that try as one might, it was impossible to escape the discourse of the master. In other words, abandon all hope, ye who enter the "symbolic realm," or language! There is no circumventing the fact that discourse itself is merely a *mechanism of domination* to which there is no "outside" or "escape." As Lacan resignedly declared in a 1969 colloquy: "The aspiration to revolution has but one conceivable issue, always, the Discourse of the Master. That is what experience has proved. What you, as revolutionaries, aspire to is a Master. You will have one!"[123] Lacan's view of language, as filtered through the exclusionary mechanisms of ego formation, or "ontogenesis," as, in essence, a "discursive penitentiary," harmonized with Foucault's critical views on the repressive function of language qua "discursive regime" or "episteme." (What both approaches neglect is a theory of the autonomy or originality of the "speech act," which by virtue of its expressive capacities possesses the ability to escape the rigid constraints of structure.) Hence, the popularity of the ethereal Christian tract penned by ex-Maoists Christian

[122] See the astute critique by Jacques Bouvresse, *Le philosophe chez les autophages* (Paris: Editions de Minuit, 1984), 44, 89.

[123] Lacan, "Impromptu at Vincennes," in *Television* (New York: Norton, 1978), 126. In fairness, Lacan's remarks are as much a critique of the repressive function of ego formation ("ontogenesis"), which he chronicles in his famous essay "Mirror Stage," as they are an indictment of the symbolic realm.

Jambet and Guy Lardreau, *L'Ange* (Angel), which argued that, in light of the "fallen" state of language, history, and politics, "transcendence" remained the sole option. The choice was clear-cut: either Stalin or Joan of Arc. There were no half measures to be found.

Those who disagreed with the New Philosophers' perspective were brusquely dismissed as "master censors" (maître-censeurs).[124] Thus, in their defense of human rights, the New Philosophers displayed an intolerance for criticism that, in many respects, mirrored their earlier, pro-Chinese ideological dogmatism.

It was ironic, then, that despite his congenital anti-Sartrism, it was Foucault who, when all was said and done, inherited Sartre's mantle as France's archetypical engaged intellectual. By the same token, the demands of commitment in a posttotalitarian epoch mandated a return to the *ethical* vocation of the intellectual as represented by Voltaire, Hugo, and Zola.[125] In 1978 François Furet had proclaimed: "The French Revolution is over."[126] With it died the prophetic intellectual, the political clairvoyant who specialized in envisioning humanity's radiant utopian future. The universal intellectual was reborn from her ashes.

[124] See Bernard-Henri Lévy, "La réponse aux maîtres-censeurs," *Le Nouvel Observateur*, June 27, 1977.

[125] On this point, see the excellent book by Bourg, *From Revolution to Ethics*.

[126] François Furet, *Interpreting the French Revolution*, trans. Elborg Forster (Cambridge: Cambridge University Press, 1979), 1.

CHAPTER 8

The Impossible Heritage: From Cultural Revolution to Associational Democracy

> The struggle against the Apparatus is no longer carried
> out in the name of political rights or workers' rights but
> in support of a population's right to choose its kind of
> life . . . which is often called *self-management*. Political
> action is all-pervasive: it enters into the health service, into
> sexuality, into education and into energy production. . . .
> *At the heart of society burns the fire of social movements.*
>
> —Alain Touraine, *The Voice and the Eye*

> In the lovely month of May 1968, the forces of order
> managed to prevent the spring from spilling over into
> summer. The crowds at the aborted celebration left
> the streets and dispersed to the universities, the high
> schools, the factories, and France's forgotten ghettos.
> The scent of Nanterre lingers in the air everywhere. A
> taste for political adventure has returned to the West. . . .
> It's the beginning of the wild struggles to come.
>
> —Bernard Kouchner and Michel-Antoine Burnier,
> *La France sauvage*

ENDGAME

In 1972 a final crisis—in many ways, the coup de grâce—befell the
Gauche prolétarienne. Since the UJC-ML's (Union des jeunesses communistes marxistes-léninistes) inception in 1966, the Maoists had
firmly supported the Palestinian cause as a gesture of solidarity with

a colonized and oppressed people. In the wake of the Six-Day War in June 1967, vows of mutual support escalated. As a result of Maoist initiatives, PLO solidarity committees mushroomed throughout France. The Maoists, for their part, hoped that by invoking the Palestinian struggle, they could induce France's large Arab immigrant community to support their own political struggle. Following May 1968, several members of the Gauche prolétarienne had traveled to the Middle East to train in PLO military camps. In 1972 talks began between the GP's armed wing, the Nouvelle résistance populaire (NRP), led by Olivier Rolin, and the Popular Front for the Liberation of Palestine (PFLP).[1] PFLP leader Ahmed Jibril hoped that the NRP would take responsibility for operations in France.

But in September 1972 everything changed as PLO commandos took eleven Israeli athletes hostage during the summer Olympics in Munich. While television viewers around the world looked on in horror, the athletes were killed during a failed German rescue attempt. The cold-blooded murder of the Israeli Olympians represented a point of no return for the Maoist delusion that gauchisme's political future lay with armed struggle. Henceforth, the image of the heroic urban guerrilla definitively lost its luster.

As we have seen, the September 14 issue of *La Cause du Peuple* condemned the PLO attack on Israeli civilians. The GP's resolute stance stood in marked contrast to the attitude of the *Tel Quel* group, which used the occasion to proclaim their undying solidarity with the Palestinian cause. By murdering Jews merely because they were Jews, the PLO had reproduced the logic of modern anti-Semitism. The macabre nature of the incident was enhanced by the fact that the attack had occurred on German soil, just a few miles from the Dachau concentration camp.

For the Maoists, the Munich episode arrived on the heels of two other major political setbacks: Pierre Overney's slaying at a Renault-plant protest in February 1972 (Overney's killer, a member of the Renault security team, was given a four-year jail sentence and released

---

[1] See Bourseiller, *Maoïstes*, 225; and Rolin's revealing fictionalized memoir *Tigre en papier* (Paris: Editions du Seuil, 2002).

after eight months); and the Bruay-en-Artois affair, in whose aftermath French Maoism's political fault lines—between "democrats," like Foucault and Sartre, and the GP rank and file; between ruthless apostles of "popular justice," like Victor, and French Maoism's more moderate "libidinal" wing—stood fully exposed.

But there was another aspect of the Munich affair that provoked soul-searching and revulsion among the Maoists. The GP leadership— Alain Geismar, André Glucksmann, Tiennot Grumbach, Benny Lévy (Pierre Victor), Tony Lévy, and Daniel Linhardt—was preponderantly Jewish. They were, albeit, archetypical "non-Jewish Jews," that is, assimilated Jews who did not self-identify as Jewish. Almost all had negligible religious training and possessed a relatively limited sense of Jewish cultural belonging. Nevertheless, the Munich massacre triggered a long-repressed religious dimension of gauchiste collective psychology. It was hardly accidental that of the four major leaders of the May student revolt—Daniel Cohn-Bendit, Alain Geismar, Alain Krivine, and Jacques Sauvageot—three were Jews. (Sauvageot, the head of the National Union of French Students, was the lone exception.)

Following the Holocaust, French Jews had grown suspicious of the republican-assimilationist, "immigrants into Frenchmen" model of citizenship, and were left to wonder whether they would ever be accepted as entirely French. Such doubts provoked more general misgivings about the virtues of French belonging and about French society in general; when all was said and done, was assimilation merely a sophisticated ruse to deprive French Jews of a Jewish identity? In private, many Jews wondered how much France had really changed since Vichy's insidious racial laws had been implemented.[2] That so many gauchistes thought of themselves as *résistants* testifies to how powerful the legacy of Vichy, collaboration, and the shameful Jewish deportations remained among postwar French youth, Jewish youth in particular. These memories were permanently etched in the political unconscious of young French activists. According to the standard Marxist interpretation of Nazism, it was German industrialists who had greased the wheels of Hitler's seizure of power in order to suppress the Left. Viewed

---

[2] See Paxton and Marrus, *Vichy France.*

from this vantage point, was the reigning constellation of political and economic forces in France *really* so different from the one that existed in Germany in 1933? By identifying profoundly with the Resistance, the Jewish leftists were in many respects seeking to win the antifascist struggle their parents' generation had lost.

Chroniclers of left-wing radicalism have frequently asked why was it in Germany and Italy that leftists crossed the line to engage in terrorist acts, whereas in France, despite gauchisme's popularity, similar tendencies were kept at bay.[3] In France the Maoists increasingly realized how unrealistic their commitment to the goals of revolutionism had become. The movement's working-class base had failed to expand, contradicting one of the fundamental tenets of the Marxist revolutionary catechism. In fact, France's industrial working class was contracting, whereas the ranks of white-collar and service-industry employees swelled. France's major trade unions seemed perfectly content to accept wage increases and improvements in working conditions. Revolution was the last thing on their minds. From the workers' perspective, why engage in the risky brinkmanship of violent political struggle when the strategy of collective bargaining proved so successful? One of the main ironies of the gauchiste interlude is that while economically privileged student radicals increasingly identified with the working class, the French workers' main objective was to accede to the ranks of the middle class.

Differences in history and national political culture also played a major role in influencing the terrorist potential of the various left-wing groups. Here, one cannot help but be struck by the fact that in the two cases where the extreme Left succumbed to terrorism—Germany and Italy—the nations in question had been compromised by fascist political pasts. In both cases, there were disturbing elements of continuity between the vanquished fascist regimes and their parliamentary successors.

The presence of the fascist past influenced political perceptions in several crucial respects. It discouraged moderation and encouraged a

---

[3] See, for example, Sommier, *La violence politique*. See also the important comparison of the German Red Army Faction and the American Weathermen by Varon, *Bringing the War Home*.

culture of political extremism. It fed the belief that liberal institutions were chronically weak—hence, incapable of thwarting a fascist relapse. In both Italy and Germany, the advent of fascism had been preceded by troubled and inept liberal polities. Both Italy's Red Brigades and Germany's Red Army Faction embraced the (erroneous) Marxist view that bourgeois democracy and fascism were natural political bedfellows. Hence, both groups adopted the strategy of attempting to "unmask" the fascist character of the state via violent provocations, a practice that ultimately became a self-fulfilling prophecy, for when confronted with violence, often the state's sole option was to respond in kind.

Both Italy and Germany were "belated nations." In both cases, political unification occurred tardily: 1861 in Italy's case, 1871 in Germany's. Neither nation possessed extensive experience with democratic political institutions. Consequently, when the fascist regimes ultimately collapsed at war's end, neither nation had at its disposal a usable political past. The lessons they had learned from their bloody brush with political dictatorship were, for the most part, negative.

France, conversely, had a very different political history. It was, after all, the birthplace of democratic republicanism. The Third Republic (1871–1940), for all its failings and difficulties, could claim a robust seventy years of political continuity. Postwar France could at least invoke the prestige of the anti-Nazi Resistance. And in the face of France's "strange defeat" (M. Bloch) of June 1940, de Gaulle's "Free French" had sought to uphold the honor of France's republican heritage.

Finally, since the student Maoists were almost all *normaliens*, educational background seemed to play a determinative role. When the chips were down, many militants found it difficult to simply jettison their training in the classic texts of French humanism and assume the role of urban guerrillas. As one ex-Maoist noted: "We had been formed more than we were willing to admit by the French university system. Besides, many of us were still preoccupied with our responsibilities at the Sorbonne, the Khâgne, and the course of study at the Ecole normale supérieure."[4] When all was said and done, for many student militants,

---

[4] Antoine Liniers, "Objections pour une prise d'armes, " in Furet, Liniers, and Raynaud's *Terrorisme et démocratie*, 197. Antoine Liniers is a pseudonym for Olivier

Montaigne's *Essais* proved more influential than Chairman Mao's Little Red Book.

REDEFINING REVOLUTION

The May revolt was a classic instance of unintended consequences. There was a fundamental disjunction between the insurrection's form and its content. Inspired by the rising tide of third worldism, the student radicals adopted a rhetoric of revolutionism that was fundamentally at odds with many of their innermost, peaceable, and transformative aims and sentiments. The student activists realized how badly the Russian Revolution had miscarried. It would take them a few more years to appreciate the fact that the worldwide anti-imperialist struggles they dutifully supported would finish just as poorly, if not worse.

From the outset the Maoists had emulated the comportment of the disciplined, professional revolutionaries vaunted in Lenin's *What Is To Be Done?* Yet Lenin's vanguard model had been tailored to the political conditions of czarist Russia, a police state where it was essentially impossible to militate openly for much-needed political change. It made little sense to transpose Bolshevik methods to Western democracies, where the rudiments of democratic pluralism allowed for more open and reputable means of political contestation.

Given the unresponsiveness of France's political system under de Gaulle's imperial presidency, Marxism remained the only rhetoric at the students' disposal—the discourse of French republicanism having been, in their eyes, discredited and co-opted. During May, in a tour de force of revolutionary theatricality, the students reenacted the entire gamut of insurrectionary possibilities and options: the revolutions of 1848, the Paris Commune, Berlin 1918, and the Kronstadt naval uprising. Trotskyists, anarchists, Maoists, and Situationists vied—for the most part, fraternally—to endow the unfolding events with meaning

---

Rolin, who during the early 1970s led the Gauche prolétarienne military wing, the Nouvelle résistance populaire. The Khâgne is a preparatory course for admission to the "grandes écoles," or France's elite educational track.

and direction. The one historical scenario they unanimously rejected was the Bolshevik-orchestrated storming of the Winter Palace of October 1917. The misdeeds of Stalinism and its sinister afterlives—the suppression of the 1956 Hungarian uprising, the crushing of the 1968 Czech experiment in "socialism with a human face"—had instructed the gauchistes in the dangers of Marxism-Leninism. To their credit, even the hardcore neo-Leninists among them (the Trotskyists and the Maoists) gainsaid this insurrectionary option.

In May's aftermath, the boundaries of "the political" in France were permanently expanded. Leftism had exploded the parameters of the Marxist revolutionary tradition.[5] During May the students proclaimed that "boredom is counterrevolutionary." Could not, then, the same be said about the fetishization of hierarchy and discipline that, from Robespierre to Stalin to Mao, had dominated the Western ideology of revolutionism? Had not Lenin's "professional revolutionaries" merely transposed the Protestant ethic's code of self-renunciation to Marxism?

During the 1950s Sartre had decreed that Marxism was the "unsurpassable horizon of our time."[6] Confuting Sartre, the May events turned out to be a crucial way station on the French Left's march toward an antitotalitarian political sensibility. Under the leadership of a handful of repentant ex-Maoists—the New Philosophers—anti-Marxism would metamorphose into the height of Parisian intellectual fashion. On several occasions, Sartre and Foucault—strange political bedfellows, to be sure—would bring up the rear.

In the post-May period the Maoist pur et dur tempered their ardor in order to merge with a variety of libertarian gauchiste currents and groups. Thereby, the Chinese trope of cultural revolution assumed an entirely new direction and meaning. "All power to the imagination" had been one of May 1968's foremost political slogans. For this reason, the surrealists would become a more important point of reference than Madame Mao (Jiang Qing) or the head of the People's Liberation Army, Lin Piao. Rimbaud's injunction "Change life!" (Changez la vie!) seemed as relevant, if not more so, than Marx's demand to

[5] For important precedents, see Gombin, *Origins of Modern Leftism*.
[6] Jean-Paul Sartre, *Critique de la raison dialectique* (Paris: Gallimard, 1960), 9.

socialize the means of production. In the student revolutionaries' febrile political imagination, Cultural Revolutionary China became inseparably fused with the American idyll of the Woodstock Nation. As one militant commented insightfully, the American counterculture taught that "class struggle is also a struggle for the expression of desire, for communication, and not simply an economic and political struggle."[7]

The workerist (ouvriériste) focus of traditional Marxism was out of step with the existential concerns of the times. One was no longer dealing with a class society as Marx described it. Instead, forces of social differentiation had ramified the parameters of struggle. Increasingly, a plurality of societal strata and groupings contended for rights and social recognition, beginning with the right to be seen and to be heard. The nineteenth-century image of the proletarian struggle was dismantled and entirely restructured: "immigrants, the young, prisoners, homosexuals, the insane—everyone who was excluded, all of the 'wretched of the earth,' all who were on the margins of society, became the object of revolutionary preoccupations."[8] The main issues motivating these groups revolved around questions of everyday life. The student militants and their followers sought to discover anew the meaning of self-actualization in a society where "leisure time" was increasingly administered by an unsavory alliance of large-scale organizations: the state bureaucracy, advertising conglomerates, magnates of mass culture, and multinational corporations. Consequently, the locus of struggle shifted from economics and questions of redistribution to the terrain of "symbolic domination," or culture. Associated individuals sought to defend the integrity of their various ways of life vis-à-vis the logic of corporate-dominated cultural administration.[9] In retrospect, the May movement represented an effort to reconquer the nodal points

[7] Guy Hocquenghem, "Pour une conception homosexuel du monde," in L'après-mai des faunes (Paris: Grasset 1974), 164.

[8] Picq, Libération des femmes, 50.

[9] For a classic essay on this theme, see Adorno, "Culture and Administration," in Culture Industry, 107–31.

of everyday life from a series of alien, heteronomous forces. As such, it represented an incipient attempt to reverse an accelerating process of "internal colonization."[10]

Thus, in May's aftermath the idea of emancipation was transformed. It was no longer synonymous with civic or political emancipation, the traditional ends of Western liberalism. In the light of contemporary political struggles, this conception of emancipation seemed inordinately restrictive. Liberalism neglected the nature of human particularity, our status as individuals with highly specific, nongeneric needs. The sixty-eighters began to inquire what it would mean to speak of emancipation in the case of a wide variety of social constituencies—women, gays, immigrants, the underclass—whose group-specific political needs and concerns had also been neglected by orthodox Marxism's stress on the universalizing framework of "class," which reduced social conflict unilaterally to the opposition between wage labor and capital.

Henceforth, radical politics stressed the ideals of authenticity and self-realization. Thereby, the meaning of political freedom expanded exponentially. An integral part of this new logic of social contestation entailed creating alternative discourses and spaces: a parallel polis or civil society. These zones subsisted at a healthy remove from the reifying effects of exchange relations or commodity society. In opposition to a modern civilization dominated by "death and boredom," the cultural revolutionaries who dominated the post-May period sought to facilitate the birth of a future society characterized by self-affirmation and libidinal fulfillment.

Nineteenth-century revolutionaries had manned the barricades. During the May insurrection, conversely, student radicals seized the "right to speak out," a fact that helps to explain the psychology behind a popular May graffito: "I have something to say, I just don't know what it is."[11] One of the unforeseen—and perhaps unforeseeable—upshots of the May revolt was that previously marginal groups dwelling on the fringes of society suddenly claimed the right to speak up and be heard.

[10] On this point, see Jürgen Habermas, *Theory of Communicative Action,* vol. 2, trans. Thomas McCarthy (Boston: Beacon Press, 1984).

[11] See Certeau, *Practice of Everyday Life.*

For conservatives in both Europe and the United States, the delegitimation of 1968 has been a key to establishing their own ideological credibility cum predominance. In 2002 French finance minister Nicolas Sarkozy dismissed the May revolt as an era when traditional values lost their meaning, when rights took precedence over duties and obligations, and when respect for authority fell by the wayside.[12] Former leftists, disappointed by the fact that the radiant utopian future heralded by May never came to pass, have joined the voluble chorus of naysayers and detractors. In their view, by removing the blockages of authority and tradition, May's end result was to enthrone a culture of possessive individualism. The counterculture's Dionysian spirit was commercially reconfigured to suit the ends of the consumer society.

One of the May revolt's enduring lessons pertained to the nature of French political culture. The May uprising embodied a resounding rejection of France's long-standing and traditional *étatiste* political model, which one could trace back to the absolutist reign of Louis XIV. Ironically, this same centralizing and hierarchical organizational mentality determined and suffused France's predominant postrevolutionary political forms: Jacobinism, republicanism, and communism. By renouncing *étatisme*, the sixty-eighters sought to nurture and develop a new political culture, one that scorned the top-down Jacobin model in favor of an approach that stressed the values of direct democracy and local autonomy.[13] The *soixante-huitards* ceased to regard the capacities of the state as a cure-all. They refused to allow their demands and concerns to be rechanneled by conventional political mechanisms and procedures: election campaigns, parliaments, trade unions, and so on. Instead, they experimented with a new spirit of self-reliance, seeking to invent a series of alternative, locally rooted cultural and political forms, attempts that culminated in the notion of the self-organization of society. If totalitarianism may be defined as the wholesale absorption of society by the political realm, the post-May revitalization of the social sphere was a resolutely antitotalitarian enterprise.

[12] Quoted in "Faut-il romper avec l'esprit de 1968?" *Le Monde*, May 19, 2002.
[13] See the classic study by Rosanvallon and Viveret, *Pour une nouvelle culture politique*.

As one historian of the May events has aptly summarized these developments, when all is said and done, it was the "cultural moment" of the May revolt that ultimately triumphed:

> A revolution in mores was attained . . . as well as a revolution of everyday life. The prior rigidity of social relations disappeared, symbolic hierarchies were loosened. . . . Bit by bit, a thaw permeated relations in the workplace and in the family; the disciplines became less rigid and behavioral codes were relaxed. Control over the body—a legacy of religious and petty bourgeois morality—slackened, thereby according Desire unprecedented latitude. . . . The traditional authority of intellectuals, notables, doctors, priests, lawyers, and judges was consistently contested, and diminished by degrees. "Dialogue" and "consensus" became the new code words among holders of power. Direct orders, incontestable instructions, and arbitrary directives were progressively relegated to the historical dustbin. In this sense, the May revolt was *cultural*, not *political*. . . . May '68 was not a failed revolution, but a great "reformist revolt," a democratic insurrection . . . and, in this way, it succeeded.[14]

ASSOCIATIONAL DEMOCRACY

One of the May movement's enduring legacies has been the regeneration of French associational life, spurring a reversal of France's long-standing heritage of political centralization.[15] The May uprising, and the new social movements that followed in its wake, succeeded in transforming the way the French understood society. No longer was society belittled as a passive object of state administration. Instead it was perceived as a locus of active citizenship, a sphere of collective will formation, sociability, identity constitution, and political participation. The traditional

[14] Joffrin, *Mai '68*, 319–20, 321–22.
[15] See, for example, Levy, *Tocqueville's Revenge*, and Schmidt, *Democratizing France*.

vertical axis of the French republican tradition was recalibrated along horizontal lines.[16] In many respects, the identity-oriented social movements such as feminism and gay liberation were merely the tip of the iceberg. The post-May period witnessed the proliferation of a wide variety of self-help societies, human rights organizations, and citizen initiatives. This unprecedented expansion of the nonprofit sector (le secteur non lucratif) of civil society transformed the nature and scope of French political activism. Ecology (Les amis de la terre, Les verts), "sans frontièrisme" (Doctors without Borders, followed by Pharmacists, Veterinarians, Agronomists, and Reporters without Borders), antinuclearism, immigrant rights advocacy (the FASTI, or Fédération des associations de soutien aux travailleurs immigrés), and regional autonomy movements also date from this period.[17] As Martine Barthélemy has noted in *The New Age of Participation*, "Associational activity takes root in everyday life"—the neighborhood, the city street, the local assembly hall—to become "the privileged locus of contestation. . . . [It] justly invokes the spirit of May '68."[18]

In *Democracy in America*, Alexis de Tocqueville famously contrasted France's weak associational capacity with the vigorous character of associational life in the United States.

> Americans of all ages, all stations in life, and all types of disposition are forever forming associations . . . of a thousand different types [Tocqueville observed], religious, moral, serious, futile, very general and very limited, immensely large and minute. . . . As soon as several Americans have conceived a sentiment or an idea that they want to produce before the world, they seek each other out, and when found, they unite. Thenceforth, they are no longer isolated individuals, but a power conspicuous from the

[16] For an alternative view of French republicanism, emphasizing its associational roots, see Nord, *Republican Moment*.

[17] See Belorgey, *Cent ans de vie associative*, 34–35. For a good survey of these movements, see Crettiez and Sommier, eds., *La France rebelle*.

[18] Barthélemy, *Associations*, 75.

distance whose actions serve as an example; when it speaks, men listen.[19]

To judge by recent evidence, however, the trend identified by *Democracy in America*'s author seems to have undergone a reversal. Although in recent years Americans have increasingly been observed "bowling alone," between 1970 and 2000, the number of new associations in France increased by 300 percent. Whereas during the 1960s an average of 20,000 new associations per year were created, since then the number of new associations has increased to a robust 60,000 per annum. In *The Demands of Liberty*, Pierre Rosanvallon interprets the transformation of French associational life as an essential heritage of the post-May era: "5,000 new associations were created annually in the 1950s; 20,000 in the 1960s; 25,000 in the 1970s; 40,000 in the 1980s; 60,000 in 1990; 68,000 in 2001." "Growth," Rosanvallon observes, "has been exponential, and it has not slackened."[20] When France celebrated the centennial of the 1901 law officially sanctioning associations, it was estimated that roughly twenty million people—40 percent of the adult population—belonged to one or more associations.

The expansion of associational life reflects the broader transformation from industrial to postindustrial society: continued migration from the countryside to the cities, the decline in union membership corresponding to Fordism's demise, the rise of white-collar professionals and "cadres" (the new managerial class), and the democratization of higher education, resulting in the cultural elevation of the general populace. Unsurprisingly, the rank and file of France's recent associational boom is composed largely of ex-sixty-eighters and members of the so-called new middle classes: teachers, professionals, middle managers, information workers, and so on. More generally, this trend reflects a new mode or register of social activism that analysts have described via the rubric of "new social citizenship": a new humanitarian consciousness

[19] Tocqueville, *Democracy in America*, 513, 516.

[20] Rosanvallon, *Demands of Liberty*, 261. On the decline of associational life in the United States, see Robert Putnam, *Bowling Alone: The Collapse and Revival of American Community* (New York: Simon and Schuster, 2000).

concerning civic responsibility for disenfranchised social groups and an approach to political engagement that differs significantly from the bourgeois-universalist ideal of citizenship as well as from traditional left-wing militancy in the name of the proletariat or a classless society.

The new social activism also bespeaks the rise of a "new individualism." Both Marxists and republicans have been quick to belittle this phenomenon as an abandonment of the universalist framework of the traditional Left in favor of an inner-directed and narcissistic cult of the self. However, this cynical characterization tells only part of the story, for the new individualism, which corresponds to the loosening of the ascriptive bonds of class, simultaneously signals an expansion of individual autonomy. Cultural attachments cease to be implacably predetermined by the ties of place, family, status, and class. Instead, today men and women are able to "individuate" themselves—to establish unique, self-chosen identities—socially, culturally, geographically, and professionally in a more autonomous and self-directed manner. This trend permits a broadening and enrichment of personality structure, a transformation that would have been impossible in more traditional status or class societies.

Such new techniques of self-individuation are not merely negative. They bespeak "individualism" in the positive sense stressed by Emile Durkheim: an enhancement of moral autonomy corresponding to increased prospects for individual choice, commitment, and experience. Moreover, since the "culture industry" seeks ideologically to shape personality structures, "work on the self" plays a crucial role in parrying introjected or internalized domination. An important legacy of the May movement's antiauthoritarianism, the new individualism correlates with the new humanitarianism—for example, the various "sans frontières" groups—that blossomed in the post-May period.[21] Inner directedness does not necessarily and inevitably translate into a renunciation of social commitment. In France its emergence has functioned as an indispensable prerequisite for a constructive mutation of forms of sociability and modes of political commitment.

[21] See Etienne Schweisguth, "La montée des valeurs individualistes," *Futuribles* 200 (July–August 1995).

The associational juggernaut proved so seductive that even French political elites tried to board it. Shortly after his election in 1974, President Valéry Giscard d'Estaing, sounding very much like a mellowed sixty-eighter, proclaimed: "The pluralist state means: power [belongs] in the hands of the citizens. That means: to men and women taken in their diversity and their complex reality, in their right to difference and their fundamental equality."[22] In 1977 the Socialist Party allied itself with the *autogestionniste,* or self-management, wing of the former Parti socialiste unifié (PSU), associated with Michel Rocard and the Left-Catholic Confédération française démocratique du travail (CFDT). Known as the "second Left" (la deuxième gauche), Rocard's followers were resolutely anti-Communist, anti-Jacobin, tolerant of the market, and Tocquevillian in their attitudes toward local democracy and the renovation of civil society. In 1983 the Socialists created the Conseil national de la vie associative in order to preserve and enhance the trend toward political decentralization and grassroots conviviality that had emerged during the previous decade. In 1988, following Mitterrand's election to a second term, Rocard was named prime minister. He boldly declared his intention to reconcile "political action and everyday life, state and civil society."[23]

Critics of the May revolt have faulted the protagonists for their social irresponsibility. Often, detractors on the political Left have been less forgiving than critics on the Right, censuring the student activists for revolutionary "playacting." The students, we are told, rashly exchanged revolutionary discipline for the lures of Dionysian revelry. The Sorbonne student commune was little more than a "socio-juvenile 1789."[24] The problem with the student militants was that they emulated André

[22] Valéry Giscard d'Estaing, *Démocratie française* (Paris: Fayard, 1976), 167.

[23] Cited in Barthélmy's *Associations*, 92. Rocard remained prime minister until 1991. For a history of the second Left, see Hervé Hamon and Patrick Rotman, *La deuxième gauche: Histoire intellectuelle et politique de la CFDT* (Paris: Editions du Seuil, 1984). See also Donzelot, *Invention du social.*

[24] See Morin, "La commune étudiante," in *Brèche,* 26–27. See also Henri Lefebvre, *The Explosion: Marxism and the French Revolution,* trans. Sacha Rabinovitch (New York: Monthly Review Press, 1969), and Le Goff, *Mai 68,* 470–72.

Breton rather than Lenin; they venerated the "Manifesto of Surrealism" rather than *The Communist Manifesto*. Thereby, they confused the desire for revolution with the "revolution of desire." Affluent progeny of "les trentes glorieuses," the student militants wished to see "l'imagination au pouvoir" (all power to the imagination). The result was that they ended up with an *imaginary revolution*. Little wonder that a mass strike numbering nine million people—France's largest demonstrations since the 1930s—degenerated into the recreational self-absorption and generational narcissism of cultural revolution. All was lost when, in the post-May period, *political* gauchisme lapsed into *cultural* gauchisme—a fall from grace from which the French Left has never recovered. In the view of France's leading historian of the May events, Jean-Pierre Le Goff, May's heirs promote

a black vision of the past, present and future that obstructs the horizon; [they] advocate a Great Refusal that would rather not confront possibilities and make choices. The over-estimation of the self as the heir of culture and a history . . . perverts the critical spirit and the opening to the Other, preferring the "angelicism" of the spineless . . . "citizen of the world." The "no" [of the Refusal] is not backed by an originary "yes," by a positive affirmation, be it implicit or explicit; it suffices unto itself. The primary relation of confidence uniting us to the world is broken, entailing a morbid paralysis of thought and action, a logic of self-destruction.[25]

Although such charges may contain a kernel of truth, when viewed against the backdrop of the May uprising's broader heritage and achievements, they stand as a classic instance of miscrecognition or mismeasure. They betray the frustrations of a left-wing superego unable to reconcile its utopian political expectations with the May revolt's more modest and reformist political legacy.

In the 1980s, with certain notable exceptions (SOS racisme and Act Up), grassroots political activism diminished. With the Socialists in power, confidence in the traditional methods of institutional reform

[25] Le Goff, *Mai 68*, 474.

increased. Only during the 1990s did the May uprising's legacy of social contestation come to genuine fruition. It was then that the "movement" politics that flourished in the post-May period—a politics that
studiously avoided the conventional institutional channels of electoral
politics and unions—reemerged in full force.

The May revolt set in motion a sequence of cultural politics that
left French mores and modes of sociability permanently transformed.
The social movements of the 1990s heralded a new humanitarianism,
what one might describe as a new "politics of social conscience." These
movements bypassed questions of group identity—what one might
term a "politics of recognition"—since these battles had largely been
fought and won during the 1970s and 1980s. Instead, the social movements of the 1990s targeted so-called second-generation economic
and social rights. They rallied around the idea of a reasonable "social
minimum," proclaiming: "People should not be allowed to starve in
the streets" and "Every citizen should be able to meet his or her basic
needs." They sought to highlight the contradiction between the Fifth
Republic's egalitarian political ideals and its glaring factual inequali-
ties. As such, the social movements of the 1990s focused on issues of
social "exclusion," problems related to the growing immiseration of
the French underclass. These problems had become especially acute
in an era of globalization and neo-laissez-faire, as the social safety net
established during the "thirty glorious years" had grown increasingly
precarious. The movement's chief intellectual benefactor was Pierre
Bourdieu, who documented the new conditions of social misery in his
important book *La misère du monde*.[26]

In an allusion to France's revolutionary heritage, the social movements of the 1990s were often referred to as "la Révolution des sans"—a
revolution of the excluded, or of "those without." Among its protagonists there figured prominently the *sans papiers*, *sans emploi*, and *sans
abri*: undocumented immigrants, the unemployed, and the homeless.

[26] Bourdieu, *Misère du monde*. See also Pierre Rosanvallon, *The New Social Question*
(Princeton, NJ: Princeton University Press, 2000), and Jean-Philippe Mathy, "The
Prophetic Exigency: Zola, Bourdieu and the Memory of Dreyfusism," *Contemporary
French Civilization* 24 (2) (Summer–Fall 2000): 321–40.

Their protests spawned influential organizations and pressure groups such as Droit au logement (DAL, or Right to Housing), Agir ensemble contre le chômage! (AC!, or Act Together against Unemployment!), and Droits devant! (Rights First!). The inaugural act of Droit au logement in 1995 was the occupation of a vacant apartment building on rue Dragon in the heart of the fashionable Saint-Germain des Près District of Paris, which the organizers transformed into an "active space of solidarities."[27] The goal of DAL activists, rather than providing handouts or charity, was to assist the homeless citizens of Paris in organizing themselves. In this respect, these militants were remarkably successful: they were able to find shelter for some three thousand Paris-area families. Moreover, their actions helped spur major legislation, such as the 1998 law against exclusion.

During the late 1990s, Act Together against Unemployment! employed a similar strategy. At the time, unemployment had reached chronic proportions. At nearly 12 percent, it was at its highest level since the Great Depression. Forty percent of the unemployed had been out of work for two years or more. Unemployment had changed from an episodic state to a permanent, long-term condition. To make matters worse, many of the long-term unemployed were either immigrants or poorly educated, or both, thus lacking the cultural resources necessary to break the cycle of social exclusion cum impoverishment.

Heretofore, the unemployed had been an "invisible class" whose members lacked both political and trade union representation. As a rule, unions were hesitant to champion their cause for fear of depriving employed workers of their jobs. Instead of providing the unemployed with enhanced temporary benefits, AC! activists helped them to appreciate the virtues of self-organization. The 1997–98 winter of protest signified the first time since the 1930s that the unemployed had mobilized as a group to challenge their marginal status by lobbying for recognition as a distinct constituency with identifiable political aims.

---

[27] On Droit au logement, see Waters, *Social Movements in France*, 126–27. On the relationship between the antiexclusion movements of the 1990s and the social egalitarian claims of the French Revolution, see Jacques Ghilhaumou, *La parole des sans: Les mouvements actuels a l'èpreuve de la révolution française* (Fontenay: Feuillets, 1998).

Thereby, they succeeded in emerging from the shadows into the sphere of social visibility. Soon, the protests initiated by AC! metamorphosed into a pan-European movement. In 1996 a congress of activists took place in Florence. It was followed by Europe-wide protests culminating in a march of some fifty thousand demonstrators in Amsterdam. In France protesters took over the Louvre pyramid and occupied social-benefit offices throughout the Hexagon.

The strategy of AC! militants was to place social rights on a par with civil and political rights. In essence, they tried to establish a new universal model of social citizenship. After all, the legitimacy of social rights was enshrined in both the 1948 UN Universal Declaration of Human Rights and the charter of the European Union. Activists therefore stressed the "right to work" and lobbied for a "Europe of full employment." In opposition to the 1993 Maastricht Treaty's narrow emphasis on monetary union and uncritical embrace of economic liberalism, AC! activists sought to ensure stronger legal guarantees for social rights at the European level: the right to health, housing, minimum income, education, and culture.

More generally, the AC! protests were directed against the social and human costs of a market-driven society that brusquely ignores the lot of its underclass. The AC! charter specifies: "While wealth has continued to grow, millions of inhabitants within Europe live below the threshold of poverty. We demand that each person have the right to a guaranteed income that corresponds to the wealth produced by society."[28]

Pierre Bourdieu referred to France's landmark winter of protest as a "social miracle." As one commentator has observed, the movement of the unemployed

> created a dynamic of political activism among a group that was otherwise disenfranchised and marginalized from society. They intervened in a diversity of ways, rehousing evicted tenants, launching European marches or responding to the critical daily needs of those out of work. They invented new alternative forms of action at a time when conventional left-wing politics was in

[28] AC!, *Actualisation de la "charte" d'AC!* (Paris: AC!, 1998), 17.

crisis and they revived grassroots mobilization within local communities. By their very existence, they pointed to the richness and
vibrancy of collective action outside the formal political domain
at the level of civil society.[29]

Spurred by these protests, Prime Minister Lionel Jospin invited the
movement's leaders to Matignon (the prime minister's residence) to
discuss their demands. When the dust had cleared, the AC! had secured
several significant concessions: (1) an infusion of new funds to offset the
economic burdens of chronic joblessness; (2) permanent representation
on several key government commissions charged with overseeing the
lot of the unemployed; and (3) the promulgation of a new law against
social exclusion, which was passed in July 1998. AC! pressure, along
with that of several associated groups, also played a crucial role in influencing Jospin's decision to adopt a thirty-five-hour workweek as a
means of creating more jobs.

The methods of extraparliamentary struggle utilized by the groups
associated with the new "politics of social conscience" originated with
the May uprising.[30] Thus, the notion of a new social citizenship, which
came to fruition in the 1990s, was one of the May movement's defining political legacies. In this context it is worth noting that one
of France's most enduring and renowned humanitarian organizations,
Médécins sans frontières—founded by current foreign minister Bernard Kouchner—was a direct outgrowth of the May movement.[31]

One of the May revolt's key political advances was its capacity to perceive domination in nontraditional ways. The movement's leaders understood that the mechanisms and modalities of power had qualitatively
expanded. These could no longer be equated with or reduced to state
repression or the negative effects of capitalism. Instead, amid a "society
of the spectacle," power's tentacles had expanded to the point where it

[29] Waters, *Social Movements in France*, 118–19.
[30] Crettiez and Sommier, eds., *La France rebelle*; see especially the discussion of "le
tournant 1968" (1968 as a turning point), 17–18.
[31] See Kouchner, *Malheurs des autres*.

was capable of infiltrating the body politic's innermost recesses. In this respect, the grassroots, tactical innovations of the Prison Information Group—established in 1971 by Maoist militants associated with Vive la révolution!—proved paradigmatic, for the GIP activists were successful in adapting the Maoist populist ideal of the "mass line" to the ends of participatory democracy. This meant forgoing obsolete models of political vanguardism in favor of the "self-organization of society," in this case prisoners, who following the GIP model and in the spirit of 1960s self-management (*autogestion*), would become the organizers and spokespersons of their own cause. Thereby, the May uprising's utopian political hopes were brought down to earth and redirected toward the ideals of democratic citizenship.

Bibliography

Adorno, Theodor. *The Culture Industry: Selected Essays on Mass Culture*. New York: Routledge, 1991.

Afary, Janet, and Kevin Anderson. *Foucault and the Iranian Revolution*. Chicago: University of Chicago Press, 2005.

Althusser, Louis. *L'avenir dure longtemps; suivi de "Les faits."* Paris: Stock/ IMEC, 1992.

———. *For Marx*. Translated by Ben Brewster. London: New Left Books, 1969.

———. *The Future Lasts Forever*. Translated by Richard Veasey. New York: New Press, 1993.

Aron, Raymond. *The Elusive Revolution: Anatomy of a Student Revolt*. Translated by Gordon Clough. New York: Praeger Publishers, 1969.

———. *Opium of the Intellectuals*. New York: Norton, 1962.

Aronson, Ronald. *Camus and Sartre: The Story of a Friendship and the Quarrel That Ended It*. Chicago: University of Chicago Press, 2003.

———. *Jean-Paul Sartre: Philosophy in the World*. London: Verso, 1980.

Auron, Yair. *Les juifs de l'extrême gauche en mai '68*. Paris: Albin Michel, 1998.

Badiou, Alain. *The Century*. Translated by Alberto Toscana. Cambridge, MA: Polity Press, 2007.

———. *Ethics: An Essay on the Understanding of Evil*. New York: Verso, 2001.

———. *Infinite Thought: Truth and the Return to Philosophy*. New York: Continuum, 2005.

———. *Metapolitics*. Translated by Jason Barker. New York: Verso, 2005.

———. "Roads to Renegacy: Interview by Eric Hazan." *New Left Review* 53 (September–October 2008): 125–33.

———. *Théorie du sujet*. Paris: Editions du Seuil, 1982.

Barker, Jason. *Alain Badiou: A Critical Introduction*. Steinberg, VA: Pluto Press, 2002.

Barthélemy, Martine. *Associations: Un nouvel âge de participation*. Paris: Presse de Sciences Po, 2000.

Barthes, Roland. *Critical Essays*. Translated by Richard Howard. Evanston, IL: Northwestern University Press, 1972.

———. *Criticism and Truth*. Translated by Katrine P. Keuneman. Minneapolis: University of Minnesota, 1987.

———. *Force of Circumstance*. Translated by Richard Howard. New York: Putnam, 1965.

———. *Tout compte fait*. Paris: Gallimard, 1972.

Belorgey, Michel. *Cent ans de vie associative*. Paris: Presses de Sciences Po, 2000.

Benda, Julien. *La trahison des clercs*. Paris: Grasset, 1927.

Bensaid, Daniel, and Henri Weber. *Mai 1968: Une répétition générale*. Paris: Maspero, 1968.

Berman, Paul. *A Tale of Two Utopias: The Political Journey of the Generation of 1968*. New York: Norton, 1996.

Berstein, Serge. *The Republic of de Gaulle*. Translated by Peter Morris. New York: Cambridge University Press, 1993.

Bloch, Ernst. *Geist der Utopie*. Frankfurt am Main: Suhrkamp, 1964.

Boisseau, Antoine de. *Pour servir le générale, 1940–1970*. Paris: Plon, 1976.

Bosteels, Bruno. "Post-Maoism: Badiou and Politics." *Positions* 13 (3) (2005).

Bourdieu, Pierre. *La misère du monde*. Paris: Editions du Seuil, 1993.

Bourdieu, Pierre, and Jean-Claude Passeron. *Les héritiers: Les étudiants et la culture*. Paris: Editions de Minuit, 1966.

Bourg, Julian. *From Revolution to Ethics: May '68 and Contemporary French Thought*. Montreal: Queens University Press, 2007.

Bourseiller, Christophe. *Les maoïstes: La folle histoire des gardes rouges français*. Paris: Plon, 1996.

Bouscasse, Sylvie, and Denis Bourgeois. *Faut-il brûler les nouveaux philosophes: Le dossier du "procès."* Paris: Nouvelles Editions Oswald, 1978.

Castoriadis, Cornelius. *Philosophy, Politics, Autonomy: Essays in Political Philosophy*. Edited by David Ames Curtis. New York: Oxford University Press, 1991.

Castro, Roland. *1989*. Paris: Barrault, 1984.

Caute, David. *The Fellow Travelers: A Post-Script to the Enlightenment*. London: Weidenfeld and Nicolson, 1973.

———. *The Year of the Barricades: A Journey through 1968*. New York: Harper and Row, 1988.

Certeau, Michel de. *The Capture of Speech and Other Political Writings*. Edited by Lucy Girard. Translated by Tom Conley. Minneapolis: University of Minnesota Press, 1997.

Chaplin, Tamara. *Turning on the Mind: French Philosophers on Television*. Chicago: University of Chicago Press, 2007.

Chevalier, Louis. *Laboring Classes and Dangerous Classes during the Nineteenth Century.* Translated by Frank Jellinek. New York: Howard Fertig, 1973.

Christofferson, Michael Scott. *French Intellectuals against the Left: The Antitotalitarian Moment of the 1970s.* New York: Berghahn Books, 2004.

Cohen-Solal, Annie. *Sartre: A Life.* Translated by Anna Cancogni. New York: Pantheon Books, 1987.

Cohn-Bendit, Daniel. *Nous l'avons tant aimée la révolution.* Paris: Barrault, 1986.

Cohn-Bendit, Daniel, et al. *The French Student Revolt: The Leaders Speak.* Translated by Ben R. Brewster. New York: Hill and Wang, 1968.

Cohn-Bendit, Daniel, and Gabriel Cohn-Bendit. *Obsolete Communism: The Left-Wing Alternative.* Translated by Arnold Pomerans. New York: McGraw-Hill, 1968.

Crettiez, Xavier, and Isabelle Sommier, eds. *La France rebelle.* Paris: Editions Michalon, 2002.

Daniels, Robert. *The Year of the Heroic Guerrilla: World Revolution and Counterrevolution in 1968.* Cambridge, MA: Harvard University Press, 1996.

De Beauvoir, Simone. *Adieux: A Farewell to Sartre.* Translated by Patrick O'Brien. New York: Pantheon Books, 1984.

Debord, Guy. *Society of the Spectacle.* Translated by Donald Nicholson-Smith. New York: Zone Books, 1994.

Debray, Régis. *Le pouvoir intellectuel en France.* Paris: Editions Ramsey, 1979.

Deleuze, Gilles, and Felix Guattari. *Anti-Oedipus: Capitalism and Schizophrenia.* Translated by Robert Hurley, Mark Seem, and Helen R. Lane. New York: Viking Press, 1977.

Descombes, Vincent. *Modern French Philosophy.* Translated by L. Scott-Fox and J. M. Harding. Cambridge: Cambridge University Press, 1980.

Dews, Peter. "The 'New Philosophers' and the End of Leftism." In *Radical Philosophy Reader,* edited by Roy Edgley and Richard Osborne, 361–84. London: Verso, 1985.

———. "The *Nouvelle Philosophie* and Foucault." *Economy and Society* 8 (2) (May 1979): 127–71.

Dollé, Jean-Paul. *L'insoumis: Vies et légendes de Pierre Goldmann.* Paris: Grasset, 1997.

Donzelot, Jacques. *L'invention du social: Essai sur le déclin des passions démocratiques.* Paris: Fayard, 1984.

Dosse, François. *History of Structuralism.* 2 vols. Translated by Deborah Glassman. Minneapolis: University of Minnesota Press, 1997.

Drake, David. *Intellectuals and Politics in Postwar France*. London: Palgrave Macmillan, 2003.

———. "Sartre and May '68." *Sartre Studies International* 3 (1) (1987): 43–65.

Dressen, Marnix. *De l'amphi à l'établi: Les étudiants maoïstes à la usine*. Paris: Belin, 1999.

Dreyfus-Armand, Geneviève, Robert Frank, Marie-Françoise Lévy, and Michelle Zancarini-Fournel, eds. *Les années 68: Le temps de la contestation*. Brussels: Editions Complexe, 2000.

Duchen, Claire. *Feminism in France: From May '68 to Mitterrand*. London: Routledge, 1986.

Dumontier, Pascal. *Les situationnistes et mai '68*. Paris: Editions Gérard Lébovici, 1990.

Eagleton, Terry. *After Theory*. New York: Basic Books, 2004.

Epistémon [Didier Anzieu]. *Ces idées qui ont ébranlé la France*. Paris: Fayard, 1968.

Eribon, Didier. *Insult and the Making of the Gay Self*. Translated by Michael Lucey. Durham, NC: Duke University Press, 2004.

———. *Michel Foucault*. Translated by Betsy Wing. Cambridge, MA: Harvard University Press, 1991.

Esmein, Jean. *La révolution culturelle chinoise*. Paris: Editions du Seuil, 1970.

Fanon, Frantz. *The Wretched of the Earth*. Preface by Jean-Paul Sartre. Translated by Constance Farrington. New York: Grove Weidenfeld, 1991.

Faye, Jean-Pierre. *Commencement d'une figure en mouvement*. Paris: Editions Stock, 1980.

Feenberg, Andrew, and Jim Freedman, eds. *When Poetry Ruled the Streets: The French May Events of 1968*. Albany: SUNY Press, 2001.

Felman, Shoshana. *Writing and Madness*. Ithaca: Cornell University Press, 1985.

Ferry, Luc. *68–86: Itinéraires de l'individu*. Paris: Gallimard, 1987.

Ferry, Luc, and Alain Renaut. *French Philosophy of the Sixties: An Essay on Antihumanism*. Translated by Mary S. Cattani. Amherst: University of Massachusetts Press, 1990.

Ffrench, Patrick. *The Time of Theory: A History of Tel Quel (1960–1983)*. New York: Oxford University Press, 1995.

Fields, A. Belden. *Trotskyism and Maoism: Theory and Practice in France and the United States*. New York: Autonomedia, 1988.

Finkielkraut, Alain. *The Imaginary Jew*. Translated by Kevin O'Neill and David Suchoff. Lincoln: University of Nebraska Press, 1994.

Forest, Philippe. *L'histoire de Tel Quel*. Paris: Editions de Minuit, 1993.

Foucault, Michel. *Dits et écrits*. Edited by Daniel Defert and François Ewald. 2 vols. Paris: Gallimard, 2001.

———. *Madness and Civilization: A History of Insanity in the Age of Reason*. Translated by Richard Howard. New York: Vintage 1965.

———. *The Order of Things: An Archaeology of the Human Sciences*. Translated by A. M. Sheridan Smith. New York: Pantheon, 1971.

———. *Power/Knowledge: Selected Interviews and Other Writings, 1972–1977*. Edited by Colin Gordon. New York: Pantheon Publishers, 1980.

———. *Remarks on Marx: Conversations with Duccio Trombadori*. New York: Semiotext(e), 1991.

Franz, Michael, and Chung-li Chang. *The Taiping Rebellion: History and Documents*. 3 vols. Seattle: University of Washington Press, 1966–1971.

Fraser, Nancy, and Sandra Lee Bartky, eds. *Revaluing French Feminism*. Bloomington: Indiana University Press, 1992.

Frei, Norbert. *1968: Jugendrevolte und globaler Protest*. Munich: Deutscher Taschenbuch Verlag, 2008.

Friedlander, Judith. *Vilna on the Seine: Jewish Intellectuals in France since 1968*. New Haven, CT: Yale University Press, 1990.

Front homosexuel d'action révolutionnaire. *Rapport contre la normalité*. Paris: Champ Libre, 1971.

Furet, François. "French Intellectuals: From Marxism to Structuralism." In *In the Workshop of History*, translated by Jonathan Mandelbaum. Chicago: University of Chicago Press, 1984.

Furet, François, Antoine Liniers [Olivier Rolin], and Philippe Raynaud. *Terrorisme et démocratie*. Paris: Fayard, 1985.

Gavi, Philippe, Jean-Paul Sartre, and Pierre Victor [Benny Lévy]. *On a raison de se révolter*. Paris: Gallimard, 1974.

Geismar, Alain, Serge July, and Erlyn Morane. *Vers la guerre civile*. Paris: Editions et publications premières, 1969.

Ghilhaumou, Jacques. *La parole des sans: Les mouvements actuels a l'èpreuve de la révolution française*. Fontenay: Feuillets, 1998.

Gide, André. *Retour de l'URSS*. Paris: Gallimard, 1936.

Glucksmann, André. *La cuisinière et le mangeur d'hommes: Essai sur l'état, le marxisme, les camps de concentration*. Paris: Editions du Seuil, 1975.

———. *The Master Thinkers*. Translated by Brian Pearce. New York: Harper and Row, 1980.

———. *Stratégie et révolution en France 1968*. Paris: Christian Bourgeois, 1968.

Godard, Jean-Luc. *Jean-Luc Godard par Jean-Luc Godard*. Vol. 1, edited by Alain Bergala. Paris: Cahiers du Cinéma, 1998.

Goldmann, Lucien. *Toward a Sociology of the Novel*. Translated by Alan Sheridan. London: Tavistock, 1977.

Gombin, Richard. *The Origins of Modern Leftism*. Translated by Michael Perl. New York: Penguin, 1975.

Grémion, Pierre. *Paris-Prague: La gauche face au renouveau et la régression tchécoslovaques, 1968–1978*. Paris: Julliard, 1985.

Groupe d'information sur les prisons: Archives d'une luttes, 1970–1972. Edited by Philippe Artières, Laurent Quero, and Michelle Zancarini-Fournel. Paris: Institut Mémoires de l'Edition Contemporaine, 2003.

Hallward, Peter, ed. *Think Again: Alain Badiou and the Future of Philosophy*. New York: Continuum, 2004.

Hamon, Hervé, and Patrick Rotman. *Génération*. 2 vols. Paris: Editions du Seuil, 1988.

———. *Les porteurs de valises: La résistance française à la guerre d'Algérie*. Paris: Albin Michel, 1979.

Hayward, Jack. *After the French Revolution: Six Critics of Democracy and Nationalism*. New York: New York University Press, 1991.

Hess, Remi. *Les maoïstes français: Une dérive institutionnelle*. Paris: Editions Anthropos, 1974.

Hocquenghem, Guy. *Homosexual Desire*. Translated by Daniella Dangoor. Durham, NC: Duke University Press, 1993.

Hollander, Paul. *Political Pilgrims: Travels of Western Intellectuals to the Soviet Union, China, and Cuba, 1928–1978*. New York: Oxford University Press, 1981.

Hollier, Denis. "1968, May. Actions, No! Words, Yes!" In *A New History of French Literature*, edited by Denis Hollier, 1034–40. Cambridge, MA: Harvard University Press, 1989.

Horkheimer, Max, and Theodor Adorno. *Dialectic of Enlightenment*. Translated by John Cumming. New York: Continuum, 1972.

Houellebecq, Michel. *L'extension du domaine de lutte*. Paris: Editions Maurice Nadeau, 1994.

Hourmant, François. *Au pays de l'avenir radieux: Voyages des intellectuels français en URSS, a Cuba et en Chine populaire*. Paris: Aubier, 2000.

———. *Le désenchantement des clercs: Figures de l'intellectuel dans l'après Mai 68*. Rennes: Presses universitaires de Rennes, 1997.

Huguenin, Jean-René. *Journal*. Paris: Editions du Seuil, 1964.

Inglehart, Ronald. *Culture Shift in Advanced Industrial Society*. Princeton, NJ: Princeton University Press, 1989.

Jambet, Christian, and Guy Lardreau. *L'Ange*. Vol. 1, *Ontologie de la révolution*. Paris: Grasset, 1976.

Jappe, Anselm. *Guy Debord*. Berkeley: University of California Press, 1994.

Jay, Martin. *Downcast Eyes: The Denigration of Vision in Twentieth-Century French Thought*. Berkeley: University of California Press, 1993.

Jeanson, Francis. *Sartre and the Problem of Morality*. Translated by Robert Stone. Bloomington: University of Indiana Press, 1980.

Jennings, Jeremy. "Of Treason, Blindness and Silence: Dilemmas of the Intellectual in Modern France." In *The Intellectual in France: From the Dreyfus Affair to Salman Rushdie*, edited by Jeremy Jennings and Anthony Kemp-Welch, 65–86. New York: Routledge, 1997.

Joffrin, Laurent. *Mai '68: Histoire des événements*. Paris: Editions du Seuil, 1988.

Judaken, Jonathan. *Sartre and the Jewish Question*. Lincoln: University of Nebraska Press, 2006.

———. "'To Be or Not to Be French': Soixante-Huitard Reflections on 'la Question Juive.'" *Journal of Modern Jewish Studies* 1 (1) (2002): 3–21.

Judt, Tony. *The Burden of Responsibility: Blum, Camus, Aron, and the French Twentieth Century*. Chicago: University of Chicago Press, 1998.

Kauppi, Nilo. *"Tel Quel": The Making of an Avant-Garde*. Amsterdam: Mouton de Gruyter, 1995.

Kessel, Patrick. *Le mouvement maoïste en France*. 2 vols. Paris: 10/18, 1972.

Khilnani, Sunil. *Arguing Revolution: The Intellectual Left in Postwar France*. New Haven, CT: Yale University Press, 1993.

Knapp, Bettina, ed. *French Novelists Speak Out*. Troy, NY: Whitston, 1976.

Kojève, Alexandre. *Introduction to the Reading of Hegel: Lectures on the Phenomenology of Spirit*. Translated by Allan Bloom. New York: Basic Books, 1969.

Kouchner, Bernard. *Le malheurs des autres*. Paris: Odile Jacob, 1991.

Kouchner, Bernard, and Michel-Antoine Burnier. *La France sauvage*. Paris: Editions Publications Premières, 1970.

Kraushaar, Wolfgang. *Achtundsechzig: Ein Bilanz*. Berlin: Propyläen Verlag, 2008.

Kristeva, Julia. *About Chinese Women*. Translated by Anita Barrows. New York: Urizen, 1977.

———. *Julia Kristeva: Interviews*. Edited by Ross Guberman. New York: Columbia University Press, 1996.

———. *The Kristeva Reader*. Edited by Toril Moi. New York: Columbia University Press, 1986.

———. *The Portable Kristeva*. Edited by Kelly Oliver. New York: Columbia University Press, 1997.

————. *Revolution in Poetic Language*. Translated by Margaret Waller. New York: Columbia University Press, 1980.

————. *The Samurai*. Translated by Barbara Bray. New York: Columbia University Press, 1992.

Kühn, Andreas. *Stalins Enkel, Maos Söhne: Die Lebenswelt der K-Gruppen in der Bundesrepublik der 70er Jahre*. Frankfurt: Campus-Verlag, 2005.

Kurlansky, Mark. *1968: The Year That Rocked the World*. New York: Random House, 2005.

Labro, Philippe. *Mai/Juin '68: Ce n'est qu'un commencement*. Paris: Editions Denoël, 1968.

Labro, Philippe, et al. *"This Is Only a Beginning."* Translated by Charles Marlmann. New York: Funk and Wagnalls, 1969.

Lacan, Jacques. *Ecrits: A Selection*. Translated by Alan Sheridan. New York: Norton, 1977.

————. *Television: A Challenge to the Psychoanalytic Establishment*. Translated by Jeffrey Mehlman. New York: Norton, 1990.

Lallement, Bernard. *Libé: L'œuvre impossible de Sartre*. Paris: Albin Michel, 2004.

Leclerc, Serge. *Un combat pour la justice*. Paris: La Découverte, 1994.

Le Dantec, Jean-Pierre. *Les dangers du soleil*. Paris: Presses d'Aujourd'hui, 1978.

Lefebvre, Henri. *Everyday Life in the Modern World*. Translated by Sacha Rabinovich. New York: Harper and Row, 1971.

————. *L'irruption de Nanterre au sommet*. Paris: Anthropos, 1968.

Le Goff, Jean-Pierre. *Mai 68: L'héritage impossible*. Paris: La Découverte, 1998.

Lemaire, Anika. *Jacques Lacan*. Translated by David Macey. New York: Routledge, 1970.

Lévy, Benny. "From Maoism to Talmud (with Sartre along the Way)." *Commentary* (December 1984): 48–53.

————. *Le nom de l'homme: Dialogue avec Sartre*. Paris: Verdier, 1984.

Lévy, Bernard-Henri. *Barbarism with a Human Face*. Translated by George Holoch. New York: Harper and Row, 1979.

Levy, Jonah. *Tocqueville's Revenge: State, Society, and Economy in Contemporary France*. Cambridge, MA: Harvard University Press, 1999.

Leys, Simon. *Chinese Shadows*. New York: Penguin, 1977.

————. *Les habits neufs du président Mao*. Paris: Editions Champs Libre, 1971.

Lilla, Mark, ed. *New French Thought*. Princeton, NJ: Princeton University Press, 1994.

Lindenberg, Daniel. *Le rappel à l'ordre: Rapport sur les nouveaux réactionnaires*. Paris: Editions du Seuil, 2002.

Linhart, Robert. *L'établi*. Paris: Editions de Minuit, 1978.

Lipovetsky, Gilles. *L'ère du vide*. Paris: Gallimard, 1983.

Lottman, Herbert. *The Left Bank: Writers, Artists, and Politics from the Popular Front to the Cold War*. Boston: Houghton Mifflin, 1982.

Macciocchi, Maria-Antonietta. *De la Chine*. Paris: Editions du Seuil, 1971.

Macey, David. *The Lives of Michel Foucault: A Biography*. New York: Vintage, 1995.

MacFarquhar, Roderick, and Michael Schoenhals. *Mao's Last Revolution*. Cambridge, MA: Harvard University Press, 2006.

Macksey, R., and E. Donato, eds. *The Language of Criticism and the Sciences of Man*. Baltimore: Johns Hopkins University Press, 1970.

Mallet, Serge. *Essays on the New Working Class*. Edited and translated by Dick Howard and Dean Savage. St. Louis: Telos Press, 1975.

Manceaux, Michèle. *Les maos en France*. Preface by Jean-Paul Sartre. Paris: Gallimard, 1972.

Mao Tse-tung. *The Mao Papers: Anthology and Bibliography*. Edited by Jerome Ch'en. Oxford: Oxford University Press, 1970.

——. *On Contradiction*. Beijing: Foreign Languages Press, 1967.

——. *Quotations from Chairman Mao*. Beijing: Foreign Languages Press, 1972.

——. *Selected Works*. Vol. 2. New York: International Publishers, 1954.

Marcellin, Raymond. *L'importune vérité: Dix ans après Mai '68 un ministre de l'intérieur parle*. Paris: Plon, 1978.

Marshall, Bill. *Guy Hocquenghem: Beyond Gay Identity*. Durham, NC: Duke University Press, 1997.

Martel, Frédéric. *The Pink and the Black: Homosexuals in France since 1968*. Translated by Jane Marie Todd. Stanford: Stanford University Press, 1999.

Marwick, Arthur. *The Sixties: Cultural Revolution in Britain, France, Italy, and the United States, 1958–1974*. New York: Oxford University Press, 1998.

Marx-Scouras, Danielle. *The Cultural Politics of* Tel Quel: *Literature and the Left in the Wake of Engagement*. University Park: Pennsylvania State University Press, 1995.

Massu, Jacques. *Baden 68*. Paris: Editions Plon, 1983.

Mendras, Henri. *Français, comment vous avez changé*. Paris: Tallandier, 2004.

—— (with Alistair Cole). *Social Change in Modern France: Toward an Anthropology of the Fifth Republic*. New York: Cambridge University Press, 1991.

Merleau-Ponty, Maurice. *Adventures of the Dialectic*. Translated by Joseph Bien. Evanston, IL: Northwestern University Press.

Michnik, Adam. *Letters from Prison and Other Essays*. Translated by Maya Latynski. Berkeley: University of California Press, 1985.

Miller, James. *The Passion of Michel Foucault*. New York: Simon and Schuster, 1993.

Monod, Jean-Claude. *Foucault et la police des conduites*. Paris: Michalon, 1997.

Moravia, Alberto. *La révolution culturelle de Mao*. Paris: Flammarion, 1967.

Moreau, Jean. "Les maos de la gauche prolétarienne." *La Nef* 48 (June–September 1972): 77–103.

Morin, Edgar, Claude Lefort, and Jean-Marc Coudray. *La brèche: Premières réflexions sur les événements*. Paris: Fayard, 1968.

Moyn, Samuel. *The Origins of the Other*. Ithaca, NY: Cornell University Press, 2006.

Nord, Philip. *The Republican Moment: The Struggle for Democracy in Nineteenth-Century France*. Cambridge, MA: Harvard University Press, 1995.

"Nouveau fascisme, nouvelle démocraties." *Les Temps Modernes*, 310 bis (1972).

Oliver, Kelly. *Reading Kristeva: Unraveling the Double-Bind*. Bloomington: Indiana University Press, 1993.

Paxton, Robert, and Michael Marrus. *Vichy France and the Jews*. New York: Basic Books, 1981.

Perrot, Michelle, ed. *L'impossible prison: Recherches sur le système pénitentiaire au XIXe siècle*. Paris: Editions du Seuil, 1980.

Picq, Françoise. *Libération des femmes: Les années mouvement*. Paris: Editions du Seuil, 1993.

Ponchaud, François. *Cambodia—Year Zero*. Translated by Nancy Amphoux. New York: Penguin, 1978.

Raynaud, Philippe. *L'extrême gauche plurielle: Entre démocratie radicale et révolution*. Paris: Autrement, 2006.

Reader, Keith, and Khursheed Wadja. *The May 1968 Events in France: Reproductions and Interpretations*. London: St. Martin's Press, 1993.

Rieffel, Remy. *Le tribu des clercs: Les intellectuels sous le Vième République, 1958–1990*. Paris: Calmann-Lévy, 1993.

Robespierre, Maximilien. *Ecrits*. Edited by Claude Mazauric. Paris: Messidor/Editions sociales, 1989.

Rolin, Olivier. *Paper Tiger*. Translated by William Cloonan. Lincoln: University of Nebraska Press, 2007.

———. *Tigre en papier*. Paris: Editions du Seuil, 2002.

Rosanvallon, Pierre. *The Demands of Liberty: Civil Society in France since the Revolution*. Translated by Alan Goldhammer. Cambridge, MA: Harvard University Press, 2007.

Rosanvallon, Pierre, and Patrick Viveret. *Vers une nouvelle culture politique*. Paris: Editions du Seuil, 1977.

Ross, Kristin. *May '68 and Its Afterlives*. Chicago: University of Chicago Press, 2003.

Roudinesco, Elisabeth. *Jacques Lacan*. Translated by Barbara Bray. New York: Columbia University Press, 1996.

———. *Jacques Lacan and Co.: A History of Psychoanalysis in France, 1925–1985*. Translated by Jeffrey Mehlman. Chicago: University of Chicago Press, 1990.

Saint-Just, Louis-Antoine. *Œuvres complètes*. Edited by Michèle Duval. Paris: Gérard Lebovici, 1984.

Samuelson, François-Marie. *Il était une fois "Libération."* Paris: Editions du Seuil, 1979.

Santoni, Ronald. *Sartre on Violence*. University Park: Pennsylvania State University Press, 1993.

Sartre, Jean-Paul. "Les Bastilles de Raymond Aron." *Le Nouvel Observateur*, June 19, 1968.

———. *Being and Nothingness: An Essay on Phenomenological Ontology*. Translated by Hazel Barnes. New York: Washington Square Press, 1966.

———. *Between Existentialism and Marxism*. Translated by J. Matthews. New York: Pantheon, 1974.

———. *Colonialism and Neocolonialism*. Translated by Azzedine Haddour. New York: Routledge, 2005.

———. *Critique of Dialectical Reason*. Translated by Alan Sheridan-Smith. London: New Left Books, 1976.

———. *Les écrits de Sartre*. Edited by Michel Contat and Michel Rybalka. Paris: Gallimard, 1970.

———. "L'idée neuve de mai 1968." *Le Nouvel Observateur*, June 26, 1968.

———. *Life/Situations: Essays Spoken and Written*. Translated by Paul Auster and Lydia Davis. New York: Pantheon, 1977.

———. *Notebooks for an Ethics*. Translated by David Pellauer. Chicago: University of Chicago Press, 1992.

———. *Situations*. Volume 8, *Autour de mai '68*. Paris: Gallimard, 1972.

———. *The Words*. Translated by Bernard Frechtman. New York: New Directions, 1964.

Sartre, Jean Paul, and Benny Lévy. *Hope Now: The 1980 Interview*. Translated by Adrian van den Hoven. Chicago: University of Chicago Press, 1996.

Schmidt, Vivien. *Democratizing France: The Political and Administrative History of Decentralization*. New York: Cambridge University Press, 1991.

Schnapp, Alain, and Pierre Vidal-Naquet. *The French Student Uprising: November 1967–June 1968*. Translated by Maris Jolas. Boston: Beacon Press, 1971.

Seale, Patrick, and Maureen McConnville. *Black Flag/Red Flag: French Revolution 1968*. New York: G. P. Putnam's Sons, 1968.

Seidman, Michael. *The Imaginary Revolution: Parisian Students and Workers in 1968*. New York: Berghahn Books, 2004.

Short, Philip. *Pol Pot: The Anatomy of a Nightmare*. New York: Henry Holt, 2006.

Situationist International. *On the Poverty of Student Life*. Berkeley: Contradiction, 1972.

———. *The Situationist International Anthology*. Edited by Ken Knabb. Berkeley: Bureau of Public Secrets, 1981.

Sollers, Philippe. *Writing and the Experience of Limits*. Translated by P. Barnard and D. Hayman. New York: Columbia University Press, 1983.

———, ed. *Théorie d'ensemble*. Paris: Editions du Seuil, 1968.

Sommier, Isabelle. *La violence politique et son deuil: L'après 68 en France et en Italie*. Rennes: Presses Universitaires de Rennes, 1998.

Spence, Jonathan. *The Search for Modern China*. New York: Norton, 1999.

Starr, John, and Nancy Dyer, eds. *Post-liberation Works of Mao Tse-tung: A Bibliography and Index*. Berkeley: Center for Chinese Studies, 1976.

Starr, Peter. *Logics of Failed Revolt: French Theory after May '68*. Stanford: Stanford University Press, 1995.

Tocqueville, Alexis de. *Democracy in America*. Translated by G. Lawrence. New York: Harper and Row, 1966.

Touraine, Alain. *The May Movement: Revolt and Reform*. Translated by Leonard Mayhew. New York: Random House, 1971.

———. *Return of the Actor: Social Theory in Postindustrial Society*. Translated by Myrna Godzich. Minneapolis: University of Minnesota Press, 1987.

Van der Poel, Ième. *Une révolution de la pensée: Maoïsme à travers Tel Quel, Les Temps Modernes, et Esprit*. Amsterdam: Editions Rodopi, 1992.

Vaneigem, Raoul. *Treatise on Living for the Use of the Young Generation*. New York: Situationist International, 1970.

Varon, Jeremy. *Bringing the War Home: The Weather Underground, the Red Army Faction, and Revolutionary Violence in the Sixties and Seventies*. Berkeley: University of California Press, 2003.

Vienet, René. *Enragés et situationnistes dans le mouvement des occupations*. Paris: Gallimard, 1968.

Wakeman, Frederic. *History and Will: Philosophical Perspectives of Mao Tse-tung's Thought*. Berkeley: University of California Press, 1973.

Waters, Sarah. *Social Movements in France: Towards a New Citizenship*. New York: Palgrave Macmillan, 2003.

Weber, Henri, *Vingt ans après: Que reste-t-il de 68?* Paris: Editions du Seuil, 1988.

Index

Act Up, 365

Adorno, Theodor, 11n, 225n, 357n9

Agir ensemble contre le chômage (AC!), 367–369

Agronomists without Borders, 361

Algeria, 39–44, 51, 69, 73, 80, 87, 93, 109, 116, 156, 178, 181–182, 201, 207–208, 220–221, 228, 230, 236, 238, 261, 303; Liberation Front (FLN), 39, 44, 80, 116, 207, 220–221, 303

Althusser, Louis, 75, 156, 159, 162n11, 164; and French Communist Party, 118–119, 121, 265, 312; and Maoism, 2–3, 27, 30, 33, 116–124, 197; and May '68, 2, 103, 106, 160, 193; and Sartre, 183, 185–186, 187n13, 193–194; and structuralism, 119–121, 160, 185–186, 242, 243n17, 244, 345

Amis de la terre, Les, 361

Arguments group, 20, 59–60, 177, 317

Aron, Raymond, 1, 8, 45, 91, 103–104, 117, 183, 206, 210, 225, 227, 285, 291, 353

Artaud, Antonin, 240, 254

Auden, W. H., 5, 236

Ayers, William, 1

Bachelard, Gaston, 185

Badiou, Alain, 17, 155–167, 219n79

Barthélemy, Martine, 361

Barthes, Roland, 49, 121, 174, 186, 187n13; and the Nouveau roman, 239–241, 247; and Tel Quel, 19, 238–241, 245–247, 279, 286; and Writing Degree Zero, 239–240

Benda, Julien, 103, 214, 287

Black Panthers, 14, 318–319

Bloch, Ernst, 209

Bloch, Marc, 354

Bloom, Allan, 6

Bourdieu, Pierre, 51n, 79n, 366, 368

Braudel, Fernand, 120–121

Breton, André, 237, 364–365

Bruay-en-Artois, 25–38, 352

Camus, Albert, 44, 75, 226–227, 285

Castoriadis, Cornelius, 57–59, 103n39, 104, 107n48, 297

Castro, Fidel, 11, 70–71, 276, 329

Castro, Roland, 25, 96–97, 123, 321

Cause du Peuple, La, 27, 34–37, 116, 140, 168, 169, 171, 179, 198–205, 221nn82 and 83, 300, 303–304, 316, 351

Centre d'études, de recherche et de formation institutionnelles (CERFI), 337

Centre Pompidou, 63

Charléty Stadium, 1, 291

Chevalier, Louis, 53n14, 62n28, 63–64, 339n103

Chiang Kai-Shek, 11, 125

Clark, Mark, 318

Clark, Ramsay, 319

Clavel, Maurice, 304, 309–310

Cohn-Bendit, Daniel, 54–55, 59, 75, 101, 103n39, 266n67; and French Communist Party, 91–92, 266–267; and March 22 Movement, 81–85, 87, 193; and May '68, 80–85, 87–89, 91–93, 190–193, 195–196, 223, 266–267, 352; and Sartre, 190–191, 195–196

Comité de liaison des étudiants révolutionnaires (CLER), 136n42
Confédération française démocratique du travail (CFDT), 91, 95, 364
Confédération générale du travail (CGT), 28, 91–92, 139, 155, 196, 266–267
Coudray, Jean-Marc. *See* Castoriadis, Cornelius

de Beauvoir, Simone, 29n4, 33, 168, 180, 182n, 194–195, 208, 218n78, 220n80, 222, 225n91, 267; and Amis du Cause du Peuple, 201; *Les Belles images*, 64–66; and Maoism, 117, 140–141, 203–204; *Second Sex*, 144, 146, 257–258; and trip to China, 203–204
de Gaulle, Charles, 7–8, 10, 16, 33, 45, 50, 55, 78, 125, 134, 137, 149, 156, 218, 237, 247, 260, 354–355; and Algerian War, 39–43, 93, 156, 181–182; and flight to Baden-Baden, 2, 99–103; as man of June 18, 39–43, 182; and May '68, 85, 87, 92–93, 99–103, 190, 196, 294, 297, 329
Debord, Guy, 60–61, 74–75
Debray, Régis, 9n5, 106, 294n13, 325, 330
Defert, Daniel, 17, 193, 299–301, 304–305, 316, 318
Deleuze, Gilles, 37, 81, 289–290, 308, 311, 313, 323, 327–328, 333–334, 337–338
Deng Xiaoping, 109–110, 157–158, 165
democracy, 51, 53, 57, 69, 73, 82, 83, 94, 99, 104–105, 107, 133, 155, 163–164, 167, 192, 196, 199, 208, 228, 236, 255–256, 283, 286, 344; associational, 350–370; bourgeois, 354; direct, 20, 82, 106, 205, 359; radical, 57, 192, 297; revolution of, 5, 12; social, 119, 196–197

democrats, 32, 34, 36, 304, 352
Derrida, Jacques, 18, 245, 257, 268
Dewevre, Brigitte, 25–28, 31–32, 36
Doctors without Borders (MSF—Médécins sans frontières), 228, 342, 361
Donzelot, Jacques, 318, 364n23
Dosse, François, 119n20, 188–189, 193n22, 247, 251n33, 288, 289n2, 333n92, 341nn106 and 107
Dreyfus Affair, 19; legacy of, 4, 21, 178, 215, 366n
Droit au logement (DAL), 367
Droits devant!, 367
Durkheim, Emile, 363
Dutschke, Rudi, 84, 191

École Nationale d'Administration (ENA), 53, 79, 296
École Normale Supérieure (ENS), 2, 15, 26, 33, 95, 117–120, 122, 124, 126, 129, 135, 136 192, 197, 354
Engels, Friedrich, 61n25, 122, 271
enquête, 18, 131, 132, 138, 303, 305–307, 315–316, 323, 330
Esmein, Jean, 155
European Union (EU), 368
existentialism, 35, 177, 181, 183, 185, 187, 235
Express, L', 199

Fanon, Frantz, 43, 206–208
Fédération des associations de soutien aux travailleurs immigrés (FASTI), 361
Fédération des cercles Marxistes-léninistes, 15
Ferry, Luc, 9n5, 105n43, 106
Figaro, Le, 8, 103, 309
Finkielkraut, Alain, 223–224
Fischer, Joschka, 2
Fordism, 362

Foucault, Michel, 4, 16–21, 53, 117,
    121, 158, 172, 185–187, 193, 233,
    240–242, 244–246, 249, 286, 352,
    356; *Discipline and Punish*, 289–290,
    338–342; and André Glucksmann,
    17, 342–347; and Lens, 29–32, 36–37,
    304; and Maoism, 117, 288–349; and
    New Philosophers, 342–349; and
    Prison Information Group (GIP),
    17, 289–290, 304–317; and Sartre,
    16, 36, 178, 186–187 , 233, 304; in
    Tunisia, 17, 178, 193, 288, 292–298;
    at Vincennes, 17, 158
French Communist Party (PCF—Parti
    Communiste Français), 14, 18, 91–92,
    102, 117, 119–128, 131, 137, 156–157,
    183, 191, 193, 196–197, 217, 245n21,
    261–270, 272, 276, 283, 312
Freud, Sigmund, 150, 184, 242, 244–
    245, 250–253, 265, 282, 313, 333–334
Front homosexual d'action révolution-
    naire (FHAR), 142, 330–333, 338;
    and Foucault, 332–333; and Guy
    Hocquenghem, 147–150, 331
Furet, François, 187–188, 349

Geismar, Alain, 87, 91, 136, 140, 169,
    201, 205, 223, 352
Genette, Gérard, 245
Gide, André, 125n28, 181, 235, 238,
    261, 331
Gingrich, Newt, 5–6
Giscard d'Estaing, Valéry, 152, 222,
    283, 322, 364
Glucksmann, André, 17, 34, 37, 118n18,
    170, 269, 281, 342–348, 352
Godard, Jean-Luc, 15, 33, 67–69, 75,
    114–117, 171, 309
Goldmann, Lucien, 50n9, 188, 240n11,
    247, 294, 330
Great Helmsman, The. *See* Mao
    Tse-Tung

Great Leap Forward, 13, 109
Groupe d'information sur les prisons
    (GIP), 17, 305, 307–308n, 315n53
Guattari, Felix, 37, 81, 330, 333–334,
    337–338
Guevara, Che, 29, 70–71, 329
Gulag Archipelago, 21, 264, 156, 227,
    342, 345

Hegel, Georg William Friedrich, 120,
    180, 207, 212, 231
Heidegger, Martin, 120, 162n14
Ho Chi Minh, 29, 329
Hocquenghem, Guy, 147–150, 331,
    334–338, 357n7
Hölderlin, Friedrich, 240
Houellebecq, Michel, 9
Hoxa, Enver, 15
Hua Ko-feng, 165
Huguenin, Jean-René, 238, 243n16
human rights, 5, 21, 36, 156, 164, 178,
    269, 276, 285, 342–343, 349, 361;
    UN Universal Declaration of, 368
Hungarian uprising (1956), 12, 59, 104,
    121, 356
Husserl, Edmund, 120

J'Accuse, 179, 221n82
Jacobinism, 211, 228, 359
Jacobins, 4, 93–94, 113, 156, 162, 165,
    208n50, 211–212, 275, 292, 359, 364
Jambet, Christian, 37, 269, 344, 349
Jeanson, Francis, 116
Jiang Qing, 356
Jim Crow, 7
Jospin, Lionel, 156, 343n109, 369
July, Serge, 16, 201, 219, 304, 342

K Gruppen (K Groups), 13
Kampuchea, Democratic (Cambodia),
    229
Kennedy, John, 118

Kennedy, Robert, 11–12, 72

Khayati , Mustapha, 75–76, 292

Khmer Rouge, 162–163, 229–230

King Jr., Martin Luther, 72

Kouchner, Bernard, 228, 342–343, 350, 369

Kravchenko, Victor, 264

Kristeva, Julia: and China, 19, 174, 234, 274–276, 279–281; and feminism, 250, 257–260, 283–284; and modernism, 254–256; and psychoanalysis, 250, 283–284; and semanalysis, 250–254; and *Tel Quel*, 233–234, 243, 247–266, 282–286

Kuomintang, 125, 137, 165

Lacan, Jacques, 242–248, 259, 286, 304; and May '68 , 103, 193; and structuralism , 121, 185–187, 243, 333–334; and the symbolic sphere, 161, 242–244, 250–253, 256, 348

Lardreau, Guy, 344, 349

Le Dantec, Jean-Pierre, 9, 37, 123, 140, 199–202

Le Goff, Jean-Pierre, 9n5, 103, 147n55, 364n24, 365

Lefebvre, Henri, 10n7, 56–57, 59–60, 62, 84, 193, 297, 364n24

Lefort, Claude, 103n39, 104, 297; and Socialism or Barbarism group, 57–59

Lenin, Vladimir, 82, 109, 123, 160, 163, 254–255, 271, 291, 302, 345, 347, 355–356, 365; and Jacobinism , 93, 113, 115, 165; and theory of the party, 20, 57, 190, 192, 196–197, 214, 226, 355; *What Is to Be Done?*, 136, 196, 355

Leninism, 20, 57–58, 127, 165, 190–191, 196–197, 214, 226, 255; Neo-, 38, 157–158, 356

Lens, 28–29, 304

Leroy, Pierre, 25–28, 31–32, 34–37

Let 100 Flowers Bloom, 13

Lévi-Strauss, Claude, 103, 120–121, 184–187, 193–194, 242, 245, 247–248

Lévy, Benny, 29, 219, 223, 352; and *Hope Now* interviews, 225–232

Lévy, Bernard-Henri, 227n93, 281–282, 349n124

Lévy, Tony, 352

Leys, Simon, 155, 277–278, 281

Libération, 16, 201, 214, 217–220, 222, 316

Ligue communiste révolutionnaire (LCR), 137

Lin Piao, 155, 356

Linhart, Robert, 95–97, 122–124, 129, 131n35, 134–135, 159

Lipovetsky, Gilles, 9n5, 105–106

Liu Shao-qui, 110, 157

Maastricht Treaty, 368

Macciocchi, Maria-Antonietta, 124, 269, 272, 275

Madame Mao. *See* Jiang Qing

Mallarmé, Stéphane, 239, 250, 254–255, 265

Mao Tse-Tung, 2–3, 11–15, 19–20, 29, 35, 116, 121–122, 124–129, 131n36, 132, 134–137, 140, 165, 193, 198, 205, 213n66, 218–219, 223, 226, 233, 255, 270–278, 281, 302, 345, 355–356; and the Cultural Revolution, 13, 15, 57, 77, 109–115, 126, 157–158, 160, 162, 203, 217n74, 270–271, 277–278, 280–281, 329; and the Great Leap Forward, 13, 109; *Little Red Book*, 14, 114, 118, 133, 355; and the Long March, 137; *On Contradiction*, 112, 122, 273

Mao Tse-Tung Thought, 111–112, 124, 131, 135, 197, 229, 302

Marcellin, Raymond, 134–135, 137, 140, 199–202, 302

March 22 Movement (22 du Mars), 56, 81–85, 87, 91–92, 190–193, 267

Marx, Karl, 10, 27, 38, 49–50, 60–61, 94, 113, 120, 184, 186–187, 193, 197, 231, 270, 273, 290, 313, 345–347, 357

Marxism, 2, 10, 12, 15, 18–20, 35, 47, 49, 57–60, 71, 95, 106, 108, 112, 133, 136, 144, 158–162, 165–166, 177, 179, 183–185, 187–188, 192–193, 197, 217, 228, 242, 244, 265, 270, 273–274, 289–290, 293–298, 302, 312, 318, 320, 327, 329–330, 342, 344–347, 352–358, 363; Althusser's conception of, 116–123, 159, 183, 242–244, 312; existential, 60, 139, 185, 215–216, 241; Freudian-, 313; Hegelian-, 29; Mao's interpretation of, 125–127, 131, 270; Soviet, 12, 15, 57, 115, 122, 188; structuralist, 160

Marxism-Leninism, 134, 206, 300, 356. *See also* Mouvement communiste français marxiste-léniniste; Union des communistes français marxiste-léniniste; Union des jeunesse communistes marxiste-léniniste

Marxiste léniniste, Le, 157

Massu, Jacques, 40, 100

Mauriac, François, 234, 309

Mendès-France, Pierre, 96, 135

McCain, John, 1

Michnik, Adam, 93

Miller, Jacques-Alain, 17, 122, 304

Miller, Judith, 158n6, 304

Mollet, Guy, 156

Monde, Le, 31, 41, 55–56, 76–77, 105n44, 109n, 114–115, 163n15, 181n3, 189, 202, 229n95, 246, 278, 279, 281, 282, 359n12

Monot, Jean-Claude, 289

Morin, Edgar, 59, 84, 103n39, 104, 364n24

Moscow show trials, 183

Mouvement communiste français marxiste-léniniste (MCF-ML), 15

Mouvement libération des femmes (MLF), 142–147, 150–151, 330–331

National Association for the Humanization of Prison Life (KRUM), 317

neoconservativism, 5

Nerval, Gérard de, 240

New Philosophers (Nouveaux Philosophes), 163, 227n92, 269, 276, 281, 342–349, 356

New Philosophy (Nouvelle Philosophie), 345. *See also* New Philosophers

new wave cinema (nouvelle vague), 14–15, 67, 69, 75, 115

Newton, Huey, 14, 321

Nietzsche, Friedrich, 36, 74, 81, 162, 234–235, 300, 313–314, 324–325, 347

normaliens. *See* École Normale Supérieure

Obama, Barack, 1

Organisation de l'armée secrète (OAS), 42, 181

Overney, Pierre, 32–34, 351

Palestinian Liberation Organization (PLO), 220–221, 351

Parti communiste français marxiste-léniniste (PCFML), 137, 157

People's Liberation Army, 155, 165, 277–278, 356

Pharmacists without Borders, 361

Plato, 6, 252

Playboy, 114

Podhoretz, Norman, 5

Pol Pot, 35, 228–230

politics: feminist, 142–146, 150–153, 218, 256–260, 283–284, 307–308n35; liberal, 72, 82, 84, 106, 152, 164, 243, 285, 312, 316, 354, 358, 368; libidinal, 38, 70–108, 141, 156, 218, 261, 352; neoliberal, 163

Poststructuralism: 233, 248, 262, 284–286

Prague Spring, 72, 119, 213–214

Red Guards, 3, 109–112, 114, 124n25, 165, 214, 217n74, 275, 277–278, 307–308n35

Renault factory, 32–33, 98, 138, 264, 351

Reporters without Borders, 361

revisionism, 15, 119, 128, 140, 157, 197, 205, 230, 270–271, 274

revolution: Cuban, 11, 70, 208; Cultural, 3, 10–15, 19–20, 29, 57, 77, 109–132, 135, 155–157, 160–163, 165–167, 178, 203, 214, 217n74, 229–230, 233–234, 269–281, 297, 301–303, 323–323, 329, 356–357; democratic, 5; of everyday life, 56–62, 77, 142, 298; French, 3, 8, 30–31, 45, 52, 85, 88–89, 94, 103, 162, 182, 207, 208n50, 227–228, 349, 367n; Industrial, 296; Iranian, 344; literary, 233–287; May as absence of, 8, 50, 70, 103–106, 164, 364; moral, 5, 7, 73, 360, 366; palace, 37; Russian, 82, 162, 165–166, 182, 355; self-limiting, 92–97; sexual, 78, 142–151, 330–338; specter of, 2; third world, 11, 13, 29, 276n89

revolutionism, 12, 32, 106, 190, 206, 209, 213, 226, 228, 231, 255, 325, 353, 355–356

Rimbaud, Jean Nicholas Arthur, 50, 123, 356

Robbé-Grillet, Alain, 18, 49–50, 64, 186, 239–240, 243

Robespierre, Maximilien, 113, 177, 182, 207, 211, 226, 229, 291, 356

Rocard, Michel, 33, 364

Rolin, Olivier, 33n8, 218, 351, 354–355n

Rosanvallon, Pierre, 359n13, 362, 366n26

Royale, Ségolène, 1

Saint-Just, Louis-Antoine, 34, 39, 115, 211, 219, 291

Salan, Raoul, 40

sans frontièrisme. *See*: Agronomists without Borders; Doctors without Borders; Pharmacists without Borders; Reporters without Borders; Veterinarians without Borders

sans papiers, 165–166, 366

Sarkozy, Nicholas, 1, 105n44, 343n109, 359

Sartre, Arlette-Elkaïm, 222, 232

Sartre, Jean-Paul, 27–36, 43–44, 60, 66, 139, 148, 159–160, 162n14, 168, 177–233, 235–241, 262, 283, 286–287, 309, 325, 338; and Althusser, 103, 117, 119, 160, 183, 185–187, 193–194, 197; and Raymond Aron, 117, 206n47, 210, 227; and Daniel Cohn-Bendit, 89, 93n26, 190–195, 223; *Critique of Dialectical Reason*, 28, 182, 184, 204, 207, 209–213, 216, 228, 230; and Michel Foucault, 16, 18–19, 29–30, 32, 36, 117, 172,178, 185–187, 233, 286, 304, 308–309, 325, 342, 349, 352, 356; *Hope Now*, 225–232; and Judaism, 219– 225, 231–232, 284; and Lens Tribunal, 27–30, 32–36, 304; and Benny Lévy (aka Pierre Victor), 16, 29–30, 35, 217, 219–226, 228, 230–232, 352; and Maoism, 3–4, 16, 18–19, 27, 29, 32–37, 139, 148, 160, 179–180, 191–193, 197–206, 212–219, 222–224, 226, 229–230, 304–305, 308; and May '68, 89, 93n26, 103, 116–117, 119, 177–179, 188–201, 206, 210n57, 214–215, 217–219, 223, 226, 267; *Les mots*, 180–181, 190, 194, 235; *On a raison de se revolter*, 16, 205n4, 213n683, 217, 219; and structuralism 179, 183–188, 193–194; and violence, 35, 43–44, 205–214

Saussure, Ferdinand, 120, 241–242, 245, 250

Section française de l'internationale ouvrière (SFIO), 156

Sichère, Bernard, 158

Sino-Soviet Rift, 12

Situationist International, 12–13, 19–20, 48n7, 56, 73–77, 82, 133, 135, 141, 177, 292, 317–318, 338, 355–356

Socialism or Barbarism (Socialisme ou barbarie), 20, 57–60, 177, 317, 344

Sollers, Philippe, 4, 18–19, 174, 382; and Tel Quel, 233–246, 261–283

Solzhenitsyn, Alexander, 21, 156, 178, 227, 264, 269, 342, 345, 347

SOS Racisme, 365

Sozialistischer Deutscher Studentenbund (SDS), 83–84, 191

Stalin, Josef, 30, 35, 57, 82, 110, 162, 191, 213, 281, 345, 347, 349, 356; pact of with Hitler, 236

Stalinism, 13–15, 57–58, 92, 110, 117–121, 125, 157, 159–160, 165–166, 178, 181–182, 197, 23–234, 245n21, 262–263, 265, 276, 347, 356

structuralism, 14, 17–19, 50, 119–121, 160, 178–179, 183–188, 193–194, 233, 235, 239, 241–251, 259, 262–263, 284–289, 309–311, 334, 342, 345

Tempes Modernes, Les, 16, 26n, 29, 139n, 222, 225n91, 309

third worldism (tiers mondisme), 11, 13, 29, 113, 118, 122, 125, 206–207, 209, 228, 234, 276n89, 325, 344, 355

Tocqueville, Alexis de, 52, 104–106, 285, 291, 361–362

Todorov, Tzvetan, 245

Torchon Brûle, Le, 146

Touraine, Alain, 70, 84, 88n, 103n39, 107n46, 108, 296–297, 350

Tout!, 141–142, 147–148, 151, 179, 201, 321, 326

Trotsky, Leon, 57, 272–273, 345

Trotskyism, 82, 96, 102, 136n42, 137, 140, 148–149, 152, 191, 272, 296, 301, 355–356

Tse-toung, Jean. See Lévy, Benny

Unified Socialist Party (PSU—Parti Socialiste Unifié), 156–157, 364

Union des communistes français marxiste-léniniste (UCF-ML), 156–159, 165

Union des étudiants communistes (UEC), 118

Union des jeunesse communistes marxiste-léniniste (UJC-ML), 96–97, 118, 123–127, 129–137, 143, 156, 158, 197–198, 292, 296, 300–301, 350

Union nationale des étudiants français (UNEF), 44–45, 87, 223n87

University of Paris X Nanterre, 19, 56, 79–80, 83–86, 95–96, 116, 135, 141, 143, 188, 194, 292, 330, 350

University of Strasbourg, 73, 76, 292

University of Vincennes (ex-Saint Denis), 17, 158, 298–300, 304, 331, 337, 348n123

Verts, Les, 361

Veterinarians without Borders, 361

Victor, Pierre. See Lévy, Benny

Vietnam War, 6–7, 11, 15, 18, 29, 44, 71–73, 83–84, 90, 118, 131, 177, 181n5, 206, 227, 260, 278, 343

Vive la révolution! (VLR), 141

Wahl, François, 174, 237, 279

Wilkins, Roy, 319

Woodstock, 357